God, Guilt, and Death

Studies in Phenomenology and Existential Philosophy

GOD, GUILT, and DEATH

AN EXISTENTIAL PHENOMENOLOGY OF RELIGION

Merold Westphal

INDIANA UNIVERSITY PRESS
Bloomington

Library of Congress Cataloging in Publication Data

Westphal, Merold.
    God, guilt, and death.

    (Studies in phenomenology and existential philosophy)
    Includes index.
    1. Religion—Philosophy. 2. Guilt—Religious aspects.
3. Death—Religious aspects. I. Title. II. Series.
BL51.W44   1984   200'.1   83-48525
ISBN 0-253-32586-2
1 2 3 4 5 88 87 86 85 84

for Carol
who taught me that
the meaning of life
is the miracle of love

Contents

3

Ambivalence, Inertia, and Resentment

4

The Existential Meaning of Guilt

5

The Existential Meaning of Death

6

The Believing Soul's Encounter with Guilt and Death

7

Religion as Means and as End

8

Prayer and Sacrifice as Useless Self-Transcendence   138

9

Guilt and Death in Exilic Religion   160

10

Guilt and Death in Mimetic Religion   194

11

Guilt and Death in Covenantal Religion   219

PREFACE

This book grew out of a course I gave during the early seventies, for three years at Yale and for two at the Purchase campus of S.U.N.Y. At first it was simply entitled "Phenomenology of Religion." Using materials written by everyone but philosophers, I tried to show how the methodology developed by Merleau-Ponty in the Preface to *The Phenomenology of Perception* and by Ricoeur in *The Symbolism of Evil* could be used to gain fresh perspective on the meaning of the religious life. That the methodology seemed to illuminate the subject matter rather than compete with it for the limelight satisfied my Hegelian sense of the proper place of method. Correspondingly the course changed its name to identify the substantive themes which came to be central. It became "God, Guilt, and Death."

The enthusiasm of my students in those classes reinforced my own excitement and enjoyment with the project and had a lot to do with the decision to try to put my findings into book form. As best I could tell, only a minority of them were practicing believers in some religious tradition, while the majority were not. This tended to confirm for me that the attempt to understand the "believing soul" from within did not presuppose that one was already a "believing soul" oneself. Students across the entire spectrum of belief and behavior in relation to religion found the enterprise worthwhile.

The term "believing soul," used here and throughout the book, is borrowed from Ricoeur. I use it, I believe, as he does, to designate more or less generically those who live the religious life. While it does imply that the religious life has its cognitive side, it is not intended to suggest that believing is the exclusive or even the primary religious activity. Nor does the term "soul" carry with it any metaphysical commitments about the nature of human existence beyond the assumption that each of us is in some sense an individual. As the following chapters will make clear, it is entirely neutral both with respect to notions of personal immortality and with respect to such issues as the primacy of subjectivity or the ultimacy of personhood. In fact, one of the striking themes which recurs throughout the text is that the sacred, both in its personal and impersonal forms, stands as a dramatic challenge to the ontological status of the personal and social selfhood we take for granted in everyday experience.

The chapters which follow can most fruitfully be read in the light of the following grouping. Chapter One stands alone. It describes the methodology I've sought to employ in both its phenomenological and its existential dimensions. It is atypical in a couple of senses. The most obvious is that it talks about the enterprise that the other chapters are engaged in doing. In addition it contains a couple of sections which are more technical philosophically than the rest of the book. Some readers may prefer to begin with Chapter Two and return to Chapter One after reading several of the non-methodological chapters.

Chapters Two and Three concern the sacred as the source of the peculiarly religious dimensions of meaning in human experience. Beyond noting that the sacred comes in many forms, only some of which are God or gods, and some of which, such as the Buddhist Nirvana, cannot very helpfully be designated as any kind of something but have to be talked about as nothing, as emptiness, or as the void, these chapters focus on the dark side of the sacred. The religious life is necessarily lived in ambivalence because it is lived in the light of that which is not only attractive but also threatening to ordinary human selfhood. Any consideration of the attractiveness of religion which diminishes or omits this motif will be, from the perspective of the believing soul, one-dimensional religion.

Chapters Four through Six concern the second dimension, the benefits or usefulness of the religious life for those who participate in it. The central thesis here is that over and above any benefits which might be subsumed under the heading of worldly good fortune, the crucial concern of the believing soul is to find in the sacred a way of solving the problem of guilt and death. The analysis of these themes in existential terms shows their intimate linkage with each other and explains why they represent more nearly a single problem than two separate problems.

Chapters Seven and Eight sketch the third dimension of the religious life. The believing soul places the attractiveness of religion as a means of solving the problem of guilt and death in dialectical tension with not one theme, but two different themes. The first we have already noticed in the tension between the attractiveness of the sacred and its repelling features. The second occurs as the tension between the attractiveness of the religious life as a means to various ends and its attractiveness as an end in itself. This latter value is described as the value of useless self-transcendence. The meaning of this concept is developed in relation to two aspects of the religious life most easily susceptible to a merely utilitarian role, namely prayer or meditation and sacrifice.

Up to this point the goal has been to understand the believing soul as such. The attempt has been to exhibit structures or patterns which can be illustrated from a wide variety of very different religious traditions, "primitive," eastern, and western, and which thereby possess at least a *prima facie* claim to belong to religion generically. I certainly do not purport to have established universality by complete enumeration, and my claim to a kind of Husserlian *Wesensschau* is a relatively soft one. If definitive counter-examples can be shown, that will not diminish the value of noting important similarities that recur in dramatically different contexts.

In Chapters Nine through Eleven attention shifts from similarities to differences. Returning to the guilt and death motif from the second of religion's three dimensions, I develop a threefold typology for interpreting religious differences and seek to show the corresponding differences in the treatment of guilt and death which follow. The case for the universality of the guilt and death problem is strengthened through a more detailed study of its meaning in systematically different types of religious life. At the same time this commonality clearly does not drive differences to the periphery of the religious life as if they were unessential. On the contrary, we find irreducibly different understandings of the relation of human life to the sacred.

The key to this particular typology, which makes no pretense of being the only illuminating one, is the concept of world. As Heidegger has shown, being in the world is utterly basic to the being that each of us has to be. But it does not follow from the givenness of this structure that we take it in the same way or give it the same value. One possibility for the religious life is to take being in the world as such to be the human predicament. Following Ricoeur, I call this anti-worldly type of religion exilic, for it views worldly existence, both physical and psychical, to be an exile from which salvation offers liberation.

Another possibility is to take worldly life for a good thing, but only as nature and not as history. I call this semi-worldly type of religion mimetic, for it finds salvation in the imitative participation in the timeless events of the natural or cosmic order, most frequently mediated through myths.

The third possibility is to take worldly life as such for a good thing and to affirm both the natural and the historical dimensions of being in the world. I call this worldly type of religion covenantal, for it seems to presuppose that the sacred is manifest not only in nature but also in history, where by virtue of a vowed partnership, historical experience is shared by human and divine participants.

These three types of religion are illustrated from medieval eastern and ancient western texts that are culturally very remote from us. They were chosen for the clarity with which they exhibit their respective types. But the types themselves are possibilities for human experience. They are neither ancient nor modern, eastern nor western. Whether they are existentially remote (dead options) or near (live options) to us is not determined by our historical situation.

My debts in connection with this volume are numerous. Heartiest thanks are owed and hereby offered:

to Hope College for summer grants supporting research on this project;

to Juniata College for appointing me J. Omar Good Visiting Professor during 1981–82, giving me extra time to write and the opportunity to teach once again the course from which this book derives, this time on the basis of draft chapters of the manuscript;

to the students at Yale, Purchase, and Juniata whose interest and questions have contributed so much;

to those who have read part or all of the manuscript and offered both their encouragement and their helpful criticisms—Wayne Boulton, Steve Dunning, Louis Dupre, Art Jentz, David Myers, Nick Perovich, Charles Scott, John Smith, Al Verhey, Dennis Voskuil, Carol Westphal, and Bruce Wilshire, and an anonymous reader for Indiana University Press;

to James Edie and David Carr of the SPEP Editorial Board for their encouragement and support of the project;

to Kathy Brink, Anne Edgin, Chriss Raak, and Diana Smith for their patient and skillful assistance in preparing the manuscript.

Hope College   MEROLD WESTPHAL

1

The Art of Understanding as an Alternative Approach in the Philosophy of Religion

Philosophy lives in the perennial danger of losing touch with the everyday experiences it seeks to illuminate. As philosophy of religion it easily overlooks the fact that "out there in the real world" the question of religious truth, important as it is, is hardly ever the first question we raise about the religious claims we encounter. Colloquially speaking, we are more apt to ask, What's that all about? or Where are they coming from? than Is it really true? For unless we understand the meaning of the assertions we are invited to believe and the ideals we are urged to adopt, how can we even begin to pose coherent questions about their truth or value?

This question of meaning is often last as well as first. It does not disappear as soon as the question of truth has been decided. If that decision has been negative, one can become all the more curious about the secret of religion's hold on people and come, like Nietzsche, to ask such questions as "What is the Meaning of Ascetic Ideals?"[1] Even more, if one has become persuaded of certain religious truths and committed to certain religious ideals, that very persuasion and commitment will, unless they are shallow, generate an ever-renewed quest to understand more deeply the life one has chosen.

The question, then, that I invite you to join me in asking is, What does it mean to be religious? Among those for whom this will be a vital question and not merely an academic exercise are likely to be both those who are religiously committed and those hostile to reli-

1

gion, as well as those in between who fall on the spectrum from the mildly curious to the seriously searching. Our task will be to understand the religious life by interpreting its various manifestations.

1A. What a descriptive philosophy of religion is not: (a) evaluation

In giving priority to the question of meaning over that of truth we will be departing from what most typically occurs as philosophy of religion. The debate about the proofs for the existence of God clearly stands at the heart of a long-standing and widespread tradition in philosophy of religion. Instead of joining that debate we shall be inquiring into the meaning of God or the Sacred for the religious life as part of the overall attempt to discover what religion is all about. In this respect our enterprise is analogous to the philosophy of science and the philosophy of art. For rather than trying to establish which scientific theories are true or which works of art are best, these modes of philosophical reflection are directed toward understanding what science is all about and what it is to create or appreciate a work of art.

It is tempting to make this distinction as that between philosophizing about God and philosophizing about religion. But this won't quite work. We cannot philosophize about religion without discussing the "object" of religion, God, the gods, the Sacred, and so forth. Nor can we philosophize about God without implying claims about religion, for example, that it is man's highest activity or that it is one of his most deeply rooted illusions. The distinction that is really seeking expression here is between an evaluative or normative approach and a descriptive approach.

As a normative discipline the philosophy of religion seeks to evaluate the truth of religious assertions (and the value of religious ideals). In the West this links up historically with (1) the tradition of natural theology, including proofs for the existence of God and the immortality of the soul; (2) the tradition of rational apologetics, seeking to establish the truth of the Christian religion from the evidence of miracles and fulfilled prophecy; (3) the negation of the first, with Hume and Kant in the foreground; and (4) the negation of the second with Hume and Lessing in the foreground. In each case the philosopher is seeking to determine whether or not there is rational justification for holding to certain religious beliefs. The question of truth or falsity prevails.[2]

If one comes to be disenchanted with these debates, either on the grounds that they cannot satisfactorily be resolved or on the grounds that they tend misleadingly to reduce religion to its cognitive dimensions, one might come to wonder whether philosophy might have other tasks vis-à-vis religion than passing verdicts on its truth claims. Such tasks might well include the one we are undertaking, that of describing the religious life from within, that is, not as an observed fact but as a possible experience.

Historically speaking, Schleiermacher's *Speeches on Religion* (1799) represent the first major move toward such a descriptive philosophy of religion. As it subsequently became clearer that the interpretative task could be more fruitfully pursued when questions of truth (and value) were deliberately set aside or bracketed (Schleiermacher had presupposed a kind of pantheism), it came to be known as the phenomenology of religion.

There are historical precedents for this title. The first is the Kantian distinction between the phenomenal and noumenal, that is, between the real insofar as it appears to our experience and the real as it is in itself or as it would appear to an infinite intellect. Kant argued that God, freedom, and immortality do not belong to the phenomenal world, that they are not facts of our perceptual-scientific experience. A "transcendent metaphysics" seeking the truth about these putative realities which fall beyond the reach of experience is, for theoretical reasons at least, not possible as a science. But an "immanent metaphysics" describing the structures of human experience remains a legitimate and important philosophical task.

Kant's own development of such an "immanent metaphysics" was quite narrowly directed upon perceptual and scientific experience. But an analysis of the structure of religious experience would also fit into such a program, for while God may transcend perceptual-scientific experience, religion is an easily observed feature of the human world. Not even the most ardent atheist could deny that there are religious phenomena and that these can be described. It would be natural to call such a description a phenomenology of religion.

This naturalness is increased by two further historical precedents. Hegel, at the beginning of the nineteenth century, and Husserl at the beginning of our own, both used the term phenomenology to designate systematic attempts to understand human experience by describing its structure and dynamics from within. Husserl is especially important for the development of two concepts related to the deliberate setting aside of truth questions of which mention has already been made.

The first of these is the intentionality of consciousness. To say that consciousness is intentional is to say that it is *of* or *about* something, that it is directed toward its object. Husserl writes, "Cognitive mental processes . . . have an *intentio*, they refer to something, they are related in this or that way to an object. This activity of relating itself to an object belongs to them *even if the object itself does not.*"³ For example, in imagination, hallucination, and dreaming consciousness directs itself toward an object which is not publicly there. How glad we often are that our dream objects turn out to be unreal and how sad that our Walter Mitty fantasies remain just that. Yet we can describe these objects as present to consciousness, even if absent from the real world.

If that is so, Husserl argues, we can also describe objects of consciousness we take to be really there without regard for their reality. We can set aside or bracket all questions and beliefs about the real existence of the objects of consciousness in order to describe the way in which they appear to consciousness. Husserl uses a Greek name for this suspension of judgment about the existence of our object. He calls it the *epoche*. This second fundamental concept of his has direct bearing on our project, for in not asking about the real existence of the objects of consciousness we are deliberately setting aside the question of the truth of falsity of claims about God's existence in order to focus attention on the ways he is present to human experience, regardless of whether that presence is to be taken as veridical perception or some kind of illusion.

On the basis of these precedents in Kant, Hegel, and Husserl, I have called this descriptive philosophy of religion a phenomenology of religion. I am greatly indebted to each of these thinkers. Still, the methodological and speculative specifics of their systems are both complicated and controversial, and I do not wish to invoke any of them in their totality. There is no reason why the difficulty in mastering the intricacies of these systems or the debate over their soundness should stand in the way of seeking to understand the religious life.

The reader who finds one of these frameworks useful, will, I suspect, have little difficulty fitting what follows into it. Other general standpoints from which easy approaches to this enterprise can be made include: Jaspers's psychology of meaning (*verstehende Psychologie*), Weber's interpretative sociology (*verstehende Sociologie*), Dilthey's critique of historical reason, Strawson's descriptive metaphysics, Austin's notion of ordinary language philosophy as "linguistic phenomenology," and post-Wittgensteinian philosophy of action.

But none of these is really necessary. One need not have a ready-made philosophical methodology worked out in order to ask, What does it mean to be religious? In fact, it may well be an advantage not to have one, for there is always the danger, against which Hegel perennially warned, that method will obscure rather than illuminate what is to be grasped. But perhaps enough has been said both to indicate that our descriptive philosophy of religion need not be wedded to any particular philosophical tradition and to distinguish it from more traditional discussions of the existence of God, the problem of evil, the verification criterion of meaning, and the evidentiary value of mystical experience, all of which focus attention on the truth question. Whatever the strengths and weaknesses of the traditional approach, I am consciously seeking to develop an alternative in which evaluation (determination of truth and value) is temporarily suspended in order that description and thereby understanding may progress the more freely.[4]

1B. What a descriptive philosophy of religion is not: (b) explanation

There is a very important sense in which *explanation* is passed over, along with *evaluation*, for the sake of *description*. This dual self-denying ordinance is clearly expressed by van der Leeuw in his attempt to interpret the religious significance of art. "We do not intend to pursue causal relationships, but rather to search for comprehensible associations. Further, we do not intend to investigate the truth behind the appearance, but we shall try to understand the phenomena themselves in their simple existence."[5]

While van der Leeuw's second sentence concerns the distinction we have just been discussing between a descriptive philosophy of religion and the tradition rooted in the debate over natural theology, his first sentence indicates that the alternative is not a kind of scientific study of religion modeled on the experimental sciences. Those sciences have causal explanation rather than understanding as their goal, a statement which itself calls for some explanation if it is to be understood.

In ordinary usage we don't normally think of explanation and understanding as related to distinct intellectual goals. We often say that we didn't understand this or that until someone explained it to us, and then we understood it perfectly. This commonsense interchangeability of the two is reinforced in the experimental context (or is it the other way around—common sense having translated into everyday obviousness an inheritance from the scientific world view?) where it is taken for granted that we really understand this or that only when a good theoretical explanation has been given.

But there are at least two philosophical contexts, relevant for our purposes, in which a fairly sharp distinction between description and interpretation on the one hand and causal explanation on the other, has been made. One is the largely German debate after Dilthey over the methodological uniqueness of the *Geisteswissenschaften*; the other is the largely Anglo-Saxon philosophy of action in the aftermath of Wittgenstein and Ryle. In both cases it has been argued that when it comes to human behavior or action as the expression of the meaningful lived experience of persons our primary cognitive tools are quite different from those of the experimental sciences. To *understand* human action is to be able to *describe* and *interpret* it in terms of the agent's motives, intentions, wishes, desires, purposes, goals, reasons, and so on. This is quite different from giving the kind of *causal explanation* implied in Hume's famous and much imitated "attempt to introduce the experimental method of reasoning into moral subjects," a method grounded in the observation of constant conjunctions.[6]

To put it in Jaspers's words, the difference between understanding and explanation is that between meaningful connections (van der Leeuw's "comprehensible associations") and causal connections. In this context *Verstehen* (understanding) becomes a technical term and it is trivially true that we do not "understand" the movements of planets or positrons.[7]

The theory of action makes much the same point by distinguishing action or behavior from movement (in Aristotelian terms, *energeia* from *kinesis*). There is an important difference between "my hand rising above my head in the shape of a fist" and either "my making a gesture of political defiance" or "my signaling, as referee, that it is fourth down." The first movement would be involved in either of the other two actions, though the movement might not involve any action at all. You might learn, for example, that my arm moves in that way at the onset of an epileptic seizure or whenever an electrical signal is sent to an electrode implanted in my brain. (Question—is my own interpretation also fallible?) We specify which action, if any, we take the movement to express, by identifying the intention of the agent. In doing so we *describe* the movement at a new level of richness and *interpret* it as a specific piece of behavior.[8]

But do we also explain behavior when we describe and interpret it in terms of its motives, intentions, and so forth? This is the point at which the German tradition makes its sharp and uncompromising distinction between understanding and explanation, saying that the kind of interpretation we've been discussing involves understanding but not explanation. Within the philosophy of action two more flex-ible responses are to be found. One is to say that we explain, but not causally. The other is to say that we explain causally, but not in the strict, that is, experimental, sense of causal explanation.

Underlying this quarrel is a fundamental agreement. Even those who argue that (1) since we give the agent's motives, intentions, and so forth, in answer to the question, Why did he raise his fist? we must be explaining, and (2) since we reply, Because he wanted to signal fourth down, we must be giving a causal explanation, are eager to preserve the distinction intended by the original, absolute dichotomy between understanding and explanation. For it is widely agreed that whatever we are doing when we say, He raised his fist because he wanted to signal fourth down, we are not giving the kind of causal explanation involved in the experimental sciences and associated with the names of Hume, Mill, and Hempel.

There are three essential features of this kind of causal explanation which are not involved in interpreting action in terms of its motives, intentions, and so forth. (1) In the experimental sense cause and effect must be contingently related to each other, which means that the two must be independently identifiable. The one may not be a nec-essary ingredient in the description of the other. But intentions are not, at least in many instances, logically independent of the actions in which they are ingredient, but are necessary conditions (concep-tually, not experimentally) of those actions. Without the intention to signal fourth down, my fist's rising over my head simply doesn't count as the action of signaling fourth down. In this sense, motives can't be causes nor interpretations causal explanations.

(2) Causal explanations are nomological-predictive. That is to say they involve reference to the kind of general or universal rules that have predictive force. I explain a particular occurrence by showing how it could have been predicted and I both use and test the law by which the explanation was made by making other predictions with its aid.

But to understand an action in terms of its motives or intentions is not to invoke a law or any other kind of prediction generating uniformity. We understand the meaningful connection between the referee's intention and his behavior, though there is no law sug-gesting that whenever someone wants to signal fourth down he raises a fist (it used to be done by raising four fingers), or vice versa that whenever someone raises his fist his intention is to signal fourth down.

It might be replied that such laws are operative, though with lesser scope than those normally associated with science. If we limit the context to referees in football games we can, with the help of a human convention (artificial law), reliably predict that whenever the referee wants to signal fourth down he will raise his fist and vice versa. In order, then, to see the force of the original point we should consider an example from outside the framework of conventionally rule-governed behavior.

Jaspers give us such an example. "When Nietzsche shows how an awareness of one's weakness, wretchedness and suffering gives rise to moral demands and religions of redemption, because in this roundabout way the psyche can gratify its will to power in spite of its weakness, we experience the force of his argument and are convinced. It strikes us as something self-evident. . . . Such conviction . . . is not acquired inductively through repetition of experience."[9] What convinces us as being self-evident in this situation is not that altruistic and ascetic morality and redemptive religion always or with any statistical regularity arise from these roots. There need be no law here nor power of prediction for us to see that there is a meaningful connection between a certain admixture of actual weakness and the will to power on the one hand, and certain moral and religious behavior on the other. The one arises intelligibly out of the other. Even if we were persuaded that this was the proper interpretation of morality and religion only in the single case of the women in Nietzsche's childhood home, his account would help us to understand what it meant for them to be religious. Such an "explanation" would not in the least depend on any predictive power in the "meaningful connection" we had "understood" in "understanding" these women. Just as there are for Weber "*non-understandable uniformities,*" the laws of physical nature, so for Jaspers there are *understandable non-uniformities,* universals or typical patterns, since they may well be applicable to many instances, which are nevertheless not lawlike and predictive in their function. They are more accurately described as possibilities than as laws. The philosophy of action takes account of just these differences when motive and intention talk is said either to be non-causally explanatory or causally explanatory but not in the strict sense.

(3) In the example just given Jaspers stresses that the means by which *meaningful* connections are grasped is not the inductive procedure of observed regularity. This is perhaps most obvious in cases where the motive or intention ("cause") and the behavior we interpret or "explain" by it ("effect") are not logically or conceptually distinct. But his own example involves motivations which are not so tightly bound to the behavior that Nietzsche seeks to understand in

terms of them. The frustrations of impotence are not related to vindictive righteousness in the same way that the intention to signal fourth down is related to signaling fourth down. Yet I understand the possible link between impotence and certain moral and religious attitudes not because I have frequently observed them together, but because I too am human. I know something of the pain of powerlessness and can see how satisfaction might be found in certain forms of vengeance masquerading as piety. I can, if I am honest, recall such behavior on my own part, or, if not, I can imagine myself deriving satisfaction from acting in that way. Thus even if there is some observable regularity which could be inductively explored, that is not how I grasp the meaningfulness of a meaningful connection. This accounts for the fact that understanding is often contrasted with causal explanation in terms of the distinction "from within" and "from outside," and why the concepts of understanding and sympathy are so often linked.[10]

We have seen that it is possible by linguistic fiat entirely to separate the understanding which comprehends through motives and intentions from all notions of causality and explanation. Such a decision, though not entirely arbitrary, is nevertheless awkward. For motives and intentions have efficacy. Because they bring it about, various actions occur. In that sense, they are forces, even causes, which explain behavior. But unlike the causal forces of experimental science they are forces with meaning, and it is their meaningfulness rather than their efficacy which concerns us.[11] For we do not seek the technical control that nomological-predictive science provides. Nor are we interested in a behavior modification technique, that we might either produce and nourish or weaken and extinguish the religious life. We seek simply to understand what it is to be religious.

1C. What a descriptive philosophy of religion is: three models

It is time to become more affirmative. In distinguishing our project from evaluative and explanatory approaches to religion, we have focused on what it is not. This has given some indirect insight into what it is, but this needs to be made direct and explicit. The best way to find out what this or any other kind of philosophical reflection is is to do it. Methodological reflection can never replace experience. As with golfing and gardening, there is a big difference between reading or talking about how it is done and actually doing it. Since in this instance "doing it" will itself be a reflective activity and not a physical activity, one of the things that would count as "doing it" would be the thoughtful reading of the remaining chapters of this book. Nothing said in this chapter about what a descriptive philosophy of religion is can replace the understanding that will arise from working through the materials themselves.

Yet either before or after working through the materials themselves, or perhaps both before and after, it is useful to attempt to say what is going on in an affirmative as well as in a negative way. Our goal is understanding, and it would be foolish to suggest that there is a method for understanding in the sense of rules or recipes to be followed. But we can notice several non-philosophical modes of activity which are sufficiently like our project to throw some light rather directly upon it.

The first thing to notice is that in laying aside the question of truth, which is by no means a matter of indifference, and in abstaining from the kind of explanation which gives the power to control, there is a distinct distancing of ourselves from the field of active involvement with religion. We do not judge, and therefore we do not defend or attack, build up or tear down the religious phenomena we consider. It is not because we have abandoned the public domain in order to live out our personal piety or secularity in undisturbed privacy. It is because we want to see the whole public and private world of religion as only a measure of detachment permits it to be seen.

The visual arts depend on such detached perception. Erwin Straus suggests that it is just the distancing feature of vision, made possible by the upright posture, which permits seeing to become beholding or contemplation and makes the visual arts possible. "The eye of man, emancipated from the bondage of catching, grabbing, and gobbling, can dwell on the things themselves. . . . In the attitude of composure we reach the visible and yet leave it as it is. Distance is the condition of seeing the other in his uniqueness. . . . The distant opens itself to our gaze in contemplative regard, not in aggressive action. . . . The first great abstraction of suchness is achieved in the beholding gaze: the *eidos* [form] discerned from the *hyle* [matter]."[12]

Some such understanding of artistic vision inspired the work of Cezanne. As Herbert Read tells it, he wanted to see the world *objectively* "without any intervention either of the tidy mind or the untidy emotions. His immediate predecessors, the Impressionists, had seen the world *subjectively*—that is to say, as it presented itself to their senses in various lights, or from various points of view. . . . But Cezanne wished to exclude this shimmering and ambiguous surface of things and penetrate to the reality that did not change, that was present beneath the bright but deceptive picture presented by the kaleidoscope of the senses."[13]

This is that discrimination of *eidos* from *hyle* (Straus) which only disengaged contemplation makes possible. In our case it is not catching, grabbing, and gobbling that need to be checked, since religion isn't edible. But our eagerness to judge, and therefore to defend or attack, build up or tear down, involves the intervention of both the "tidy mind" and the "untidy emotions." While our lives would be poor indeed without either of these, it might well be richer if we were able to step back from both in the attempt to see things afresh. We could perhaps do worse than take this conception of artistic vision as one model for understanding our project of understanding.

A second model comes directly from a philosopher involved in developing a descriptive philosophy of religion. Paul Ricoeur's goal is "the interpretation of living experience," specifically the confession of fault. He calls his work "a purely descriptive phenomenology that permits the believing soul to speak. The philosopher adopts provisionally the motivations and intentions of the believing soul. He does not 'feel' them in their first naïveté; he 're-feels' them in a neutralized mode, in the mode of 'as if.' It is in this sense that phenomenology is a re-enactment in sympathetic imagination."[14]

The model here is that of the actor. When a great actress plays Lady Macbeth, she interprets the latter's experience by re-enacting it; and the success of her interpretation depends on her powers of sympathetic imagination. She gets inside the experience of her subject to such a degree that for a great performance it is as true to say that she becomes Lady Macbeth as it is to say that, of course, she doesn't. The aspect of imagination, of as if, of *re*-enactment is never completely transcended. The spontaneity of the original experience (in our case the religious life) is never simply duplicated. Yet the great actress (re)*feels* the motivations and intentions of Lady Macbeth and (re)*enacts* her deeds and her consequent torment. In doing so, both she and her audience come to understand Lady Macbeth.

The idea that our philosophical task involves something of the creative skills of the painter and the actress may be at once exhilarating and intimidating. There are dangers in both responses. If we are over-exhilarated, we may form such a grandiose image of our task that anything short of Sophoclean or Shakespearean grandeur will seem insignificant; while if we are over-intimidated, we may become afraid to get involved at all. In either case, it will be helpful to notice that the artistic skills we find ourselves in need of are related to another skill which comes from everyday life, rare and extraordinary as it is. This will be our third model, and we are led to it by Ricoeur's reminder that as we seek to employ the craft of the painter and the actress our goal is simply to "permit the believing soul to speak." What we need for this is the skill of the good listener.

If I am a good listener, I don't interrupt the other nor plan my own next speech while pretending to be listening. I try to hear what is said, but I listen just as hard for what is not said and for what is said between the lines. I am not in a hurry, for there is no pre-appointed destination for the conversation. There is no need to get there, for we are already here; and in this present I am able to be fully present to the one who speaks. The speaker is not an object to be categorized or manipulated, but a subject whose life situation is enough like my own that I can understand it in spite of the differences between us. If I am a good listener, what we have in common will seem more important than what we have in conflict.[15]

This does not mean that I never say anything, but I am more likely to ask questions than to issue manifestos or make accusations. All the same, some of the questions I ask will seem to the other to be hostile questions . They will be the kind of questions the prosecuting attorney asks on cross examination, but they will not be asked in a prosecuting manner. They will rather be asked as a confessor or therapist asks them. For the purpose is not to win the case but to free understanding from self-deception. Though the goal is to "permit the believing soul to speak," it does not follow that the believing soul is automatically taken at face value.[16]

1D. Whether this philosophical task is worth the effort

The ability to distinguish descriptive philosophy of religion from evaluative and explanatory approaches and to characterize it positively with the help of our painter, actor, and good listener models does not guarantee that the enterprise will seem worthwhile. Some tasks are not worth undertaking and some books are not worth reading. This may be one of them. So I hope that by this time you are asking yourself not just what it is I'm up to, but whether it will be worth your time and effort to accept the invitation to join me in asking what it means to be religious. You might, of course, read the book anyway, because it's been directly or indirectly assigned, or you've agreed to review it. But reading about the project in this book will be intrinsically valuable to you only if you find the project to be worth attempting yourself. Neither I nor anyone else can answer that question for you, but I can indicate why I have found this mode of philosophical reflection to be unusually fruitful both personally and pedagogically.

The central point has to do with noticing what is too obvious to be seen, with finding the glasses we've been wearing, or discovering that all our lives we've been speaking prose. This is what Hegel had in mind when he wrote, "The familiar, just because it is familiar, is not really understood."[17] Because he saw this to be a major concern of philosophy, he praised Bacon's empiricism, crude as it was, for having "entirely set aside and rejected the scholastic method of reasoning from remote abstractions and being blind to what lies before one's eyes."[18] It is the possibility of this blindness which makes possible the following provocative definition of discovery: to see what everyone has always seen and to think what no one has yet thought.

In our own time Merleau-Ponty has challenged philosophy to define itself in just these terms. "True philosophy consists in relearning to look at the world." For this to occur "we must break with our familiar acceptance of it. . . ." For his philosophical purposes "reflection does not withdraw from the world towards the unity of consciousness as the world's basis . . . it slackens the intentional threads which attach us to the world and thus brings them to our notice."[19]

The idea that philosophy consists in getting acquainted with the familiar is closely related to the earlier idea that philosophical method can consist in imitating the painter, the actress, and the good listener. For the skills of the painter, actor, and good listener consist in large part of noticing and making explicit what is there to be seen by all but is for the most part overlooked.

My own experience has been that the religious life provides a thoroughly convincing example of this wisdom. Surely a major reason why I've spent more time in philosophy of religion than in philosophy of science or of art is that I came to philosophy more familiar with religion than with science or art. But stopping to ask the simple question about something so familiar, What does it mean to be religious? has initiated a process of relearning to look at the world of religion. I haven't ceased to be religious nor changed my religion; and yet the process has been anything but conservative. For I see so many things so differently. At times discovery has been exhilarating; at other times personally painful. At the same time I've been able to see students of every conceivable religious and non-religious attitude discover how such a simple question can open up avenues of understanding previously shut off by the familiarity of the subject matter.

It is just this goal of noticing what is so often overlooked which calls for the bracketing of evaluation and explanation. For the habits of mind which blind us to what is before our eyes (to give as good a definition of prejudice as any) are deeply rooted in the categories and purposes at work when we ask those kinds of questions.

Suppose, for example, we wish to explore the significance of myth for religious life. If we are scientists before we are artists we may get ourselves into trouble. Schelling warns of this in his own monumental study of mythology, noting that the desire to explain brings with it the temptation to "suppress, devaluate, diminish, or truncate" our subject matter, thereby making explanation easier. "It is not a question what notion must be derived from the appearance in order that it may easily be explained by some philosophy or other; but on the contrary, what philosophy is required to grow to the same height as the object. We must not ask how the phenomenon must be turned, twisted, made one-sided, or stunted so that it may still be explained by principles that we once determined not to transcend; but rather, in what direction our own thought must expand itself in order to keep in touch with the phenomenon."[20] One might summarize by saying that we will understand mythology only if we are good listeners.

The critical urge as well as the explanatory urge can be a source of blindness. The problem here is one of intellectual territoriality. The desire to justify to myself and to others the position I have adopted can easily get in the way of noticing what is there. Have you, for example, ever seen a good listener in a dormitory bull-session on religion?

Freud was especially sensitive to this problem in a related context. His therapeutic task was to get his patients to see what was going on in their own experience entirely unobserved. He found the critical faculty to be a major obstacle to close self-observation, for ideas which were in some way personally threatening were either not allowed to arise at all or were given such short shrift that their significance was not discovered. So he prescribed a deliberate suspension of evaluative attitudes which bears a striking resemblance to our own bracketing, particularly in its purposive and temporary character. "The self-observer on the other hand need only take the trouble to suppress his critical faculty. . . . In the state used for the analysis of dreams and pathological ideas, the patient purposely and deliberately abandons this [critical] activity and employs the psychical energy thus saved . . . in attentively following the involuntary thoughts which now emerge. . . ."[21] In other words, self-knowledge arises only when the non-judgmental attitude of the therapist is paralleled in the patient as well.

The underlying rationale for this procedure is obvious and by no means limited to the pathological dimensions of experience. We all have a strong tendency to see what we want to see and not to see what we wish weren't there. That being so we can only assume that the influence of desire upon perception is a major cause of our not noticing what is directly before our eyes. Putting our desires out of play should improve our vision. We do that not by pretending we don't have desires, but by asking the kind of questions they are less likely to influence.

This, then, is the shape of my own reply to the question whether a descriptive philosophy of religion is worthy of my time and effort. I value the enterprise because I value its single, basic goal, becoming acquainted with a familiar but not always very well understood possibility for my own life and for our life together. If I abstain from evaluation and explanation in the process this is not an end in itself but simply a means to that goal.

1E. Warnings

In undertaking this task I am flying in the face of warnings from three philosophers for whom I have the greatest respect, Hegel, Kierkegaard, and Nietzsche. Since Kierkegaard's objection can be treated most briefly we shall consider it first. He argues that while it is possible to understand what Christianity is without being a Christian, it is not similarly possible to understand what it is to be a Christian without being one.[22] We can safely assume that he would generalize from this to the claim that we cannot understand what it means to be religious unless we are religious. That pinches. The invitation for you to join me in asking what it means to be religious assumes that whether or not you are already living the religious life in some form you already have some understanding of it and can broaden and deepen that understanding through a disciplined interpretation of the religious life as others have expressed it. The very notion of sympathetic imagination involves the claim that we can comprehend beyond the limits of our own experience. As Weber puts it, "One need not have been Caesar in order to understand Caesar."[23]

This disagreement with Kierkegaard is not total, however, and we would do well to heed his warning. There is a real difference between understanding the objective meaning of doctrinal propositions and understanding the subjective meaning of a life grounded in them.[24] Objective understanding may be a necessary condition for subjective understanding, but it is not a sufficient condition. When a bank president says, "I embezzled half a million dollars," we understand immediately what is said, though we may not comprehend nearly so well what the person who says it is going through. Or when a friend tells us her fiancé has been killed in an automobile accident, we know what has happened but may not realize very thoroughly what she is living through.

But though subjective understanding is clearly more difficult (and often more important) than objective understanding, it is clearly not impossible. We do not normally assume that we are cut off from the meaningful lived experiences of others unless we have experienced the same thing (an impossibility in any case). Just the opposite. Even if we've never been an executive, nor an embezzler, nor a bereaved lover, we can imagine ourselves in those situations and gain some idea of what such a person is going through, just as we can in some measure understand Lady Macbeth without having first to become adulterers and murderers.

The situations where this is not true are the exceptions rather than the rule, and we call attention to their unusual nature by saying, "I just can't imagine what it would be like to be. . . ." Even if there are cases where this is literally true, we would normally be speaking more accurately if we said, "I find it extraordinarily difficult to imagine what it would be like to be. . . ."

My own conclusion is that (1) we should learn from Kierkegaard not to confuse the relatively easy task of understanding objective meanings with the much more difficult goal we have given ourselves of understanding what it means to be religious, and (2) we should continue to assume that whether or not we are religious we can deepen our understanding of the religious life. Kierkegaard's distinction is an important one, but it does not separate an impossible from a possible task.

Nietzsche's objection is perhaps more formidable. Aware of the power of unconscious motives and of our endless capacity for bad faith and self-deception, he asks whether it is sufficient to "let the believing soul speak," to search out that motive "which seems to the actor himself the meaningful ground of his behavior," or to interpret behavior "under its intentional description for the agent."[25] Do not such phrases define a philosophy of consciousness which dogmatically affirms with Descartes the mind's transparency to itself?

Like the prophet Jeremiah, Nietzsche knows that "The heart is deceitful above all things and desperately corrupt," and he wonders out loud whether we can ever really understand ourselves. "But how do we recognize ourselves? How can man know himself? He is a dark and hidden thing; whereas the hare is said to have seven skins, man can take off seven times seventy skins and still not be able to say: 'That is you as you really are, that is no longer mere external appearance.' Besides, it is a painful and dangerous undertaking to dig down into oneself in this way to descend violently and directly into the core of one's being."[26]

It follows for Nietzsche that the philosopher in search of self-knowledge "has a duty to suspicion today, to squint maliciously out of every abyss of suspicion." To be sure we don't miss the point, he spells out this suspicion in detail. ". . . we immoralists have the suspicion that the decisive value of an action lies precisely in what is unintentional in it, while everything that is intention, everything about it that can be seen, known, 'conscious' still belongs to its surface and skin—which, like every skin, betrays something but conceals even more. In short, we believe that the intention is merely a sign and a symptom that still requires interpretation—moreover, a sign that means too much and therefore, taken by itself alone, almost nothing."

Nietzsche's suspicion about intentions can take a weak or a strong form, corresponding to two quite different meanings we can give to the question, Why are they doing that? In one case the question is equivalent to, What are they doing? We see movement that we cannot understand as meaningful behavior and use either question to request that the action be identified. But suppose the answer is that they are doing a tribal rain dance and that we already know this when we ask, Why are they doing that? We wonder whether they are trying to make it rain or to impress some talent scouts or to discover the aerobic value of such dancing. In this case our *Why* question is not equivalent to the *What* question. We are not inquiring about the intention which makes the action the action it is, but about a contingently related motive which leads to the performance of that action.

In its weaker version, Nietzschean suspicion suggests that we cannot simply let the believing souls speak, because while they may well know *what* they are doing, they don't always know *why*. Hidden motives may well be at work. The stronger version would be that they don't even know *what* they are doing. This wouldn't mean that they couldn't answer questions about what they are doing, but rather that because of the influence of unnoticed motives, these answers might very well be wrong. The believer might say, I am worshipping God, while the suspicious critic might conclude, No, you are only seeking the approval of your peers, or No, you're not expressing your love of God but only your fear.

It seems to be the stronger thesis which leads Scheler to write that "men may be firmly convinced with their conscious judgment that they profess the Christian idea of God. . . . But at the same time, as to the actual form of their Weltanschauung, they may be ruled by a totally different idea of God. For the structure of the natural religious consciousness can only include God's love . . . if men live with a sense that *love* is what leads, governs, prevails in their midst—not if completely different things (power, economic expansion, etc.), are so 'felt'. Therefore not the slightest inference as to a community's true natural beliefs may be drawn from the fact that its intellectuals (philosophers, theologians) *teach* in schools the Christian concept of God and reject in theory, say, Nietzsche's doctrine of power."[27]

In replying to Nietzsche two important facts need to be noted. First, the idea that behavior often arises from motives and intentions not noticed by the agent is not the special thesis of a particular philosophical school. One need not be a Freudian or a Nietzschean to talk about unconscious motives and self-deception. The idea has more nearly the status of a self-evident commonplace in the discussion of human action. It is, for example, casually assumed in the *Verstehen* tradition, in the philosophy of action, and in phenomenology, even where the special theories of Freud and Nietzsche about the nature of unconscious motives are not accepted.

Second, suspicion of religion based on this idea does not arise only from the anti-religious. Ricoeur, it is true, adds the name of Marx to those of Nietzsche and Freud and calls them the "school of suspicion," a group conspicuously hostile to religion.[28] But he might well have included Kierkegaard, and there are few more passionately believing souls. Kierkegaard writes that for true piety "seriousness consists precisely in having this honest suspicion of thyself, treating thyself as a suspicious character, as a capitalist treats an insolvent person. . . ." Many of his writings are best understood in the light of this statement.[29] Similarly, we have already seen the suspicion of Scheler, who is as friendly to religion in *On the Eternal in Man* as Nietzsche is hostile; and we have already compared Nietzsche to Jeremiah, which should remind us that the Hebrew prophets, like Jesus in their tradition, were highly suspicious of much of the religion surrounding them.[30] Whether Marx, Nietzsche, and Freud really added much to their discoveries is a question without an immediately obvious answer.

So the question posed by Nietzsche is not (1) whether behavior has unconscious motives or (2) whether we must seek to downplay this factor of religious life if we are to remain free from prejudice against religion. We have not committed ourselves to the transparency of consciousness to itself. On the contrary, we have questioned whether the agent's interpretation of his behavior is infallible and have implied that it is not, by allowing the good listener to cross-examine the believing soul, whose speech is not automatically to be taken at face value. We are prepared for the idea that the full meaning of the religious life can be grasped only through understanding believing souls better than they understand themselves.

Our problem arises at another point. Whether in the hands of ardent prophets or militant atheists, suspicion has typically been used for evaluative rather than descriptive purposes. Prophets use it to discredit the religious lives of those whose religion they take to be inauthentic, and atheists seek to go a step further and discredit the beliefs as well as the believers. In doing so, they open themselves to the question whether they are guilty of the genetic fallacy, but that won't be our problem, since we are not seeking to evaluate at either level. What we need to know is whether suspicion can be incorporated into a *descriptive* philosophy of religion. Can the believer be cross-examined as well as allowed to speak, while the goal still remains simply to understand the religious life?

At this point Peter Berger's idea of "methodological atheism" will be helpful to us. He seeks to bring the insights of a functionalist sociology to bear on religion, while at the same time carefully bracketing all truth questions. The sociological glasses through which he looks at religion are clearly not those of the believer. They reveal religion to be "an immense projection of human meanings into the empty vastness of the universe."[31] This notion of projection, which Berger relates to the school of suspicion and behind them to Feuerbach, has been the basic tool of much modern atheism. For if it tells the whole story about religion, religion would be a human invention and not a discovery or a response. We would have created God in our own image rather than vice versa.

But Berger insists that while it is undeniable that the religious affirmation of meaning is a human act, it is just not an empirical question whether this act is an invention or a discovery, illusory or revelatory. In describing religion as a projection the sociologist highlights its observable characteristic of being a human act. But it would be presumptuous for the sociologist as empirical observer to assume either that this human act is nothing but a human act or that it is something much more. Correspondingly "rigorous brackets have to be placed around the question as to whether these projections may not *also* be something else than that (or, more accurately, *refer to* something else than the human world in which they empirically originate). In other words, every inquiry into religious matters that limits itself to the empirically available must necessarily be based on a 'methodological atheism.' "[32]

Though our philosophy of religion does not seek to be "empirical" in Berger's sense, our interest in remaining descriptive places us under similar restraints. We might well view our letting the believing soul speak as *methodological* theism, since we are not committed to taking what is said at face value on either the question of meaning or truth, just as our cross-examination of the believing soul is *methodological* atheism, since we are no more committed to the thesis that self-deception is the basic fact about the religious life.

This incorporation of suspicion into our methodology is an acknowledgment that Nietzsche's critique is not simply to be repudiated, any more than Kierkegaard's. But we will incorporate it in our own way, much as Ricoeur seeks to incorporate Freudian suspicion into a phenomenological interpretation of religion. "My working hypothesis," he writes, ". . . is that psychoanalysis is necessarily iconoclastic, regardless of the faith or non-faith of the psychoanalyst, and that this 'destruction' of religion can be the counterpart of a faith purified of all idolatry. Psychoanalysis as such cannot go beyond the necessity of iconoclasm. This necessity is open to a double necessity, that of faith and that of non-faith, but the decision about these two possibilities does not rest with psychoanalysis. . . . The question remains open for every man whether the destruction of idols is without remainder; this question no longer falls within the competency of psychoanalysis."[33]

Needless to say, the descriptive philosopher of religion is no more in a position to answer this question than the sociologist or psychoanalyst. This may generate a measure of anxiety in the believer and unbeliever alike. Both are asked to enter into a conversation devoid of the assuring assumption that their own stances are justified.

We come now to Hegel's warning. Like the "third wave" in Plato's *Republic* this difficulty may be the most challenging of all. If, as Keith Campbell suggests, the move from questions of truth to questions of meaning defines "philosophy's new bad image," can a descriptive philosophy of religion be more than just another instance of contemporary philosophy's lapse into "pedantic triviality"?[34] Worse yet, does not the bracketing of truth questions involve a posture of timid detachment and fastidious objectivity so distant from religious attitudes themselves as to constitute a prejudice against them, even if, *mirabile dictu*, we come to understand the religious life in the process?

This, I believe, is the heart of the question Hegel raises in the aftermath of Hume and Kant, whose assault on the proofs of God's existence provided, as we have briefly noted, the historical setting in which our own project originally had its roots. He finds that assault to have generated the assumption that "we do not know God," an assumption which "permits us to speak merely of our relation to him, to speak of religion and not of God Himself. It does not permit a theology, a doctrine of God, though it certainly does allow a doctrine of religion. . . . We at least hear much talk . . . about religion, and therefore all the less about God Himself." This complaint from just two years before Hegel's death echoes one from an early essay. "Since the firm standpoint which the almighty age and its culture have fixed for philosophy is one of reason dependent upon sensibility, it follows that such philosophy can proceed to knowing, not God, but what one calls Man."[35]

What Hegel has in mind is the move from what Kant called "transcendent metaphysics" to "immanent metaphysics," from religious-philosophical affirmation to the description of human experience. In the context of an empiricist repudiation of metaphysics it is clear that what bothers Hegel is not primarily the re-direction of attention from God to man and his religion, as if he thought the two must be forever kept separate; it is rather the attitude which underlies this re-direction. Just as Hume wanted "to introduce the *experimental* method of reasoning into moral subjects," so Kant wanted to find the royal road to metaphysics as a *science*. In other words, it seems to be the desire for the detached objectivity of the natural sciences which motivates the move to the descriptive, and Hegel suspects that the result is an attitude alien to the true aims of both religion and philosophy. Might not that pursuit of objectivity which limits itself to the phenomenal, observable, perhaps even to the testable domain be a fear of error which turns out to be a fear of truth?[36] Is not a descriptive philosophy of religion methodologically prejudiced against its subject matter, just as much in its methodological theism as in its methodological atheism?

To be methodologically prejudiced against a subject matter is to be committed by one's method to an approach so alien to the subject matter as to preclude the possibility of any deep understanding. To study love with a microscope or electrons with the tools of a literary critic is to be methodologically prejudiced against one's subject matter.

This problem comes sharply to light in one of the classics in the descriptive philosophy of religion. In the opening paragraph of *Religion in Essence and Manifestation*, Gerardus van der Leeuw writes, "That which those sciences concerned with Religion regard as the *Object* of Religion is, for Religion itself, the active and primary Agent in the situation or, in this sense of the term, the *Subject*. In other words, the religious man perceives that with which his religion deals as primal, as originative or causal; and only to reflective thought does this become the Object of the experience that is contemplated. For Religion, then, God is the active Agent in relation to man, while the sciences in question can concern themselves only with the activity of man in his relation to God; of the acts of God himself they can give no account whatever."

This stark antithesis of agent and spectator perspectives on religion enables us to see that on this point at least there is important agreement between Hegel and the nineteenth-century existentialists. For Kierkegaard and Nietzsche can gladly join in and even push the point a step further. Both would agree with Antonin Artaud when he says, "If our life lacks brimstone, i.e., a constant magic, it is because we choose to observe our acts and lose ourselves in considerations of their imagined form instead of being impelled by their force."[37]

One would have to be intrepid to the point of foolhardiness simply to dismiss this danger of methodological prejudice. Even more than the previous warnings this one has too much substance to be ignored. We are in danger of being put out of business at the start by becoming persuaded of the incoherence of our project. There is, I believe, only one way to avoid this result. That is to establish that the stance of detachment and disengagement which defines the descriptive attitude is not motivated by the desire to be rigorously scientific, but rather by a passion for self-understanding that is itself neither detached nor disengaged. There are two ways of practicing the Platonic dialectic which finds the world too much with us and withdraws from the gallimaufry of the cave. There is the Socratic way arising from a deep, inner need which supersedes the rights of business as usual, and there is the Aristotelian practice which turns into a luxury of the leisure class. Our own transcendence of the cave, our stepping back from the immediacy of everyday involvements must take Socrates and not Aristotle as its mentor.

In our own time it is Merleau-Ponty who has perhaps expressed this best. Against Husserl's ideal of a descriptive philosophy which would be a rigorous science he presents the alternative of an existential phenomenology in which the phenomenological or descriptive component is not an end in itself but is in the service of existential, personal needs. As in our use of the painter model, Merleau-Ponty notices the role of *theoria* or contemplation in the detachment of essence or possibility from existence or fact (cf. Straus in 1C. above). But he places that entire process in its larger context, which is not the pursuit of scientific security. "That means that we cannot subject our perception of the world to philosophical scrutiny without ceasing to be identified with that act of positing the world, with that interest in it which delimits us, without drawing aback from our commitment which is itself thus made to appear as a spectacle, without passing from the *fact* of our existence to its *nature*, from the Dasein to the Wesen. But it is clear that the essence is here not the end, but a means, that our effective involvement in the world is precisely what has to be understood and made amenable to conceptualization, for it is what polarizes all our conceptual particularizations. The need to proceed by way of essences does not mean that philosophy takes them as its object, but on the contrary, that our existence is too tightly held in the world to be able to know itself as such at the moment of its involvement, and that it requires the field of ideality in order to become acquainted with and to prevail over its facticity."[38]

This brings us back to our earlier theme of self-knowledge through becoming acquainted with the familiar. The familiarity of this theme by now must not hide from us, however, the doubly radical way in which Merleau-Ponty develops it. First, it is not merely our beliefs and assertions about the world which are to be subjected to philosophical scrutiny; it is our *perception* of the world, the way we see and feel it. We have already learned, especially from Scheler, that we must dig beneath the level of theory and creed to the experience which these express and sometimes disguise. Second, this deep digging pursuit of self-understanding does not arise from purely theoretical motives, nor does it arise out of idle curiosity. We seek to understand our effective involvement in the world, not to fill the storehouse of knowledge, but in order to prevail over the facticity of our existence, *to preside over our lives.* Freud once wrote, "We are lived by unknown and uncontrollable forces."[39] Knowing how true this is so much of the time, Merleau-Ponty points us to philosophical reflection in the descriptive mode as an active struggle against that kind of inert living. In doing so he leads us back to the perennial source of the best philosophical inspiration, to Socrates.

2

Ambivalence
and the Sacred

2A. Ambivalence and ontological inadequacy

Perhaps you have watched a toddler in the presence of a large dog who is not part of the family. The child is frightened and fascinated at the same time. This ambivalence is visible in the uncertainty of its bodily movements, which are an indecisive alternation between reaching out and withdrawing to safety. It is equally visible in the face of the child and in its oral response which cannot quite resolve itself into either laughing or crying.

Or perhaps you have stood on the Canadian Side of Niagara Falls at that point where you can stand so close to the edge of the falls as to be nearly on top of them. Did not the edge, like the edge of any cliff, draw you irresistibly toward it while at the same time it terrified you and made you want to keep at quite a safe distance? And did you suddenly understand those daredevils who go over the falls in steel balls as you felt the urge, not merely to get close to the edge, but to become part of that awesome demonstration of power and grace by jumping in and hurtling over the edge yourself? The very thought is enough to make you shudder and to see the falls as a seductive power from which you instinctively keep, again, a safe distance.

These complex but by no means esoteric experiences of ambivalence in the face of the awesome have their parallels in the religious life. It is in attempting to name such an experience that Rudolf Otto describes the holy as the *mysterium tremendum et fascinans*. This much-cited formula will be explored in Section 2C, but at present we need to give attention to the kinds of experience it seeks to interpret. Here's an example from medieval Jewish mysticism. It is from the autobiographical account of an anonymous disciple of Abulafia, a major Kabbalist writer of the thirteenth century. In pursuit of "progress to spiritualization" he had been taught to meditate on the letters

24

in the seventy-two names which make up the Great Name of God according to Kabbalist teaching. "But when I had done this for a little while, behold, the letters took on in my eyes the shape of great mountains, strong trembling seized me and I could summon no strength, my hair stood on end, and it was as if I were not in this world. At once I fell down, for I no longer felt the least strength in any of my limbs. And behold, something resembling speech emerged from my heart and came to my lips and forced them to move. I thought—perhaps this is, God forbid, a spirit of madness that has entered into me? But behold, I saw it uttering wisdom. I said: 'This is indeed the spirit of wisdom.' "

In the morning he told his teacher about it, who "wanted to free me of it for he saw my face had changed. But I said to him: 'In heaven's name, can you perhaps impart to me some power to enable me to bear this force emerging from my heart and receive influx from it?' For I wanted to draw this force towards me and receive influx from it, for it much resembles a spring filling a great basin with water. If a man (not being properly prepared for it) should open the dam, he would be drowned in its waters and his soul would desert him. He said to me; 'My son, it is the Lord who must bestow such power upon you for such power is not within man's control.' "[1]

From the tribal religion of Brazil, where the Sun God is worshipped as "my father," comes this account of his appearance to a village chief. "I recognized at once that it was he. Then I lost all courage. My hair stood on end, and my knees were trembling. I put my gun aside, for I thought to myself that I should have to address him, but I could not utter a sound because he was looking at me unwaveringly. Then I lowered my head in order to get hold of myself and stood thus for a long time. When I had grown somewhat calmer, I raised my head. He was still standing and looking at me. Then I pulled myself together and walked several steps toward him, then I could not go any further for my knees gave way."[2]

An equally dramatic instance occurs in Chapter 11 of the *Bhagavad-Gita*, probably the most popular and widely read of all Hindu texts. Krishna, a divine manifestation in human form, has appeared to Arjuna at a time of personal distress. After lengthy conversation, Arjuna asks "to see Thy divine form, O Supreme Person." Krishna is transfigured and Arjuna beholds "the whole universe, with its manifold division gathered together in one, in the body of the God of gods." He is "struck with amazement, his hair standing on end," and he says, "I behold Thee, infinite in form on all sides, with numberless arms, bellies, faces and eyes, but I see not Thy end or Thy middle

or Thy beginning, O Lord of the universe, O Form Universal . . .
Thou art the Imperishable, The Supreme to be realized. Thou art
the ultimate resting place of the universe; Thou art the undying
guardian of the eternal law. Thou art the Primal Person, I think. I
behold Thee as one without beginning, middle or end, of infinite
power, of numberless arms, with the moon and the sun as Thine
eyes, with Thy face as a flaming fire, whose radiance burns up this
universe. . . . Seeing Thy great form . . . the worlds tremble and so
do I . . . my inmost soul trembles in fear and I find neither steadiness
nor peace . . . I lose sense of the directions and find no peace. . . .
Tell me who Thou art with form so terrible."

Krishna's strange reply follows: "Time am I, world-destroying,
grown mature, engaged here in subduing the world." Arjuna, "with
folded hands and trembling, saluted again and prostrating himself
with great fear," replies, "Rightly does the world rejoice and delight
in Thy magnificence. The Raksasas are fleeing in terror in all directions and all the hosts of perfected ones are bowing down before
Thee (in adoration). . . . O Infinite Being, Lord of the gods, Refuge
of the universe, Thou art the Imperishable, the being and the nonbeing and what is beyond that . . . boundless in power and immeasurable in might, Thou dost penetrate all therefore Thou art All. . . .
I have seen what was never seen before and I rejoice but my heart
is shaken with fear."[3]

Of course the point of these examples is not to suggest that being
religious consists in having one's hair stand on end.[4] It is rather that
the sacred is perceived as simultaneously attractive and repellent,
"delectable" and "distressing,"[5] evoking such contradictory emotions as joy and fear. This kind of ambivalence appears in less spec-
tacular forms within the quietness of the contemplative life. Speaking
of the monk reading the scriptures and reciting the liturgy, Thomas
Merton writes, "The Word of God which is his *comfort* is also his
distress. The liturgy, which is his *joy*, and which reveals to him the
glory of God, cannot fill a heart that has not previously been humbled
and emptied by *dread*."[6] From the Hesychast tradition, whose very
name means quietness and repose, we hear that prayer brings a consciousness "of two things at the same time: on the one hand, of *joy*
and *consolation*; on the other, of *trembling* and *fear* and *mourning*."[7]

The same tension appears in Augustine's account of his intellectual
discovery, by no means devoid of emotion, of God as truth. "Eternal
Truth, true Love, beloved Eternity—all this, my God, you are. . . . I
gazed on you with eyes too weak to resist the dazzle of your splendor.

Your light shone upon me in its brilliance, and *I thrilled with love and dread alike.*"[8]

Augustine continues his account by giving us an important clue to the meaning of the fear and trembling, dread and distress which seem to accompany the joy and delight experienced in the presence of the Sacred. "Far off, I heard your voice saying 'I am the God who IS' . . . and at once I had no cause to doubt. *I might more easily have doubted that I was alive than that Truth had being.*"[9]

It was, to repeat, as much an intellectual discovery as a mystical vision which led Augustine to sense that he was in touch with something more real than himself. But it comes as no surprise that mystical ecstasy might express itself in the same way. William James gives us a vivid example from the account of an anonymous clergyman, "I remember the night, and almost the very spot on the hilltop, where my soul opened out, as it were, into the Infinite, and there was a rushing together of the two worlds, the inner and the outer. It was deep calling unto deep . . . I stood alone with Him who had made me . . . I did not seek him, but felt the perfect unison of my spirit with his. The ordinary sense of things around me faded. . . . The darkness held a presence that was all the more felt because it was not seen. I could not any more have doubted that He was there than that I was. Indeed, *I felt myself to be, if possible, the less real of the two.*"[10]

Mahatma Gandhi's experience leads to the same result. "But I worship God as Truth only. I have not yet found him, but I am seeking after him. . . . Often in my progress I have had faint glimpses of the Absolute Truth, God, and daily the conviction is growing upon me that *He alone is real and all else is unreal.*"[11]

Maurice Friedman tells of the Hasidic rebbe who seeks to transmit something of this experience to his pupil, Moshe, whom he asks, "What do we mean by God?" Three times the question is met by silence because, as Moshe explains, "I do not know." "Do you think I know?" says the rebbe. "But I must say it, for it is so, and therefore I must say it. *He is definitely there, and except for Him nothing is definitely there—and this is He.*"[12]

Most of the time most of us are more inclined to agree with Descartes. The meaning of his famous "I think, therefore I am" is simply that while everything else may be doubtful I cannot doubt my own reality; for it is the unshakable foundation for all my experiences. Everything else is relative to it. But the religious experiences we've been reviewing have just the opposite structure. They are based on a sense of the presence of something that is more real than I myself and the world of my immediate experience. I become what is relative, and in relation to this something I find myself to be suddenly doubt-ful, less real and not definitely there.

We might use an honorable old scholastic term to draw the con-trast, saying that for profane consciousness the self is the *ens realis-simum*, the most real being, while the rebbe, Gandhi, the anonymous clergyman, and Augustine live a religious life grounded in the ex-periential denial of this assumption. This denial is itself grounded in the experiential affirmation of something else as the truly real. To speak here of experiential affirmation and denial is simply to say that we are dealing not with theories or beliefs in tension with each other, but with perceptions which deny each other. Profane consciousness *sees* itself to be what another mode of consciousness, quite clearly religious in nature, *sees* itself not to be.

The sense of selfhood involved here need not be highly indivi-dualized. The self, whose ultimacy is at stake, may be a collective (tribal or national) self as easily as a personal self. The sense of human nothingness before the sacred can even extend to the whole human race and all its history.

> Why, to him nations are but drops from a bucket,
>   no more than moisture on the scales;
> coasts and islands weigh as light as specks of dust. . . .
>   All nations dwindle to nothing before him,
>   he reckons them mere nothings, less than nought.[13]

Such a conflict of perceptions is bound to generate profound ten-sion within experience. Emotional ambivalence is sure to accompany it, and we can hardly be surprised to find the self responding "with love and dread alike." Or, to put it another way, what could be more fascinating than that which is so real that everything else *including myself* seems somehow unreal? And what could be more threatening to the security systems in which I constantly enwrap myself? Like the toddler before a large dog and the adult at the edge of Niagara, the believing soul is inevitably caught between the impulse to embrace and the impulse to flee, to rejoice and to tremble, to love and to hate.[14]

2B. Ontological inadequacy and paradoxical expression

This ambivalence and its groundedness in the very nature of the sacred come to a variety of expressions in the collective testimony of the believing soul, the religious text we are seeking to understand and interpret. One of the simplest expressions of the spontaneous sense of one's own tenuous reality is the contrast between human weakness and divine power, as in the words of the children's song: "Little ones to Him belong; they are weak but he is strong." In this same vein, among the cattle-breeding Nuer tribes of the southern Sudan "above all else God is thought of as the giver and sustainer of life. He also brings death. Nuer say that since it is his world he can take away what he has given." One must therefore not complain nor grieve too much at the loss of a child or of cattle.[15]

It is no wonder the anthropologist studying the Nuer cannot help thinking of the biblical Job. For his is perhaps the most dramatic expression of God as the ultimate giver and taker and of man's corresponding impotence.

> Naked I came from the womb,
> naked I shall return whence I came.
> The Lord gives and the Lord takes away;
> blessed be the name of the Lord.[16]

Expressions of this sort led Schleiermacher to his celebrated definition of religion as the "feeling of absolute dependence."[17] But this way of putting it is never fully adequate to the experience of the believing soul. For the movement from the relative dependence we experience in relations to other finite realities to the absolute dependence experienced in relation to the sacred takes the believing soul beyond questions of power to questions of status and worth. Correspondingly, the sense of ontological inadequacy comes to expression in strong metaphors of self-depreciation.

Thus the Nuer speak of themselves as *doar*, stupid or foolish, before God, the spirit or spirits of the sky, and they liken themselves to *cok*, small black ants. Though they are a proud people in relation to other humans, "All of us are *like little ants in the sight of God*."[18] In like manner the Sioux Indian humbles himself when he prays, "remembering his nothingness in the presence of the Great Spirit" and making himself *"lower than even the smallest ant."* As another Sioux puts it, "We raise our hands (when we pray) because we are wholly dependent on the Great Spirit; it is His liberal hand that supplies all our wants. We strike the ground afterward, we are *miserable beings, worms crawling before His face*."[19] And Abraham, wanting to pray for wicked Sodom, asks, "May I presume to speak to the Lord, *dust and ashes that I am. . . .* "[20]

But straightforward metaphors of self-depreciation are as little adequate to the expressive task at hand as are those of dependency. Psyche is a believing soul who discovers this in C.S. Lewis's retelling of the ancient myth of Cupid and Psyche. She has just seen the god of the wind, West-wind himself in human form but most clearly not a man. She is trying to explain it all to her sister. She begins by suggesting that "we, beside the gods, are like lepers beside us." But she realizes this hasn't conveyed her meaning. So she confesses that in the presence of the god and the spirits accompanying him she felt ashamed, "Ashamed of looking like a mortal—ashamed of being a mortal. . . . This shame has nothing to do with He or She. It's the being mortal—being, how shall I say it? . . . insufficient. Don't you think a dream would feel shy if it were seen walking about in the waking world?"[21]

It is surely strange to speak of being ashamed, not of what I have done but of what I am, or, to speak more precisely, of what I am not. Psyche's attempt to give expression to her experience of ontological inadequacy (her term is insufficiency) results in a very peculiar statement and a radically new kind of metaphor. A leper is every bit as real as a healthy person, though not as beautiful or capable. But a dream in relation to the reality of the waking world, that is a wholly different matter. Like the metaphors of dust and ashes, of the worm, and of the ant, the leper metaphor is striking and vivid. But the dream metaphor is downright paradoxical. So counter is it to everyday common sense that it's hard to be sure just what it means or whether it can mean anything at all.

It turns out that Psyche is the rule rather than the exception. The believing soul is regularly led to paradoxical forms of expression in the attempt to give words to the sense of ontological inadequacy which underlies the rest of its experience.[22] Thus we should not be surprised to find the straightforward picture of God as the ultimate giver and taker transformed into a paradoxical variation on the same theme, as in the following Muslim prayer:

> Sometimes He gives while depriving you,
> and sometimes He deprives you in giving.[23]

The frequency of paradox in the religious text has not gone unnoticed. But since the discussion of this phenomenon usually occurs in the context of a philosophy of religion oriented toward evaluation, it usually falls under the heading, Paradox and Logical Consistency. A phenomenology of religion which gives priority to understanding will proceed differently. Taking the experience of ontological inadequacy as a clue, it will pose a new problem, that of Paradox and Emotional Ambivalence. For the latter gives rise to paradoxical expression and is in turn reinforced thereby. The remainder of this section will briefly explore two prevalent forms of paradoxical religious expression with a view to their rootedness in the ambivalence of ontological inadequacy.

The first of these is the metaphysics of appearance and reality or of degrees of being. This is already hinted at in Psyche's suggestion that in the presence of the god she felt like a dream wandering in the waking world. In the West and the East alike, this sense is transformed into full-fledged metaphysical systems. Right after Augustine confesses that "I might more easily have doubted that I was alive than that Truth had being," he describes the ensuing reflection. "Also I considered all the other things that are of a lower order than yourself, and I saw that they have not absolute being in themselves, nor are they entirely without being. They are real insofar as they have their being from you, but unreal in the sense that they are not what you are. For it is only that which remains in being without change that truly is."[24] In texts like this and in Anselm's description of God as "that than which a greater cannot be conceived" and "that which cannot be conceived not to exist" we have the foundations for the medieval theology of God as *ens realissimum*. Such a metaphysics can look like sterile speculation only when it becomes separated from the experience it seeks to express. Anselm was himself keenly aware of that possibility, for he no sooner concludes his own famous ontological proof of the existence of God, grounded in the two descriptions just cited, than he cries out, "If you have found him, why is it that you do not *perceive* what you have found? O Lord God, why does my soul not *perceive* you if it has found You?"[25] Anselm is eager to complete the circle from experience to concept and back to experience. This is perhaps why both he and Augustine develop their metaphysical speculations in the form of prayer, constantly addressing God in the first person.

The concept of *maya* in Hinduism's Advaita (non-dualist) Vedanta and the contrast between Samsara and Nirvana in Buddhism represent even more radical versions of the metaphysics of appearance and reality. For the former, *Brahman*, one without a second, is all there is. Any duality or plurality in our experience is ignorance in the active sense of misperception. The whole realm of distinct beings of name and form, *including myself*, is *maya*, appearance. It is as with a mirage or as when in the dark we mistake a rope for a snake or a post for a man or mother-of-pearl for silver. What we think we see simply isn't there. Thus "for him who has reached the state of truth and reality the whole apparent world does not exist."[26] Naturally the distinctions we make with the help of name and form are "valid, as far as the phenomenal world is concerned," but that world has been deprived of its ultimacy, even, in some strong sense, of its very being.

In like manner much of Buddhist metaphysics lies in explaining the three marks which characterize everything in Samsara, the worldly domain ruled by the law of Karma and the cycle of birth, death, and rebirth. That whole world and all its parts are (1) impermanent, (2) sorrowful or filled with misery, and (3) lacking in self or ego. It is the latter point which especially concerns us here. In seeking to explicate the non-selfhood of everything which falls within our normal experience, including most religious experience, Buddhist texts resort to a proliferation of metaphors which fall into two general categories. One category parallels the Advaita Vedantist tradition in Hinduism exactly. The "emptiness" of things, *including myself,* is to be understood in terms of my awareness of them being likened to a magical illusion, a mirage, a misperception due to eye disease, or a dream. In short, what I see simply isn't there, and I am not either. The other set of metaphors likens all such things, including once again, myself, to the most insubstantial items of experience, bubbles, foam, echoes, and so on. The *Dhammapada* sums it up rather succinctly. "Knowing that this body is like froth, knowing that it is of the nature of a mirage, breaking the flowery shafts of Mara, he will go where the king of death will not see him. . . . Look upon the world as a bubble; look upon it as a mirage. Him who looks thus upon the world the king of death does not see."[27] Here too, it is clear that we are not dealing with speculation for its own sake, for what is at issue is how to be able to face death without fear.

The believing soul's sense of not being (fully) real has taken on elaborate expression in the Christian Platonism of Augustine and Anselm and the illusionist doctrines of Hindu and Buddhist metaphysics.[28] A fundamental religious experience has been taken as the decisive clue to the nature of reality, and the systematic articulation of this takes the form of paradoxical expression. For what could be more paradoxical than the statement, "I am not (fully) real"? By speaking (to or about the sacred) the self asserts its own reality, but by what it says (to or about the sacred) it undercuts the original assertion. The Cartesian experience of the self as absolute center is simultaneously given and taken away.

The result of this is twofold. First, the original experience has been expressed with an adequacy which nothing short of this paradoxical language could achieve. The emotional tension of ambivalence has been mirrored in the conceptual tension of paradox. Second, the original experience is reinforced and recapitulated. Whereas the original sense of tenuous selfhood occurred in the immediacy of direct experience, it has now been translated into the reflective mode. What was first encountered in feeling and perception is now met in conceptual articulation made available to the intellect. This opens the door to a great deal of definition, dialectic, and debate, but in the final analysis serves to integrate the believing soul (whose status is so problematical) by bringing feeling and intellect together.

The fragility of being human comes to expression in a second paradoxical way which exhibits ambivalence, namely in the representation of the holy as simultaneously attractive and repulsive. The gods are at once creative and destructive, the source of life and of death, beautiful and ugly, tender and terrifying, intimate and remote, and so forth. Among the Sioux, for example, the sacred pipe which is central to their religious rites was brought to the people by a very beautiful woman, dressed in white buckskin. She suddenly appeared to two hunters, one of whom immediately recognized her as *wakan* (sacred), though the other had lustful intentions toward her. As she approached she asked the latter to join her. "They were both covered by a great cloud, and soon when it lifted the sacred woman was standing there, and at her feet was the man with the bad thoughts who was now nothing but bones, and terrible snakes were eating him." At the same time it is she through whom the pipe and thereby the gift of life itself is given to the people from *Wakan-Tanka*, the Great Spirit.[29]

Though the moral element of judgment is present in this instance it need not be. There is perhaps nowhere to be found a stronger link between God and the moral law than in the story of the giving of the Ten Commandments at Mount Sinai. It is all the more striking that it is just in that context that the destructive power of God in his sheer being, apart from any element of moral judgment, is experienced. Immediately after the listing of the Ten Commandments, the narrative continues, "When all the people saw how it thundered and the lightning flashed, when they heard the trumpet sound and saw the mountain smoking, they trembled and stood at a distance. 'Speak to us yourself,' they said to Moses, 'and we will listen; but if God speaks to us we shall die.' " Shortly afterward, when Moses says to God, "Show me thy glory," the reply is, "My face you cannot see, for no mortal man may see me and live."[30] It is human mortality not human sinfulness which constitutes the danger here. It is not God's anger at his people's disobedience but the sheer energy of his divine reality which makes him dangerous. Yet this God is loved as the giver and preserver of life, who lovingly enters into covenant relationship with his people.

Whenever Hindu piety represents the holy as gods this same unity of creator and destroyer is close at hand. This is dramatically true for Krishna, the most beloved of the Hindu gods. We have already seen him in the *Bhagavad-Gita* present himself as "world destroying time." There he also tells Arjuna, "I am the origin of all; from Me all (the whole creation) proceeds." Nor does he hesitate to combine these features: "I am the origin and the dissolution . . . I am immortality and also death; I am being as well as non-being. . . . I am death, the all devouring and (am) the origin of things that are yet to be."[31]

In the later history of Hindu devotional religion the attractiveness and repulsiveness of the divine receive independent development. Krishna in his boyhood and youth becomes the focus of the former, while the goddess Kali expresses the latter. Though the *Gita* remains an ever-popular text, the cult of Krishna comes to revolve almost entirely on the child whom all can coddle and cuddle and especially the youth whose sexual cavortings with the equally young and beautiful cowherdesses, Radha in particular, can only be described as a "carnival of joy."[32] Krishna and his world are filled with freedom and spontaneity, beauty and grace, fragrance and harmony, wildness and play, warmth and intimacy. He is approachable, irresistible, hypnotizing, intoxicating, bewitching, and spellbinding. He embodies the bliss of ecstatic love. The mood he creates is captured in a love song devoted to him.

> Blue lotuses
> Flower everywhere
> And black *kokilas* sing
> King of the seasons,
> Spring has come
> And wild with longing
> The bee goes to his love.
> Birds flight in the air
> And cowherd girls
> Smile face to face
> Krishna has entered
> The great forest.[33]

If the flute is the symbol of the intoxicating beauty of the eternally youthful Krishna, the sword is the symbol of Kali, who represents all the "hair-raising, horrifying aspects of destructive forces."[34] Descriptions of her seem to compete with one another in portraying her as bloodthirsty, ruthless, and fierce. "Of terrible face and fearful aspect is Kali the awful. Four-armed, garlanded with skulls, with disheveled hair, she holds a freshly cut human head and a bloodied scimitar in her left hands. . . . Her neck adorned with a garland of severed human heads dripping blood, her earrings two dangling severed heads, her girdle a string of severed human hands, she is dark and naked. Terrible, fanglike teeth, full, prominent breasts, a smile on her lips glistening with blood, she is Kali whose laugh is terrifying . . . she lives in the cremation ground, surrrounded by screaming jackals. She stands on Shiva, who lies corpselike beneath her. . . . In her left hand she holds a cup filled with wine and meat, and in her right hand she holds a freshly cut human head. She smiles and eats rotten meat."[35]

It is important to remember that we are not dealing with two religions, or even two denominations or sects within one religion. Though the cults and mythologies of Krishna and Kali have a measure of independence within the Hindu tradition, both remaining extremely popular over centuries of time, the point is by no means to separate them from each other. We have already noted that it is the same Krishna who cavorts with the cowherdesses and who makes Arjuna's hair stand on end, who is both the life-giving origin of all and the destroyer of all. The same is true of Kali, to whom the faithful pray, "Thou art the Beginning of all, Creatrix, Protectress, and Destructress that Thou art."[36]

The nineteenth-century Hindu saint, Sri Ramakrishna, a passionate devotee of Kali, the Divine Mother, expresses the unity of opposites in this goddess most dramatically. In the temple where he worships her she stands in basalt, spectacularly bedecked in gold and jewels, upon the prostrate body of Shiva in white marble. "She has four arms. The lower left hand holds a severed human head and the upper grips a bloodstained sabre. One right hand offers boons to her children; the other allays their fear. The majesty of Her posture can hardly be described. It combines the terror of destruction with the reassurance of motherly tenderness. For she is the Cosmic Power, the totality of the universe, a glorious harmony of the pairs of opposites. She deals out death, as She creates and preserves."[37] In an early vision of Ramakrishna, Kali emerged from the Ganges, came to the land, and presently gave birth to a child, which she began to nurse tenderly. "A moment later she assumed a terrible aspect, seized the child between her grim jaws, and crushed it. As she swallowed the child, she re-entered the waters of the Ganges."[38] The paradox is all but unbearable.[39]

In a very different quarter we find the same mixture of maternal tenderness with vicious terror. The cult of Dionysus in ancient Greece was celebrated at night in wild mountaintop frenzies. With the help of rhythmic dancing and wine the maenads, female followers of Dionysus, came to a state of ecstatic enthusiasm in which they were possessed by him. In this condition they would give their breasts to suckle young animals, wild and otherwise, only to turn on them and tear them to pieces with their bare hands. Such was the dual nature of the god whose influence had overcome them, whom Euripides describes as

> Dionysus, son of Zeus, consummate god,
> most terrible, and yet most gentle, to mankind.[40]

There is another recurring paradox in accounts of human response to the sacred which may be more closely related to the foregoing than a superficial glance would reveal. Just as the divine is experienced as a unity of opposites in terms of tender, creative, life-giving power and terrifying, destructive, death-dealing power, so it is perceived as a unity of delightful nearness and dreadful remoteness. Gerardus van der Leeuw says, "It allows us to become aware of infinite distance and feel a never suspected nearness."[41]

The contexts we have been exploring abound with indications of this experience. Augustine confesses, "You are the most hidden from us and yet the most present amongst us."[42] The Nuer see God as sometimes present in the here and now, but only sometimes and incompletely, for the distance between his dwelling in the sky and man's on earth is too great to be bridged.[43] Ramakrishna was driven to a mad frenzy in his devotion to Krishna, seeking to follow the Bhagavata Purana, for Krishna "would tease and taunt, now and then revealing Himself, but always keeping at a distance."[44] In response to Moses' request for a vision of God's glory he is told, "Take your stand on the rock and when my glory passes by, I will put you in a crevice of the rock and cover you with my hand until I have passed by. Then I will take away my hand, and you shall see my back, but my face shall not be seen."[45]

The Advaita Vedantist seeking absolute unity with Brahman and the Buddhist seeking Nirvana are pursuing a goal so remote that it requires great effort and quite possibly many, many lifetimes. And yet what they seek is right there to be seen and realized, if only they would see the rope instead of the snake, the landscape instead of a mirage. So the Vedantist learns the meaning of the Upanishadic formula, That art Thou, meaning that I myself am the Brahman I seek, and the Buddhist comes to say that Samsara is Nirvana, understanding by this that "the infinitely Far-away is not only near, but it is *infinitely near*. It is nowhere, and nowhere it is not. This is the mystical identity of opposites."[46] The Muslim sage teaches the same thing when he writes

> Only His extreme nearness to you
> is what veils God from you.[47]

This teaching points to the surpassing greatness of God, whose capacity for nearness exceeds our capacity to receive. The following dialogue between a master and pupil emphasizes the limitation on the human side, but the point is the same, and is equally paradoxical.

> What is the Tao?
> It is right before your eyes.
> So why can't I see it?
> Because you have a Me.[48]

In these contexts, the paradox of near and far is virtually identical with the metaphysics of appearance and reality. The one is a commentary on the other. The nearness stems from the ontological excellence of the sacred, while the farness expresses the ontological poverty of the believing soul.

2C. Rudolph Otto's interpretation of ambivalence

At this point we are in danger of being overwhelmed with data. We need to pause for recapitulation and analysis. If we are right in suspecting (1) that human ambivalence before the sacred is grounded in a sense of ontological inadequacy, (2) that this complex and volatile experience comes to expression in the language of paradox, and (3) that the rich variety of such expressions nevertheless arises out of a single experiential core which remains significantly the same in them all, then it would be helpful to bring this single, unified though complex mode of experience to conceptual unity, to name the idea (*eidos*) which manifests itself in so many different ways. This is the task that Rudolph Otto undertakes in his masterpiece, *The Idea of the Holy*.

Since experience is always someone's experience, his analysis begins with the believing soul's consciousness of creaturehood. This is to be distinguished from the consciousness of createdness, for what is involved is not necessarily a conception of creation in which God is conceived as maker by analogy with the human artisan. The idea that "it is He that hath made us and not we ourselves" is indeed a very common and widespread one,[49] and it no doubt gives expression to the experience we are talking about. But it is important to notice the inadequacy of that analogy to this experience. For normally we think of cause and effect as equally real, whereas creaturehood here suggests a deficiency of being. It is not primarily a question of how I have come to be here (though it may well be related to that) as much as it is a question of what I am, my nature rather than my origin.[50] (Psyche is ashamed of being *mortal*, not of being made.)

Directing our attention from the experience to the "object" intended in the experience,[51] Otto suggests that we speak of "the holy" and "the numinous" to indicate whatever it is whose apprehension evokes the consciousness of creaturehood, of ontological deficiency. He then specifies the meaning of these terms with his celebrated formula, *mysterium tremendum et fascinans*, the aweful and fascinating mystery. The holy is a mystery, not because it is a puzzle to be solved, but because it is something out of the ordinary. Thus it is, in Otto's oft quoted phrase, "wholly other." Affectively, it strikes us with "blank wonder and astonishment." Conceptually, it finds expression in positive theologies as the supernatural or transcendent and in negative theologies as nothingness, silence, or the void. Both of these are ways of trying to talk about what goes beyond the adequacy of human language, as if one were trying to describe a three-dimensional world in the language of two-dimensional creatures.[52]

The two adjectives in Otto's formula indicate that the wholly other repels and attracts. As *tremendum* the holy is the uncanny in the presence of which we experience fear, terror, shuddering, dread, and horror. It is this aspect of the numinous that the Bible expresses as the wrath of God, that the Greeks refer to as the jealousy of the gods, and that Indian art portrays as the grotesqueness of the gods. Otto speaks of the holy as "absolutely unapproachable" and "absolutely overpowering." This is right at the heart of the consciousness of creaturehood in which we apprehend ourselves as "not perfectly or essentially real." This ontological self-depreciation or annihilation of the self expresses itself by saying in one way or another, "I am naught, Thou art all." When Kierkegaard speaks of "the shudder which is the first experience of worship," he is talking about what Otto calls the *tremendum*.[53]

But the holy is also overwhelmingly attractive, "an object of horror and dread, but at the same time it is no less something that allures with a potent charm, and the creature who trembles before it, utterly cowed and cast down, has always at the same time the impulse to turn to it, nay even to make it somehow his own."[54] It isn't just a matter of wrath and jealousy, but of love, mercy, grace, comfort, and bliss. Hence there is a deep, nearly incomprehensible desire and yearning in the believing soul to be "with" the holy;[55] and where the believing soul and the holy are properly "together" there is talk of exaltation, ecstasy, rapture, beatitude and bliss unspeakable. Language seems, if anything, less adequate to the *fascinans* than to the *tremendum*.

Otto's claim is that the numinous lies at the very heart of the religious life, and "there is no religion in which it does not live as the real innermost core, and without it no religion would be worthy of the name."[56] He asks, in effect, what it is that unites the various religious intentionalities as religious and distinguishes them from those which are not. He is careful not to suggest that it is God or the gods, for he knows that there can be religion without gods or spirits. It may be, as the history of Buddhism suggests, that there is an ineluctable tendency within the religious sphere to move toward a personal God or gods, but there are phenomena which we tend to classify as religious which involve little or no involvement of personal gods or spirits of any sort. In spite of the proliferation of gods in many popular forms of Buddhism, there are modes of Buddhism from which this element is entirely missing—to mention only the most frequently cited example.

Much of the strength and appeal of Otto's concept lies in just this ability to understand religion in terms of whatever it is which evokes the consciousness of creaturehood and the ambivalence which is an inevitable part of such a sense. Whether this "whatever" is God or gods or spirits or the impersonal power called *mana* or an absolute so far beyond the finite categories of being and non-being as to be nothing at all, the religious nature of the life built around such experience need not be questioned. God in the monotheistic sense associated with Judaism, Christianity, and Islam would be a special case of the numinous, the holy, the sacred, the divine.[57] Whether from an historical-explanatory point of view monotheism appears early or late in human history, and whether from a teleological-evaluative perspective it represents some kind of goal toward which all religious expressions move for their fulfillment—these are questions that our descriptive method has bracketed.

There are, however, at least two serious objections to taking Otto's notion of the holy, as developed to this point, as a generic concept applicable to religion in all its forms. First, it will not have gone unnoticed that up to this point the hallmark of the holy seems to be power. In speaking of the wrath of God in the Bible and the Hindu scriptures, Otto speaks of the holy as "like stored-up electricity, discharging itself upon anyone who comes too near. It is 'incalculable' and 'arbitrary.'"[58] Therefore the ancient Israelites were warned to stay away from Mount Sinai on the day when the Lord would give the law to Moses "for fear that the Lord may break out against them," and Uzzah, who reached out and touched the Ark of God to steady it when the oxen stumbled, was struck down and died on the spot.[59] The electricity metaphor has come to be a commonplace for describing the impersonal power which is the numinous for a wide variety of preliterate tribes throughout the world, often referred to generically by its Melanesian name, *mana*.[60]

In his classic work, *Religion in Essence and Manifestation*, G. van der Leeuw makes *mana* his point of departure for interpreting "the object of religion." The result is that his account is completely dominated by the concept of power, of which he says, "Power enjoys no moral value whatever. . . . It remains merely dynamic, and not in the slightest degree ethical or 'spiritual.'"[61]

There is something disconcerting about the possibility that the very essence of religion lies in a power "incalculable" and "arbitrary," entirely free of moral, ethical, or spiritual significance. Almost all the religious people you and I know would vigorously repudiate the notion that they worship raw power. It may well be that they have domesticated the divine and filtered out of their scriptures anything about the wrath of God or the fear of the Lord which is the beginning of wisdom. In doing so, they refuse to equate the sacred with a kind of supernatural electricity?

The first thing to notice in this regard is that the ontological perfection of the sacred has not been exclusively a matter of power up to this point. We have seen that for Gandhi and Augustine God is Truth, while for Anselm he is the "supreme and inaccessible Light." Otto himself quotes, in part, a passage from Augustine in which the ambivalence we've been looking at relates to God as wisdom and light. "What is that light whose gentle beams now and again strike through to my heart, causing me to shudder in awe yet firing me with their warmth? I shudder to feel how different I am from it: yet in so far as I am like it I am aglow with its fire. It is the light of Wisdom."[62]

Second, and more importantly, Otto explicitly raises the objection before us and insists that there is more than power involved in the numinous. He devotes an important chapter to "The Holy as a Category of Value." The *mysterium tremendum et fascinans* is "not simply absolute might, making its claims and compelling their fulfillment, but a might that has at the same time the supreme *right* to make the highest claim to service and receives praise because it is in an absolute sense worthy to be praised. 'Thou art worthy to receive praise and honour and power.' "[63]

The "numinous worth" attributed to the holy and the respect it evokes generate another dimension to the disvaluation of the believer's own self from what we have previously considered. Now, instead of being *unable* to stand in the presence of the holy ("for no mortal can see me and live"), the believing soul feels unworthy to do so. (Psyche is *ashamed* of being mortal.)

We can illustrate this new element from two of our earlier examples. In response to Krishna's transfiguration, Arjuna replies, "Boundless in power and immeasurable in might, Thou dost penetrate all and therefore Thou art All. For whatsoever I have spoken in rashness to Thee thinking that Thou art my companion and unaware of this (fact of) Thy greatness, O Krishna . . . out of my negligence or maybe through fondness, and for whatsoever disrespect was shown to Thee in jest . . . I pray, O Unshaken One, forgiveness from Thee, the Immeasurable."[64] Arjuna feels Krishna not only to be "boundless in power" but also worthy of a respect that he has quite possibly not shown.

The hypothetical element is entirely missing from the otherwise very similar response of Job to the manifestation of God which climaxes his story.

> I know that thou canst do all things
> and that no purpose is beyond thee.
> But I have spoken of great things which I have
> not understood,
> things too wonderful for me to know.
> I knew of thee then only by report,
> but now I see thee with my own eyes.
> Therefore I melt away;
> I repent in dust and ashes.[65]

It is clear that "the holy" has ceased to signify an ontology where fact is cleanly separated from value. It is not merely as the ultimate power but as the ultimate worth that the sacred is experienced, with the result that the believing soul not only becomes intensely aware of the impotence of finitude but also of personal and corporate unworthiness.

Otto, however, is reluctant to label the new dimension the moral or ethical. There are two reasons for this. First, the depreciation of the self as somehow unworthy can have an immediacy which makes it more nearly a spontaneous response to what the holy is than a comparison of itself with the moral law. There is nothing here of remorse for specific misdeeds. The examples transcend the moral realm in that sense, for it is not in relation to the moral law but before the holy as "the power and the glory" that Arjuna and Job find themselves repenting, acknowledging their defiled and sinful condition, and asking forgiveness.

Second, there is no synonymity here between "You alone are holy" and "You alone are good". The sacred is not worthy because it is in tune with the moral law. Rather the moral law derives whatever sanctity it has from its ties to the sacred.[66] When these ties are broken, morality becomes merely a matter of social convention and expedience. Unlawfulness, moral or legal, is one thing; sin is quite another. The religious sense of guilt or impurity has a depth to it of which "the merely moral" person knows nothing. So in spite of his reluctance to speak about *moral* worth and unworthiness, Otto would be sympathetic with Paul Ricoeur and Kierkegaard when they ask, "Does not sin make God the Wholly Other?"[67]

For Otto, then, the *mysterium tremendum et fascinans* is not simply raw power but absolute worth as well, evoking a sense of ontological inadequacy which involves not only impotence but defilement and sinfulness as well. There remains, however, a second objection to viewing the "numinous" as present in all religious phenomena. It is often argued that a distinction should be made between numinous experience and mystical experience.[68] The idea is that numinous experience remains within the subject-object structure in which the believing soul encounters a being different and independent from his or her own being, while in certain forms of mystical experience the difference between self and other is entirely obliterated. For a Hindu to become one with Nirguna Brahman, beyond all name and form, or for a Buddhist to attain Nirvana is not to encounter something numinous and stand in fascinated fear and trembling before the power, personal or impersonal. It is rather to lose all sense of personal identity as the finite self is absorbed or extinguished in an undifferentiated All or Nothing. Bliss there is, but no "I am blissful," for the I in all its particularity as something other than anything else no longer functions.

There is unquestionably a major difference between the view that our highest eternal destiny consists in a heavenly life of worship and praise before the throne of God, something like the angels in the vision of Isaiah, and the Vedantist or Buddhist view that it consists in dissolving and transcending all sense of personal identity. But we are not asking about different conceptions of life beyond the here and now. We are asking what it means to be religious precisely in the here and now. For the Vedantist the religious life does not consist in experienced undifferentiated oneness with Brahman, one only without a second. It consists in the striving for this goal from a situation in which the world, including the finite self, is always too much with us. There may be moments of mystical trance in which the mirage of maya vanishes and the snake of subject-object experience is replaced by the rope of undifferentiated oneness. But for the most part the religious life is walked by faith and not by sight, that is, the believing soul believes with a greater or lesser degree of conviction in a oneness which is not directly experienced just because the self remains discrete enough as an individual to believe, to doubt, and to yearn.[69]

In Ramakrishna's harmony of Bhakti piety with Vedantist metaphysics, Kali, the Divine Mother aids in attaining oneness with Brahman. "If it so pleases Her, She takes away the last trace of ego from created beings and merges it in the consciousness of the Absolute, the undifferentiated Godhead. Through Her grace the finite ego loses itself in the illimitable Ego—Atman—Brahman."[70] The terror and the threat which Brahman represents remains unchanged if Kali is left out of the picture and one seeks unity with Brahman through breath control and meditation rather than through personal devotion. The Brahman in whom I seek to drown myself as a drop of rain drowns itself in the ocean will become for me the bliss I seek only at the cost of something very dear to me, not simply my selfishness, which is hard enough to part with, but with the whole structure of my self as a discrete and identifiable ego. My very being-in-the-world is threatened.

The same can be said, *mutatis mutandis*, about the Buddhist and Nirvana, and this has major importance for the universality of Otto's category. In his extraordinary book of Buddhism, T.R.V. Murti has argued that early Buddhism is not a religion. "Religion is the consciousness of the Super-mundane Presence immanent in all things, the consciousness of what Otto happily calls the 'mysterium tremendum'. Early Buddhism . . . was not a religion in this sense. It was an order of monks held together by certain rules of discipline (vinaya) and reverence for the *human* Teacher. It enjoined a very austere moral code, primarily for the ordained. But there was no element of worship, no religious fervour, no devotion to a transcendent being. No cosmic function was assigned to Buddha; he was just an exalted person and no more."[71]

Murti acknowledges that this was changed in later Buddhism, that Buddha becomes a cosmic savior, and that he becomes an object of worship and devotion. But that is to miss the point. For the form of the *mysterium tremendum et fascinans* common to all expressions of Buddhism is not Buddha, but Nirvana. To be sure, Nirvana is not an object of worship and devotion. It is not even an object at all in the sense in which a sacred mountain or a god is. But it is the ultimate intentional object of Buddhism in all its modes and, what is crucial here, it is the *mysterium tremendum et fascinans*. About the *mysterium* and the *fascinans* there can be no question at all. What is here talked about is that which is so wholly other that it cannot be talked about at all, for it is beyond the very structure of subject-object experience. If anything, early Buddhism is more keenly aware of this than the later systems. That Nirvana is at the same time overwhelmingly fascinating is clear from the enthusiastic descriptions of the bliss of attainment and the extraordinary striving evoked toward this end.

Still there is good reason to keep at a safe distance from this bliss. For Nirvana (blowing out, burning out, extinction) can be attained only through the snuffing out of the flame of my desires, not merely my evil desires in the ordinary sense, but desire as such, even the desire for Nirvana. Since even for early Buddhism the very heart of my being in the world is inextricably tied to the structure of desire, Nirvana is viewed as the void in which the whole of my individual self and my world are evaporated.

Schopenhauer understood clearly how empty nothingness could be as numinous as any powerful something. He knows that to an essentially Buddhist position the objection will inevitably be raised that once "we have before our eyes in perfect saintliness the denial and surrender of all willing, and thus a deliverance from a world whose whole existence presented itself to us as suffering, this now appears to us as a transition into empty *nothingness.* . . ." Philosophical analysis can show us that this is a "peace that is higher than all reason," an "ocean-like calmness of the spirit," and an "unshakable confidence and serenity" which we desire with a "painful yearning." Those who have had temporary experience of this state call it "ecstasy, rapture, illumination, union with God, and so on," though such experience is neither knowledge nor communicable, since it "no longer has the form of subject and object." If the world were not so much with us another perspective would be possible which "would cause the signs to be changed, and would show what exists for us as nothing and this nothing as that which exists. But so long as we ourselves are the will-to-live, this last, namely the nothing as that which exists, can be known and expressed by us only negatively," and, what is here the crucial point, it can only be understood, as a condition of no will and therefore no world, as an ultimate threat which "we fear as children fear darkness." The paradoxical situation which results is that progress toward will-lessness can be made only if we "banish the dark impression of that nothingness," though it is clear that such banishment can only be the result of the will-lessness it is supposed to produce.[72]

There is no denying that the *tremendum* is importantly different for the Vedantist and the Buddhist from what it is for Arjuna before Krishna or Isaiah before Yahweh. But it clearly remains the *tremendum* and we need not have gone very far in our understanding of these traditions to understand why Brahman and Nirvana might repel. The task will be to see how they come to be so overwhelmingly attractive. For the present we can simply note that even where the "object" of religion isn't really an object at all in the sense of being someone or something that along with everyone and everything else, myself included, makes up all there is, that toward which the believer's attention is directed is numinous in the sense of being the *mysterium tremendum et fascinans* and the believing soul is bound to be ambivalent toward it.

Ambivalence, Inertia, and Resentment

3A. Ambivalence and inertia

Bound to be ambivalent! If religion always involves the holy in some form, if the religious life is always rooted in an awareness of the *mysterium tremendum et fascinans*,[1] then there is something inevitable about the ambivalence of the believing soul. Does the believing soul love God? He also hates him. Does she strive earnestly to attain Moksha (enlightenment, liberation)? She also fears and dreads it, and clings to the security of everyday suffering. Is there a passion to live in harmony with the Tao? There is also an aversion to the strenuousness of learning so to relax.

The *Tao Te Ching* knows of ambivalence toward the Tao, the Way. But as is so frequently the case, it overlooks the necessity.

> When the man of highest capacities hears Tao
> He does his best to put it into practice.
> When the man of middling capacity hears Tao
> He is of two minds about it.
> When the man of low capacity hears Tao
> He laughs loudly at it.[2]

To laugh loudly in this context is simply to deny the religious perception, thereby avoiding (or seeking to avoid) the ambivalence it generates. The one who laughs loudly is thus the unbelieving soul. We shall have occasion shortly to raise the question whether the unbeliever is all of one mind about this or whether the laughter may partly be a defense against an inward tendency to believe. But for the moment our attention is on the believing soul, who does not laugh, at least not loudly. According to this text such as a person has two possibilities, either to be of two minds about the Tao or single-mindedly to live it. The latter is naturally praised as a person "of highest capacities," but in the light of our previous discussion it remains an open question whether one can truly apprehend the Tao in all its sacredness and not turn out to be the person "of middling capacity" who is "of two minds about it." The Tao as the Way and its Power is that before which I experience a deficiency of being with respect to both the power and worth of my being; at the same time it holds out to me the possibility of the only true happiness and my own highest fulfillment. Would I not have to be more than human not to be ambivalent toward it, if I take it seriously at all?

In the same way, when Kierkegaard entitles one of his edifying books *Purity of Heart Is To Will One Thing*, we are led to expect that if he really understands the religious life his purpose will not so much be to portray a goal we might actually achieve as to uncover the pervasive doublemindedness of even our deepest piety.

If we are to understand what it means to be religious we shall have to keep human ambivalence before the sacred constantly in mind. Failure to do so will not only lead to serious misunderstanding of the religious life, but this, in turn, can easily lead us, when we make evaluative judgments about that life, to praise or condemn something that isn't authentically religious at all.

For example, if we eliminate the ambivalence by seeing only the attractive side of religion we may too easily affirm it without counting the cost or noting how deeply irreligious our motives are as we shame-lessly reduce the sacred to but a means in the pursuit of our own self-interest. On the other hand, if we notice only the repelling fea-tures we may too quickly repudiate religion as a kind of masochistic escape from selfhood, not noticing that the believer finds fulfillment not in abasement for its own sake, but in the integrity of finding his or her rightful place in the overall scheme of things.[3] In order to avoid "cheap grace" in our religious affirmation and "cheap shots" in our religious criticism we will have to keep before us the tension in which the believer perpetually lives.[4] This is not to say that cheap grace and masochistic piety are nowhere to be found on the religious scene. It is simply to deny that they are authentically religious and to emphasize the importance of informing our pro and con attitudes toward religion of that fact.

This task will prove easier if we can pursue the meaning of am-bivalence before the sacred beyond the point to which Otto has gone. Instead of being satisfied with noting that the believer's attention is always directed toward that which is at once attractive and repelling because of its overwhelming power and worth, we will need to in-vestigate more closely both the nature and the necessity of this am-bivalence. In the process we'll discover that the unbeliever is indeed as likely to be ambivalent as the believer, though perhaps in a different way.

Of all the believing souls to whom we might turn for deeper insight into the ambivalence we are seeking to understand, perhaps none is so well suited to help us as Kierkegaard. No one who wrote books about religion entitled *Fear and Trembling* and *The Concept of Anxiety* is likely to have overlooked the *tremendum* aspect of the holy; and we have already noticed that Kierkegaard understands worship to begin with a shudder.[5] Yet one has to look far and wide to find a more lyrical expression of the tender loveliness of God, the *fascinans*, than is to be found in his writings. And he is extraordinarily articulate.

Most helpful for our concern is his analysis of "existential pathos" in the *Concluding Unscientific Postscript*.[6] His ultimate goal is to talk about what it means to be a Christian; but only a tiny fraction of his very big book is devoted to describing a distinctly Christian piety. Most of it is given over to spelling out the categories of ethico-religious subjectivity within which any life must be lived if it is to be authentically religious. It was his judgment that much of the Christianity of his day was so rooted in aesthetic and speculative detachment that it wasn't even a genuinely religious phenomenon, as if one were trying to play chess on a Monopoly board. The pieces might be chessmen, but the game could hardly be chess.

The analysis of "existential pathos" comes when Kierkegaard seeks to isolate the distinctly religious aspect of ethico-religious subjectivity. This section is therefore properly read as his account of what it means to be religious in a generic or universal sense. His account begins, "In relation to *an eternal happiness as the absolute good,* pathos is not a matter of words, but of permitting this conception *to transform the entire existence of the individual.* . . . If in relating itself to the individual's existence the absolute *telos* [goal] fails *to transform it absolutely,* the relationship is not one of existential pathos. . . . "[7] One is not religious automatically or by default, but only as one's existence is fundamentally changed from what it would naturally be. The radical nature of this transformation is indicated both in its scope—the entire existence of the individual—and in its intensity—absolutely.

This reorientation is brought about by bringing life into relation with an absolute good or goal, which by definition subordinates and relativizes all other goals and purposes of life. Kierkegaard calls this goal "eternal happiness." No doubt the term primarily connotes for him life after death in heaven with God, but it has an elasticity which permits it to apply to other conceptions of post mortem bliss such as oneness with Brahman and Nirvana, and even to conceptions of the absolute good without reference to life after death, such as harmony with the Tao. No particular eschatology is required, only that there be a goal conceived as the absolute good. Such a good Jesus had in mind when he said, "The kingdom of Heaven is like treasure lying buried in a field. The man who found it, buried it again; and for sheer joy went and sold everything he had, and bought that field. Here is another picture of the kingdom of Heaven. A merchant looking out for fine pearls found one of very special value; so he went and sold everything he had, and bought it.'[8]

Kierkegaard calls the transformation involved here *resignation* and labels it the *initial expression* of existential pathos. He means simply that for the sake of the absolute good "all finite satisfactions are volitionally relegated to the status of what may have to be renounced in favor of an eternal happiness."[9] The believing soul is the one who has "deprived the finite of its unchecked vitality." Whether fortunate or unfortunate with respect to finite goods, the believer says " 'Oh, well,—and this 'Oh, well' means the absolute respect for the absolute *telos*. Men do not exist in this fashion when they live immediately in the finite." Rather, "the significance of worship is, that God is absolutely all for the worshipper."[10]

This resignation need not take the form of stoical indifference toward the world of finite goods nor of monastic isolation from the world. After all, Abraham is the father of the faithful, yet he is "the heir apparent to the finite," and "finiteness tastes to him just as good as to one who never knew anything higher." Furthermore, the true knight of faith may well appear on the scene as one who "belongs entirely to the world," the all too familiar tax collector, clerk, shopkeeper, postman, capitalist, and so on.[11] What is essential is a clean break with the comical madness of being absolutely committed to relative goods. The task is "simultaneously to sustain an absolute relationship to the absolute end, and a relative relationship to relative ends."[12]

The second moment of existential pathos is *suffering*, its *essential expression*. It arises directly out of the fact that resignation is possible only by means of the self's transformation and is not the natural or normal condition of the self. When it awakens to self-consciousness before the holy, it finds itself in a condition Kierkegaard calls immediacy. This consists in being absolutely committed to relative ends. Thus the holy confronts the self with the task of *perpetually dying to immediacy*. The difficulty and painfulness of the reorientation is indicated by calling it a form of dying.[13] We might use the same metaphor in talking about a chain smoker dying to his tobacco habit or an alcoholic dying to her drinking habit.

This example, however, lacks the crucial element of Kierkegaard's description. There is a threshold in breaking such habits beyond which the battle is essentially won and it is possible to relax. One may still need to abstain entirely from the addictive materials, but it becomes relatively easy to do so by comparison with the agony of the initial quitting. In describing the religious life as a *perpetual* dying to immediacy, Kierkegaard denies, in effect, that immediacy ever loses its spell upon us. The goal of being at once absolutely related to the absolute end and relatively related to relative ends is never fully achieved and remains a continual struggle throughout the whole of the believer's life. The attitude of resignation is something that needs to be renewed again and again, for the self's natural tendency is to relapse into immediacy after even the most thrilling spiritual victories.[14]

This perpetual dying to immediacy is the *essential* expression of the religious life because the suffering which it defines is neither optional nor accidental. Within the framework of fortune and misfortune, some people suffer sometimes. Within the authentically religious context, all believing souls suffer all the time. Of course, it is a different suffering, inward rather than outward, and it means not only dying to my absolute commitment to this or that finite goal, but also transcending the whole attitude in which fortune and misfortune are the primary categories for evaluating my life. Success and failure, gaining and losing, as these are usually measured, cease to be the gods of my life. My addiction to them is to be broken.

There is a final aspect of dying to immediacy beyond breaking off my absolute commitment to particular finite ends and to the whole framework of values defined by the categories of fortune and misfortune. Seriously to undertake this task, to accept this suffering, is to undermine my confidence in myself. It is to discover that immediacy, which includes "the wish to have the power to do anything," is itself a power over which there are no final victories. It is to discover "that the individual can do absolutely nothing of himself, but is as nothing before God." For the task which is set to me by the holy is simply too great. From its own spiritual life, the believing soul learns that "self-annihilation is the essential form for the God-relationship" and that without "this consciousness of impotence" religiosity itself has vanished.[15] This is the sense of nothingness and impotence which was central to the previous chapter. Only here it is not the mere presence or thought of the sacred which evokes a sense of ontological inadequacy. It is the explicit thought that the sacred makes a claim upon my life which I find myself unable to fulfill, even when I have decided that I want to. Or, to put it a bit differently, I discover that I cannot satisfy the claim because I discover that I cannot unreservedly want to.

It is therefore not surprising that Kierkegaard moves directly from *suffering* as the *essential expression* of ethico-religious subjectivity to *guilt* as the *decisive expression*. The crucial thing about this guilt is that it is total or essential guilt.[16] I do not divide myself into some behaviors which happen to be evil, in comparison with other behaviors which happen to be good. More fundamental than this distinction and functionally prior to it is the fact that my fundamental project, my deepest intention, is at best partially committed to what I recognize as the good. This makes my "moral" deficiency total, for my good deeds are contaminated by my qualified willing of them, just as my evil deeds are presumably corrupt in themselves. Similarly, my guilt is no longer accidental but essential, for given my ambivalent will, the difference between behaviors which "happen to be" either good or evil has been superseded by the unity of a fundamental project which is never what it ought to be vis-à-vis the sacred. What is at issue is the quality of my being and not the quantity of my (good or evil) behavior. Here again we can see why Kierkegaard would be among those who ask, "Does not sin make God the Wholly Other?"[17]

In the context of developing this dimension of what it means to be religious, Kierkegaard talks about "the special type of religious conflict the Germans call *Anfechtung*." It is tempting to translate the word as temptation, but that won't quite work. For normally to be tempted means to be attracted by what is lower, while here to be tempted means to be frightened back by the higher, that is, tempted to flee.[18] *Anfechtung* is not the whole story. The God before whom the believing soul is annihilated is also the one from whom strength and consolation are to be sought.[19] But *Anfechtung* is an essential part of the story. Therefore this consolation is no opiate of the masses. For while it may heal the pain of misfortune it perennially co-exists with the essential religious suffering.

To summarize: Kierkegaard suggests that to orient oneself toward eternal happiness as the absolute good is to be called to resignation and suffering and guilt. The holy reveals the radical limitations of my moral power and goodness, for it shows me to be reluctant and unable wholeheartedly to choose that which I myself consider to be the best. The question is put to me—What do you really want?—and my answer turns out to be an ambivalent one. I see the limited value of my everyday goals, but my insight doesn't fully persuade me, nor am I able to act and feel in harmony with it. It leads me to the pain of resignation, suffering, and guilt, and in this respect I would gladly dispense with the whole business. But I cannot, for precisely what produces this existential discomfort is what I apprehend to be intimately involved in my eternal happiness. My awareness of the sacred both rankles and assuages. By it I am both annihilated and comforted.[20] If I am the believing soul who takes seriously the claim of the sacred upon my life and the promise of happiness it offers, I am bound to be ambivalent.

I propose that we call the ambivalence which Kierkegaard describes the ambivalence of inertia. He does not himself use the term in the *Concluding Unscientific Postscript*, from which the foregoing analysis has been taken. But almost simultaneously with the *Postscript* he published a long review of a Danish novel which appeared just as he was concluding his own book and which fascinated him by providing an occasion for dealing with some of the same themes in a different setting. It is in *Two Ages* (the review now bearing the same title as the novel reviewed) that he introduces inertia as a physical metaphor for the spiritual resistance to that dying to immediacy that the sacred seems to demand of us.[21]

The spiritual inertia, which in the *Postscript* he presents as the inevitable response of human individuals to the sacred, is portrayed in *Two Ages* as a conspicuous mark of society at large in "the present age." He views his age as "prudentially relaxing in indolence," one which "relaxes temporarily in complete indolence." That prudence, a virtue of highest rank, and relaxation, a value of highest regard, should turn out to be masks for "indolence," "torpor," and "apathy" is something fully hidden from the present age, which is too inert to come to self-awareness. It is to be likened to the "stay-abed" who hasn't the energy to make it out of bed or to an overfed Roman emperor "suffering from boredom" and "more sluggish than he is evil." Even with regard to matters of less importance than the transformation of existence called for by the sacred, "a proposal to consider the matter further is received with rising enthusiasm, and a proposal for action is met with indolence."[22]

This is the spiritual condition Kierkegaard has in mind when he introduces the metaphor of inertia. In speaking of the ambivalence of inertia as unavoidable for the believing soul who takes seriously both the claim and the promise of the sacred, it is not implied that the believing soul is necessarily as decadent as "the present age" in Kierkegaard's view. The point is simply that the believing soul is by no means free from those tendencies which, when uncontested, result in total spiritual indolence.

In language quite different from Kierkegaard's, Augustine and Heidegger offer interpretations of spiritual inertia which complement his. For Augustine the central concept is that of habit. For Heidegger it is the notion of everydayness.

Augustine's account of habit occurs in that part of the *Confessions* in which his conversion comes to completion. Shortly after those passages which we have examined in Sections 2A and 2B, he returns to a description of the ambivalence he experienced as a newly converted believing soul. "And I felt wonder at the thought that now I loved you. . . . But I did not stay in the enjoyment of my God; I was swept away to you by your own beauty, and then I was torn away from you by my own weight and fell back groaning toward these lower things. Carnal habit was this weight."[23]

This account is all the more striking since it comes immediately after Augustine announces the result of his long struggle to understand the origin of evil. He had found "that it is not a substance but a perversity of the will turning away from you, God, the supreme substance, toward lower things. . . ." Yet what keeps him from staying in the enjoyment of God is not so much the active perversity of his will as it is a passive bondage in the mode of habit; indeed, it is not long afterward that he is speaking of being held back from a transformation of self for which he longs by "the iron bondage of my own will," which he again identifies as habit, a crucial link in the chain which "held me fast in a hard slavery."[24]

In addition to the metaphor of habit as a weight, to which Augustine returns repeatedly in Books VII and VIII, and this additional metaphor of habit as an iron chain, he adds a third way of speaking about habit, the image of sleep. All three come together in this dramatic account: "Now I could see [the truth] perfectly clearly. But I was still tied down to earth and refused to take my place in your army. And I was just as frightened of being freed from all my hampering baggage as I ought to have been frightened of being hampered. The pack of this world was a kind of pleasant weight upon me, as happens in sleep, and the thoughts in which I meditated on you were like the efforts of someone who tries to get up but is so overcome with drowsiness that he sinks back again into sleep. Of course no one wants to sleep forever, and everyone in his senses would agree that it is better to be awake; yet all the same, when we feel a sort of lethargy in our limbs, we often put off the moment of shaking off sleep. . . . For I had no answer to make to you when you called me: *Awake, thou that sleepest, and arise from the dead, and Christ shall give thee light.* And, while you showed me wherever I looked that what you said was true, I, convinced by the truth, could still find nothing at all to say except lazy words spoken half asleep: 'A minute,' 'just a minute,' 'just a little time longer'. . . . For the law of sin is the strong force of habit, which drags the mind along and controls it even against its will. . . ."[25]

Sometimes Augustine describes the ambivalence in which habit plays such a large role as the conflict between his two wills, the old and the new. There is something experientially obvious about this imagery, and it has its biblical foundation in Paul's epistle to the Romans. But in his subtler moments he speaks of only a single will, divided absurdly against itself. "What can be the explanation of such an absurdity? The mind gives an order to the body, and the order is obeyed immediately: *the mind gives an order to itself, and there is resistance.* . . . The mind orders the mind to will; *it is the same mind yet it does not obey.* . . . The fact is that it does not will the thing entirely; consequently it does not give the order entirely. The force of the order is the force of the will, and disobedience to the order results from insufficiency of the will. . . . So it is not an absurdity partly to will and partly not to will; it is rather a sickness of the soul which is *weighted down with habit* so that it cannot rise up in its entirety. . . ."[26]

In spite of important differences from Kierkegaard and Augustine, Heidegger's notion of everydayness is intimately related to the foregoing descriptions. Though he does not acknowledge Kierkegaard in his notes, Heidegger's language strongly suggests the influence of the former's analysis of "the present age" in *Two Ages.* And he speaks of everydayness in language which is just as strongly reminiscent of Augustine's account of the "bondage of the will." Everydayness is, for example, "the real dictatorship of the 'they'." Because "they" are a very indefinite set of others they exercise an "inconspicuous domination," which is, on that account, not the least bit less a "stubborn domination." Everydayness is a power in which we become "entangled" and which "holds [us] fast in its fallenness."[27] It looks as if everydayness may be a mode of spiritual inertia. We must back up and start from the beginning to see how this is so.

The question Heidegger is asking is the same one which leads Kierkegaard to speak of immediacy. He is not asking how we have come to be but how we always find ourselves already to be. Prior to any perception or action in the world is that basic structure of being-in-the-world which makes perception or action possible.[28] The everydayness of *Dasein* (Heidegger's name for human being-in-the-world) shapes "the basic way in which Dasein lets the world 'matter' to it," thereby determining "what and how one 'sees' " as well as what and how one does.[29]

Because everyday *Dasein* is already "absorbed in the 'they' and mastered by it," it sees what they see, reads what they read, says what they say, and thinks what they think. This has its effects on both the subject and object poles of experience. On the side of *Dasein* itself everydayness "deprives the particular Dasein of its answerability. . . . It 'was' always the 'they' who did it." This disburdening of *Dasein* encourages any tendencies in *Dasein* "to take things easily and make them easy," that is, not to swim upstream. Thus life is made easier by this "failure to stand by one's Self."[30]

This applies with equal force to the object side of experience. Everydayness smooths off the rough edges of the world. It makes it possible to conduct the business of life without any real contact with the subject matter of living. It provides "the possibility of understanding everything without previously making the thing one's own." Because everything is already understood, *Dasein* looks, not to understand, but merely to see, to be distracted from its boredom, to be entertained. It has neither the time nor the energy for "grasping something and being knowingly in the truth," for "the leisure of tarrying observantly," for "observing entities and marveling at them. . . ."[31] It goes without saying that any action responding to the world so perceived will be equally mindless.

Heidegger speaks of everydayness as "inauthenticity," as "Being-lost," as "falling." He even describes it as "this kind of *not-Being* [which] has to be conceived as that kind of Being which is closest to *Dasein* and in which *Dasein* maintains itself for the most part." But he insists that he "is far removed from any moralizing critique of everyday Dasein," that his terminology has no "disparaging signification" and "does not express any negative evaluation." Everydayness is not "a bad and deplorable ontical [empirical] property of which, perhaps, more advanced stages of human culture might be able to rid themselves," nor does his description of it make any "ontical assertion about the 'corruption of human Nature'. . . ."[32] It is extremely difficult to take Heidegger seriously on this point, but we must see why he is so insistent upon it. There are two reasons. One concerns what we can't see, the other what we can.

In the first place, we cannot "take the fallenness of Dasein as a 'fall' from a purer and higher 'primal status'. Not only do we lack any experience of this ontically, but ontologically we lack any possibilities or clues for interpreting it."[33] (In this context "ontic" refers to particular, accidental facts, while "ontological" refers to universal, necessary structures.)[34]

This leads to Heidegger's second point, the one which rests on what we do know rather than on what we don't. His claim that he is not moralizing or giving a negative evaluation rests on the claim to an eidetic insight into the inescapability of everydayness. As an essential structure of human existence as such it is not a contingent condition which "more advanced stages of human culture" or morally superior individuals might leave behind. The possibility of authentic *Dasein* is quite real for Heidegger, but it "does not rest upon an exceptional condition of the subject, a condition that has been detached from the 'they'. . . ." Instead it is a "*modification*" of the "they" as an essential mark of *Dasein's* being.". . . authentic existence is not something which floats above falling everydayness; existentially, it is only a modified way in which such everydayness is seized upon." This is why the relationship of "all genuine understanding, interpreting, and communicating, all re-discovering and appropriating anew" are triply related to "falling everydayness." They are "in it, out of it, and against it. . . ."[35] The two are related like Helen Keller's achievements to her blindness. Authenticity, being my own true self, is always a struggle against a lostness in the "they" which is as ineradicable as it is ineluctable.

We can now see why Heidegger's everydayness represents a bondage of the will even more fundamental than the acquired habits which weighed Augustine down. Heidegger has not been talking about the believing soul, but about human existence as such. But the significance of his account for the religious life is not hard to see. If I should become aware of the sacred and be powerfully drawn toward its promise of an eternal happiness and toward the transformation of my existence which goes with that, I will find everydayness to be a power resisting that movement and that change. But it is not a power in the sense of something other than myself working against me. The power which resists all movement and change is a fundamental characteristic of myself. In the physical world we speak of inertia when the very constitution of the thing provides a resistance to movement. Heidegger's analysis of everydayness helps us see the appropriateness of Kierkegaard's metaphor of spiritual inertia. The believing soul is bound to be ambivalent toward the sacred because the very act of acknowledging its claims reveals a built-in resistance to any moral and spiritual transformation of the self.

3B. Ambivalence and resentment

It may seem strange to turn next to Freud for further interpretation of our ambivalence before the sacred. He is not even as open to religion as the skeptic. He *knows* that religion is a big mistake. In argument with Wundt about the origins of taboo he writes, "It would be another matter if demons really existed. But we know that, like gods, they are creations of the human mind."[36] Freud is, moreover, implacably hostile toward religion. Philip Rieff describes him this way: "It is on the subject of religion that the judicious clinician grows vehement and disputatious. Against no other strong-point of repressive culture are the reductive weapons of psychoanalysis deployed in such open hostility. Freud's customary detachment fails him here. Confronting religion, psychoanalysis shows itself for what it is: the last great formulation of nineteenth century secularism. . . . Here and here alone, the grand Freudian animus, otherwise concealed behind the immediacies of case histories and the emergencies of practical therapeutics, breaks out."[37]

We need not, however, be disappointed that Freud turns out to be no more a detached observer of the religious scene than Augustine or Kierkegaard, nor that his attitude is as negative as theirs is positive. For our method suggests that we should try to understand what it means to be religious not only by listening carefully to the believing soul, but also by hearing the critical cross-examination to which piety is put by its enemies.[38]

Freud's starting point is the observation that human conception is not immaculate, that reason is often the slave of the passions. "Do you suppose that human thought has no practical motives, that it is simply the expression of a disinterested curiosity? That is surely very improbable."[39] In other words, we often believe what we would like to believe, and our convictions, like our dreams and neurotic symptoms, are all too often wish-fulfillments. Such beliefs Freud calls illusions. This indicates that wish-fulfillment is a "prominent factor" in their motivation. They need not necessarily be false, but when we discover them to be illusions in this sense we have good reason to be suspicious of them.[40] (Freud at times seems almost to be an epistemological Puritan. If the Puritans can be caricatured as believing that nothing can be good unless it is unpleasant, Freud sometimes talks as if nothing can be true unless it goes against our wishes.)

Religion is an illusion in this sense. Hence the little book, *The Future of an Illusion.* Since the primary target of Freud's critique is Jewish and Christian theism, it is God as heavenly father at whom he particularly takes aim. In the helplessness of infancy the child learns to rely upon the mother, "who satisfies the child's hunger, becomes its first love-object and certainly also its first protection against all the undefined dangers which threaten it in the external world. . . ." But in this role "the mother is soon replaced by the stronger father, who retains that position for the rest of childhood."[41]

With the coming of adulthood "man's helplessness remains, and with it his longing for his father, and the gods." Nature is cold, cruel, and pitiless. It confronts us as fate and as the ultimate misfortune, death. The need to feel at home in the world means that "life and the universe must be robbed of their terror. . . . And thus a store of ideas is created, born from man's need to make his helplessness tolerable and built up from the memories of the helplessness of his own childhood. . . ." In building up this store of ideas man "makes the forces of nature not simply into persons with whom he can associate as he would with his equals—that would not do justice to the overpowering impression which these forces make on him—but he gives them the character of a father. He turns them into gods. . . ." Hebrew monotheism completes the process. Freud's own people "laid open to view the father who had all along been hidden behind every divine figure as its nucleus. Fundamentally this was a return to the historical beginnings of the idea of God. Now that God was a single person, man's relations to him could recover the intimacy and intensity of the child's relation to his father."[42]

In short, the believing soul believes in God because "it would indeed be very nice if there were a God,"[43] a heavenly father. But would it be nice? According to both Freud's personal experience and his psychoanalytic theories, the answer would have to be, "Well, of course it would—and of course it wouldn't at all." For Freud knows full well that "the child's attitude to its father is coloured by a peculiar ambivalence. The father himself constitutes a danger for the child. . . . Thus it fears him no less than it longs for him and admires him. The indications of this ambivalence in the attitude to the father are deeply imprinted in every religion."[44] At this point he makes reference to his own earlier study of ambivalence in the totemism of preliterate tribes he calls savages, the opening chapters of *Totem and Taboo*, to which we shall return shortly.

Without noticing it, Freud has undermined his project of discrediting religion. For if God is a heavenly father to whom we transfer the longing and admiration we feel for our earthly fathers, he will also be the object of our fear and, as we shall see, hatred. If belief can be seen as a wish-fulfilling illusion grounded in our longing for protection and help, disbelief can just as easily be seen as a wish-fulfilling illusion expressing our rebellion against the father's supremacy. We might say that the illusion of lingering childhood and the illusion of lingering adolescence cancel each other out (though Freud traces hostility toward the father back to earliest childhood). As Dostoyevsky pointedly remarks during the trial scene in *The Brothers Karamazov*, the psychological argument cuts both ways. We are left with no way of using the notion of wish-motivated beliefs to test whether religious beliefs are true or not.

But while such testing may have been Freud's purpose, it is not ours. In spite of this difference Freud might still help us better to understand the ambivalence of which he is so keenly aware. Let us consider his personal life first.[45] His own father died in 1896. During the years 1897 to 1900 he was struggling with a neurosis of his own and developing the theory of dreams he would publish in 1900 as *The Interpretation of Dreams*. In the process of interpreting his own dreams he discovered a very deep, jealous hatred toward his father, long hidden because of its incompatibility with an equally real love and affection for him. His father had always been the strict parent, while his mother was the indulgent one, the reality principle and the pleasure principle as it were, but Freud remembered three specific incidents which are undoubtedly related to the hostility he was so surprised to discover in himself.

When he was but seven or eight, his father accompanied a reprimand for misbehavior with the comment, "That boy will never amount to anything." The sting was lasting. Freud wrote of it, "This must have been a terrible affront to my ambition, for allusions to this scene occur again and again in my dreams, and are constantly coupled with enumerations of my accomplishments and successes, as if I wanted to say: 'You see, I have amounted to something after all.'" Then when he was twelve his father reported that a Gentile had knocked off his new fur hat and shouted, "Jew, get off the pavement." One can imagine the twelve-year-old's disappointment when in answer to the question of what he had done in response, his father replied that he had stepped to the gutter and picked the hat up again. At sixteen he fell in love with a certain Gisela, while the family was visiting his birthplace. Though she had been a childhood companion of his, they had moved away and the all too brief visit was but a tantalizing taste of what might have been. Somehow he seemed to blame his father for thwarting the promise of young love.

We need not assume that these incidents were the beginning or the deepest root of Freud's hostility toward his father. But they do seem to be the dust particles around which raindrops of hatred gathered during approximately a decade of his later childhood.

A closer look at the three incidents reveals that they embody two sources of an antipathy which turns into resentment. One concerns worthiness, the other happiness. We naturally resent anyone who calls our worth into question. With equals or inferiors we seek to dissipate the feeling by deflecting the judgment. "What do they know?" we say, or "It takes one to know one." But when the judgment comes from one whose moral stature tends to reduce all our defensive devices to silence, the judgment tends to stand for us and to generate resentment. Such is the situation of a boy whose father says he will never amount to anything and who meekly lets stand the abusive belittlement of a crude anti-Semitic gesture which is directed not merely toward him but toward all Jews as such. The former is a more direct blow to the boy's sense of worth, but the latter may be even harder to deal with, for, as Scheler has pointed out, resentment increases "the more the injury is experienced as a destiny."[46]

Where a sense of diminished worth leads us to feel hostile toward one we otherwise love and respect we can speak of the *ambivalence of resentment*. In the believing soul this resentment may well be completely covered over, as Freud's hatred of his father was for so many years. In the unbelieving soul just the opposite may have occured. The hostility may have taken over so completely that all tendencies toward affirming the sacred have been driven into the unconscious. But in neither case does absence from immediate view indicate the actual absence of the opposing attitude. It looks as if respect and resentment may dialectically imply one another. This is only a special case of what playwrights and novelists have known and shown for years, that love and hate are often inseparable.

The anti-Semite incident and the Gisela incident show that happiness is at stake as well as worthiness. Most concretely put, the question is this: Why did my father not use his physical strength to teach that haughty Gentile a lesson he would never forget? And why did he not arrange things so Gisela and I could be together rather than separated? More generally, why does my father not use his power to secure my happiness? When the questions are formulated in this way they closely parallel the traditional problem of evil, which comes to expression in anguished questions like these: Why did you let my child die? or Why do you let the children suffer? Both in personal experience and in philosophical reflection this kind of question is one of the most serious obstacles to trusting belief in God. It leads Dostoyevsky's Ivan to deny God, while Job stays with his "Though he slay me, yet will I trust him." Yet we would be mistaken if we think Job free of the resentment Ivan feels. For he immediately continues, "But I will defend mine own ways before him."[47] Such a defense is in effect an accusation of God, one of which Job eventually repents, but from which he is not wholly able to free himself.

We have been led to speak again of resentment, and there is no reason why we should not speak again of the *ambivalence of resentment*. But it must be noticed that here the resentment is grounded in my perceived lack of *power* rather than lack of *worth*. If I had the power of my (heavenly) father, I would surely have arranged things differently. We can distinguish the question of happiness from the question of worth. There is an important difference between resenting the father's use of his power in ways which do not meet with my approval and resenting the fact that I do not myself meet with his approval. Neither of these resentments is incompatible with genuine love and admiration. Love and respect may drive the resentment underground, or vice versa, but it does not seem possible for either love or hatred completely to eliminate its rival.

Freud himself is an especially interesting case in this respect. Though it is clear he was genuinely ambivalent toward his father, one might, on the basis of his published writings deny that he was ambivalent about God. There seems to be an implacable hatred, unrelieved by any affirmative attitudes whatever. Ernest Becker, however, points to a number of indications that something in Freud flirted with God and the supernatural. He affirms the judgment of Zilboorg, who has written, "It becomes also clear that Freud fought deliberately against certain spiritual trends within himself. . . . [He] seems to have been in a state of searching and painful conflict in which the positivist scholar (conscious) and the potential believer (unconscious) fought an open battle."[48]

When we turn from Freud's own life to his theorizing we find ambivalence if anything more prominent. In his *Introductory Lectures on Psycho-Analysis*[49] he presents psychoanalytic theory as a theory of dreams and a related theory of neurotic symptoms, introduced by observations on everyday errors such as slips of the tongue or pen. The key to each of these three fields of investigation, and with them the entire Freudian theory of the unconscious, is the psychic tension generated by conflicting attitudes within the person, or, in short, ambivalence. Freudian theory is like a massive sermon on the text, "A double minded man is unstable in all his ways."[50]

At the very heart of Freud's thought is the Oedipal complex, the child's ambivalence toward the parent. The child loves the parent with a love which is part awful admiration and part appreciation for benefits received. But the child also comes to view the parent of his or her own sex as a rival for the love and possession of the other parent. Hence jealousy and hatred toward one loved and respected. Freud insists that this has a sexual meaning, and though the point has been hotly disputed, we need not debate that issue here. What is clear is that there is a deeper meaning, of which any sexual meanings are but the vehicle of expression. It is not fundamentally a matter of sexual pleasure but of *power*. Who has the *ability* and *authority* to satisfy his or her desire?

Becker sees this as already true of the child's relation to the mother. "On the one hand the mother is a pure source of pleasure and satisfaction, a secure power to lean on . . . But on the other hand the child has to strain against this very dependency, or he loses the feeling that he has aegis over his own powers. That is another way of saying that the mother, by representing secure biological dependence, is also a fundamental threat." It is the "power of the parents in their awesome miraculousness" that the child must fight against, while enjoying it at the same time.[51]

This theme of power is found in Freud's own account of the Oedipal ambivalence. "More than one occasion for hostility lies concealed in the relation between parents and children—a relation which affords the most ample opportunities for wishes to arise which cannot pass the censorship. Let us consider first the relation between father and son. The sanctity which we attribute to the rules laid down in the Decalogue has, I think, blunted our powers of perceiving the real facts. We seem scarcely to venture to observe that the majority of mankind disobey the Fifth Commandment [Honor your father and mother]. . . . The obscure information which is brought to us by mythology and legend from the primaeval ages of human society gives an unpleasing picture of the father's despotic power and of the ruthlessness with which he made use of it. Kronos devoured his children . . . while Zeus emasculated his father and made himself ruler in his place. The more unrestricted was the rule of the father in the ancient family, the more must the son, as his destined successor, have found himself in the position of an enemy, and the more impatient must he have been to become ruler himself through his father's death. Even in our middle-class families fathers are as a rule inclined to refuse their sons independence and the means necessary to secure it and thus to foster the growth of the germ of hostility which is inherent in their relation. A physician will often be in a position to notice how a son's grief at the loss of his father cannot suppress his satisfaction at having at length won his freedom. In our society today fathers are apt to cling desperately to what is left of a now sadly antiquated *potestas patris familias*; and an author who, like Ibsen, brings the immemorial struggle between fathers and sons into prominence in his writings may be certain of producing his effect."[52]

Power is both ability and authority, as has already been noted. In Becker's account of the child and mother it is the former sense that prevails, the notion of the mother as strength, capacity, self-sufficiency. In Freud's account of the son and father it is the latter sense that prevails. From our earlier account of the nature of the numinous we should be hesitant to assume that these two aspects of power are always neatly separable or even distinguishable. When we're dealing with the wholly other (and surely the parents are that to the child), might and right do not come neatly labeled and sorted out. But even when we have drawn the difference between ability and authority quite sharply, what we need to notice is that both kinds of power are something we badly want. Each is an essential ingredient in both our happiness and our sense of personal worth. We experience the lack of either as a deficiency of being.

It is tempting to suggest at this point that Freud's life highlights the ambivalence of resentment, directed toward the use of power, while his theory points to the ambivalence of envy, directed toward its mere possession. We shall shortly see that resentment and envy are more closely related than this, but the distinction between the use and possession of power already introduces a crucial new aspect to our understanding. Reflection on the three incidents in Freud's childhood might suggest that Freud's hatred of his father could have been avoided if his father had simply exercised his ability more courageously and his authority more sensitively. Or, to put it a bit differently, Freud would have gladly played the role of son to a father who played his role better. This is what the theory of the Oedipal complex denies, which is why Norman O. Brown has suggested that we speak of the Oedipal project rather than Oedipal complex. "The Oedipal project is not, as Freud's earlier formulations suggest, a natural love of the mother, but as his later writings recognize, a product of the conflict of ambivalence and an attempt to overcome that conflict by narcissistic inflation. The essence of the Oedipal complex is the project of becoming God—in Spinoza's formula, *causa sui* [one's own cause]." In other words, says Becker, the child wants to be "*father of himself*, the creator and sustainer of his own life."[53]

Envy in a more directly religious context is a central theme of *Totem and Taboo*, whose second, lengthy chapter is entitled, "Taboo and Emotional Ambivalence." Freud discovered among his neurotic patients behavior habits which seemed to him strikingly like the taboo practices of pre-literate tribal religions which were being described in a rapidly growing anthropological literature. Wishing to explore this and other parallels he subtitled his essays "Some Points of Agreement between the Mental Lives of Savages and Neurotics."

Writing before Otto, he seems to have the concept of the numinous fully in hand except for the word itself. He speaks of *mana* as that which generates taboo, and sees this power as evoking a fear which "has not yet split up into the two forms into which it later develops: veneration and horror."[54] Though *mana* is clearly a power concept, Freud recognizes that it is also "a category of value" (Otto), for he notices that it is intimately tied up with ceremonies of purification and atonement, and he speculates that the taboo it generates lies at the root of our own understanding of moral imperatives as categorical.[55]

Convinced that the taboo behavior of neurotics is rooted in ambivalence, the strength of the prohibition being required to counterbalance a powerful desire for what is forbidden, he looks for the ambivalence underlying the religious taboos of primitive peoples. What is especially interesting for our purposes is his account of the taboos surrounding kings and rulers. They seem to be objects of considerable affection and veneration, but also targets of aggression and hostility, for the taboos pertaining to their person simultaneously honor them as special and harass them in ways which can only be described as sadistic. Freud finds nothing mysterious about the fact that the king should be honored. What needs to be understood is the hatred which seems so regularly to accompany affection and respect. His solution is simple—envy. Those who are not the ruler recognize the ruler as possessor of greater *mana* than they, else he would not be king. They are grateful that he has this power and they bask in its splendor and beneficence. But at the same time they want more of it for themselves. This envy generates ambivalence. Here again it is not a question of how the power is used. Envy finds the mere possession of it by someone else to be objectionable, and it finds ways to express its feelings, even in the midst of honoring.[56]

In summary, Freud reminds us that we have ample reasons for thinking "it would indeed be very nice if there were a God." At the same time he helps us to recognize, perhaps with surprise, that we not only understand but also sympathize with Nietzsche's Zarathustra, when he says, "But let me reveal my heart to you entirely, my friends: *if there were gods how could I endure not to be a god!* Hence there are no gods. . . ."[57]

Up to this point we have been looking at resentment and envy in relatively concrete embodiments, Freud's resentment toward his father, the child's envy of the parent, the "savage's" envy of political authority, and so on. We have not focused on resentment and envy themselves so as to bring them to eidetic clarity. A brief phenomenology of these two affects will not only deepen our comprehension of the materials taken from Freud's life and theory and their significance for the religious life; it will also provide the promised clarification of the relation of the two feelings to each other.

Resentment can be directed toward a wide variety of objects, including groups of persons, social institutions, and even values. But in its simplest form it is the relation of one person to another, and we can focus our attention on that mode, guided by Scheler's descriptions. The first thing to notice about resentment is that it is not a primary feeling. It presupposes that some other feeling, a hostile one, is already directed toward its object. The other key element in the genesis of resentment is the repression of the primary feeling.

"Repression" here does not have its technical Freudian sense, involving censorship and the driving of the primary feeling into the unconscious. It simply means that the original antipathy cannot be adequately discharged through action which gives expression to it. Hostile feelings will result in resentment "only if there occurs neither a moral self-conquest (such as *genuine* forgiveness in the case of revenge) nor an act or some other adequate expression of emotion (such as verbal abuse or shaking one's fist), and if this restraint is caused by a pronounced awareness of impotence."[58] This impotence, which can arise from either weakness or fear, is absolutely fundamental to Scheler's account of resentment. This is of special significance for our investigation in view of the importance of power in the human experience of the holy and in the Freudian account of envy.

If a sense of impotence is the source of the repression that produces resentment, its result is the continued presence of the original hostile feelings. Sometimes Scheler's language makes resentment sound more episodic than the notion of continued presence expresses. But hostile feelings which have not been discharged do not pass into non-being when they leave center stage. They pass from the foreground of consciousness to the background, which, in turn, functions as the transcendental condition of the possible experience of anything else which may come to the foreground or focus of our awareness. For this reason Scheler perceptively speaks of resentment as "the continual reliving of the emotion [which] sinks it more deeply into the center of the personality." From the security of this inconspicuousness the original hostile feelings "become fixed attitudes, detached from all determinate objects. Independently of his will, this man's attention will be instinctively drawn by all events which can set these affects in motion. The resentment attitude even plays a role in the formation of perceptions, expectations, and memories. It automatically selects those aspects of experience which can justify the factual application of this pattern of feeling."[59] From the surface, resentment may look like a volcano which blows its top only occasionally. But the geologist of the soul knows that such episodes are but the conspicuous visibility of processes which go on continually.

The basic structure of resentment, then, is this: feelings of hostility are repressed because a perception of impotence does not allow them to be discharged, with the result that they take up (semi)permanent residence in psychic life.[60]

We are now in a position to see how envy is related to resentment. Up to this point the original feelings whose repression produces resentment have only been described quite generically as feelings of hostility or antipathy. Scheler is careful, however, to specify quite a number of distinct feelings which can become resentment through suppression. These include revenge, hatred, malice, the impulse to detract, spite, rancor, wrath, joy at another's misfortune, and envy. Resentment and envy are related more or less as form to matter. This implies not only that there can be resentment without envy and vice versa, but also that resentment will be the form which envy takes when it cannot be dissipated. When our investigation of what Freud can show us about ambivalence before the numinous leads us sometimes to speak of resentment and sometimes of envy, we need not think we are dealing with two separate phenomena. There is a more than ample role for envy to play in what has here been called the ambivalence of resentment.

Of envy itself we can say that it comes to expression by reversing what John the Baptist said about Jesus, "He must become greater; I must become less."[61] Envy says, "I must become greater at the other's expense." To understand envy we must grasp both the preoccupation with oneself with which it begins and then the relation to others which it entails.

Kierkegaard speaks of "selfish envy,"[62] but the phrase is a redundancy. Envy is simply the form self-centeredness takes in relation to another's possessions. In this context "possessions" refers to another's properties as much as to another's property, especially where those properties are some form of excellence, and thus something esteemed.

One of the easiest ways to discover the thoroughly egocentric character of envy is to notice how difficult it is to admire others, admiration being the opposite of envy.[63] Even if we have trouble finding ourselves in the earlier descriptions of envy as expressed in primitive taboos, neurotic symptoms, and raving rebels like Nietzche, we might recognize ourselves in the dramatist friend of Marcel who told him "that admiration was for him a humiliating state which he resisted with all his force." Marcel sees this as expressing "the tendency to view with suspicion any acknowledged mark of superiority. An analysis similar to the one Scheler has given of resentment should disclose that there is a burning preoccupation with self at the bottom of this suspicion, a 'but what about me, what becomes of me in that case?' " Since "the function of admiration is to tear us away from ourselves and from the thoughts we have of ourselves," to view admiration as humiliating "is the same as to treat the subject as a power existing for itself and taking itself as a center. To proclaim on the other hand, that it is an exalted state is to start from the inverse notion that the proper function of the subject is to emerge from itself and realize itself primarily in the gift of oneself and in the various forms of creativity."[64] In the language of Kierkegaard, envy keeps us from self-sacrifice.[65] In the language of Section 2A, above, we can say that envy is the response to any challenge to my ordinary sense (so clearly articulated by Cartesian philosophy) of myself as the absolute center to which all else is properly relative. Since the life of the believing soul is grounded in the experience of the sacred as the *ens realissimum*, that life is bound to be caught in the tension between two conflicting experiences and most unlikely to be free of the envy we would expect to result.

But we must not lose our focus on envy as such. As we have just seen, it is a special form of preoccupation with self, but it is anything but solipsistic or narcissistic. It is essentially and intensely comparative.[66] This is what distinguishes it from greed. Greed is directed toward that which I wish to possess. Envy is directed toward the one who possesses what I wish to possess. We acknowledge this without noticing when we say, not I envy her good looks, but I envy her her good looks. Where simple greed is at issue, I can be satisfied merely by coming to possess. But if it is a case of envy my possession must be at your expense.

Envy has as a basic assumption that life is a zero-sum game, one in which the total winnings equal the total losings. This was especially clear to Spinoza. He defines envy as "hatred in so far as it affects a man so that he is sad at the good fortune of another person and is glad when any evil happens to him." Since men are "naturally envious," he expects that "a man's joy in contemplating himself will therefore be greatest when he comtemplates something in himself which he denies of other people."[67]

A special consequence of envy, thus understood, is that "if we imagine that a person enjoys a thing which only one can possess, we do all we can to prevent his possessing it."[68] If this is true then we will be especially prone to hostility (and thus ambivalence) toward God in a monotheistic context, though we have already seen Nietzsche's Zarathustra give expression to essentially this same sentiment in a polytheistic context. Sartre's claim that we are fundamentally the desire to be God and Spinoza's that we are naturally envious turn out to be virtually synonymous.

Envy then is selfish desire turned into hostility in a comparative, zero-sum context. Like other forms of hostility, it will produce resentment if it cannot be discharged, and it will produce a tense ambivalence if the inability to discharge envy is in part due to genuine admiration. If we remember with all this that envy can be directed toward another's ontological excellence as well as toward accidental and external possessions, we will understand both the basis of Scheler's most profound comment about resentment and its significance for understanding religion. "Therefore *existential envy*, which is directed against the other person's very *nature*, is the strongest source of resentment. It is as if it whispers continually: 'I can forgive everything but not that you *are*—that you are *what* you are—that I am not what you are—indeed that I am not *you*.' This form of envy strips the opponent of his very existence, for this existence as such is felt to be a 'pressure,' a 'reproach,' and an unbearable humiliation. . . . Here lies the meaning of Goethe's reflection that 'against another's great merits, there is no remedy but love.' "[69]

We will also understand why this remedy is not likely ever to be complete.

The Existential
Meaning of Guilt

4A. Guilt and death as the believing soul's ultimate concern

The discovery of the preceding chapter, if we have been on the right track, is that being religious means being ambivalent because it means being open to what is at once attractive and repelling. Sometimes the believing soul is taken to stand in a lasting relation to a personal God or gods or to that impersonal, quasi-electric power known as *mana*. At other times the relational nature of the believing soul is taken to be in need of dissolution, for example, in the oneness of Brahman or in the emptiness of Nirvana. In either case the presently experiencing finite self, which answers to its own proper name, is confronted by that which surpasses it, bringing its own being and value into question and destroying its Cartesian certainty of itself. Whether the challenge is to become identical with this surpassing reality (or unreality), to become harmoniously attuned to it, or to enter loving fellowship with it, the believing soul can only be drawn toward it as toward its own highest prize and offended by it as the ultimate put down of its beloved self.

By speaking of inertia and resentment as two different aspects of this ambivalence we have emphasized the negative or repelling moment, all too easily overlooked by believer and unbeliever alike. Only by seeing from the outset that the blessings of the religious life are themselves a threat to the human, all too human, self each of us is, can we hope to avoid reducing the religious life to its attractive dimension, the only one which gets acknowledged by some of its critics and by those of its devotees who have themselves lost touch with the Holy.[1] Such a reduction is wishful thinking in either case. In point of fact, the believing brother and sister pay a high price for whatever it is they get out of their religion.

But whatever is it they get out of their religion? What makes it seem worthwhile to struggle against the inertia, the resentment, and

69

the envy which the Sacred inevitably evokes and to make it one's highest good? Does not every religion have its own version of the claim that "to know Christ means to know his benefits"?[2] What are the benefits of religion?

Some light will be thrown on this question by comparing two conflicting attempts by anthropologists to distinguish religion from magic. In *The Golden Bough*, Frazer describes magic as being like science in assuming an impersonal uniformity of nature which can be manipulated by those who know its laws. By contrast, religion involves the belief that the course of nature and human life is controlled by personal and conscious beings, more powerful than we, and that we can win the favor of these spirits or gods through such acts as *prayers* or *sacrifices* and thereby "persuade or induce the mighty beings who control [the course of nature] to deflect, for our benefit, the current of events from the channel in which they would otherwise flow."[3] By making personal forces ultimate, religion differs from both magic and science. But the difference concerns only the means, not the ends. While magic works directly on nature and religion indirectly, both seek to control nature "for our benefit." In other words, both are concerned with the fertility of the soil and success in the hunt, with healing and life for oneself and one's friends and death for one's enemies, and, in general, with the securing of good fortune and the avoidance of misfortune.

The distinction of religion from magic is made rather differently by Malinowski. He asks about the purpose or function of the rites which are such a prominent feature of both and asks us to compare a rite carried out to prevent the death of a child with a ceremony celebrating the birth of a child. "The first rite is carried out as a means to an end, it has a definite practical purpose which is known to all who practice it and can be easily elicited from any native informant. The post natal ceremony . . . has no purpose: it is not a means to an end, but an end in itself . . . there is no future event which this ceremony foreshadows, which it is meant to bring about or prevent."[4] For Malinowski, this is what differentiates religion from magic. Whereas Frazer sees it to be a different means to the same ends as magic, he sees religious activities to be their own end rather than instrumentalities directed toward some result other than the activities themselves.

Neither of these distinctions will really work. We have already seen, in contrast to Frazer, that the (1) believing soul does not always *believe* in personal and conscious powers presiding over nature and (2) that the categories of fortune and misfortune are by no means ultimate for the religious life. Furthermore, Malinowski (3) warns us not to overlook those religious activities which are their own end, indicating that religion is not simply an instrumental or utilitarian concern.

Nevertheless, Frazer reminds us that the believing soul does pray for healing and rain and protection from enemies, that the question of personal or group benefits is not wholly foreign to religious concern. This reminder serves as a corrective against Malinowski's attempt to see religion exclusively in terms of activities which are their own reward and not means to any beneficial end. The situation is actually more complicated than either Frazer or Malinowski recognizes. Religion is both a means to various ends and an end in itself. In trying to understand the attractiveness of religion, therefore, we will have to speak of both the instrumental and the instrinsic value of the religious life to the believing soul. The activities which make up the religious life are valued sometimes for the benefits they bring, sometimes for their own sake, and sometimes, as we shall see, both ways at once.

It will be the task of Chapters Seven and Eight to explore the intrinsic value of religion, the various ways in which its activities, like play and aesthetic contemplation, are prized for their own sake and not for their consequences or results. But first we shall turn our attention, in this chapter and the next two, to the instrumental value of religion, seeking to understand the way it functions as a means for dealing with the fundamental human problems of guilt and death.

After noting the affinity between religion and magic as means for gaining health and wealth, it may seem strange to describe the goal-oriented nature of the religious life in terms of guilt and death. But the believing soul will understand, and if we let him speak he may help us to understand as well.

In this instance his name is Zechariah, whose son we know as John the Baptist. He has become persuaded that God has designated this son of his to be Messiah's forerunner, announcing to all Israel this long-awaited, great new act of salvation. Inspired, he speaks.

> Praise to the God of Israel!
> For he has turned to his people, saved them and set them free,
> and has raised up a deliverer of victorious power
>   from the house of his servant David.

> So he promised: age after age he proclaimed
>   by the lips of his holy prophets,
> that he would deliver us from our enemies,
>   out of the hands of all who hate us;

that he would deal mercifully with our fathers,
    calling to mind his solemn covenant.

Such was the oath he swore to our father Abraham,
    to rescue us from enemy hands,
and grant us, free from fear, to worship him
    with a holy worship, with uprightness of heart,
    in his presence, our whole life long.

And you, my child, you shall be called Prophet of the Highest,
for you will be the Lord's forerunner, to prepare his way
    and lead his people to salvation through knowledge of him,
    by the forgiveness of their sins:
for in the tender compassion of our God
    the morning sun from heaven will rise upon us,
to shine on those who live in darkness, under the cloud of death,
    and to guide our feet into the way of peace.[5]

A strange transformation occurs in this hymn. It begins with praise
and ends with a reference to peace. For the first three stanzas that
peace is described in terms of national liberation. In the first, though
speaking of the present, Zechariah evokes the two primary symbols
of Israel's earlier national independence: the Exodus, when God saved
his people and set them free from slavery in Egypt, and the Davidic
kingship. In the second and third stanzas he talks about God's promise (covenant, oath) to deliver the people from their enemies in such
a way as to make an immediate reference to the hated occupation
of the Jewish homeland by the Romans unmistakable. The great new
act of salvation seems ineluctably modeled on the people's deliverance from the Egyptians under Moses and from the Philistines under
David. Just as the Egyptians lost their firstborn sons and had their
army drowned in the sea, and just as Goliath lost his head and his
followers their heart, so now the Romans are going to get what's
coming to them.

But in the final stanza the enemy turns out to be not the Romans,
but guilt and death, and peace is identified not with national liberation, but with the life of those whose sins are forgiven and who no
longer live under the dark cloud of death, but in the light which
shines from heaven.

It is as if the believing soul confesses, almost in spite of national
longing, that peace and prosperity in the political and economic sense
are only penultimate concerns and that what is most needed from
God is deliverance, at the level of ultimate existential concerns, from
guilt and death.

The more widely I examine the phenomena of religion from animism to Zen the more persuaded I become that on this point Zechariah is not just a believing soul, but the believing soul, fully typical of religion as such. He is, unashamedly, interested in what we might call worldly good fortune, in this case national liberation. But, when the chips are down, he willingly acknowledges that his ultimate concern is of a different order, that being able to face death with a clear conscience is more important to him than getting rid of the wretched Romans.

We cannot say what attitude Zechariah and his believing brothers and sisters will take at this point. They may live penultimately, devoting most of their energies to the pursuit of worldly good fortune and turning their religious life into the magical manipulation of the Sacred as a means to that end. Or they may decide that asceticism is the only way to preserve the ultimacy of the ultimate, cultivating a thorough-going disinterest in and contempt for all worldly good fortune. Or they may seek simultaneously to be absolutely committed to the absolute and relatively committed to the relative,[6] humbly trusting for the health and wealth they need and thankfully refusing to despise these blessings, but concentrating their religious energies on meeting needs they take to be both deeper and higher. They will all agree, however, at least in their most lucid moments, that it is these deeper and higher needs which are the real heart of their religious life.

Mention was just made of facing death with a clear conscience. We have yet to see that this has not one meaning, but many different meanings. But already the phrase suggests what will subsequently be shown in some detail, that the problems of guilt and death are intimately related and can only be understood together. The present chapter and the next will explore the existential meaning of guilt and death, seeking to enrich our understanding of how they might be counted among the most problematic aspects of human life. With this preparation we will be ready in Chapter Six to consider religion as a means to freedom from guilt and victory over death.

4B. The existential meaning of guilt

It may seem puzzling, or to some outright implausible, to say that guilt lies at the heart of religious concern and that religion is regularly a means of solving the problem of guilt. But let us stick to the methodology we have adopted and seek to understand what is being said before we evaluate it. Unless we know rather precisely what is meant by guilt in this context we will not be able to see for ourselves whether it in fact shapes a fundamental religious interest, just as we cannot tell whether the influence of snyks on the economy is rising or falling unless we know what snyks are.

We can, perhaps, best spell out the meaning of guilt, as it will be used from here on, by reflecting on the relation of guilt to punishment. To begin with, there is the objective sense of guilt. Here we are talking about being found guilty (as distinguished from feeling guilty) by a parent, teacher, court of law, or some such authority. To be guilty in this sense is to be liable to punishment. According to the dictionary, liable means, "subject, exposed, or open to something possible or likely, esp. something undesirable."[7]

Naturally, a person can be guilty in this sense and be entirely unaware of it. In that case there might be objective guilt without any accompanying subjective guilt or guilt feeling. But the person who is aware of being liable to punishment will almost automatically, if the punishment amounts to anything, feel a fear or dread of it.

Since both punishment and the fear of punishment are painful, our natural desire is to avoid or eliminate both. Usually they come and go more or less together, but that is not essential. Fear of punishment can be a terrible ordeal, even if the punishment never actually comes. And a punishment which comes so unexpectedly as to permit no prior fears is scarcely for that reason less unpleasant.

But unless we get beyond punishment and the fear of punishment to a third dimension of the problem we will not fully understand the meaning of guilt as the believing soul experiences it. This third dimension is so fundamental that we should call it guilt proper. (In what follows I shall regularly refer to it simply as guilt.) For while the believing soul is as eager as anyone to be free from punishment and the fear of it, neither of these is the heart of the problem.

This third dimension is another subjective aspect, guilt in the sense of guilt feeling or guilt consciousness. We can perhaps get at it best through a concrete example. Consider the sixth grade lad who has gotten too big, as they say, for his britches.[8] Looking forward to summer heroics in Little League, he and his buddies have found the school gym teacher's program somewhat beneath their professional dignity. So throughout the spring they have engaged in what we might euphemistically call systematic non-cooperation. The unexpected toleration of the gym teacher only serves to increase the shenanigans. But he is only biding his time; for he knows that the report cards call for two grades in every subject, one for achievement and one for "comportment." The latter is a pass-fail proposition. The student has either behaved satisfactorily or has not. And suddenly there it is, staring our lad in the face. Not one, but two check marks in the box marked Unsatisfactory.

Up until this time he has not felt especially troubled about his behavior. Now, in the face of certain punishment, he feels terrible. He knows that lightning will strike quickly. It won't take his father long to find out what the two check marks signify and even less time to turn the son over his knee so as to continue their dialogue at the level of non-verbal, but ever so unambiguous communication.

The exigencies of the situation transform the boy into an instant presidential press secretary. To his father's inquiry about the double check mark he replies with as obfuscatory a half-truth as was ever served up to the White House press corps. To his utter disbelief and enormous relief, the topic is dropped. This cover-up has worked completely.

Is our hero suddenly at peace again with the world and himself? Hardly! As he gets a little distance from the immediate situation the sense of relief fades and is gradually replaced by a puzzled disappointment in his father. What was the matter with him anyway, that he had failed so conspicuously in his fatherly responsibility? Against the background of this disappointment there sounds the voice of the boy's guilty conscience. This voice is much quieter than the loud shouting which accompanied him home with the report card. Now that the fear of punishment is gone there remains only the pure sense of guilt, or guilt proper. No doubt it was present before, but we can only now see it clearly for what it is. In particular we can see as we reflect on this experience, which might have been our own, that the experience of guilt (guilt proper) is qualitatively different from the fear of punishment and is in no intelligible sense derived from that fear.

For, in the first place, fear looks forward toward what will or may happen, while guilt looks backward to what I have done or become.[9] Furthermore, fear is object oriented while guilt is subject oriented. That is to say that in fear my awareness is directed outward to the source from which some unpleasant consequence is expected, while in guilt my awareness is directed toward myself. It is a mode of self-consciousness or self-knowledge in which, to use Buber's phrase, "the bearer of guilt is visited by the shudder of identity with himself" and comes to the "humble knowledge of the identity of the present person with the person of that time," that is, the time of the action in question.[10]

It will be objected by some that it is just this turning inward by which fear is transformed into guilt. Guilt is simply the fear of punishment which remains when no external threat is on the horizon. It can either be said to be an objectless fear or the fear of an internal punisher. But this familiar interpretation of the second difference between fear and guilt is entirely undermined when a third difference is noted. Put in Kantian language it is this: in fear I am concerned about my happiness, while in guilt I am concerned about my *worthiness* to be happy. The uneasiness which eats away the original sense of relief that our young friend experienced when his father let him off the hook is not the fear of an invisible or interiorized father. It is the gradual dawning of the awareness of himself as thoroughly *deserving* the punishment he did not receive. He is not so much afraid of anything as he is ashamed of himself.[11]

Luther is a particularly clear example of this. Because he speaks so much about the wrath of God and because he believes in eternal punishment it is easy to make Scheler's mistake and assume that when he speaks of the terrors of conscience he simply expresses his fear of hell.[12] What drove Luther, however, first to despair and then to grace was not a fear of suffering in hell, but the overwhelming sense that this is what he *deserved*. Not the mere fact of God's wrath, but its uncontestable rightness brought his existence to its crisis.[13] For man can face enormous suffering with nobility and courage if with Job he is sure of his innocence or with Prometheus he is sure of God's guilt. What defines Luther's experience as that of guilt is precisely the absence of these comforts.

"I have often experienced," he writes, "and still do every day, how difficult it is to believe, especially amid struggles of conscience, that Christ was given, not for the holy, righteous, and deserving, or for those who were His friends, but for the godless, sinful, and undeserving, for those who were His enemies, who *deserved the wrath of God and eternal wrath.*"[14]

These two examples, of Luther and our Little League friend, forbid us to equate guilt with the fear of punishment. But they also suggest a twofold relation between the two. In the first place, fear of punishment can occasion the experience of guilt. Guilt essentially involves the awareness of myself[15] as less worthy of happiness than I would like to be. Punishment presents itself as an unhappiness which I (allegedly) deserve, thereby raising the question of my worthiness. Where the answer to this question is patently unfavorable to my pride I am likely to deceive myself more successfully by avoiding the question altogether than by stubbornly affirming my innocence to myself.

In that situation punishment tends to force the issue. I can defend myself from the *moral* pain of punishment[16] only by consciously denying that I deserve it, thereby reducing it to misfortune or persecution. But even to consider that option is to raise the question which up to that time had been effectively tabled and which *ex hypothesi* has an obvious and unfavorable answer. This is clearly what happened to our schoolboy. He had managed to avoid feeling guilty by repressing any evaluation of his behavior whatever, until the defense mechanisms he had so diligently erected self-destructed in the face of impending punishment. Part of what he felt on his way home was guilt proper, though we were able to see it clearly only when it outlived the fear that originally was fused with it.

This fusion represents a second relation between guilt and the fear of punishment. In his discussion of defilement as a symbol of evil as fault Ricoeur calls this fusion dread. Reference is to the primitive understanding of taboo, prior to any conceptions of divine or social agents of retribution. Yet the violation of a taboo is a violation against an impersonal order which is effective and will certainly strike back in vengeance. Since this order is also prior to any division between the merely natural and the moral order, the offender does not merely anticipate an unpleasant response as inevitable, but also as somehow appropriate. In an inarticulate way he is already in possession of the Socratic wisdom that "to escape punishment is worse than to suffer it." In this case "fear of vengeance is not a simple passive fear; already it involves a demand, the demand for a just punishment."[17]

The fear of punishment which demands precisely the punishment it fears is clearly not a simple fear. It is the radical ambivalence of desperately wanting to avoid just what we deeply want to happen. This was the state of mind which comes to light in the autobiographical elements of Luther's theology. Since this is a unified, if complex, mode of consciousness, it would be useful if there were a standard term for referring to it. Ricoeur's use of "dread" for this purpose runs the risk of introducing extraneous connotations from more firmly fixed existentialist usages, but this meaning is at least as close to pre-technical usage as the existentialist meanings.

This concept of dread serves two purposes. As already indicated, it enables us to acknowledge the close relationship between guilt proper and fear of punishment without identifying the two. Second, by preserving a clear distinction between the guilt and fear components, it provides us with a working definition of guilt. In this context guilt is an affirmative attitude toward the verdict which renders me liable to punishment.[18] Since punishment is an unhappiness

I (allegedly) deserve, it represents a negative judgment on my worth coming from outside me. Since in guilt I affirm this judgment, we can say that *in guilt I approve the other's disapproval of me*. To illuminate and confirm this initial result we shall take a closer look at the phenomenon of guilt from three quite different perspectives: the sociology of deviance, the literature of morbid inwardness, and the psychology of false consciousness.

4C. Guilt and the sociology of deviance

It would appear from the foregoing that Nietzsche was mistaken in saying that punishment does not awaken the feeling of guilt.[19] When he says that the sting of conscience is extremely rare among criminals and convicts, he confuses guilt with repentance. It may be that our correctional systems make men hard and cold; but this very hardness and coldness is more accurately seen as a defensive reaction to the dawning of an unpleasant awareness than as the calm assurance that all is quiet on the worthiness-to-be-happy front. It may equally be true that the knowledge convicts gain of the cruelty and hypocrisy practiced in the name of justice helps to distract attention from their own guilt; but only those in whom guilty self-consciousness has dawned can find comfort in finding others to be just as bad or worse.[20]

My own experience with those who have served time in prison does not suggest that they have come through the experience with an unscathed sense of personal worth. In their bitterness toward the system and its agents, as justified as it may be, they come through as willing, but never quite able, to justify themselves. From the point of view of public policy the problem is not that our penal system fails to awaken guilt, but rather that it fails to engender repentance. The law is simply a taskmaster when it should be a schoolmaster.

While it is mistaken, then, to think that the criminal has invincible defenses against guilt, it is nevertheless true that his avoidance mechanisms make up an awesome armory. For if it is true that punishment forces the question which gives rise to experienced guilt, those who live in the shadow of punishment will be able to sustain a viable self-image only by neutralizing most of the guilt they would normally feel. A closer look at the way they (and the rest of us, if we're honest about it) avoid being destroyed by the guilt that their deeds seem to call for may further illuminate the meaning of guilt. The soldier, too, has need of such "techniques of neutralization."[21] These parallel those of the delinquent so strikingly that they can be presented together.

Does the juvenile delinquent live in an inverted world where all norms and values are the opposite from those prevailing in straight society? No, we are told. He shares the values of the larger society, at least abstractly, but is especially skillful at rendering them inoperative in relation to his own behavior. Five distinct techniques of neutralization can be specified. The first is *Denial of Responsibility*. The delinquent quickly learns to take the point of view of the social scientist and humane jurist who see him as a product of his environment. In the important sense that guilt requires, his deeds are not really his own. The soldier gets the same effect by viewing himself as merely part of a larger organic whole. Not only are thousands of others doing the same thing; it is others who are giving the orders and directing the show.[22] His deeds are not really his, but those of this supra-personal entity known as The Army or My Country. Or he may submerge himself in a sub-personal entity, the machinery which immediately does the killing, and come to see himself more nearly as an extension of the weapons he uses than as their user. Once again his deeds cease to be his own and he can say, It wasn't really I who did it.

A second technique is called the *Denial of Injury*. The delinquent tells himself that vandalism is merely a prank which harms no one and that his stealing is from those who can afford it anyway. The soldier can hardly avail himself of these ploys, but in modern warfare he is often so spatially distant from his victims that it is easy for him not to notice that his shells and bombs will inevitably destroy children not unlike those who anxiously await his safe return home.

In this way no one gets hurt, except the Enemy, which brings us to a third technique, *Denial of the Victim*, or more precisely, the denial of the victims' innocence. In other words, they had it coming so why should I feel guilty about what happened. Delinquency and war depend heavily on our capacity to view the other as evil. Where the Enemy is to be found, there is war; and all is fair in war.

If we pause now and ask what self-awareness these devices are intended to ward off it would have to be expressed like this: I am responsible for injuring or harming an innocent victim. With this awareness there may or may not be a fear of anticipated unpleasant consequences. That is quite contingent. What is necessarily associated with this awareness is a depleted sense of personal worth that we call guilt or shame. In the likely event that the first three techniques are not totally effective, some further mitigating factor will be sought for. The required mitigation would have to be a supervening value which could drive a wedge between the awareness of myself as having harmed an innocent victim and the guilt which would otherwise be an inevitable part of that awareness.

This brings us to a fourth technique: *Appeal to Higher Loyalties.* The delinquent seeks to justify his assault on the larger society by reference to his loyalty to the smaller group to which he belongs, the gang, his buddies. The soldier does the same. Loyalty to his buddy or his unit or the Fatherland in its hour of need serves to transform acts that he could not normally perform at all, much less without guilt, into courageous deeds of valor. What was *prima facie* evil has now become justified, even obligatory. William Calley scarcely feels the guilt a healthy person would feel, not just because the women and children of My Lei are the Enemy, but also because he is there to protect his Friends.

The four defenses so far presented can be summed up colloquially as follows: I didn't do it, and anyway nobody got hurt. Besides, they had it coming, and you wouldn't want me to abandon my friends, would you? I had to do it! This is not a model of calm coherence, but of a desperate struggle against that diminution of self-esteem which might be expressed in a number of ways; I am worthy to be punished, I am not worthy to be loved, I am not worthy of happiness. The defense is all the more passionate because the confession would be so painful. But to whom is the defense offered in lieu of a confession?

The fifth, and for the present analysis, final protection from guilt indicates that the defendant has not been talking merely to himself, but to the Other. This technique can be called *Condemnation of the Condemners* or *Rejection of the Rejectors.* "The delinquent shifts the focus of attention from his own deviant acts to the motives and behavior of those who disapprove of his violations."[23] Once again, there is an Other who must be viewed as the Enemy if guilt is to be avoided. But this time it is not simply the victim who must be so conceived. It is the whole class of those who disapprove of the behavior in question. The attitude of veterans groups to war resisters indicates that this remains a necessity for soldiers, even decades after their war has ended.[24]

It is worth stressing that this technique is not one of persuading the disapprovers, but of rejecting them. Persuasion would be nice, but it is not necessary. There is no need to eliminate the disapproval. All that is required, if the sense of guilt is to be avoided, is that I not find it necessary to approve the other's disapproval. For this purpose it is sufficient to discredit the other in my own eyes. This involves an element of persuasion, to be sure, since I must persuade myself that the other is the Enemy and can be disregarded. Under the circumstances I can probably persuade myself more easily than the other.

Although I end up talking to myself in order to persuade myself, this technique highlights the essential presence of the other in the experience of guilt. Where guilt is confused with fear of punishment its intersubjective nature is inescapable. But closer attention to the phenomena has led us to separate fear from guilt proper and to discover guilt as a form of self-consciousness. The other has gradually disappeared. We have seen conscience as the self saying to itself, Thou art the man (and trying to persuade itself that it is not). But this final aspect of the social scientific theory of delinquency confirms the suggestion of the two earlier examples that this is not the whole story, that the voice of conscience is not a soliloquy.[25] If guilt essentially involves this reference to the other's disapproval, this aspect of the fear theory needs to be rescued in order to be faithful to the full concreteness of the phenomenon before us.

Yet there may be a lingering doubt whether the suggestion which has emerged from two examples and from social scientific theory can be confirmed by genuine eidetic insight. May it not be that the other seems to be essential to the experience of guilt only because in the cases before us external sanctions are actually at hand in the persons of the boy's father, Luther's God, and the penal system of the state? Since it has been argued that this element is only an occasion for guilt and not part of its essential structure and that guilt must be sharply distinguished from the fear of punishment, is it not possible that we have allowed punishment, which obviously involves the other, to play too large a role in our exploration? May there not after all be an experience of conscience as pure soliloquy, as unmediated self-consciousness? May it not be only the element of fear which brings the other on the scene?

Perhaps it is time to shift our focus briefly. Instead of trying to get at guilt from below, as it were, through specific cases or types of cases, we might approach it from above, from the general theory of self-consciousness. It seems to me that one of the most firmly established phenomenological insights into the nature of self-consciousness is the Hegelian and Sartrean discovery that self-consciousness is always mediated by consciousness of the other. I first come to see myself when I see you looking at me. In opposition to the abstract and unmediated self-consciousness of transcendental philosophy from Descartes to Fichte, any awareness rich enough to be described as self-esteem is never an act of unconditioned self-positing. It is always a response to the other's attitude toward me. Empirical psychology has increasingly come to recognize this fact, but for our purposes the point is that it is not simply a fact but part of the essential structure of the finite self-consciousness we are. If this be indeed the case for self-consciousness as such, then guilt, which we have come to see as a mode of self-consciousness, is but a special case of the same necessity. As self-consciousness, it remains distinct from fear, but like every self-consciousness it is mediated through the self's relation to the other. David needs Nathan after all. The voice which accusingly tells the self, Thou art the man, is in the first instance the other's voice. Guilt is a kind of echo effect; for when that voice resounds off the walls of the self's inner life it has been transformed into the self's own voice.[26]

This fusion of voices is but another way of indicating that in guilt I recognize (even when I cannot bring myself to acknowledge) the justification of the other's judgment upon me. If we would keep guilt before us whole, we will have to preserve this unity of self-consciousness and other-consciousness.

4D. Guilt and the literature of morbid inwardness

What would be helpful at this point would be to return to the concrete to see anew the whole structure of guilt in both its complexity and its unity. It would be especially helpful if we could imagine or find an experience of guilt which, unlike Luther's, is thoroughly secular, and unlike all three cases considered to this point, is not staring punishment in the face. From among the candidates already worked out by the literary imagination of others, Dostoyevsky's Underground Man is perhaps best suited to our purpose. That his problem is guilt is indicated in numerous ways, among them the frequency with which he discusses the possibility of finding forgiveness for himself and the overt recollection that "at the very moment when I was most capable of recognizing every refinement of 'all the sublime and beautiful,' as we used to say at one time, I would, as though purposely, not only feel but do such hideous things. . . . The more conscious I was of goodness, and of all that 'sublime and beautiful'; the more deeply I sank into my mire and the more capable I became of sinking into it completely."[27]

To begin with, it is clear that the ailment from which he suffers is not the fear of punishment, but a special form of self-awareness. Positively this is indicated by the name he gives to the morbid introspectiveness displayed in the opening monologue, hyper-consciousness. Negatively this is seen in the fact that far from fearing or seeking to avoid any humiliation overt enough to be considered a punishment, he positively longs for such and actively seeks it out. He would be delighted to be slapped in the face, to be thrown out of the tavern, or to be beaten up. Although he never succeeds in evoking anything physical, he does manage in each of the three episodes narrated in Part II to expose himself to extreme social humiliation, to which he is especially sensitive.

The one persistent feature of Underground Man's hyperconsciousness is the overwhelming sense of his own worthlessness. Symbolically this is expressed throughout the narrative by his description of himself as a mouse, a fly, a beetle, an eel, a spider, and a worm.[28] But even this drastic symbolism is inadequate to the situation. Underground Man is thoroughly impotent. He cannot do anything, and the reason is that he cannot be anything. If only he could be something, he feels, his life would be saved. His demands are not inordinate. He once knew a man who was a connoisseur of Lafitte and who died triumphantly in the assurance that he was something. Underground Man would be more than happy if he could be sure he was a loafer, or someone spiteful, but he lacks what it takes. "Now I want to tell you gentlemen," he writes, ". . . why I could not even become an insect. I tell you solemnly that I wanted to become an insect many times. But I was not even worthy of that." After such a statement his repeated announcements that he is totally lacking in self-respect are a bit redundant.

In spite of an existence which he describes as "solitary to the point of savagery," Underground Man lives in the constant presence of others. They are, like Simonnet in the childhood experience of Sartre, "absent in the flesh." As such they are more oppressively present than anything physically present.[29] "For forty years," he writes, "I have been listening to your words through a crack under the floor. I have invented them myself." It would be false to suppose that his guilt was first a self-contained self-relation which only came to involve others when he invented them and put words in their mouth. Rather, from the start he felt his existence to be under judgment by others and when, due to his own withdrawn style of life, the others were no longer empirically present he found it necessary to "invent" them, for they simply did not go away.[30] The solitude of his existence is only the subsequently attempted ratification at the empirical level of what had come to be an existential fact for him—the total break with the other due to a disapproval which he could only approve.[31]

The three episodes of Part II show us this situation before he had actually taken up his underground life, though, as he tells us, he already had the underground in his soul. Throughout these three episodes three themes recur constantly. (1) While Part I recounts his lack of self-respect, the temporally prior Part II describes his desperate and unfulfilled longing for respect from others. (2) Beyond this he longs for a complete healing of the break between himself and others, and in each of the episodes he fantasizes a reconciliation which culminates in either friendship or love. (3) But it all remains at the level of desire and daydream, for the one all pervasive fact is his inability even to look anyone in the face. He not only feels their disdain; he feels it is justified. So much is this the case that when the prostitute Liza begins to respond to his compassion with what he rightly detects as love, he immediately withdraws. He lies to her cruelly and tells her he is nothing but a scoundrel who didn't really care for her for a moment, but was only laughing at her, using her psychologically after having used her physically.

All this confirms that the self-loathing to which Underground Man is addicted is his approval of the other's disapproval, his acknowledgment that others have the right, even the duty, to view him as worthless. His guilt separates him not only from himself, but from the rest of humanity as well. Like anyone who experiences guilt, he encounters the temptation to defend himself by somehow neutralizing the low esteem in which he and others see him. The intensity of his guilt indicates that he has failed to succumb to these temptations, two of which he recounts for us.

There is first of all the temptation to Reject the Rejectors. From start to finish this tendency emerges in the form of Underground Man's inner sense of infinite superiority to everyone else. Of course, he is visibly not very high on the socio-economic ladder, but he almost finds his hyper-consciousness to be an adequate remedy for this, giving him understanding of the whole scene which puts him in the know, leaving others out in the dark just as he is socially out in the cold. At the point where this comes to fullest expression, he suddenly screams at his readers, "Hurrah for underground!" But immediately he takes it all back. He knows that there is something truly better than the complacency and stupidity around him, but that it is not underground. So he shouts again, "Damn underground!" The intellectual superiority that his hyper-consciousness gives him does nothing to invalidate the reproaches he feels from every direction. Even when these are social, rather than moral, he experiences them not just as embarrassment or social shame but, like Milton's Adam and Eve in their nakedness, as "guilty shame."

More prominent is the battle Underground Man wages against the Denial of Responsibility which can be gained by seeing oneself as merely the expression of a larger necessity. The stubborn refusal to bow to the laws of nature and view himself as a piano key on which they play whatever tune they will is matched by an equally stubborn refusal to place his hopes in the social utopias symbolized by the crystal palace. He is unwilling to shift the blame for what he is to either natural or social necessity, and he is most explicitly articulate about this. Man's "most advantageous advantage" is not reason, but the freedom to be responsible for himself, even when unreasonable. No doubt it is the energy with which Underground Man holds himself open to his guilt, refusing the comfort to be found in rejecting his rejectors or in denying his own responsibility, which makes him such an unforgettable character.

4E. Guilt and the psychology of false consciousness

From the point of view of the preceding analyses one might seek to discredit Freud and Nietzsche as phenomenologists of guilt. But a closer look will show that in spite of their heavy investment in a model which represents guilt quite differently from the foregoing, they provide still further confirmation of our previous results.

The case against them would go like this. Both are too concerned to explain guilt in terms of introverted aggression to notice that guilt is a question of worth, of what I deserve. The aggression which is orginally directed outward on their theories is not valuational in this sense. For Nietzsche it is a spontaneous cruelty and desire to dominate which entails nothing whatever about the victim's merits. Similarly for Freud the impetus toward destruction is simply a biological instinct and wholly void of moral judgment. In fact, Freud's metapsychology is nowhere more thoroughly biological than in *Beyond the Pleasure Principle*, on which his theory of guilt depends. The turning inward of this aggression is supposed to be guilt. But no account is given of the miracle (should we speak here of transubstantiation or alchemy?) by which this non-judgmental outward aggression is suddenly inseparable from questions of worth when directed inward toward myself. The basic thesis of the aggression theory systematically overlooks this aspect of guilt for the sake of causal explanation, with the awkward consequence that whatever is explained, if anything, is not guilt. At neither the descriptive nor the explanatory level does the aggression theory survive close scrutiny.

Since few can claim to match Freud and Nietzsche when it comes to powers of careful observation, we would be faced with an awkward dilemma if this were all there were to say on the subject. We would either have the difficult task of explaining how they failed so completely as phenomenologists or we would have to begin doubting the results of our own investigation, which seem to be strongly confirmed. But neither Freud nor Nietzsche limited his interpretation of guilt to the mechanical model just summarized. Both present a theory of guilt from dammed up aggression in the fairly crude form in which I have presented it; but they also have a good deal more to say about the subject.

Let us consider Nietzsche first. He calls attention to all the essential elements of guilt according to the previous analysis, namely that it is a relation to oneself, that it involves the question of worth, and that it essentially involves relation to others.

That guilt is a relation to oneself is already implicit in the theory of introverted aggression, though the fact that the relation is one of self-consciousness is hidden. When Nietzsche describes it as "an animal soul turned against itself, taking sides against itself,"[32] it sounds as if something more than the interplay of biological forces may be involved, though this could be just a metaphor for the inward flooding of a cruelty whose outward flow has been dammed up. But when he goes on to speak of "a soul voluntarily at odds with itself,"[33] the previous ambiguity is surpassed. Only as self-consciousness can a soul be voluntarily at odds with itself.

The question of worth enters Nietzsche's account only when guilt has become guilt before God; but at least in this context it comes through loud and clear. In the face of the ideal of a holy God the individual comes "to feel the palpable certainty of his own unworthiness." This is the context in which nihilism and nausea are explicitly present as guilt phenomena, for "existence in general" comes to be "considered worthless as such."[34] Although he has a rather different view from Luther's on how we are to be delivered from this dreadful disease, he is too acute an observer to let this aspect of the data pass unnoticed.

From a theological perspective, guilt is always in the final analysis guilt before God, and conscience is always in some sense the voice of God. That guilt involves relation to another is never in question. Just for this reason the suspicion may well arise that the attempt to find this relation as an essential part of guilt may stem less from careful observation of human experience than from theological assumptions. To the previous attempts to deal with this suspicion with help from Hegel, Sartre, and Dostoyevsky, we can now add the insights of Nietzsche. He is especially helpful in this respect, for while God comes on the guilt scene rather late in the day on his account, the other is there from the start, and ineluctably so.

"To breed an animal with the right to make promises"[35]—it is this intersubjectivity of promise making that is the starting point for his analysis of guilt and bad conscience. Although he does not equate guilt with fear of punishment, he recognizes the close connection between guilt and punishment, since objectively guilt is the liability to punishment. Punishment he seeks to understand in terms of contract and the relation of creditor and debtor, a special sort of promise making. Hence the intimate connection between guilt and debt, embedded in German consciousness by the word *Schuld*, and not wholly missing from the English-speaking world, where many Christians continue to pray, "Forgive us our debts as we forgive our debtors."[36]

Nietzsche seeks to derive guilt and justice in the moral sense from the realm of legal rights and contract by means of a "transfer."[37] To those of us for whom moral and legal obligation have gone their separate ways this seems to introduce another miracle of transformation. For the knowledge that the other has the right to collect thirty dollars from me, since I have promised to pay it, does not necessarily involve any diminished self-esteem on my part, while the knowledge that the other has the right to punish me clearly does. But the fact remains that language retains a term we take to be pre-ethical for use in the ethical domain. Nietzsche calls our attention to an important symbolic usage whose significance needs to be explored. In what way is debt an appropriate symbol for guilt? The primary answer must be that both involve the violation of a relation to another. I become a debtor in a weak sense when I promise to pay someone for something; but in Nietzsche's strong sense, which involves liability to punishment, this occurs only when I break that promise and do not pay when I have promised to do so. In contract, the promise represents a bond of agreement between buyer and seller, making them in a specified respect one. The debtor (in the strong sense) breaks that bond (possibly through no personal fault) and creates a conflict between the two parties in place of harmony. Similarly, when guilty I see myself as moral debtor in having broken the promise implicit in my membership in the human community or explicit in some particular relationship. I know that this breaking of the bond between myself and the other is a wrong which confers on the other a right, possibly to punish, certainly to judge. Having failed to pay my neighbor the respect I owe, I confer on the neighbor the right to foreclose and collect what is due from the moral resources remaining to me, my own self-respect. Such is the essentially intersubjective nature of guilt from a Nietzschean perspective.

Freudian theory seems, if anything, more heavily laden with difficulty than Nietzschean. For not only does Freud have the problems inherent in the aggression theory; by consistently treating the super-ego as an internalized punisher, whose sadistic extravagances the most violent rhetoric can never quite adequately express, he regularly identifies guilt with fear of the super-ego. There is first the fear of external dangers such as the threat of castration. Even prior to internalization of any kind, Freud identifies this fear with guilt. It is, therefore, not surprising that when parental authority is introjected and (mysteriously) supplied with aggressive energy through blockage of the outward flow of aggression by social restraint, the resultant super-ego is not only portrayed as an internal aggressor, but guilt is said to coincide completely with the fear of it.[38] In this equation of guilt with fear the question of worth seems to be completely subordinated to the question of happiness. Furthermore, the super-ego becomes as other to the self as the id and the external world, so that the moment of self-consciousness seems lost as well.

But again these aspects of the guilt phenomenon are too conspicuous to be overlooked, even in the presence of metaphors unfriendly to their discovery. The picture of Freud presented so far is selectively abstract and incomplete. For example, the super-ego is not just presented as an aggressor, but as a judicial and critical agency and even as a faculty of self-judgment and self-criticism involving moral censorship and humility. And in spite of passages making guilt completely coincide with fear of punishment, Freud regularly speaks of guilt as the need of punishment, suggesting an approval of negative judgments against me, even if it is not fully conscious. In both cases Freud clearly sees guilt as a question of worth.[39]

At the same time the complex unity of self-consciousness and other-consciousness previously described with the echo metaphor is present in Freud's account of the super-ego's origin through identification or introjection and in his original description of it as the ego ideal. Although the role of parents and other external authority figures is a powerful one and the voice which speaks within can sound as harsh and hostile as an external voice, the latter represents values with which I have identified and is undeniably my own voice. This interplay of self-consciousness and relation to the other is probably best expressed when Freud writes, "A child feels inferior if he notices that he is not loved, and so does an adult. . . . Altogether, it is hard to separate the sense of inferiority and the sense of guilt."[40] In both cases we are dealing with a process in which I come to view myself as the other sees me, to adopt the other's sense of my worth.

Let us recapitulate. Objectively guilt is (1) liability to punishment. Subjectively it is (2) fear of punishment, and (3) approval of my own punishment, or, more carefully stated, approval of the other's disapproval of me which may render me liable to punishment. Even if it does not lead to punishment, the other's disapproval is a painful assault on my self-esteem made all the more so when I am compelled to approve of it, that is, to acknowledge its legitimacy. We have spent a lot of time exploring this third dimension of guilt, a focus made necessary because this aspect is both so easily overlooked and so central. It is just this element which leaves both our Little League friend and Underground Man with such big guilt problems in spite of their having no punishment nor fear of punishment to deal with.

Yet it would be a mistake to assume that the believing soul is only troubled by this final element we have called guilt proper. For the Sacred is experienced not just as judge, but also as punisher. This may seem most obvious in the context of a personal God or gods as enforcers of the moral law, but it is no less present in impersonal manifestations of the Sacred. As primitives fear the *mana* which punishes the violations of taboos and as the ancient Greeks feared the *Nemesis* which punished every human act of *hybris*, so devout Hindus and Buddhists fear the *Karma* which makes them pay for every wrong they have done, no matter how many lifetimes it may take them.

If guilt, then, is an experience, especially conducive to the manifestation of the Sacred as the *mysterium tremendum*, its meaning as *fascinans* will come to light as it helps us deal with guilt in all three of its dimensions. We remain with ambivalence. Religion will be repelling as it gives focus and new intensity to human guilt.[41] But it will be attractive just to the degree that it (1) helps us to avoid the punishment we would otherwise be liable to, (2) gives us sufficient assurance of this to free us from the fear of punishment, and (3) heals the wounded self-consciousness which can only approve the other's disapproval, which knows how vastly its desire for happiness exceeds its worthiness.

The Existential
Meaning of Death

5A. Death and the literature of dying

We turn now to the question, What kind of problem is death for human experience? Biologically considered, it is that against which the instincts of self-preservation and species-preservation are directed. It should not be thought that by speaking of "the believing soul" there is any implication of soul as distinct from body, as if the religious person were not an embodied person. Since each of us is a living organism we should not be surprised that death concerns us in terms of the instincts just mentioned. But human existence is more than its biological dimension, and our concern in the face of death is not simply with the preservation of life. Gabriel Marcel has written, "As long as death plays no further role than that of providing man with an incentive to evade it, man behaves as a mere living being, not as an existing being."[1] Just as we have had to look beyond the fear of punishment to get to the heart of the problem of guilt, so we will have to look beyond the lust for life, biologically defined, if we would understand the existential meaning of death

Once again we turn to fiction as a helpful source of insight. There is a large body of novels and plays which make the human confrontation with death a central theme. A thorough investigation of the best of them would be an exciting project in itself. For my money, the best of the best is Tolstoy's *The Death of Ivan Ilich*. In this masterful story we see death as an enemy which (1) leads us to deceive ourselves, (2) robs us of the meaning of life, and (3) puts us in solitary confinement.

Our earlier excursion into the sociology of deviance brought to light a whole battery of defense mechanisms by which we defend ourselves from guilt by deceiving ourselves about it. Death, too, evokes systematic self-deception. Like Big Daddy in *Cat on a Hot Tin Roof*,

Ivan discovers that his impending death produces a whole house full of mendacity. In school he had studied the syllogism

Caius is a man.
All men are mortal.
Therefore, Caius is mortal.

But this had always seemed to him to involve only Caius and not himself. In this respect he is no different from one of his "nearest friends," Peter Ivanovich, who calmly asks, "about the details of Ivan Ilich's end, as though death was an accident which was peculiar to Ivan Ilich, but by no means to him."[2]

At times it seemed as if Ivan's "chief suffering was from a lie . . . for some reason accepted by all . . . that he was only sick and not dying. . . . And he was tormented by this lie and by this, that they would not confess what all, and he, too, knew, but insisted on lying about him in this terrible situation, and wanted and compelled him to take part in this lie." He felt that this life "was becoming so entangled that it was getting hard to make out anything."

But it is not just "they" who will not speak the truth; nor is he "compelled" to participate in the farce. The lie is "dreadfully painful for Ivan" and he is often "within a hair's breadth of shouting out to them: 'Stop lying! You know, and I, too, know that I am dying,—so stop at least your lying.' But he had never the courage to do it." In fact, he comes to spend "the greater part of his time in these endeavors to reestablish his former trains of feeling, which had veiled death from him." Like the delinquent whose techniques of justification tend to break down in the face of punishment, Ivan finds it harder and harder to deceive himself about his own death. So, while his family and friends are in perennial fear "that now the decent lie would somehow be broken, and everyone would see clearly how it all was," Ivan is ever more desperately and unsuccessfully trying to compel himself to take part in it.

Not even the Sacred is exempted from the lie. Ivan's wife begs him to let the priest come, hear his confession, and give him communion. He agrees, not out of any conviction or sense of need, but to pacify her. She returns afterward, and "her attire, her figure, the expression of her face, the sound of her voice,—everything told him one and the same thing: 'It is not the right thing. Everything which you have lived by is a lie, a deception, which conceals from you life and death.' " While playing games on his deathbed he learns that this lie didn't start with his illness, but has been going on all his life.

Moreover, the primary consequence is that it is not just death from which he has been hiding. He has concealed life from himself as well.

Thus, as death becomes a reality about which self-deception becomes increasingly difficult, the meaningfulness of Ivan's life becomes increasingly dubious. We learn from the narrator that Ivan's life has been spent in the pursuit of social status, "but Ivan Ilich's real joys were the joys of the game of vint." Yet things are different now. He draws a hand with seven diamonds. His partner supports with two more. "What else could one wish? It ought to be jolly and lively,—a clean sweep. And suddenly Ivan Ilich feels such a gnawing pain, such a bad taste in his mouth, and it feels so queer to him to be able, with all that, to find any pleasure in a clean sweep."

This episode is symbolic, not just for the reader, but for Ivan as well. He enters into dialogue with the voice of his soul, which asks him what he really wants, after all. He replies that he wants to live, more precisely to live as he lived before, well and pleasantly. " 'As you lived before, well and pleasantly?' asked a voice. And he began in imagination to pass in review the best minutes of his pleasant life. But, strange to say, all these best minutes of his pleasant life now seemed to him to be different from what they had seemed to him to be before,—all of them, except the first recollections of his childhood. . . . Everything which then had appeared as joys now melted in his sight and changed into something insignificant and even abominable. . . .

" 'Perhaps I did not live the proper way,' it suddenly occurred to him. 'But how can that be, since I did everything that was demanded of me?. . . .'

" 'What do you want now? To live? To live how? To live as you live in the court, when the bailiff proclaims, 'The court is coming!' he shouted in anger. 'For what?' And he stopped weeping and, turning his face to the wall, began to think of nothing but this one thing: 'Why, for what is all this terror?'

"But, no matter how much he thought, he found no answer. And when the thought occurred to him, and it occurred to him often, that all this was due to the fact that he had not lived in the proper way, he immediately recalled all the regularity of his life, and dispelled this strange thought."

Ivan had been consumed all his life with gaining the approval of his peers. Now, in the face of death, he finds that he can only disapprove their approval. For while his life has met their expectations it melts before his eyes as he finds himself suddenly in a court whose disapproval he can only approve. His angrily shouted pleas of Not

Guilty convince no one, least of all himself, though it is clear that he had not given up the attempt to deceive himself, futile though he finds it. All it does is make it clear to all that for Ivan the question of death is also the question of guilt.

His technique for neutralizing guilt is an interesting one. It goes all the way back to law school days, when he had committed acts "which had presented themselves to him as great abominations and had inspired him with contempt for himself at the time that he had committed them, but later, when he observed that such acts were also committed by distinguished personages and were not considered to be bad, he, without acknowledging them to be good, completely forgot them and was by no means grieved at the thought of them." In other words, to avoid noticing the disapproval he knows should be directed toward him and which he would have to approve, he finds a peer group from whom he receives actual approval. This single technique seems to have worked for him throughout his adult life. He has been as untroubled by critical self-evaluation as our Little League friend (Section 3B, above) during the course of his springtime shenanigans. But just as this oblivion is shattered by impending punishment in the one case, so in the other it dissipates before impending death. Ivan has hidden from death and guilt together, and it is together that they break through his defenses as both become too obvious any longer to be overlooked.

Though we have already been told that his chief suffering comes from the lie he wants to help perpetuate, much as he hates it, we are also told that "his chief agony," greater even than the physical suffering which requires opium to alleviate, is the moral suffering which consists in asking, "What if indeed my whole life, my conscious life, was not the right thing?"

Eventually Ivan gives up resisting the question, and instead of resting on an approval he can only disapprove, he asks his family, stammeringly, for forgiveness. It is only when he had dealt with his guilt in this way that he is able to die in peace, giving dramatic expression to the linkage of the two issues in his experience.

In addition to being a story of self-deception and guilt, the story of Ivan's death is a story of isolation and loneliness to the point of solitary confinement. It is on this note that the narrative opens. The announcement of Ivan's death brings into focus those who loved him most, his family and his "nearest friends." Instead of grief, we find the most shameless self-preoccupation imaginable. They are thinking only of the promotions they might win, of the money they will inherit, of the tedious tasks they must perform, and especially of what *they* have suffered. They are filled with joy that it is Ivan who has died rather than themselves, and with anxiety lest the proper fulfillment of their social duties should interfere with the vint game scheduled for that evening. It is clear that the bond between them and Ivan has been extremely superficial.

The reader can see from the outset that this estrangement has been there for a long time, though like guilt and death itself, Ivan has somehow managed not to notice it. As death becomes more and more obvious to him, however, he finds himself more and more alone. ". . . he had to live by himself on the edge of perdition, without a single man to understand or pity him." When he went to lie down he "was again left alone with it, face to face with *it*. . . ." Even in the presence of his family he saw that "no one wanted even to understand his position. Gerasim [the servant who emptied his bed pan] was the only one who understood this position and pitied him. And so Ivan Ilich never felt happy except when he was with Gerasim." We are also told, significantly, that "Gerasim was the only one who did not lie."

There had been a time when, as a prosecuting attorney, Ivan had been passed over for two promotions in a row. "He felt that all had abandoned him." But that was quite a different sense of aloneness from what he now experiences, which Tolstoy describes as "that loneliness amidst a populous city and his numerous acquaintances and his family,—a loneliness fuller than which can nowhere be found,— neither at the bottom of the sea, nor in the earth." The doctor is indifferent to his condition, and his wife seems to view his dying as an annoyance for which he is to blame. For Ivan, dying is an experience which exposes and intensifies the personal isolation of a life lived in the forgetfulness of death and guilt. The question which all this poses for Ivan is whether there is an Other to whom he could confidently entrust himself in death, an Other with whom he need not flee from the truth in order to find understanding and acceptance.

In view of the importance in religious contexts of the question of life after death and self's destiny in any afterlife, it is of interest that this question is largely overlooked by Ivan. On one occasion, as the fact of his death gets clearer, he does say to himself, "I was here until now, but now I am going thither. Whither?" Ivan is too human not to be concerned with this question, but he is also too human to experience it as the heart of the matter. For only if there is a life free from self-deception, from guilt, and from loneliness in the crowd would any life after death be heaven instead of hell. If these are inseparable from personal existence, then the quietness of dreamless sleep might be the goal of life. But in any case, there would remain the question about this life. When death is looked squarely in the face, what is the meaning of this life, and how should it be lived? The answer to that question will be the key to any hopes and aspirations for what lies on the far side of death.

5B. Death and the philosophy of finite freedom

"Ordinary people seem not to realize that those who really apply themselves in the right way to philosophy are directly and of their own accord preparing themselves for dying and death."[3] Not all philosophers have shared with Socrates this view of what it is to do philosophy. But in our own time it has been the existentialists above all who have sought to philosophize in this spirit. Beginning with Kierkegaard, who devotes a brief, but crucial four and a half pages to the problem of "what it means to die" in his *Concluding Unscientific Postscript*,[4] they have not only regularly addressed themselves to the theme of death, but have tried to do so in the Socratic manner, making their reflection practical and not merely theoretical, preparing for death and not merely speculating about it.

The philosophical tradition of existentialism is much like the literary tradition of romanticism. That there is such a tradition and that certain central figures are at the heart of it cannot be denied. But to define it with any precision seems impossible. Without claiming that this characterization is an adequate definition, I suggest we think of existentialism as the philosophy of finite freedom. It is a philosophy of freedom, not in the simple assertion of human freedom, but in the claim that our being is not so much given to us as it is something we choose. Freedom is an awesome gift, or perhaps a dreadful responsibility, for it is ours to choose who we will be. But it is not ours to choose whether we shall be. Ours is a finite freedom and the existentialists give equal attention to the limitations within which we choose who we will be.

Death is clearly one such limitation. We cannot choose to keep on being, to sustain our present life indefinitely. Yet it is just this fact which gives added poignancy to the choice of how we live our life. Had we an infinite amount of time to play with, it would not matter so much what we did with any particular day or "lifetime." But when we remember that

> The years of our life are threescore and ten,
> or even by reason of strength fourscore;

we can easily understand the Psalmist's prayer

So teach us to number our days
that we may get a heart of wisdom.[5]

Of course, death is not the only significant limit within which human freedom functions. Sartre is unquestionably right when he writes that "human reality would remain finite even if it were immortal. . . ."[6] Yet death highlights the structure of finite freedom so vividly that it is not surprising to find the existentialists regularly turning their attention to it. Probably the most significant discussions by twentieth-century existentialists are those of Jaspers and Heidegger.

Because of its close links to the story of Ivan Ilich we shall begin with Heidegger's analysis. He acknowledges his indebtedness in a footnote which credits Tolstoy's story with presenting "the phenomenon of the disruption and breakdown of having 'someone die'."[7] One finds many themes from Tolstoy echoed in Heidegger, especially the self-deception theme. He describes the "evasive concealment" of "tranquilized everydayness" in which we say things like this to ourselves: "One of these days one will die too, in the end; but right now it has nothing to do with us." Or, "One dies too, sometime, but not right away." Or, "Death certainly comes, but not right away."[8]

It has been offered as a criticism of Heidegger's treatment of death that it is, "for the most part an unacknowledged commentary on *The Death of Ivan Ilich.*"[9] It is not only true that much of what Heidegger says can be found in Tolstoy, but also that the latter's fiction is both more vivid and more easily accessible than the former's often tortured philosophical prose. In spite of this, Heidegger's famous discussion of Being-toward-Death in *Being and Time* (1927) can further our understanding of "what it means to die."

In the first place, he universalizes the problem. What is the story of a particular individual for Tolstoy becomes the human condition for Heidegger. This is not to challenge Aristotle's dictum that "poetry is something more philosophic and of graver import than history, since its statements are of the nature rather of universals, whereas those of history are singulars."[10] In this case that simply means that Ivan would not interest us if he were utterly unique, if there were nothing typically human about him. But to be typically human is one thing; to be the paradigm of the human situation is another. Or, to put it another way, Ivan is scarcely unique, but not everyone lives as he did, nor responds in the face of death as he did.

But does it follow from this that there is nothing universally human which comes to light in Ivan's story? And is the attempt to see Everyman in Ivan merely the illegitimate projection of the anxiety of Weimar Germany onto the whole of the unsuspecting human race?[11] I think not, but we must be careful to sort things out. While it may be true that not everyone lives as Ivan lived, can we say with any confidence that the temptation to evasive concealment, and even the tendency toward it, are completely missing from anyone's experience? Probably no one lives a life which never lapses into tranquillized everydayness, but even those whose lives might be said to be for the most part open to death and only occasionally self-deceiving will not have found themselves in that situation through inertia. They will have had to rise above the temptation and tendency toward that of which Ivan is an extreme case.

The same can probably be said about the guilt and loneliness we encountered with Ivan. Not everyone will deal with them in the same way. Some will have dealt better with them during their lifetimes than he did and will not, therefore, collapse as he did in the face of death. But they will have had to deal with just those issues. It is in the nature of the problem to be dealt with rather than in the method of dealing with it that Ivan is Everyman. The evidence in support of this conclusion will be developed in the following section and in the following chapter. But already Heidegger has helped us by calling to our attention that it is nothing automatic, but a "fantastical exaction" to be wholly free from the defensive self-deception in the face of death which we meet in Ivan.[12]

There is a second point on which Heidegger furthers our understanding. It has to do with the role of the other. For both Tolstoy and Heidegger, death individuates. But for Tolstoy this is a story of bitter loneliness and the desperate attempt to make contact with friends and loved ones, whereas for Heidegger it is an heroic human achievement. In the evasive concealment of tranquillized everydayness we are part of an anonymous crowd which knows not only that one dies, indeed, that everyone dies, but also, that I don't, at least not now. This shared lie, to which Ivan becomes so deeply sensitive at the end, involves a depersonalizing of human existence in which truth is not only concealed, but choices avoided. Tolstoy helps us to see how superficial are human relations in this artificial world, and how painful is the discovery, forced upon Ivan by his imminent death, that one is and has been alone in a crowd.

But the pain is extreme because of the extreme way in which Ivan has mis-lived his life. It belongs to what is particular about Ivan, not what is universal. By focusing on the universal, Heidegger helps us to see that becoming an authentic self in the sense of resisting the temptation and tendency to be part of an anonymous corporate self, which wears what "everyone" is wearing and sees this movie because "they" say it's good, is a task that each of us inherits. Whether or not it is as painful as it was for Ivan, it is a difficult and challenging task. It is the task of freeing ourselves from others and standing alone, accepting responsibility for ourselves by willingly choosing who we will be. Among the reasons that Heidegger speaks of this individuation in the face of death as freedom toward death is that in it "one is liberated from one's lostness in those possibilities which may accidentally thrust themselves upon one; and one is liberated in such a way that for the first time, one can authentically understand and choose among the factical possibilities lying ahead of that possibility which is not to be outstripped." This freedom to choose is in turn made possible by the experience which "shatters all one's tenaciousness to whatever existence one has reached."[13] This is the freedom which is possible only to those who have the "courage to be as oneself."[14] This is the loneliness before death which is not to be dreaded and avoided at all costs, but to be chosen and achieved at all costs. Death not only threatens us with that isolation which is already perdition; it also challenges us to that isolation without which we cannot be ourselves, without which the term "self" is applied to us only out of politeness.

Naturally the need to flee from an inauthentic being-with-others does not deny the possibility of an authentic form of relatedness nor imply that existential loneliness is the highest human achievement. It may be that existential loneliness is but the half-way house required on the path from everyday loneliness to genuine togetherness. But we dare not underestimate the importance of this moment in reaction to those existentialists, Heidegger probably among them, who leave the impression that the courage to stand alone is what it's all about. Tillich helpfully suggests that the "courage to be as oneself" needs to be supplemented by the "courage to be as a part" and the "courage to accept acceptance."[15]

Turning to Jaspers, we find the philosophy of finite freedom expressed in terms of the notion of boundary situations.[16] He introduces into the existentialist vocabulary this concept of being in a situation as a way of talking about the givens which confront, surround, and hedge in all human action. Human freedom is never creation *ex nihilo*, but always the response to a context which includes elements I did not choose.

There is a certain mobility with respect to situations. I can often get out of one and into another. I can leave my school, my job, my family, my country, my religion, and so forth. In each case I substitute a new situation for the old one. But I can never, so long as I continue to exist, get to the place of being in no situation at all. Just as being in a situation is a permanent feature of my life, so there are features such as guilt, suffering, and death which belong to every situation. "They *never change*, except in appearance. . . . They are like a wall we run into, a wall on which we founder. We cannot modify them. . . . They go with existence itself."[17] Because of this wall-like character, Jaspers calls these unsurpassable situations "boundary situations." They are the impenetrable limits within which human freedom of choice operates.

But my response to these givens is not given. It is rather mine to make. For that reason the shift in emphasis from finitude to freedom takes the form of exploring whether and how I let myself be conscious of the boundary situations in which I function, whether I notice them or not.

Jaspers indicates the important difference between facing one's finitude and fleeing from it by talking about the rather sudden transition from ignoring boundary situations to noticing them. We will find it difficult not to think of Ivan again. When I open my eyes to the boundary situations, "I even *face my own existence as if it were a stranger's*. . . . This conquest of my own being occurs in absolute *solitude*. Whatever happens in the world is doubtful; everything fades away, my own existence included. . . . Nothing is of real concern to me." The overriding feeling is that "nothing means anything."[18]

Again, the point is not that everyone has a shattering existential awakening. It is rather that many of us are in need of such an experience and that the gap between this consciousness and an all too prevalent oblivion is an enormous one. For that reason Jaspers uses Kierkegaard's notion of the leap, not to describe the passionate affirmation of a particular religious reality, but simply to designate the full awareness of the problem of, in our case, death. For him a major task of philosophical reflection is the "elucidative contemplation" which makes boundary situations, which we cannot plan and calculate to overcome, simply lucid.[19] The entire second volume of *Philosophy* is subtitled "Existential Elucidations."

What then is the "elucidative contemplation" of death? If we remember that it is a leap, we will not be tempted to think of it as mere gazing. It is a reflection which allows the self to be transformed by its reflection. If we ask about this self-transformation, we will discover an important difference between Jaspers and Heidegger. For the most part, Heidegger speaks as if the leap to a full open-eyed awareness of my death is itself both an end in itself and the self-transformation which is effected by true philosophical thinking (though he is embarrassed by the thought that his book will be edifying). Jaspers doesn't deny that the leap to lucidity is already an intrinsically valuable reorientation of the self. But he pushes further with the pragmatic question. What difference does it make? And the answer he gives to this question once again brings the problem of guilt into intimate contact with the problem of death.

The difference it makes is this. As I allow myself to become fully aware of death as a boundary situation it becomes "a *challenge* . . . to live and to test my life in view of death." When this happens, "death is then the *mirror* of Existenz . . . the *test* that proves Existenz and relativizes mere existence."[20] The idea of death as a mirror that challenges and tests my life is already familiar to us from *The Death of Ivan Ilich*. Under the best of circumstances it is hard to look death in the face and be fully complacent about one's life. In Ivan's case, this is a test that he simply flunks outright. What we need to focus on, if we are to learn more from Jaspers, is the distinction we might have overlooked above, between Existenz and existence. Death is "the test that proves Existenz and relativizes mere existence."

Mere existence is perhaps best understood in terms of functions. Each of us is made up of various biological, intellectual, and social functions without which we wouldn't be human. These are the more nearly objective aspects of our selfhood. They can be studied scientifically and, to a considerable degree, predicted and controlled. But we wouldn't really be human selves if we were nothing but these objective functions and processes. If we were not also the one who presides over them, within limits, and who must take up an attitude toward those limits beyond which we cannot preside over our lives—or to be more concrete, if we were not the one who takes care of our health or neglects it and must come to grips with a physical handicap suffered in an automobile accident—then we wouldn't be a truly human self. We would be a *homo sapien* masquerading as a human being. It is this subjective, self-determining aspect of the self, the freedom at the core of who we are, that Jaspers call Existenz.

Death is the test that proves Existenz. It does so in two ways, if we look it in the face. It asks us whether we have made the leap to Existenz, whether we have acknowledged and accepted the freedom that we are and the responsibility which goes with it, and it asks us whether we have exercised such freedom wisely, lovingly, and honestly. Have you fulfilled the task of becoming a self and have you used the gift of self-hood rightly?[21]

At the same time that death proves Existenz it relativizes existence. That is simply to say that the kind of questions just asked take priority over questions about how well I am functioning biologically, intellectually, and socially. More important than the biological success certified by doctors and coaches, more important than the intellectual success certified by teachers and learned societies, and more important than the social success certified by bosses and in-groups is the ability to pass the test by which Death proves Existenz. It is not that these other functions cease, nor that I necessarily lose all interest in them. It is rather that they are now only of relative and not of absolute importance to me.

This distinction between existence and Existenz corresponds to the difference from our discussion of guilt between fear of punishment and guilt proper, the sense of being worthy of punishment. Jaspers finds in turn that the fear of death is a twofold fear, matching the dual structure of our selfhood. Existenz knows "a despair that may befall it despite its vital existence and in contrast to its simultaneous vigor and abundance. The *fear of existential nonbeing* is so different in kind from the fear of vital nonbeing that despite our use of the identical words, nonbeing and death, only one fear can truly reign. . . . Existential death . . . is what turns the prospect of biological death into utter despair." Corresponding to this twofold fear, death takes on a twofold form "as unexistential existence and as radical nonbeing." "An *existence coupled with the nonbeing of Existenz* [Have you fulfilled the task of being a self?] raises the specter of an endless life without potential, without effect and communication. I have died, and it is thus that I must live forever; I do not live, and so my possible Existenz suffers the agony of being unable to die. The peace of radical nonbeing would be a deliverance from this horror of continual death. . . . *Total nonbeing* will horrify an Existenz to the extent to which in existence it has betrayed its potential. . . . [Have you used the gift of selfhood rightly?]"[22]

What finally comes to light in Jaspers's elucidative contemplation of death is that, if allowed, it asks just those questions most likely to evoke a sense of guilt. Have you fulfilled the task of becoming a self and have you used the gift of selfhood wisely? I will be able to die in peace only if I can answer these questions without guilt or if I can find a way of dealing with the guilt they are more likely to arouse. And it is just at this point where the problems of guilt and death merge, that the problem of death becomes a fully human problem and my selfhood in the truest sense becomes involved, not merely my objective functions.

That being the case, death is finally a question of freedom rather than of necessity. That is to say, it is not a question about what will happen to me, but about what I will do with my life. Since the first form that question takes concerns whether or not I even allow myself to become fully cognizant of death as a boundary situation, the very notion of boundary situation takes on a new meaning. At first, the adjective, boundary, indicated an unsurpassable limit, a wall beyond which I can never pass. Now, without losing that significance, it also comes to stand for a boundary in the sense of a frontier, through or over which I pass enroute from one place to another. Boundary situations are gates through which we may pass from existence to Existenz, from self-deception and oblivion to honesty and lucidity, from pseudo-selfhood to genuine selfhood. Here again we meet the paradox of finite freedom, for the absolute and unsurpassable limits of human existence show themselves to be possible vehicles for entering into freedom.[23]

5C. Death and the social-psychology of heroism

"Every human society is, in the last resort, men banded together in the face of death. The power of religion depends, in the last resort, upon the credibility of the banners it puts in the hands of men as they stand before death, or more accurately, as they walk, inevitably, toward it."[24] In the next chapter we shall begin to look at religion's concern with death. For the present we need to consider the suggestion that in their loneliness before death men and women join hands to help each other and that the result is what we call society. Obviously this cannot merely mean, for example, that we will die if we don't get enough food and that society is a more effective means of assuring the food supply than leaving us all on our own. Here as before it is not fundamentally a question of biological, but of existential survival. The enemy is not hunger, but terror and despair and guilt. How does society, or, if you prefer, human culture, relate to death as a boundary situation?

Ernest Becker gives an answer to this question in *The Denial of Death* which is at once startling and simple. "The fact is that this is what society is and always has been: a symbolic action system, a structure of statuses and roles, customs and rules for behavior, designed to serve as a *vehicle for earthly heroism*. . . . Society itself is a *codified hero system*. . . ."[25]

The first step toward understanding the link between heroism and death is the description of human narcissism. "The problem of heroics is the central one of human life" just because we are all still the child whose "need for self-esteem [is] *the* condition for his life." This need for a sense of value of self-worth is so strong and limitless that we all demand some sense of "cosmic significance," and even sibling rivalry "expresses the heart of the creature: the desire to stand out, to be *the* one in creation."[26]

The term narcissism may not be entirely appropriate here, for what is at issue is not merely the ability to admire myself, but to esteem myself on the basis of another's approval which I can approve. I need someone else to justify or validate my existence. That is why, for example, in the modern world, some for whom God no longer is the other who justifies, have turned to the cult of romantic love with an urgency that no biological understanding of sex can make intelligible. A Hindu song gets right to the point, however: "My lover is like God; if he accepts me, my existence is utilized."[27]

There is nothing particularly new in all of this. Aristotle recognized the desire for honor as a fundamental human need.[28] And Hegel based his famous analysis of the life and death struggle which culminates in master-slave relations on the fundamental human desire for recognition.[29] Perhaps Thomas Hobbes has put it most vividly. "For every man looketh that his companion should value him at the same rate he sets upon himself; and upon all signs of contempt, or undervaluing, naturally endeavors, as far as he dares (which amongst them that have no common power to keep them in quiet, is far enough to make them destroy each other), to extort a greater value from his contemners by damage, and from others by the example." Thus, it is that the desire for "glory" or "reputation" is one of the three principal causes of quarrels among us.[30]

What Becker adds to these observations is the second and crucial step toward linking heroism with death. It is the suggestion that the apparently insatiable appetite for approval and esteem from those around us is not itself unmotivated like the so-called hunger and sex drives, but is directed toward "transcending death by qualifying for immortality." We try to solve the problems of the meaning of life "by addressing our performance of heroics to another human being, knowing thus daily whether this performance is good enough to earn us eternity." Or, as Otto Rank puts it, "Here we come upon the age-old problem of good and evil, originally designated eligibility for immortality, in its emotional significance of being liked or disliked by the other person. On this place . . . personality is shaped and formed according to the vital need to please the other person whom we make our 'God,' and not incur his or her displeasure."[31] This is why Becker can say that "heroism is first and foremost a reflex of the terror of death."[32]

We can now more easily see how society is "men banded together in the face of death." It can provide a publicly validated system of "techniques for earning glory," thereby becoming "a vehicle for earthly heroism" or a "codified hero system."[33]

The cultural hero system may be a religious one; but then again it may be secular. We've already noted how the cult of romantic love, not to speak of its modern variation as the "*Playboy* mystique,"[34] can be a desperate pursuit of self-justification. Ludicrous as it sounds when one says it outright, the attempt to earn immortality by being good in bed may be the terms in which it is possible to understand the contemporary compulsion about sexual performance.

In this light we can also understand the workaholic, for the Performance Principle[35] can be applied to work as easily as to sex. Becker, in fact, gives Freud as an example here, suggesting that his life-work as founder of the psychoanalytic movement was for him the heroic task which would qualify him for immortality.[36]

It is not just in specific activities like sex and work that heroism functions. Character-formation itself, often referred to as the socialization process, provides each of us with characteristics which enable us to feel that we are somebody and to be recognized as such.[37] At the same time, society certifies various symbols of the glory or grandeur we would like others to attribute to us. Then the mere possession of these or association with them comes to signify heroic accomplishment. How else explain our infatuation with money and goods, our loyalty to the flag or the proletariat, our passion for sports cars and atomic missiles, and our thirst for success in the corporation or university. If it seems strange to us that Becker includes skill at the pinball machine as a symbolic heroics, it would not have seemed so to Underground Man. He tells us, "I knew a gentleman who prided himself all his life on being a connoisseur of Lafitte. He considered this as his positive virtue, and never doubted himself. He died, not simply with a tranquil, but *with a triumphant conscience*, and he was completely right." Then he reflects on what might have happened if he had chosen a career for himself, perhaps being a sentimental spokesman for the sublime and the beautiful. "I would demand respect for doing so, I would persecute anyone who would not show me respect. I would live at ease, *I would die triumphantly*."[38]

Most of us would probably require a more robust heroism than that in order to triumph over death and guilt. (It should be clear from the foregoing that the pursuit of self-esteem derived from the approval of the other is the attempt to deal with guilt in the face of death. Becker goes so far as to define guilt as the failure of heroics.)[39] The fact that society provides a variety of "techniques for earning glory" does not guarantee that they will work. This makes it possible to understand the phenomenon of alienation as the eclipse of any "convincing dramas of heroic apotheosis." "The crisis of modern society is precisely that the youth no longer feel heroic in the plan for action that their culture has set up. . . . The great perplexity of our time, the churning of our age, is that the youth have sensed— for better or for worse—a great social-historical truth: that just as there are useless self-sacrifices in unjust wars, so too is there an ignoble heroics of whole societies: it can be the viciously destructive heroics of Hitler's Germany or the plain debasing and silly heroics of the acquisition and display of consumer goods, the piling up of money and privileges that now characterizes whole ways of life, capitalist and Soviet."[40]

Becker's understanding of heroism and death is not in conflict with the existentialist analysis. Jaspers, in fact, includes heroism in his own account. For when he writes "I feel dread to the extent to which I failed to live—failed, that is, to make decisions and thus to come to myself," he continues, "and I feel at peace insofar as I realized my potential. The clearer my accomplishments are in the certainty of my self-being . . . the closer will my Existenz come to a posture of welcoming death in existence. . . ."[41] Beyond this, however, Becker provides a confirmation of the existentialist universalizing of Ivan Ilich. For if society itself functions as a cultural hero system in order to provide *each* of us with "techniques for earning glory" that we might die triumphantly, it can only be because *each* of us has to confront the challenge from which Ivan fled so desperately all his life until the very end.

The poet Hölderlin is one who preaches heroism as the remedy for death and its terror. The speaker in the following poem, whether it be Hölderlin as he was or as he wishes to be, is one who does not come apart at the seams in the face of death as Ivan did. Yet the poem expresses far more eloquently than I can that this is not because he has not had to encounter death as a threat to his worthiness for life. Quite the contrary.

> A single summer grant me, great powers, and
> A single autumn for full ripened song
>   That, sated with the sweetness of my
>   Playing, my heart may more willingly die.
> The soul that, living, did not attain its divine

Right cannot respose in the nether world.
Holy, my poetry, is accomplished,
Be welcome then, stillness of the shadows' world!
I shall be satisfied though my lyre will not
Accompany me down there. Once I
Lived like the gods, and more is not needed.[42]

The Believing Soul's Encounter with Guilt and Death

6A. Guilt and death in biblical religion

For most of the last two chapters we have parted company with the believing soul. You may recall that Zechariah is to blame for this. For it was his suggestion that guilt and death are central concerns of the religious life that set us to exploring the nature of guilt and death as human problems.

The context in which Zechariah's suggestion came before us was that of attempting to distinguish religion from magic. Magic may be understood as the attempt to dominate and manipulate the Sacred Power for the sake of good fortune for oneself and one's people. Religion is to be distinguished from magic, not by its lack of concern for good fortune (since the believing soul does pray for rain), but by (1) a more humble, non-manipulative attitude toward the Sacred Power and (2) by the quality of its concerns.

The qualitative distinctiveness of these concerns is twofold. First, when asked the question, What are the benefits of the religious life? the believing soul will answer at least in part by saying, "The religious life itself." That is to say that unlike magic, religion has a non-instrumental, non-utilitarian dimension in which activities are valued for their own sake and not for the results they produce, as ends in themselves and not as means to an end. The exploration of this part of what it means to be religious lies ahead of us in Chapters Seven and Eight.

But religion is also a means to various ends, and it is in the nature of these ends that its concerns show themselves to be distinctive in a second way. For the magician devotes himself to the production of those economic, medical, and military benefits, which in our day it

107

is the role of the politician to promise. We look to politics to provide us with peace and prosperity, health and wealth, in short, with happiness in what we often describe as the material, as distinct from the spiritual, sense. But the believing soul wants more than the magician and politician can promise. Guilt and death represent spiritual or existential needs which are somehow deeper or higher. At least that seemed to be the suggestion of Zechariah.

It was to explore the nature of these "deeper" or "higher" needs that we have interrupted our conversation with the believing soul for the last two chapters. It is time now to return to the religious context first to see how pervasive concern about guilt and death as we have come to understand them actually is, and then to explore the fundamentally different ways in which religion deals with them. These two tasks cannot be entirely separated, but it is to the first of them that the present chapter is devoted. Its task is to support the suggestion that Zechariah's prophecy introduces us not just to a believing soul but to *the* believing soul.

This is perhaps most obvious if we move from Zechariah the individual to the tradition to which he belongs. I am calling this the tradition of biblical religion, for it consists of the ancient Judaism and the primitive Christianity which are presented to us in the Bible. Zechariah himself stands right at the boundary between the two. For while his poem appears in one of the canonical writings of the Christian faith, he speaks not as a Christian but as a devout Jew awaiting Messiah. There are important differences between biblical Judaism and biblical Christianity.[1] Yet they belong to a single tradition, as can be seen from the fact that the New Testament is quite unintelligible, even unimaginable, apart from the tradition recorded in the books that Christians call the Old Testament and Jews call simply the Bible.

There is perhaps no more succinct summary of biblical religion's view of guilt and death than Luther's, when he writes, "If sins are forgiven, death is gone."[2] From start to finish the two issues are linked. This occurs already in the narratives of Genesis 2 and 3 about the Garden of Eden and the fall of Adam and Eve. In the story of the garden God warns them not to eat of the tree of the knowledge of good and evil, "for in the day that you eat of it you shall die."[3] In the story of the fall Eve tells the serpent that God had promised death even for touching the forbidden fruit. Thus for biblical faith death enters human experience explicitly as a punishment for sin. It is because Adam and Eve are guilty that they must die.

They continue to live, however, long after that day on which God had promised them death. Yet nowhere is there the suggestion that this confirms the serpent's claim to Eve that God didn't really mean to carry through on his threat. We must rather look to see what did happen to them on the day that they ate in order to see in what sense death was theirs from that day on.

The first thing we are told is that their eyes were opened and they were ashamed of their nakedness. They made aprons of fig leaves, but even these were insufficient; for when God came walking in the garden in the cool of the day, they hid themselves, Adam explaining later, "I was afraid, because I was naked; and I hid myself."

The point is not that there is some special link between sin and sexuality. It is rather that physical nakedness has become an all-but-inevitable symbol for the spiritual nakedness that they feel, having lost their intimacy with God. Just as we normally hide our naked bodies from the other's view, so they wished to hide their naked selves from God's. For they could only approve the disapproval which rendered them liable to punishment. And knowing the punishment God had promised, they were, as Adam says, afraid.

This is the kind of fear that Ricoeur calls dread in speaking of the archaic sense of taboo. It is "not a simple passive fear; already it involves a *demand*, the demand for a just punishment."[4] It is just this fear that the naughty little leaguer felt on his way home with the incriminating report card.[5] Before God curses them and expels them from the garden they anticipate a death sentence they cannot dispute but only approve, and they know this death as punishment. It is no natural fact (at least not any longer) but a sign of their unworthiness in God's eyes to live. They continue to live, but on death row.

The next thing that occurs on the day they sinned is that the sentence they anticipate is actually pronounced. First the serpent, then the man and woman are cursed. The pain and difficulty of their labor in childbirth and food production, which might otherwise be treated as misfortunes, are explicitly labeled punishments; and this extends to the final words as well, "you are dust and to dust you shall return." This leads one commentator to write that "*it is not indeed the simple fact of dying which is here proclaimed as the punishment of sin but the enslavement of all life to the hostile powers of death*—suffering, pain, toil, struggle—by which it is worn out before its time."[6]

The third and last event of that day is the expulsion from the garden. We lock behind bars prisoners who have been sentenced to death until it is time for the sentence to be carried out. Adam and

Eve are locked out rather than in, and because of their sin the whole world becomes death row, where they live under sentence of death.

If we think of death exclusively in biological terms we will say that Adam and Eve did not die on the day they ate of the forbidden fruit. But having seen in Chapter Four that death is not simply a biological issue, we can see how death overtook and conquered them that very day. When Luther later says that "there is no greater pain than the gnawing pangs of conscience," that "to feel and to experience the intolerable burden of the wrath of God" is already to be in hell, and that anyone who actually goes to hell "would be in God's disfavor. This would be more unwelcome and painful to him than the pain itself," he expresses the meaning of the story of the fall.[7]

It has often been noted that the story of the fall does not have the prominence in the Jewish tradition that it comes to have in the Christian. But the themes from that story echo throughout the literature of ancient Israel, perhaps nowhere more forcefully than in Psalm 90.

1   Lord, thou hast been our dwelling place in all generations.
2   Before the mountains were brought forth,
         or ever thou hadst formed the earth and the world,
         from everlasting to everlasting thou art God.

3   Thou turnest man back to the dust
         and sayest, "Turn back, O children of men!"
4   For a thousand years in thy sight are but as yesterday when it
         is past, or as a watch in the night.

5   Thou dost sweep men away; they are like a dream,
         like grass which is renewed in the morning:
6   in the morning it flourishes and is renewed;
         in the evening it fades and withers.

7   For we are consumed by thy anger;
         by thy wrath we are overwhelmed.
8   Thou hast set our iniquities before thee,
         our secret sins in the light of thy countenance.

9   For all our days pass away under thy wrath,
         our years come to an end like a sigh.

10   The years of our life are threescore and ten,
         or even by reason of strength fourscore;
         yet their span is but toil and trouble;
         they are soon gone, and we fly away.

11   Who considers the power of thy anger,
         and thy wrath according to the fear of thee?
12   So teach us to number our days
         that we may get a heart of wisdom.

For the first six verses and again in verse 10, the Psalm seems to
be a reflection on the fleetingness of human life, accentuated by
contrast with the everlastingness of God. We are reminded of the
Greeks who simply used the terms mortals and immortals to distinguish human from divine persons. But the sensitive ear wonders
whether verse 3 might be an echo of Genesis 3 with its "you are dust
and to dust you shall return." Verses 7 to 9 confirm this suspicion
and make it clear that "where the antithesis between God and man
comes to light in this way, there sin is also clearly manifested," that
is, that the issue of human mortality is a "*moral* issue." Beyond that,
the "shallowness and futility of human life" not only become obvious
but show themselves as "the necessary result of a wrong attitude to
life and to its divine background, as having an all too intelligible
connection with human guilt and sin."[8]

In this Psalm death shows itself to be a boundary situation in both
of the senses this notion has in Jaspers. It is an inescapable situation.
But at the same time it can be the checkpoint through which we pass
from inauthentic to authentic existence, or, in the Psalmist's language, from foolishness to wisdom. For the request of verse 12 is
not for long life but for wisdom. The experience of this believing
soul is that it is in the full consciousness of death and of its integral
link with human sin and guilt that human life can attain to the wisdom
that makes it meaningful.

That the central issue is the meaningfulness of life and not its
prolongation is clear from the final verse of the Psalm.

> Let the favor of the Lord our God be upon us,
>   and establish thou the work of our hands upon us,
>   yea, the work of our hands establish thou it.

The prayer is to avoid the experience of Ivan Ilich, who found the
work of his entire lifetime to be worthless, and of Underground Man,
whose life work was so worthless in his own eyes that he could envy
someone with no greater accomplishment than being a connoisseur
of Lafitte.

Finally we should note the request for the Lord's favor. As the
Psalmist proceeds toward seeing the shortness and shallowness of life
as an expression of the wrath of God who sees all too clearly the

extent of human sinfulness, there is no complaint about being un-
fairly judged. Verse 8 is in the same spirit as another Psalmist, who
prays,

> Against thee, thee only, have I sinned,
> and done that which is evil in thy sight,
> so that thou art justified in thy sentence
> and blameless in thy judgment.[9]

But while there can only be approval of the disapproval which expresses itself in God's anger, there remains the hope of finding a
divine favor which can somehow be accepted.

If we turn to the New Testament and read that "the wages of sin
is death" and that "the sting of death is sin,"[10] nothing new is happening. The first phrase might be seen as a capsule summary of
Genesis 3, the second of Psalm 90. The apostle Paul, whose phrases
these are, is the one who develops a theology of sin and salvation
based on the Genesis story of the fall. "Therefore as sin came into
the world through one man and death through sin, so death spread
to all men because all sinned. . . ." Jesus is the Savior because he
frees us "from the law of sin and death."[11]

This is true in the gospels as well as in the epistles. Already in the
birth narratives of Jesus the point is made. We've already noted that
in the gospel according to Luke, from which the prophecy of Zechariah comes. In Matthew, too, the angel tells Joseph that Mary will
have a son, "and you shall call his name Jesus, for he will save his
people from their sins."[12] Jesus himself links this issue to that of death
in his teachings concerning the last judgment[13] and in his conversation with Nicodemus. Whereas in the former the Son of Man is
pictured as the judge who condemns the wicked, the latter stresses
that for the present the Son is not sent into the world to condemn
it, but to bring eternal life rather than death.[14] Eternal life, which
the gospel of John presents as both the present and future victory
over death is a victory over guilt at the same time, for it is presented
as the alternative to the judgment which condemns. At the same time
those who reject the son are pictured as "condemned already," a
phrase likely to recall the story of Genesis 3 to Nicodemus, a learned
Jewish theologian.

Turning finally to the last book of the Bible, known as the book
of Revelation or the Apocalypse, we find a synthesis of themes from
the gospels and epistles. More vivid and extensive than anything in
the teaching of Jesus is its imagery depicting the last judgment which
awaits all after death. At the same time it can be interpreted as a

visionary commentary on the Pauline text, "The last enemy to be destroyed is death."[15] It begins with the presentation of "Jesus Christ the faithful witness, the firstborn of the dead." He introduces himself as "the living one. I died, and behold I am alive forevermore, and I have the keys of Death and Hades."[16] As in the gospels and epistles, his resurrection is seen to be the foundation for human victory over death.

The vision of this victory culminates in the final two chapters of the book in the vision of the new heaven, the new earth, and the new Jerusalem. It is a vision of the reversal of Genesis 3. Whereas Adam and Eve through their sin had been exiled from the intimate presence of God, the new Jerusalem is introduced with these words: "Behold, the dwelling of God is with men. He will dwell with them, and they shall be his people, and God himself will be with them." This reunion means a rescinding of the curse, for the vision continues, "He will wipe away every tear from their eyes, and death shall be no more, neither shall there be mourning nor crying nor pain any more, for the former things have passed away."[17]

Whereas the exile had meant separation from the tree of life as punishment for sin, the new Jerusalem has a tree of life watered by the water of life. Under its shade, "There shall no more be anything accursed. . . ."[18] The explicit lifting of the curse is not the only reminder, however, of the linkage between the problems of guilt and death in the biblical tradition. For no less than three separate times in this final vision comes the reminder that residence in the new Jerusalem is not automatic. Those who are unclean, who have not washed their robes, that is, those who remain stained and polluted by a life of evil about which they have done nothing but to persist in it do not have "the right to the tree of life." They are kept outside the city and "their lot shall be in the lake that burns with fire and brimstone, which is the second death."[19]

6B. Beyond the biblical tradition

The foregoing has been but the sketchiest survey of the guilt and death themes in biblical religion. It could easily be worked out in much greater detail. But for some even the briefest summary is likely to be more than is necessary. They will be thinking something like this. "You say that concern about guilt and death is central for the believing soul. As soon as you say that, we know that your roots are in the biblical tradition, and we begin to suspect that you are suffering from cultural myopia, mistaking a particular religious tradition for religion as such. That guilt and death are central concerns of the believing soul in the biblical tradition is too obvious a point to need any demonstration. But there are whole traditions and cultures which are free from these concerns. Zechariah may be *the* believing soul so far as biblical religion is concerned, but beyond the biblical tradition it's a very different story. At least you haven't given us any reason to suppose otherwise."

Just as it was the task of Chapter Two to make plausible, if not to prove conclusively (how would one do that?), that ambivalence vis-à-vis the Sacred as the *mysterium tremendum et fascinans* is involved in the religious life as such and not just in particular forms of it, so now the task is to show that guilt and death have the importance they do in biblical religion because it is religious and not because it is biblical. Note carefully! This is not to deny that there are important differences in the ways different religious traditions deal with these issues. It is rather to assert that in some way or other religion has to take notice of these issues and deal with them if it is to be religion at all. At this point the focus is on the generic features rather than on the specific differences. The time will come for us to ask what kinds of differences are really fundamental. But for a little while longer the task will be to see the many as one rather than the one as many.

The first step toward expanding our horizon will be to follow up on two clues from the conclusion of the previous section. The apocalyptic vision of the new Jerusalem invokes a symbol and a picture which are central to our theme, though they are anything but unique to the biblical tradition. The symbol is that of defilement, stain, and pollution as a representation of human sin and guilt. The picture is that of a judgment of the dead which leads to punishment for the wicked and paradise for the righteous.

It is not only in the Bible that this symbol and this picture are united. If one reads Plato or Virgil, or the even more ancient *Egyptian Book of the Dead*, or, moving eastward, the ancient sacred writings of the Hindus and Buddhists, including the *Tibetan Book of the Dead*, one reads of how those who die pure are led to the joys of a heavenly paradise, while the wicked must be purified through torments in hell or purgatory which exceed any earthly misfortune.[20] In each case the advice is that with which Socrates brings the *Republic* to a close. If we would learn to face death with equanimity, we must "keep our soul unspotted from the world."

It is not, however, the juxtaposition of these two ideas which is of primary importance, interesting and important as it is. Each in its own right can enable us to view the problem of guilt and death in religious traditions quite distinct from the biblical traditions.

Consider the symbol of defilement first of all. Paul Ricoeur in particular has brought to sharp focus the significance of this notion in the symbolism of evil. His phenomenology of confession opens with the claim that "dread of the impure and rites of purification are in the background of all our feelings and all our behavior relating to fault."[21] The reference to "our" feelings and behavior must not be taken to refer to those of us who, like Ricoeur himself, live in an advanced, western civilization with a Judeo-Christian heritage. It would be more appropriate to hear that "our" as a reference to human experience as such. For defilement as a symbol of human evil is to be found, not only in the West, but just as intensively and extensively throughout the high cultures of the East; it saturates the sacred writings of Hinduism and Buddhism. Furthermore, it flourishes not only in advanced civilizations, but especially among the preliterate peoples we often refer to as archaic or primitive. In fact, the symbol is best understood as an archaic or primitive symbol which has a remarkable ability to survive in cultural contexts we tend to think of as "higher." From the "primitive," impersonal, dynamistic religion of *mana* and taboo, to the highly personalized ethical monotheism of the biblical traditions, to the most sophisticated metaphysical speculation, that is, from sorcerer to prophet to sage, the human sense of fault expresses itself in the language of purity and impurity.[22]

One key to the flexible usage of the symbolism of defilement is an idea which lies at its very heart, the idea of touching. It is by contact with what is to be avoided that one becomes impure. For that reason writers trying to give an account of the primitive notions of *mana* and taboo use the images of contagion and electricity, where disease and shock are the products of contact with the dangerous. Thus one typically becomes impure through touching a corpse.

Though the touching is literal in such a case, the defilement is already symbolic. This is clear from the fact that it will not do as a remedy simply to wash with soap and water. To be defiled is not literally to be dirty, even when it is literal contact which defiles. So one can be cleansed only through a ritual purification, a specifically prescribed and sanctioned ceremony, which may, of course, include acts of washing, but need not.

This symbolism is easily extended, so that the touching is symbolic as well. Thomas Aquinas gives an explanation of how the symbol can live on long after people feel defiled by actual physical contact. "Now, when the soul cleaves to things by love, there is a kind of contact in the soul; and when man sins, he cleaves to certain things against the light of reason and of the divine law. . . . Therefore the loss of splendor, occasioned by this contact, is metaphorically called a stain on the soul."[23]

This idea is what enables David to confess his murder and adultery with the prayer

> Wash me thoroughly from my iniquity,
>   and cleanse me from my sin. . . .
> Purge me with hyssop, and I shall be clean;
>   wash me and I shall be whiter than snow.[24]

The same thinking underlies the Sioux Indian prayer, "O *Wakan-Tanka*, we are now purifying ourselves, that we may be worthy to raise our hands to you."[25] It also grounds the Hindu and Buddhist teaching that anger, greed, and hatred defile the mind.

To understand the ground of this metaphor and the ease with which those who understand sin to be an affair of the heart talk about washing it away, we need to explore the differences and similarities between the experience of defilement in the "primitive" *mana*-taboo setting and the experience of fault in the more fully "developed" moral consciousness. This will enable us to see that "the representation of defilement dwells in the half-light of a quasi-physical infection that points toward a quasi-moral unworthiness" and that it involves a "half-physical, half-ethical fear" because it belongs to a world "anterior to the division between the ethical and physical" in which "the evil of suffering is linked synthetically with the evil of fault; the very ambiguity of the word "evil" is a grounded ambiguity. . . ."[26] This is why Ricoeur with his sympathy for the believing soul and Freud with his hostility can agree in seeing in primitive taboos clues to the nature and origin of conscience.[27]

The most conspicuous difference between taboo and moral conscience as we understand it is the former's lack of concern about intent. As the metaphors of contagion and shock by contact indicate, one need not have meant to come in contact with the virus or the live wire. It matters only that the act has occurred. The agent is not a fully personal moral agent.

Neither is that which is violated and strikes back personalized in the manner presupposed by our understanding of punishment. We usually think of some person or group of persons (God, parent, teacher, society) whose right in a given context to make demands of us corresponds to our obligation to obey them and their right in turn to punish us when we don't. We have already seen that fear of punishment in this setting is an important part of the subjective meaning of guilt. But just as taboo is violated by mere contact, whether intended or not, so the power of *mana* strikes back automatically and unintentionally. We must speak here of "anonymous wrath."[28]

Because of these differences van der Leeuw suggests that we not speak of guilt and punishment at all when speaking of *mana* and taboo.[29] This is a helpful reminder that we are dealing with experiences different from our own. But it obscures the equally important similarities between this experience and ours. For, in this experience, just as in the more "developed" moral awareness, according to which I am responsible for what I intended but not for what I could in no way have foreseen, the act remains mine. Rather than disown it I accept responsibility for it. I resist the modern temptation to engage in the Denial of Responsibility.[30]

Closely related to this is a second fact. Although the vengeance which follows the violation of taboo stems from anonymous wrath it still has an important character of punishment. It is not a mere fact of misfortune, but somehow right. The order which has been violated is as much an ethical as a physical order. We are not dealing with pre-moral experience, but with experience in which the moral and physical have not been clearly distinguished by the abstractive powers of the intellect. Thus the "fear of vengeance is not a simple passive fear; already it involves a *demand*, the demand for a just punishment."[31] It is just this sense that punishment is somehow deserved which makes it punishment and not simply misfortune.

Oedipus is a good example of this. His crimes of murder and of incest were entirely unintentional. He can with ease attribute them to ignorance and fate. But rather than disown them he accepts full responsibility for them. There are, to be sure, gods on the scene, primarily Phoebus Apollo, who "in plain words commanded us to drive out a pollution from our land . . .," and to whom the question is addressed, "What is the rite of purification?" But he is not punishing Thebes for breaking his law as Yahweh punished Israel for breaking his. He is rather the one to whom the Thebans turn for help in dealing with a more mysterious power. The Chorus speaks as if this were a god, "a savage God who burns us." But he is not one of the Olympians, "for the God that is our enemy is a God unhonoured among the Gods."[32] He is rather that "anonymous wrath" which is seeking a name, the primitive, inchoate power of taboo seeking entrance into the ordered world of Olympian forms.

Teiresias tells Oedipus, "You are the land's pollution." As it gradually dawns on him that he is, simply by virtue of actions he committed without the slightest intention of doing so, he speaks. "And
I pollute the bed of him I killed by the hands that killed him. Was
I not born evil? Am I not utterly unclean? . . . Now I am godless and
child of impurity . . . I do not know with what eyes I could look upon
my father when I die and go under the earth, nor yet my wretched
mother—those two to whom I have done things deserving worse
punishment than hanging. . . . To this guilt I bore witness against
myself. . . . Now I am found to be a sinner and a son of sinners."[33]

Thus it is misleading to deny that defilement has anything to do
with guilt and punishment. The unwanted consequences of pollution
are punishment insofar as they are seen as somehow deserved. This
in turn means not only that we have to do with subjective guilt as
fear of punishment, but also with subjective guilt proper, the question
of a person's worth as distinct from happiness. This is why Otto
speaks of self-depreciation and Freud of self-reproach while describing the quasi-moral sense of defilement.[34] The impure person can
only approve the disapproval of gods and men that defilement evokes.
Because the act which pollutes need not have been intentional, it
might be better to speak of the consequent self-depreciation as
loathing rather than as remorse, as Otto suggests, but that does not
lessen the sense that one's "own entire personal unworthiness might
defile even holiness itself."[35] When the Sioux Indians purify themselves in order to be worthy of *Waken-Tanka*, they express the essential link between the symbolism of defilement and guilt as we have
come to understand it. Since this symbolism is, if not ubiquitous in
religious experience, at least one of the most widely spread of religious phenomena, we must be careful not to deny that guilt is a
fundamental concern of the believing soul just because it does not
always take exactly the form we may be familiar with from the biblical
tradition. Whenever we find religion providing the believing soul
with means of purification, whether ritual or moral or meditational,
we can be sure we have found it in some way taking on that enemy
that Zechariah found more threatening than the Romans, the sense
of being unworthy before the Sacred.

We have noted that this anxiety is particularly acute in the presence
of death. One of the most vivid expressions of this is the idea that
"it is appointed for men to die once, and after that comes judgment."[36] It is to the picture of the judgment of the dead that we turn
after our brief look at the symbolism of defilement.

Ibsen's Master Builder, Halvard Solness, is charged by the youthful Hilda with being afraid to climb the scaffold of the magnificent tower he has built. He admits it.

HILDA	Afraid of falling and killing yourself?
SOLNESS	No, not that.
HILDA	What, then?
SOLNESS	Afraid of retribution, Hilda.

Solness's buildings had become towers of Babel, symbols of his rivalry with God. Having come from a pious, country home, "I pretty well got the idea that He wasn't pleased with me." Thus, it is not death as such that frightens him, but the thought that his death might be or lead to retribution.[37]

Hamlet is even more explicit. Suicide would be a welcome end to the slings and arrows of outrageous fortune

> But that the dread of something after death,
> The undiscover'd country from whose bourn
> No traveler returns, puzzles the will,
> And makes us rather bear those ills we have
> Than fly to others that we know not of?
> Thus conscience does make cowards of us all. . . .[38]

It is the same conscience which makes of the aged Cephalus, who has found life a good thing, a man of justice. At the opening of the *Republic* he tells Socrates that the greatest benefit of his considerable wealth is that he can pay his debts to gods and men. For "when a man begins to realize that he is going to die, he is filled with apprehensions and concern about matters that before did not occur to him. The tales that are told of the world below and how the men who have done wrong here must pay the penalty there, though he may have laughed them down hitherto, then begin to torture his soul with the doubt that there may be some truth in them . . . he is filled with doubt, surprises, and alarms and begins to reckon up and consider whether he has ever wronged anyone."[39]

Solness, Hamlet, and Cephalus have been exposed to religious traditions in which the picture of the judgment of the dead is sufficiently prominent to have made a lasting impression on them, though none of them is particularly devout.

These images give expression to a need they do not create. By giving focus to issues which otherwise might remain inarticulate they serve to intensify human concern in the face of guilt and death. This may give the impression that they have produced that concern. But we have already seen that the basic human desire to be happy and to be worthy of happiness are sufficient to that end and that anxiety over guilt and death do not even require belief in an afterlife, much less is some sort of heaven or hell.

Just as the picture of a judgment of the dead is not a necessary condition of guilt and death being problematic, so it is not a universal or ubiquitous element in religion as a means to defeating these enemies. Although it comes to play an important role in China, Japan, ancient Greece, and ancient Israel, there seem to be important, early periods in each of these cultures which are quite free of it. The Egyptians developed the idea in pre-biblical times, but the parallel civilization in Mesopotamia did not.

What is striking about this picture, however, is how widespread it is. By itself it is sufficient to refute the suggestion that a central concern with guilt and death is distinctive of only the biblical tradition. In this regard S.G.F. Brandon's book *The Judgment of the Dead* is of major importance. He documents the development of this idea not only in the biblical tradition, but also in ancient Egypt, in Graeco-Roman culture, in Iran, throughout the world of Islam, and in India, China, and Japan under the influence of Hinduism and Buddhism. Among his conclusions two stand out. First, that this picture is by no means restricted to monotheistic or even theistic contexts, and second, that there is a good deal of uniformity from one tradition to the next. On the second point he writes, "While the representation of the joys of the just has generally tended to be of a rather symbolical kind, the sufferings of the damned have been depicted with such brutal realism that, except for a difference of artistic idiom, a medieval Christian picture of Hell might well have portrayed Orphic, Muslim, Tibetan, Chinese or Japanese expectations of the fate of the damned."[40] It would seem that the Puritan and revivalist preachers we are familiar with, at least from the movies and television, do not stand alone.

Just as the symbolism of defilement helps us to see religious concern about guilt in places we might easily overlook, so the picture of a judgment of the dead shows that concern linked with anxiety before death not only within but beyond the biblical tradition as well. Perhaps the suggestion that guilt and death are concerns belonging to religion as such is not a piece of ethnocentric projection after all.

This suggestion can be rendered more specific by the examination of the role guilt and death play in different types of religious experience. To that end the final three chapters of this essay will develop a threefold typology of religious life-worlds in terms of which very different experiences of guilt and death in relation to the Sacred can be understood. But just as it would be a misunderstanding to view religion's usefulness solely in terms of the goods of worldly fortune, overlooking its value to the believing soul as a means of overcoming the threat of guilt and death, so it would be a misunderstanding to think of religion's value to the believing soul entirely in terms of usefulness, overlooking the striking way in which the religious life is an end in itself. The believing soul's insistence upon this point is a crucial part of the context within which the battle with guilt and death is fought, and it is to this dimension of religion that we turn in Chapters Seven and Eight.

7
Religion as Means and as End

7A. Does Job fear God for nought?

It has been said that the concept of need is a powerful tool in the task of understanding religion, perhaps the most important element in the generic structure of religion, and that "what is common to all religions is . . . people and their needs."[1] Even where magical manipulation of the Sacred is not involved these needs include the mundane needs of medical, political, and economic good fortune (health, peace, and prosperity). But the categories of worldly fortune and misfortune are not ultimate for the believing soul, and at the very heart of religious concern we have found the more fundamental issues of guilt and death. The believing soul is erotic in the broad Platonic sense. It is impelled toward the Sacred by the awareness of its own deficiencies.

It is in these terms that Ricoeur understands the significance of myth and ritual. They point, according to Ricoeur, to a plenitude and wholeness in which man and the Sacred are united, but which "are not *given* but simply *aimed at*." The believing soul is "an unhappy consciousness; for him, unity, conciliation, and reconciliation are things to be *spoken of* and *acted out*, precisely because they are not *given* . . . [because] participation is signified rather than experienced."[2] The unhappy consciousness is a needy (erotic) consciousness which knows itself to be such. Its religious life is simply the attempt to meet that need.

There is another account of the meaning of myth and cult which is not so much incompatible with Ricoeur's as a challenge to its ability to tell the whole story. It must be remembered that Ricoeur is focusing particularly on the problem of guilt in its various forms. That the believing soul feels the need for purification, forgiveness, and reconciliation, and so forth, in the face of fault is undeniable. But

122

are this and the parallel concern for resolving the problem of death the extent of true piety?

Walter Otto thinks not. It looks to him as if *celebration* is even more important to religion than *yearning*. For example, when cultic action takes the form of dancing, as it so often does, the believing soul is not so much dealing with the gods as imitating them. Even when we talk about sacrifice, that element of the cult most easily susceptible of a *do ut des* (I give to you in order that you give to me) analysis, utilitarian and contractual models are inadequate for understanding religion. Not that Otto is oblivious of "man's natural wish to be blessed by the good will of the deity." But he finds something else to be more basic. "Man must give utterance to the feeling of awe which has seized him," to express the emotion which is aroused by his proximity to the Sacred. "The concept of utility, however early it may have attached itself to the cult act, is always secondary and contributes nothing to the understanding of the origins of the act. The more it moves into the foreground, the greater the distance becomes between ritual and the spirit in which it was conceived."[3]

How is this possible, in the face of the staggering needs, temporal and eternal, of which the believing soul is so keenly aware? Otto's answer is direct. Despite widespread opinion to the contrary, "it is not the application of unusual means to the achievement of a thoroughly natural aim, but the absence of expediency which makes cult practices so alien and strange to the modern mind. The basic character of these acts is not determined by the fact that the men who first participated in them wished to bring about some desirable objective, but by the fact that they already possessed the most desirable of objectives—the imminence of deity." In other words, it is *encounter* not *utility*, *contact* and not *contract* which lies at the heart of true piety. "That a faith in future salvation should associate itself with an activity which sprang from such plenitude is natural and inevitable."[4] But *salvation* remains secondary to something else that we might simply call *worship* or *ecstasy*, and the "spontaneous overflow of powerful emotion" prevails over calculating self-interest.

Evelyn Underhill's account of worship is quite similar. Where Otto takes celebration to be the central religious act, she defines worship in terms of adoration, and says of it, "It is true that from first to last self-regarding elements are mixed with human worship; but they are no real part of it. Not man's needs and wishes, but God's presence and incitement, first evoke it. As it rises toward purity and leaves egotistic piety behind, He becomes more and more the only Fact of existence, the one Reality. . . ." Worship is thus a response "to a

Wholeness, a Perfection already fully present . . . not because this august Reality consoles or succours men, not because worship enriches and completes our natural life, but for Its own sake."[5]

Worship ultimately leads to "that union with God which is the beatitude of the soul," and it is easy for worship to "decline from adoration to demand." But we are never to engage in it for this "or any other reason which is tainted by self-regard." Instead we are to allow its practice to lead us out from our "inveterate self-occupation" to "unconditioned self-oblation" and "selfless adoration." The "unconditioned" nature of the cultic act means "that even though God gave nothing of Himself to the soul, yet the soul must give the whole of itself to Him." In this light, worship is to be viewed as a "useless" activity.[6]

The premise of Ricoeur's account is the absence or remoteness of the divine while the premise of Otto's and Underhill's is its presence or proximity. If we recall (from Chapter Two) the dialectic of absence and presence which characterizes the Sacred, we will realize that it is not here a question whether one premise is right or the other, for both are. If this is so then both accounts are misleading and abstract by virtue of presenting one moment apart from its dialectically necessary opposite.[7] And if that is true, then the latter account (Otto and Underhill) will be useful to us in pointing to a dimension of the religious life which we have not yet explored, a non-erotic dimension that springs from fullness rather than emptiness.

Otto introduces the new dimension by giving expression to a complaint commonly directed against any *do ut des* piety exclusively devoted to meeting the believer's needs. "Yet if we suspect self-interest, we consider the giver's sentiments to be base or his piety unwarranted," and "whenever the concept of utility reigns supreme, cult actions have become completely superficial."[8] Modern versions of the argument that religion is either unworthy (base) or illusory (unwarranted) on these grounds abound, from Hume and the French Enlightenment to Feuerbach and Marx to Nietzsche and Freud. But the *locus classicus* remains the story of Job. When Yahweh points to the faithfulness of his servant Job, Satan replies, "Does Job fear God for nought? Thou hast blessed the work of his hands, and his possessions have increased in the land. But put forth thy hand now, and touch all he has, and he will curse thee to thy face."[9] In short, Job's religion is simply the best policy, his way of looking out for Number One. God needn't be too pleased, nor Job much admired.

It's clear that Satan's concern is not the mundane nature of Job's blessings, as if a spiritual materialism concerned only about guilt and death would be acceptable where a worldly materialism is rejected. The question, as Otto properly puts it, is whether self-interest and utility, either spiritual or material, are the ground of Job's religious life. By enduring the disasters that God then permits Satan to bring to him in the spirit of his outcry, "Though He slay me, yet will I trust him,"[10] Job shows that they are not. He demonstrates that his own faith is not a case of piety for profit. When he says, "The Lord gave, and the Lord has taken away; blessed be the name of the Lord,"[11] he makes it clear that what really matters to him is not God's gifts but God himself. Nor is God himself simply the greatest gift in the sense of being the answer to his needs. For he is the God who gives and takes away on his own terms, not Job's. And when in answer to Job's loud subpoenas at the end of the story God finally shows up, he does not answer Job's questions nor give an account of himself. He rather buries Job under an avalanche of questions whose effect is to relativize Job entirely. Job learns that his salvation consists not in having God solve his problems or answer his questions but simply in being addressed by God. This relationship is its own end and not a means to anything else.

There can be little doubt that the Jewish and Christian traditions have loved the story of Job for just this reason. For the critique of commercial piety belongs to religion itself. It arises from the believing soul and not just from Satan and suspicious skeptics. This is already clear in the story of Job. For in the story it is The Adversary who raises the question, but the story itself is told from the perspective of the believing soul in order to express a faith which has risen or is trying to rise above self-interest and utility.

Luther is an especially interesting witness on this point. The depth of his concern about guilt and death make him a prime candidate for the spiritual materialism in which religion is merely a means to innocence and immortality. But he resists this fiercely. One of his complaints against a theology of merit or salvation by good works is that "this is to make God a merchant and to tell Him, 'If you give, I will give.'" He calls it an "evil, false, and deceitful guile" when someone is pious "not for God's sake but for his own sake"; and when someone is pious "out of fear of hell or hope of heaven, not because of God," he calls this "the wicked filth that theologians call 'self-love.'" Believers of this work lack "a clean heart or a right Spirit. They are lovers of themselves more than of God."[12]

The same concern is on the lips of the pious Socrates. In the *Euthyphro* he comes through as the believing soul who knows that true religion consists in more than the meeting of even the deepest of

human needs. Though he has never given a moment's serious thought
to the matter, Euthyphro volunteers to instruct Socrates on the nature of piety. After his first three definitions self-destruct under Socratic questioning, he offers a fourth: "If any man knows that his
words and actions in prayer and sacrifice are acceptable to the gods,
that is what is pious; and it preserves the state, as it does private
families." Socrates takes Euthyphro to understand sacrifice as giving
things to the gods and prayer as getting things from them, so he
reformulates this notion of piety as "the art of carrying on business
between gods and men."[13]

This notion of piety as reciprocal commerce between gods and
men is not always criticized in Platonic contexts.[14] For this reason it
has been argued that the mutual self-interest conception of religion
in the *Euthyphro* is not "intended to be rejected as conveying a selfish
and sordid conception of religion. . . . If we think rightly of the
blessings for which it is proper to pray, it will be a worthy conception
of religion that it *is* an intercourse between man and God in which
we offer 'acceptable sacrifice' and receive in return the true goods
of soul and body."[15]

In the light of our own analysis of the needs which are central to
religious concern we can appreciate such a suggestion. For there is
not necessarily anything selfish or sordid about the believing soul's
longing for freedom from guilt and death. Yet in the context of the
Euthyphro, Socrates does not respond to the definition of piety as "the
art of carrying on business between gods and men" by reflecting on
what benefits it is proper to seek from the gods. Subtly and indirectly
in his own inimitable way, he ignores the distinction between crass
commerce and existentially serious asking and giving in order to
bring all forms of *do ut des* piety under critical scrutiny. Since he does
this not by a direct assault on the crude calculation of profit and loss
to which such religion can degenerate but rather by hinting at dimensions of the religious life which just don't fit into even the noblest
forms of spiritual need fulfillment, his point seems less to discredit
all religious asking and giving as such than to discredit that religion
which knows nothing more than asking and giving.

There are two indications of this. First, Socrates asks what gifts
we give the gods and how they are benefited by them. He gets Euthyphro to list such items as honor, thanks, and gratitude and to see
that his commercial metaphor implies a neediness inappropriate to
the gods. The suggestion is that these gifts may be acceptable to the
gods without being useful to them, that is, that they enter into relationship with humans apart from any needs which would lead to

bartering. Euthyphro can't make much of this and is led skillfully away from it by Socrates, who seems to prefer leaving us with but a tantalizing hint.

The other indication comes earlier in the dialogue though its full significance only now becomes apparent. Euthyphro had abandoned the idea that piety is the service of the gods as slaves serve masters because he could not answer Socrates' question about the result the gods achieve with the help of our services. The conversation points to the suggestion that we enter into relation with the gods not in order to solve our problems and meet our needs but to serve in carrying out divine purposes. When this is combined with the notion that the gods meet us not out of need but from some other motivation, the presuppositions of religion as good business for both parties has been undercut from both sides. Socrates would have understood the piety which prays

> Hallowed be Thy name,
> Thy kingdom come,
> Thy will be done,
> On earth as it is in heaven[16]

before it prays for its own daily bread and the forgiveness of sins.

A final example of the believing soul's own struggle against instrumental piety is drawn from the most beloved of Hindu scriptures, the *Bhagavad-Gita*. Vedic religion centered around sacrificial rituals and was therefore easily viewed as commerce between gods and humans. Hindu scriptures, including the *Gita* itself abound with *do ut des* conceptions of the religious life. But at the same time the tradition seeks to keep sight of that other dimension and is nowhere more articulate about it than in the *Gita*.

The only truly proper sacrifice is that offered "by those who expect no reward and believe firmly that it is their duty to offer the sacrifice."[17] This turns out to be the case not only for sacrifice and other specifically religious acts, but all of human action. All human actions are to be done as a sacrifice, that is, sacramentally. Krishna instructs Arjuna, "Save work done as and for a sacrifice this world is in bondage to work [Karma]. Therefore . . . do thy work as a sacrifice, becoming free from all attachment."[18] That freedom from attachment means the same as expecting no reward is clear from an accompanying instruction, "Let not the fruits of action be thy motive."[19]

The foundation for this view of the religious life in which the barrier between cultic and secular acts is deliberately breached, is the "Buddhist" notion that desire is the root of all human troubles. It is the natural tendency of human desire to give undue importance to one's own self, or, in other words, the human predicament is an egocentric predicament. "He who abandons all desires and acts free from longing, without any sense of mineness or egotism—he attains to peace."[20] This renunciation of "selfish purpose" makes possible "unselfish performance."[21]

There is no denial that benefits flow to those who live properly. Their sins are cleansed, they enjoy the favor of the gods, and they ultimately win liberation from the cycle of death and rebirth. The point is simply and directly stated, that desire for these benefits is not to be the motive of the religious life. What motives, then, should take the place of these?

At least three are suggested in the *Gita*. One we've already noted, the sense of duty. One should do this or that simply because the scriptures teach that it is right. One should not have to be bribed to do one's duty by the prospect of personal benefit.[22] Alongside the notion of duty is that of a gift of love, a notion that takes two familiar forms, love to God and neighbor. The very notion of sacrifice involves the notion of a gift to God, and Krishna, speaking as an incarnation of deity, tells Arjuna, "Whatever thou doest . . . do that . . . as an offering to Me."[23] If this is not done for the sake of the giver, it can be done for the sake of the recipient. The point is to direct attention away from myself, my needs, and my concerns to God, making him and not myself the center of my life. This has a natural parallel in relation to my neighbor. Krishna tells Arjuna to imitate him in working so as to maintain the world order. But just as Krishna does this out of no sense of personal need, so Arjuna is to make his own world-maintaining activity a kind of spontaneous gift to the world once again directing his energies away from himself.[24] That is the connecting link between motivation from duty and motivation from love. One might say that in the *Gita* duty serves as a mediator between eros and agape.

Socrates and those other ancients who gave us the stories of Job and Krishna with Arjuna would have appreciated a much later expression of their central point. The third and fourth stanzas of a sixteenth-century metrical version of Psalm 100 are as follows:

> O enter then his gates with praise,
> Approach with joy his courts unto;
> Praise, laud, and bless His name always,
> For it is seemly so to do.

> For why? the Lord our God is good,
> His mercy is forever sure;
> His truth at all times firmly stood,
> And shall from age to age endure.

We are confronted here with a kind of sacrifice, the gift of praise to God. Twice the question Why? is asked, and in both cases we are led away from any suggestion that we praise God in order to get something from him. Why should we enter his temple with joyous praise and always bless his name? Because it is *seemly* to do so. It is fitting, somehow appropriate. If we wish to ask Why? again the question is taken to be, Why is it seemly? and the reply to this is in terms of the character of God, his unchanging goodness, mercy, and truth. The believing soul knows (or learns) that the motivation of the religious life transcends that calculation of benefits that social scientists curiously insist upon calling rational behavior.

7B. Three models

The believing soul resists the reduction of the religious life to utility, expediency, and the instrumental. The calculating self-interest which makes the Sacred a means for dealing with fear and hope, desire and aversion is recognized as the self-love that religion seeks to transcend. There may be benefits to the faithful in this life and the life to come, but if the bottom line of piety is simply profit, then Satan's question about Job is a devastating rebuke. With commercial and contractual categories inadequate for understanding religion, what concepts shall we use? Are there models from outside the religious life which could be helpful to us?

The believing soul's attempt to keep from lapsing into instrumentalism and magic has powerful parallels in Aristotle's attempt to distinguish the moral life from the technologies of production. He takes it to be trivially true that our goal in life is happiness, since we all call what we're seeking by that name. But we disagree as to just what it is we so label. Aristotle finds honor (prestige, power), pleasure, and wealth to be among the most frequent concrete meanings of happiness in the popular mind. Raising objections to the identification of each of these with genuine happiness, he suggests that virtue or excellence is the true happiness. Virtue is doubly distinguished from the other candidates for happiness. First, while honor, pleasure, and wealth refer to what I possess or what happens to me, virtue involves what I do. If happiness is virtue, then it will be an activity of a certain sort. Second, while there are techniques for winning honor, pleasure, and wealth, there are no techniques for the excellent realization of our contemplative and active capacities.

The reason for this latter point is that the realm of technique involves a distinction between means and ends which is foreign to the moral life. To make this clear Aristotle sharply distinguishes making (*poiesis*) from acting (*praxis*), "for while making has an end other than itself, action cannot; for good action itself is its end."[25] Making (and the know-how which goes with it, *techne* or technique) concern the intelligent adaptation of means to ends. Acting (and its know-how, *phronesis* or practical wisdom) concern the intelligent shaping of activities whose value does not lie outside themselves in their consequences but in the very activity itself.

Technology is not machines; it is technique, the skillful employment of means to the end of controlling our environment. As such it pervades our lives. Aristotle's theory of the moral life calls our attention to a different human domain in which we act not in order to . . . but because it is seemly so to do. It calls to mind Krishna's instruction not to let the fruit of action be its motive, as well as Malinowski's distinction between magic and religion (Section 3A, above). The notion of action that springs from self-sufficiency rather than need reminds us of Otto's and Underhill's accounts of the non-erotic nature of religious celebration. As a model which seems to share an important structure with that part of the religious life we are now exploring, it gives us a look at that structure outside the religious context. In addition, it helps us to see how radically different it is from the goal-oriented nature of so much of our activity. It would be an even more illuminating model were it not for two factors.

The first of these is that instrumental or utilitarian thinking has come so deeply to shape our understanding of the moral life. The near ubiquity of calculative thinking in the world of our everyday experience includes the rise of utilitarian ethics. Nor is this just an event in the history of philosophy. People who couldn't name a single work written by Jeremy Bentham or John Stuart Mill know instinctively that the goodness of an action, public or private, is to be measured by the desirability of its consequences. Because this is true to such a large degree, Aristotle's theory of the moral life is just that, a theory. Whether and to what degree it corresponds to anything in our own moral experience is a serious question. Unless we already feel its truth in our moral muscles, so to speak, which cannot be unreservedly assumed, it may not be all that much help to us.

The second problem is a bit more subtle. A recurring theme in our preliminary encounter with the believing soul's critique of instrumental piety was the attempt to shift attention away from preoccupation with oneself. Luther was typically violent in denouncing those who are pious for their own sake rather than God's. Socrates hints that true piety consists in working for God's kingdom rather than our own. And Krishna teaches that all human activity is to be a sacrifice offered as a gift to God. Common to these expressions is the conviction that human self-centeredness is a prime barrier to true religion. While Aristotle seeks to direct attention from goal-oriented to intrinsically valuable activity, he offers nothing which corresponds to this religious concern about self-interest. His moral theory is properly understood as a theory of self-realization, and the question of human happiness stands unchallenged at its center.

A second model which may be helpful is the notion that aesthetic perception is essentially "disinterested." This idea takes its rise in eighteenth-century England with Shaftesbury, Hutcheson, Burke, and Alison; it is central to the aesthetic theories of Kant and Schopenhauer, and in our own century no less so to Croce's famous *Encyclopedia Britannica* article, "Aesthetics," Edward Bullough's influential concept of "psychical distance," and C.S. Lewis's gem, *An Experiment in Criticism*, where the idea is ever so succinctly summarized: "the many *use* art and the few *receive* it."[26]

Shaftesbury, who stands at the fountainhead of this tradition, uses four examples to make his point: viewing the sea with the desire to command it, viewing land with the desire to own it, viewing a tree with the desire to eat of its fruit, and viewing a human body with the desire to possess it sexually.[27] The desire to touch sexually, to eat, to own, and to command— each of these is an instance of what Shaftesbury means by interest. To view a beautiful object with a view to satisfying one of these desires, whether in the mode of planning or fantasizing, is to be distracted from the object's beauty toward its usefulness to me. Thus a genuine appreciation of the beauty at hand must be disinterested, free from the dominance of those desires or interests.

The totality of such desires Shaftesbury calls "the private system." Thus interest is "private interest," the pursuit of "private good," and interchangeably identified as "self-interest," "self-passion," "self-love," or simply "selfishness." Disinterested activities, then, are not means to the satisfaction of some need or desire; instead they occur when people transcend "cool and deliberate selfishness" and are "drawn out of themselves," to serve "purposes (other) than their own."[28]

This notion of getting beyond preoccupation with myself and my wishes receives a slightly different formulation when Shaftesbury further illustrates disinterestedness with reference to the aesthetic component in mathematics. Here the emphasis is not on purposes other than my own but upon objects other than myself.[29]

Following Shaftesbury's lead, Hutcheson and Burke seek to give a more precise and unified account of the desire whose absence or subordinate role constitutes disinterested attention. They focus on the notion of *use* and *possession*.[30] Interest is the desire to possess an object so as to use it. Since possession and use require real objects, this permits Kant to define disinterestedness as indifference to the object's existence.[31] C.S. Lewis brings us back from abstraction to experience with a personal illustration of the point. As a child he had been especially fond of illustrations by Beatrix Potter and Arthur Rackham. "Clearly, the pictures of both artists appealed to me because of what they represented. They were substitutes. If (at one age) I could really have seen humanized animals or (at another) could really have seen Valkyries, I should greatly have preferred it. Similarly, I admired the picture of a landscape only if, and only because, it represented country such as I would have liked to walk through in reality. A little later I admired a picture of a woman only if, and only because, it represented a woman who would have attracted me if she were really present."[32]

Kant's definition has an important implication. Taste, as the appreciation of beauty, is not only to be distinguished from "satisfaction in the pleasant" but also from "satisfaction in the good." For moral devotion to the good is no less interested in the real existence of its object, for example, justice, than the hedonism which seeks to possess and use whatever gives me pleasure. Since moral interest is not, especially for Kant, the self-centered desire upon which Shaftesbury focused attention, it turns out that it is desire or wish as such, and not merely selfish desire that Kant wishes to exclude from disinterested perception.[33] Freed from all desire "either of reason or of sense," the disinterested "judgment of taste is merely contemplative."[34]

Schopenhauer gives this radical dichotomy between desire and pure contemplation an eastern flavor through the identification of desire with pain and suffering. "All *willing* arises from want, therefore from deficiency, and therefore from suffering."[35] By contrast the mother of the fine arts is "superfluity."[36] Their appreciation occurs when the mind "is no longer directed to the motives of willing, but comprehends things free from their relation to the will, and thus observes

them without personal interest, without subjectivity, purely objectively, gives itself entirely up to them. . . ." Thus delivered from our
"miserable self," we are able to experience peace and blessedness.
A very important feature of this for Schopenhauer is "the forgetting
of self as an individual" which he calls "the transcending of our own
individuality. . . ."[37]

It is time to look at this model of aesthetic contemplation as disinterested in relation to the believing soul and at the question whether
piety isn't sanctified self-interest. Like Aristotle's account of the virtuous life, this model is one of non-instrumental activity. Disinterested activity is "terminal" rather than "anticipatory."[38] And just as
such activity is possible for Aristotle when it springs from self-
sufficiency rather than lack, so disinterested perception arises from
superfluity rather than want. In both cases the non-instrumental
character or activity is grounded in the non-erotic dimensions of the
self, reminding us once again of the picture of the believing soul
celebrating the presence of the Sacred.

There are, however, two differences between this model and the
first which bear on our subject. One of the problems with using
Aristotelian ethics as a paradigm of the religious life is that the former
is so clearly and unreservedly an answer to the question, How can I
be happy? By contrast, disinterested contemplation tends to displace
the self from the center of attention, reminding us of the anti-Carte-
sian experience (described in Section 1B). We are caught up into
purposes other than our own (Shaftesbury). We become attentive to
the qualities of the object rather than its relation to ourselves
(Shaftesbury, Kant, Schopenhauer).[39] We open ourselves to receive
the object rather than to use it. (Lewis—"The first demand any work
of art makes upon us is surrender. Look. Listen. Receive. Get yourself
out of the way."[40]) We learn to give ourselves completely to the object
of our attention (Schopenhauer).[41]

It is Schopenhauer who sums up all these ideas in the notions of
self-forgetfulness and transcending our individuality. This is only
part of a larger story. He constantly uses metaphors of elevation to
describe the passage from everyday experience to a thoroughly different world of experience in which space, time, and causality as well
as individuation as we know them are transcended. He calls this "spiritual exaltation."[42] Drawing on Platonic rather than Indian sources,
Schaftesbury describes the love of beauty as ecstasy and even enthusiasm.[43] And Clive Bell, drawing on the tradition we've been exploring, writes, "Art transports us from the world of man's activity
to a world of aesthetic exaltation. For a moment we are shut off from

human interests; our anticipations and memories are arrested; we
are lifted above the stream of life. . . . A good work of visual art
carries a person who is capable of appreciating it out of life into
ecstasy. . . . Great art remains stable and unobscure because the feelings that it awakens are independent of time and place, because its
kingdom is not of this world. . . . The forms of art are inexhaustible;
but all lead by the same road of aesthetic emotion to the same world
of aesthetic ecstasy."[44]

The link between self-forgetfulness and ecstatic world transcendence is not really very mysterious. The everyday world is the Cartesian world in which I am myself more certain and central than anything else. Everything revolves around me. If and when aesthetic
experience occurs in which I move into the background instead of
the foreground and for a while cease referring everything to myself
and my desires, this is quite literally the transition from one world
of experience to another. If Luther, Socrates, and Krishna have guided
us well, the believing soul is committed to something quite similar.

There is a second difference between the Aristotelian and aesthetic
models. The former is a theory of the active life, the latter of the
contemplative. We can speak in both senses of activity (*energeia*) in
the sense of actualizing possibilities; but in terms of the distinction
between theory and practice, the theory of aesthetic disinterest is an
account of perception rather than action, of seeing rather than doing.
Bullough sums up the entire tradition by saying that we achieve disinterest or physical distance "by putting the phenomenon, so to speak,
out of gear with our practical, actual self."[45] And throughout this
entire discussion we may well have been reminded of the account of
contemplation given by Straus (Section 1C, above) as being "emancipated from the bondage of catching, grabbing and gobbling." We
must ask what bearing this has on understanding religion.

We might be tempted to say something like this. The religious life
has both its active and its contemplative dimensions. The Aristotelian
model can help illuminate the active side, with its account of intrinsic
rather than instrumental action. But this still remains self-oriented.
The believing soul can transcend that only in the contemplative and
theoretical dimensions of faith, by analogy with the theory of disinterested perception. But this would be to misunderstand our second
model. Two qualifications should make this clear.

In the first place the self-forgetfulness that's been mentioned is
not an automatic result of shifting from the practical to the theoretical side of life. Theory, too, has its interests, and these may mit-
igate against that giving of ourselves to the object of our attention

in such a way as to receive it rather than use it for our purposes. Kant knew this well when he virtually defined natural science as "constraining nature to give answer to questions of reason's own determining," replacing the assumption that "our knowledge must conform to objects" with the assumption that "objects must conform to our knowledge."[46] This is why Kant is so careful to deny the priority of concepts in aesthetic perception, making the judgment of taste a reflective rather than determinant judgment, since only the former "allows the content to suggest its own concept."[47] Similarly Croce warns that "while philosophy transcends the image and uses it for its own purposes, art lives in it as in a kingdom."[48] The obvious consequence is that even in its contemplative and theoretical activities, the religious life may or may not achieve disinterestedness, self-forgetfulness, and world transcendence.

The second qualification is even more important. The notion of disinterestedness is not exclusively linked to the contemplative domain. It is true that is has developed as a theory of aesthetic perception and is known almost exclusively in that context. But Shaftesbury stands at the head of this tradition, and for him it is not first and foremost a matter of aesthetics. Rather he seeks to refute the Hobbesian claim that "interest rules the world," that we are machines fueled solely by self-interest.[49] Hobbes' is a general theory of human behavior, not an aesthetics, and Shaftesbury is especially eager to dispute it in relation to moral and religious behavior, to show that self-interest is "an obstacle to piety, as well as to virtue" and that there is more to be found in them than just another "bargain of interest."[50]

Horace's oft-quoted lines, "Sweet and fitting [*Dulce et decorum*] it is to die for one's country," becomes for Shaftesbury a kind of one line summary of his anti-Hobbesian theory that virtue is properly "inviting" only because it is "becoming." And he compares the piety of those inspired by fear of punishment or hope of reward to "the meekness or gentleness of a tiger strongly chained, or the innocence and sobriety in a monkey under the discipline of the whip." In such cases "the obedience is servile."[51]

Since the categories of disinterestedness were developed in the first place by Shaftesbury to protect the active life of virtue and piety from Hobbesian analysis, there is no reason not to use them in our attempt to understand the believing soul. The theory of aesthetic contemplation which developed subsequently can serve as a model for the religious life in both its active and contemplative aspects.

Our third model is play. It is not unrelated to the first two. Aristotle, though not very enthusiastic about "pleasant amusements," notices that they resemble virtuous activity in that "we choose them not for the sake of other things."[52] And Hans-Georg Gadamer, whose phenomenology of play concerns us here, not only takes note of the importance of the concept of play in the aesthetic theories of Kant and Schiller; he offers his own analysis as a "clue" to a deeper understanding of art and aesthetic experience.

Following the lead of Johan Huizinga in *Homo Ludens*, Gadamer emphasizes the non-instrumental character of play. Play involves a "to-and-fro movement which is not tied to any goal which would bring it to an end." For this reason the effort that is expended is experienced as relaxation rather than as strain. Of course, there are goals set up within various games, but the meaning of the game is not in the achieving of these, but in the trying. Thus play is an "energeia which has its telos within itself."[53]

Even more attention is given to the self-transcending character of play. "Play fulfills its purpose only if the player loses himself in his play." Because of this "the players are not the subjects of play."[54] Instead, "even for human subjectivity the real experience of the game consists in the fact that something that obeys its own set of laws gains ascendency in the game."[55] Thus, "the primacy of the game over the players engaged in it is experienced by the players themselves. . . . All playing is a being played. The attraction of a game, the fascination it exerts, consists precisely in the fact that the game tends to master the players. . . . The real subject of the game . . . is not the player, but instead the game itself. . . . The player experiences the game as a reality that surpasses him."[56] Here Gadamer finds it necessary to speak of "transposition into another world" and to claim that the player's "absorption into the game is an ecstatic self-forgetting that is experienced not as a *loss* of self-possession, but as the free buoyancy of an elevation above oneself."[57]

It is this element of self-transcendence that leads Gadamer to link the religious life to his description of play. Noting that the Greek concept of theory is derived from that of one who witnesses a religious festival, he notes that the presence involved in religious ritual as well as what the Greeks called theory arises from the fact "that in attending to something it is possible to forget one's own purposes." There is something passive in this, yet passivity is not quite the right notion either. "To be present, as a subjective act of a human attitude, has the character of being outside oneself. . . . In fact, being outside oneself is the positive possibility of being wholly with something else.

This kind of being present is a self-forgetfulness, and it is the nature of the spectator to give himself in self-forgetfulness to what he is watching. Self-forgetfulness here is anything but a primitive condition, for it arises from the attention to the object, which is the positive act of the spectator." This kind of presence makes possible the hearing of a claim. "The application to lutheran theology is that the claim of the call to faith persists since the proclamation of the gospel and is made afresh in preaching. The words of the sermon perform this total mediation which otherwise is the work of the religious rite, say, of the mass."[58]

Here the invitation is explicit to use the notion of play not only to understand aesthetic experience but the religious life as well. Though this model introduces no new elements not already brought out in the first two models, it may well be closer to the experience of many of us than the moral life as Aristotle understands it or the aesthetic ecstasies described by Schopenhauer and Bell. Together these three models provide us with examples of human experience which are not instrumental and self-centered. They may help us better to understand the believing soul's answer to Satan's question, "Would Job worship you if he got nothing out of it?"[59]

Prayer and Sacrifice as Useless Self-Transcendence

The world knows only the usefulness of the useful,
but does not know the usefulness of the useless.[1]

Being useless and silent in the presence of our God
belongs to the core of all prayer.[2]

8A. Prayer and Presence

We have seen religion conceived as celestial commerce, the
attempt of mortals to control or win the favor of the Sacred Power
for the increase of their earthly welfare.[3] The believing soul prays
for rain. We have also seen, with help from Zechariah, that human
involvement with the Sacred also concerns itself with spiritual welfare. Josiah Royce has summarized the view of religion which corresponds to this aspect. "The gods, as man conceives the gods, live
upon spiritual food; but, viewed in the light of history, they appear
as beings who must earn their bread by supplying, in their turn, the
equally spiritual sustenance which their worshippers need."[4] Finally,
we have seen religion claim to rise above self-interest in both its
material and spiritual forms. Before turning to the religious life itself
to see whether or not this claim can be validated, we looked outside
the religious life for clues about what to look for if the skeletal hints
of Otto, Underhill, Luther, Socrates, and Krishna are to be fleshed
out. Two such clues have emerged from that look at the moral life,
at aesthetic contemplation, and at play. Religion can be viewed as
something more than a means for dealing with our various needs to
the degree that it consists of (1) "terminal" activities, valued for their
own sake, and (2) activities in which the self's attention is directed
away from itself and thus from its own needs. We can call such ac-

138

tivities Useless Self-Transcendence. Of course, by using the term "useless" to highlight the non-instrumental character of the activities in question, it is not meant that they are worthless. The frequent identification of useless with worthless expresses the attitude that only what can be used has worth. By describing the religious life as consisting in part of "useless" activities, we are reminded that the believing soul, like the child at play, does not share this viewpoint.

Otto's notion of celebration and Underhill's of adoration, both rooted in the sense of the Sacred as present, refer to activities of useless self-transcendence. What is especially noteworthy, however, is the degree to which these structures inform prayer and sacrifice. It is noteworthy because these are the religious acts where the believing soul is most clearly instrumentally self-concerned. Prayer is praying for this or that benefit. It is asking and receiving. And sacrifice consists in giving gifts to the gods in hope that they will give blessings material and spiritual in return. It was prayer and sacrifice that Euthyphro had in mind when he described piety as commerce with the gods, and it was against the commercializing of prayer and sacrifice that Plato protests in *Republic* Book II. But it was also prayer and sacrifice that Otto and Underhill explicitly mention in rejecting this reduction. If prayer should consist significantly of adoration and sacrifice become celebration and not simply commerce, this would indicate most dramatically the degree to which the religious life is an end in itself and not just a means of meeting needs.

Consider the three following prayers, not without stature in their respective traditions. The Lord's Prayer is, of course, the most familiar prayer of Christendom. The second prayer, often called the Lord's Prayer of Islam, is the opening text of the Koran, and is prayed by the Muslim faithful at least twenty times a day. The third prayer is from Shankara, the Hindu philosopher-saint, an Indian St. Thomas Aquinas.

> Our Father who art in heaven,
> Hallowed be thy name.
> Thy kingdom come,
> Thy will be done,
> On earth as it is in heaven.
> Give us this day our daily bread;
> And forgive us our debts,
> As we also have forgiven our debtors;
> And lead us not into temptation,
> But deliver us from evil.
> For thine is the kingdom and the power and the glory, forever.
> Amen.[5]

In the Name of God, the Merciful, the Compassionate

Praise belongs to God, the Lord of all Being.
the All-merciful, the All-Compassionate,
the Master of the Day of Doom

Thee only we serve; to Thee alone we pray for succour.
Guide us in the straight path,
the path of those whom Thou hast blessed,
not of those against whom Thou art wrathful,
nor of those who are astray.[6]

A Mahadeva! O Thou Auspicious One, with the moon shining in Thy
    crest!

Slayer of Madana! Wielder of the trident! Unmoving One! Lord of
    the Himalayas!
O Consort of Durga! Lord of all creatures! Thou who scatterest the
    distress of the fearful!
Rescue me, helpless as I am, from the trackless forest of this miserable
    world. . . .

Lord of the universe! Refuge of the whole world! O Thou of infinite
    forms!
Soul of the universe! O Thou in whom repose the infinite virtues of
    the world!
O Thou adored by all! Compassionate One! O Friend of the poor!
Rescue me, helpless as I am, from the trackless forest of this miserable
    world.[7]

Each prayer involves at least one petition for the spiritual or material benefit of the one who prays. The Hindu prays for salvation
in the form of liberation from samsara, the cycle of death and rebirth.
The Muslim prays for guidance and help in living a right life, almost
as if thinking of Ivan Ilich. And the Christian adds to the prayer for
guidance away from evil a request for forgiveness and for daily bread.
So far prayer is simply the means of winning these favors from God
by asking for them.

But each prayer begins on a very different note. The believing soul
is directed away from personal needs to the majesty and greatness
of God. The deeds, character, and worth of God are brought into
focus through praise. In the case of the Lord's Prayer, the petition
for God's kingdom to come has already come to our attention in
connection with Socrates' suggestion that true piety consists in ded-

ication to purposes other than our own. The believing soul looks away from self-preoccupation to consider God and his kingdom, and at the end of the prayer, having made the other petitions, comes back to these thoughts.

There are times when the elements of awe and adoration take over completely. The result is the hymn of praise, a liturgical form for private and public prayer entirely free from self-interest. Many of the Psalms of ancient Israel have this character, and hymns to the gods are widespread throughout theistic and polytheistic religions.[8]

The cynical eye of suspicion will see nothing but flattery in all this, buttering up the deity so as to win more divine favors. There is nothing to guarantee that adoration will not degenerate into adulation. But the believing soul protests that prayer has been unfaithful to its own truest nature whenever this happens. The faithful are encouraged to "Praise, laud, and bless His name always, For it is seemly so to do."[9] Thus, when St. John of the Cross asks one of his penitents in what her prayer consists, she replies, "In considering the Beauty of God, and in rejoicing that He has such beauty," and Evelyn Underhill comments, "Such disinterested delight is the perfection of worship."[10] Another believing soul sat alone each day in the dark of a church. When asked by a friend what he did there, he replied, "I just look at Him and He looks at me."[11]

These last two items come from the tradition of contemplative prayer in which prayer, meditation, and contemplation are blended into one. Henri Nouwen, writing out of that tradition, takes note of the possibility that prayer is merely self-seeking. "Prayer is often considered a weakness, a support system, which is used when we can no longer help ourselves. But this is only true when the God of our prayers is created in our own image and adapted to our own needs and concerns. When, however, prayer makes us reach out to God, not on our own but on his terms, then prayer pulls us away from self-preoccupations. . . . The movement from illusion to prayer is hard to make since it leads us . . . from an easy support system to a risky surrender."[12]

Thomas Merton similarly stresses the theme of prayer as surrender and submission rather than self-seeking.[13] As he sees it, it is just the transcendence of self-interest that keeps the surrender of the self to God from being servile. "If we remain in our ego, clenched upon ourselves, trying to draw down to ourselves gifts which we then incorporate in our own limited selfish life, then prayer does remain servile. Servility has its root in self-serving. Servility, in a strange way, really consists in trying to make God serve our own needs . . . authentic prayer enables us to emerge from our servility into freedom in God, because it no longer strives to manipulate him by superstitious 'deals.' " It is not that we deny our neediness. Rather we acknowledge it "at the beginning of prayer in order to rise above it. . . ."[14]

This freedom of self-surrendering praise of which the Christian monk speaks would be instantly understood by the Hindu saint, Ramakrishna. It comes to expression in this hymn which he loved.

Upon the sea of the world unfolds the lotus of the New Day.
And there the Mother sits enshrined in blissful majesty.
See how the bees are mad with joy, sipping the nectar there.

Behold the Mother's radiant face, which so enchants the heart
and captivates the universe. About Her Lotus Feet
Bands of ecstatic holy men are dancing in delight.

What matchless loveliness is Hers! What infinite content
Pervades the heart when She appears! O brothers, says Premdas,
I humbly beg you one and all, to sing the Mother's praise.[15]

But the freedom that comes from rising above our neediness is not restricted to moments of ecstatic, dancing praise. It also transforms the other moment of prayer, as Underhill has noted. Prayer is not wholly disinterested; it asks for blessings. "But as the genuine religious impulse becomes dominant, adoration more and more takes charge . . . whenever the envisaged end is not man's comfort, security, or personal success, but His glory and purpose, the more perfect doing of His Will, then the prayer of petition itself . . . becomes a true 'hallowing of the Name'."[16] Thus it is that the Sioux Indian, who prays to Wakan-Tanka for good crops and good hunting, "that I may live" or "that my people may live," also makes this kind of petition. "Wakan-Tanka, You are everything, and yet above everything! You are first. You have always been. . . . O Wakan-Tanka, You are the truth. The two-legged peoples who put their mouths to this pipe will become the truth itself; there will be in them nothing impure. Help us to walk the sacred path of life without difficulty, with our minds and hearts continually fixed on You."[17]

Even the prayer of confession, in which the believing soul's interest in forgiveness is patent, gains a new dimension as "adoration more and more takes charge." "In the worshipper's view that ultimate purpose of the recognition of sin is to be sought in the first place not in his own person but in God. The purpose which the recognition of sin must serve is that God is known to be God, and that he is acknowledged as such. . . ."[18]

The believing soul is committed to a radical form of self-transcendence in this notion that prayer reaches its perfection in asking for daily bread and the forgiveness of sins for the sake of God and his kingdom and not simply to satisfy our own stomach or psyche. Sometimes this is expressed as the need to "make God our only thought," or to "fill the mind with God alone."[19] In the words of *The Cloud of Unknowing*, "A naked intention directed to God, and himself alone, is wholly sufficient."[20] That is easier said than done. One exercise prescribed as preparatory training in contemplative prayer is the following: "Choose something in the created order and for 10 minutes each day practice the outpouring of yourself toward it. It does not matter what you choose—a cup of water, a slice of bread, a leaf, a tree, a building, a piece of machinery. Then, using your will, energy and powers of concentration defend the object chosen against all other claims for your attention."[21]

The purpose of such an exercise is clear. It is to relax the self from its anxious grasping so it can be open to reality, at first the reality of finite things, but ultimately the reality of the Sacred. The transition from eros to openness involves the paradoxical notion that even the desire for God is to be left behind. "Only when we are able to 'let go' of everything within us, all desire to see, to know, to taste and to experience the presence of God, do we truly become able to experience that presence with the overwhelming conviction and reality that revolutionize our entire inner life." This has an important consequence. "In proportion as meditation takes on a more contemplative character, we see that it is not only a *means* to an end, but also has something of the nature of an *end*. Hence monastic prayer, especially meditation and contemplative prayer, is not so much a way to find God as a way of *resting* in him whom we have *found*, who loves us, who is *near* to us, who comes to us to draw us to himself."[22]

It is precisely because self-transcendence in prayer culminates in openness to the divine presence that it can be called useless. Adoration and self-surrender are "the practice of the presence of God."[23] As such they are "terminal" activites with no goal beyond themselves. Contemplative prayer is the antithesis of calculative planning. As desire gives place to openness, striving gives place to rest.

It has been said that as prayer is the heartbeat of Christianity, so meditation is the heartbeat of Buddhism.[24] It might be more to the point to describe prayer as the heartbeat of monotheism, for it is no less important to Jewish, Muslim, or Sioux piety than to Christian.

But the comparison is important. What has been said about prayer presupposes that the Sacred is a personal being (or beings in the case of polytheism) with whom mortals can speak. The grammar of prayer is second person singular. What about a religion like Buddhism which views reality as ultimately being not only impersonal but unsubstantial? Nothing is permanent. Everything is empty. In the final analysis there can be no God or gods to pray to.

But this is only in the final analysis. Though the Buddhas and Bodhisattvas are not strictly speaking gods, they are prayed to for help and assistance in gaining Enlightenment. In fact, faith is the first of the five cardinal virtues of Buddhism, and the faithful are to live full of faith in the Buddha, the Dharma (law, teaching, doctrine, norm), and the Sangha (order, community, "church").[25] The beginning of faith for the Buddhist is the simple prayer

> I go to the Buddha for refuge.
> I go to the Dharma for refuge.
> I go to the Sangha for refuge.

But faith for the Buddhist means more than turning to the "three treasures" for refuge and praying to the Buddhas and Bodhisattvas for help. It also involves worshipful meditation on the supreme excellence and worth of the three. Thus Buddhist meditation begins with devotional exercises which consist in considering the beauty of the treasures and in rejoicing that they have it. In quiet seclusion adoration takes on words.

> This Lord is truly the Arahat, fully enlightened, perfect in his knowledge and conduct, well-gone, world-knower, supreme, leader of men to be tamed, teacher of gods and men, the Buddha, the Lord. . . . (I) Well-behaved is the Community of the Lord's disciples, straight is their behavior, proper and correct. (II) The four pairs of men, the eight persons,—these are the Community of the Lord's disciples. (III) Worthy they are of offerings, worthy of hospitality, worthy of gifts, worthy of respectful salutation, they, the world's peerless field of merit.[26]

Exercises such as these play a role similar to meditation on some finite object in Christian meditation. Just as neither alp nor insect is God, so no object of meditation is ultimate for the Buddhist, since every thing is like a bubble or mirage, empty. "Concentration on an object naturally forms the starting point of the process which leads to the abolition of the object in trance."[27] This includes the object of faith. Yet the purpose of these preliminary exercises is clear.

Buddhism, is, if anything, more radical than Judaism, Christianity, and Islam in viewing self-interest as the fatal flaw in human existence. As the Christian is encouraged to "pour yourself out" and "surrender yourself" to a finite object, so the Buddhist is taught to worship and adore realities which are empty. In this way the self begins to be removed from center stage, while the greed and anger, desire and aversion which express the self's infatuation with itself, begin to melt away.

The last three of the five cardinal virtues of Buddhism all have to do with meditation which seeks to go beyond faith to the full realization (seeing and feeling, not merely believing) of the emptiness of all things. This Gestalt switch in consciousness extinguishes the flame of self and desire. It is Nirvana. The subtle differences between Mindfulness, Concentration, and Wisdom are not as important in this context as their common character, lessening and finally eliminating the sense of I and mine.[28] All Buddhist meditation, whether devotional or not, moves toward the wisdom of Nagasena. When King Milinda asked his name, he gave it as follows. "Your majesty, I am called Nagasena . . . it is, nevertheless, your majesty, but a way of counting, a term, an appellation, a convenient designation, a mere name, this Nagasena; for this is no ego here to be found . . . in the absolute sense there is no ego here to be found."[29]

There can be no question that Buddhist meditation, in spite of metaphysical differences with the monotheistic traditions, is an exercise in self-transcendence. There remains the question whether it is viewed as intrinsically valuable or as a means to an end. The latter seems at first the obvious answer, since the goal of Nirvana, both as bliss itself and as permanent release from Samsara, the cycle of death and rebirth according to the law of Karma, is central. This is the Buddhist equivalent to being religious in this life in hopes of heaven, the happy hunting grounds, or the Elysian fields in the life to come. It is solving the problems of guilt and death, and Buddhism presents itself precisely as the solution to these human needs.

But the believing soul resists seeing the religious life exclusively in these terms in the Buddhist tradition too and seeks to go beyond them. The metaphysics of emptiness becomes helpful here. "The Path exists, but not the traveler on it,"[30] and Nagarjuna teaches that "*samsara* and *nirvana* have no real substance," which means that

> There is no difference at all
> Between *nirvana* and *samsara*.
> There is no difference at all
> Between *samsara* and *nirvana*.[31]

If there is a Path but neither traveler nor point of departure nor destination, then the Path cannot be the means or instrument by which the traveler gets from one place to another. In the process of seeking salvation, the believer is taught that the very framework of a self in need of salvation and making use of the "means of grace" to that end is an illusion. To the degree that this wisdom becomes experience and not merely doctrine, the journey along the Path loses its future, goal-oriented character and each moment is absolute unto itself.

Within the Buddhist tradition it is Zen which has developed this possibility most systematically. Like other forms of Buddhism it includes petitionary prayer to the Buddhas and worship of them as "a way of horizontalizing the mast of ego."[32] And like them it gives central importance to overcoming the egocentric perspective on the world.[33] But it tends to give stronger emphasis to Nirvana in Samsara, to redeeming the here and now. Thus Dogen, who founded the Soto school of Zen in Japan after thirteenth-century travels in China, "emphasized both the complete adequacy of 'just sitting in Zen fashion'—what he called *shikantaza*—and the oneness of practice and achievement. In his statement that 'in Buddhism practice and enlightenment are one and the same,' Dogen eliminates all notions of Zazen or Zensitting as 'means' to an end apart from itself—Satori or enlightenment—and expresses something in total harmony with his principle that there is complete fullness in every moment rather than the utilization of one moment to gain the benefits in another one."[34] Just as the Christian is taught to give up the desire for God in order to be genuinely open to Him, the Buddhist is here taught to abandon the search for Enlightenment and to rest in the moment.

When the Buddhist tradition of meditation is taken as a whole, we can probably say that in comparison with the monotheistic traditions of contemplative prayer the element of self-transcendence is more radical while that of its uselessness is less pronounced. The point is not that prayer and meditation are identical; it is rather that in both cases it is just where the religious life is most obviously a means to various ends that it shows itself also to be an end in itself.

8B. Sacrifice and Love

The same can be said about sacrifice, a phenomenon ever so closely linked to prayer. Not only is the sacrificial rite virtually inconceivable without accompanying prayer; the two acts are all but interchangeable. Sacrifice can be viewed as "a prayer which is acted."[35] On the

other hand, prayers can be viewed as sacrifices, as both the Rig Veda
and the Hebrew Psalms attest.

Oh Daughter of the Sky, I have offered my hymn as a cow is offered.
Oh Night, accept my sacrifice as praise to my conqueror.[36]

Let my prayer be counted as incense before thee,
and the lifting up of my hands as an evening sacrifice![37]

Sacrifice further resembles prayer in bringing the believing soul's
self-interest to unconstrained expression. "Here is the butter; where
are your gifts?"[38] Giving something to the gods in hopes of getting
something from them is what sacrifice seems to be all about. "The
sacrificer gives up something of himself but he does not give himself.
Prudently, he sets himself aside. This is because if he gives, it is partly
in order to receive. Thus sacrifice shows itself in a dual light; it is a
useful act and it is an obligation. Disinterestedness is mingled with
self-interest. That is why it has so frequently been conceived of as a
form of contract. Fundamentally there is perhaps no sacrifice that
has not some contractual element."[39]

In this passage from their important study of sacrifice, Hubert and
Mauss acknowledge the disinterested element in sacrifice but place
emphasis on its *do ut des* character. Our purpose is the opposite.
Without in any way denying or diminishing the interested nature of
sacrifice, we want to take note of the way in which the religious life
seeks to protect itself from becoming nothing more than this.

The three most prominent ideas in discussions of the nature of
sacrifice are gift, communion, and expiation or propitiation. The gift
theory of sacrifice is associated especially with the name of Sir Edward
B. Tylor.[40] As Tylor himself noted, the giving of a gift to the gods
sometimes involved the expectation of some blessing in return. But
it could also be an act of giving homage to the gods and renouncing
the self's claim to be primary with no expectation of any benefit
beyond the act itself. Of course, these two types of giving, while
conceptually distinct enough, are not always easily distinguished in
practice. The distance in reality between "honoraria" and "bribes"
is not all that great.[41] From our own experience of Christmas- and
birthday-giving we all understand this relationship between giving in
hopes of receiving and giving for the sheer joy of giving.

W. Robertson Smith developed the communion theory of sacrifice,
focused on the notion that sacrifice was a meal shared by the divine
recipient and the worshippers.[42] Again our own experience leads us
to a ready understanding of the two elements residing in sacrifices

having the character of shared feasts. We sometimes invite dinner guests (the boss, business clients) primarily because of the benefits we hope to attain from socializing with them. On other occasions we entertain simply for the sake of fellowship with those whose presence we value. Similarly, sacrifice as communal meal can be an attempt to gain personal or tribal benefit from closeness to the Sacred; or, in the language of Walter Otto, it can be the celebration of a presence which is loved for its own sake.

Finally, there is the notion of expiation or propitiation. No single theorist has been necessary to call attention to a feature of sacrifice as prominent as this. Piacular sacrifices, as they are also called, are clearly means to the end of getting rid of the guilt which accompanies fault, or of the punishment which accompanies guilt, or both. Here the offering of sacrifice is all but inescapably seen as the paying of a fine or even a bribe so as to get the cosmic court off my back in spite of some offense I have committed. Yet, just as the prayer of confession in the context of adoration can be more than merely self-interested, so the sacrifice of expiation has the possibility of being as much the acknowledgment of the rightness of the divine order and a celebration of its supremacy as it is a device for getting out of a jam.

By looking at these three elements of sacrifice we have only encountered understandable possibilities for the believing soul to transcend the level of celestial commerce in sacrifice. What we need to do now is see how this possibility comes to fruition in ritual life.

Among the most carefully studied pre-literate peoples who practice sacrifice are the Nuer, a cattle-breeding people of the upper Nile. They are said to spend "nearly all their waking time in acts of worship," and sacrifice is the most fundamental of these acts of worship.[43]

The language in which the Nuer talk about their sacrifices is that of contract. "The ideas of purchase, redemption, indemnification, ransom, exchange, bargain, and payment are very evident in Nuer sacrifices." They use the same word for sacrifice that they use for making a purchase from an Arab merchant; and while they also use language which suggests the payment of a debt, they view the sacrifice as placing the recipient in their debt. Thus the Nuer woman says, "God, take thy cow and give me a child."[44]

Among primitive peoples who sacrifice, it is often assumed that supernatural beings "covet the same things which men consider desirable" and even that the gods "catch" people in order to receive these goods in the form of sacrifice.[45] When dealing with the lesser spirits, the Nuer acknowledge they operate at this level. The result is that their sacrifices represent a totally shameless bargaining and "huckstering."[46] But when they are dealing with the God they consider to be the Supreme Being, there is a difference. Contractuality in the sense of reciprocal giving and receiving does not by any means disappear. But "if they include, they go beyond, the dialectic of exchange and contract . . . for we can hardly speak of simple exchange or contract when one side in reality gets nothing and the other side may get nothing too."[47]

What can this mean? It is the divine side which can be said to get nothing. It is true that some gift is offered to him, but he gains nothing thereby, for the Nuer recognize all things as already belonging rightfully to him. Thus they offer him "thy cow" and not "my cow" or "our cow." The side which may gain nothing is the human side. While sacrifice may place the lesser spirits under a kind of contractual obligation, this is not true of the supreme spirit, God. For "apart from there being no means by which bargaining with God can be conducted, it is no use trying to haggle with him, because he is master of everything and can want nothing. Nor is there any idea that God is at fault if he does not give what is asked for in sacrifice; in his dealings with man he always has the *cuong*, is in the right."[48]

It becomes necessary, then, to interpret sacrifice not so much in terms of what the two parties gain, but in terms of what the human party loses. One element of this loss is already before us. Sacrifice for the Nuer is the acknowledgment that God is supreme, that everything is properly his, that "we give Thee but Thine own, whate'er the gift may be," and that "as against God we are always in the wrong."[49] In the act of sacrifice the believing soul loses by freely giving up that Cartesian centrality of self which defines the secular life.

The other human loss is the literal one, the cow, the cucumber, or whatever, that is sacrificed. Should the value of the sacrifice then be determined by the value of the gift? Not at all. The Nuer are clear that what matters is the intention of the heart. "All gifts are symbols of inner states, and in this sense *one can only give oneself*; there is no other kind of giving. . . . When Nuer give their cattle in sacrifice they are very much, and in a very intimate way, giving part of themselves."[50] Thus it seems to be less than the whole truth when Hubert and Mauss say that the sacrificer "does not give himself. Prudently, he sets himself aside." At one level this is clearly true. The Nuer do not spear their own sides or slit their own throats. But at another level just the opposite is the case. Through the symbolism of identification with the sacrificed gift, the Nuer give themselves to God, placing themselves at his disposal and acknowledging his supremacy over all they are and have. Thus the two aspects of loss are not really separable. The material loss is the symbolization or incarnation of the spiritual loss, of self-abnegation before the Sacred. Like the mystics one can use sacrificial language itself here and speak of self-oblation.

We are talking here about piacular sacrifices. This means that sacrifice is made in the hope of receiving a benefit. But the language with which the Nuer talk about their sacrifices makes it clear that there is another motivation. They give themselves to God in this way because it is right to do so and because the beliefs expressed in these acts are true. It is fitting so to do (and it may be helpful as well). Sacrificial self-transcendence is both a useful and a useless activity. This is perhaps only a first step but it is nevertheless a real step along the path Underhill calls "the most significant development in human religion . . . the movement of the idea of sacrifice from propitiation to love."[51]

If we look for another religious context as thoroughly focused on sacrifice as Nuer religion, Vedic India would surely have as strong a claim as any. From the hymns which accompany the sacrificial rites we gain further (scarcely needed) indications of the interested and instrumental nature of sacrifice.

Grant us great riches, fair in form, of all good things, wealth which
    light labour may attain. . . .
So grant thou us a dwelling wide and free from foes.
    O goddess, give us food with kine.
Bring us wealth abundant, sent in every shape. . . .

May that for which we desiring have invoked thee be ours.
    May we become lords of wealth.

Make me immortal in that realm where they move even as they list. . . .
Make me immortal in that realm of eager wish and strong desire. . . .
Make me immortal in that realm where happiness and transports, where
Joys and felicities combine, and longing wishes are fulfilled.[52]

It is not surprising to find Vedic religion described as "a scientific method of acquiring immortality as well as temporal blessings . . . a system of authorized magic or sacred science controlling all worlds, if properly understood."[53]

Yet the same author insists that already in the period of the Brahmanas, Vedic sacrifice moved beyond the *do ut des* principle. The

Brahmanas represent the total triumph of sacrifice and the Brahmin or priestly class (eventually caste) in the Hindu religion. But this very fact affects the meaning of the rituals. "In this period of the Brahmanas, beginning approximately in the tenth century B.C., the gods of the Samhitas have lost their former significance. Instead, the sacrifice now takes the place of the ruling powers in the universe. 'The sacrifice is here no longer the means to an end, but it is an aim in itself, indeed, the highest aim of existence.' "[54]

The process by which sacrificial ritual gains importance at the expense of the gods is one in which sacrifice becomes the root metaphor for viewing all reality. "The universe appeared to the Vedic Aryan as a constant ritual of sacrifice."[55] Both the original creation of the universe and its ongoing processes come to be viewed as a sacrifice in which life is maintained through the consumption of food and drink. This "cosmic sacrifice" finds its microcosmic re-enactment or imitation in sacrifice as a human ritual. Thus it can be said that "through the voluntary ritual of sacrifice man takes his place in the cosmic symphony as an equal. The main purpose of his existence is the performance of this ritual."[56] The status of equal comes from the fact that the gods, too, are viewed as offering sacrifice and even as the sacrificial victim.[57] There is a shift away from seeing them as the sovereign dispensers of good or ill fortune to viewing them as co-workers with mortals in the task of maintaining the cosmic order through imitative re-enactment. That these sacrifices could be thought of as the main purpose of human existence, and thus an end in themselves, stems from viewing them less as techniques for gaining benefits from the gods and more as acts by which the faithful attune themselves to the sacred cosmic order, *Rta*, and put themselves at its service. Since this impersonal order, like the Chinese *Tao* and the Egyptian *Maat*, has moral as well as physical connotations, and since it is often viewed as the ultimate power and authority to which even the gods are subordinate, it is not inappropriate to call it a sacred order. Maintaining and imitating such an order is but fitting and seemly.

But the same texts in which these ideas can be found include the much less subtle interpretation of sacrifice we noted earlier: "Here is the butter; where are your gifts." Given the ease of viewing sacrifice in this way, it is not surprising that there should be reactions against the notion of sacrifice itself. In India the Nastika (heterodox) religions of Buddhism and Jainism repudiate sacrifice altogether. There is no doubt a socio-political factor at work here, a protest against the Brahmins' sacerdotal monopoly over the whole of society. But there is a religious factor as well, and these "protestant" movements are testimony to the believing soul's unwillingness to reduce the religious life to the search for personal profit. They are not, however, pertinent to our immediate task, which is to discover that refusal within the practice of sacrifice itself. Within the orthodox tradition the same tendencies which led Buddhism and Jainism to abandon sacrifice completely turn up in the Upanishads and the *Bhagavad-Gita*. But since orthodoxy in India is not defined by this or that doctrinal content but by recognition of the Vedas as authoritative scripture, and since the earliest strata of the Vedas make sacrifice central to the religious life, sacrifice will have to be transformed rather than abolished.

The "sublimation" of sacrifice in the Upanishads is not consistently sustained, for they are very complex and diverse texts.[58] One finds in them the idea of sacrifice to please the gods and win favors from them, as well as the broader notion of the cosmic sacrifice of which human sacrifices are imitations. There are even passages which sound like Nastika attacks on sacrifice and the Brahmins.[59] The theme central to the "sublimation" of sacrifice is the superiority of knowledge to sacrifice.[60] The knowledge in question here is that of Atman-Brahman, the absolute one beyond duality. It can be taught doctrinally through teachings such as the Upanishads, but like the related Buddhist notion of emptiness, it can be realized only through meditation. The famous Upanishadic formula, "that art thou," means that Atman-Brahman is not some being distinct from the human self which knows it. The two are actually identical. But this metaphysics involves a radical self-transcendence. For the self which is one with the Absolute is not the finite self in its empirical discreteness. The realization of oneness with Atman-Brahman is the realization that the finite, everyday self is not fully real, and consequently, that it finds its fulfillment not in the satisfaction of its desires as a finite self, but in its identity with the infinite, non-erotic One.

Consistent with this view, the Upanishads teach that sacrifice in its original form cannot be ultimate since it presupposes the duality of gods and mortals and it fails to take seriously the priority of the heart over external reality.[61] Further, the grounds for *do ut des* sacrifice are undercut by the teaching that we should not desire wealth and that all finite goods are to be treasured "for the love of Atman."[62] It follows that "one should not offer sacrifice [merely] to secure a wish."[63] Sacrifice itself has its source in Atman and is to be viewed as offered to Atman. Thus "Brahminhood has deserted him who knows Brahminhood in aught else than *Atman*."[64]

Sacrifice is not to be repudiated; but neither can it be left to run its own course. The rites are to continue, but they are to be inter-

preted in a new way. Sacrifice is not to be viewed simply as a device
for gaining material and spiritual benefits from the gods. It is rather
an act in which the self symbolically offers itself up to the Self (*Atman*),
forsaking its own desires for the sake of the Sacred. It seems as if
the sophisticated Upanishadic seers share with the simple Nuer people a sense that "one can only give oneself."

The tolerance of orthodox Hinduism for both sacrifice as self-
interest and sacrifice as disinterested self-transcendence is nowhere
more dramatically expressed than in the portion of the *Bhagavad-
Gita* we considered in Section 7A. There we read:

> In ancient days the Lord of creatures created men along with sacrifice,
> and said, By this shall ye bring forth and this shall be unto you that
> which will yield the milk of your desires.
> By this foster ye the gods and let the gods foster you; thus fostering
> each other you shall attain to the supreme good.
> Fostered by sacrifice, the gods will give the enjoyments you desire.
> He who enjoys these gifts without giving to them in return is verily
> a thief.[65]

Without any suggestion of there being a debate or conflict, this
passage is immediately preceded by the suggestion that all work is
to be done as a sacrifice, that is, free from attachment. Here an
entirely different conception of sacrifice is presupposed, one familiar
from the Upanishads, and extended to be the model for all of human
activities. It reappears almost immediately after the verses cited above:

> But the man whose delight is in the Self [*Atman*] alone, who is content
> with the Self, who is satisfied with the Self—for him there exists no
> work that needs to be done.
> Similarly, in this world he has no interest whatever to gain by the
> actions that he has done. . . .[66]

The logician's mind may complain that the *Gita* is confused, or
even wishy-washy. But it faithfully reflects the believing soul, who
on the issue of sacrifice as on that of prayer is never wholly free from
Euthyphro's view of piety and never too far from Socrates'.

A very similar story can be told from China. There it was sacrifice
to ancestors which was the center of the cult, and the liturgy is familiar.

> We make wine and sweet spirits
> And offer them to our ancestors, male and female,
> Thus to fulfill at the rites,
> And bring down blessings to all.[67]

Mo Tzu and the Mohists following him repudiated these practices. But the Confucian tradition sought to sublimate them.

Confucius himself sacrificed to ancestors and other spirits, testifying that when he did so he felt as if they were actually present. He taught his followers to do the same as an act of filial piety. And when Tzu-kung wanted to abolish a monthly sacrifice to the ancestors, Confucius replied, "You love the lamb but I love the ceremony."[68] But he placed the ceremony, along with all human acts, within the framework of ethical principles quite contrary to any sacrifice-is-the-best-policy mentality.

The first principle of this ethics concerns motivation. Actions are to be done because they are proper and right, not because they are personally beneficial. Hence the essential antithesis between *yi* (righteousness) and *li* (profit). "The superior man understands righteousness, the inferior man understands profit."[69]

The second principle concerns the content of action. It is the principle of humanity (*jen*). Asked to define it, Confucius replied, "It is to love men" and "Do not do to others what you do not want them to do to you."[70] The great neo-Confucian Chu Hsi puts the two principles together and teaches, "*Jen* is uncalculating and has nothing in view."[71]

In short, proper action is useless self-transcendence. It is useless because it is not done with an eye to its results. And it is self-transcendent because it focuses on the welfare of the other rather than on my own. Sacrifices should be maintained as an act of filial obedience. But like all human action, ritual should consist of acts of *yi* and *jen* rather than *li*.[72]

Turning finally to the biblical tradition, which is likely to be the most familiar, we find that sacrifice was the central cultic act of ancient Judaism until the destruction of the second temple in 70 A.D. Some of the sacrifices had a rather directly *do ut des* character. The burnt offering or holocaust and the sin offering were both expiatory sacrifices whose purpose was the atonement of sins.[73] In addition, there was the peace offering (also called the communion sacrifice, the shared offering, or the fellowship offering), a meal shared among God, the priest, and the sacrificer, along with his family and any guests he may wish to bring. This sacrifice could be offered as a votive offering, the payment of vow, in which case it had a kind of retroactively instrumental character; for it arose from a solemn promise of the form, If you will help me out of this mess, I'll offer you a sacrifice.

But the two other types of peace offering have a different motivation.[74] This sacrifice may be offered as a freewill offering or as an act of thanksgiving. The former "is an example of a free act of homage, which voices man's humble recognition of and submission to his divine Lord," while the latter "springs spontaneously from man's need to give public and material expression to his gratitude for some deliverance or marvelous benefit. . . . The ideas which actuated these sacrificial rites are the very ones to be found in the hymns and thanksgivings of the Psalter, which may indeed for the most part have been composed for just these occasions and which form some of the most beautiful expressions of Old Testament piety."[75]

Closely related to these forms of peace offering is the offering of the firstfruits (the firstborn of the livestock and the earliest grain, olives, wine to be produced each year). The motive for such a sacrifice "may be either to obtain God's blessing and sanctification of all one's property, or else to acknowledge that God is the real owner of all things. . . ."[76] The sense that God is the owner of all things and in need of nothing is strong in Hebrew piety.[77] The offering of firstfruits serves to acknowledge Israel's dependence on God and to thank him for their freedom, for the original gift of their land, and for its current fruitfulness.[78] These examples should suffice to indicate that both the interested and the disinterested aspects of sacrifice we have been tracing elsewhere are built into the Israelite cult.

At least as prominent in the Jewish scriptures as prescriptions for sacrifice are polemics against it. This protest is associated especially with the pre-exilic writing prophets, but it predates them and is not found exclusively in the books attributed to them. Unlike the Buddhist and Mohist rejection of sacrifice and like the Upanishadic and Confucian reinterpretations, the prophetic protest does not aim at eliminating the ritual altogether, though sometimes the rhetoric is so strong as to suggest that.[79]

The paradigm for the critique of sacrifice is the story of King Saul and the Amalekites. God had commanded him to destroy them completely. But he couldn't resist bringing back some booty with him, so he spared the lives of King Agag and the best of the enemy's livestock. When challenged by the prophet Samuel, Saul replied that he had brought the sheep and oxen to sacrifice to God. To which Samuel replied

> Has the Lord as great delight in burnt offerings and sacrifices as in obeying the voice of the Lord? Behold, to obey is better than sacrifice, and to hearken than the fat of rams.[80]

Samuel's answer echoed throughout Israel's subsequent history.
The form of the anti-sacrifice strains in the Jewish Bible is always to
point to something which is more important to God than sacrifice.
Sometimes it is the same things Samuel mentioned, an open recep-
tiveness to the voice of God and a willingness to obey it.[81] Often it
is economic justice for the poor and oppressed.[82] On other occasions
it is attitudes of praise and thanksgiving or of contrition and humility.[83] Hosea may be said to summarize it in these words of the
Lord

> For I desire steadfast love and not sacrifice,
> the knowledge of God, rather than burnt offerings.[84]

Speaking of this last passage, Martin Buber summarizes the prophetic protest. "It is for the prophet to plead unremittingly against
the degenerate sacrificial cult, in which the offering is changed from
being a sign of the extreme self-devotion and becomes a ransom from
all true self-devotion."[85] Buber rightly sees that one must be more
specific than to talk simply about the difference between external act
and internal attitude. The question is whether the giving of animal
or plant life to God truthfully signifies the giving of oneself to him.
"But he who accumulates at his altar offering upon offering devoid
of intention, without the will to offer himself, offends Him."[86] It
seems that the Jewish believing soul wants to join the Nuer believing
soul in telling Hubert and Mauss they are wrong in claiming that
those who sacrifice withhold themselves in giving something else.

Hubert and Mauss acknowledge an exception to their claim. "There
is, however, one case from which all selfish calculation is absent. This
is the case of the sacrifice of the god, for the god who sacrifices
himself gives himself irrevocably."[87] The Christian faith takes this as
the central theme in its understanding of sacrifice. In drawing on
the Old Testament theology of sacrifice it does not only interpret
the death of Jesus as a sacrifice for sin, presenting him as "the Lamb
of God, who takes away the sin of the world!" and announcing that
"Christ, our paschal lamb, has been sacrificed." It also goes back to
the Old Testament picture of the Suffering Servant of Yahweh who
"makes himself an offering for sin" and presents Christ as the one
who "has appeared once for all at the end of the age to put away
sin by the sacrifice of himself."[88]

That the sacrificial death of Christ to atone for sin was a "once
for all" event, permanently ending the need for animal sacrifices,
might suggest that for the Christian sacrifice has a role only in mem-

ory. But this is not the case at all. It is precisely as the one who voluntarily sacrificed himself that Christ is seen as a model and example for his followers.[89] "Whoever does not bear his own cross and come after me, cannot be my disciple."[90] This does not mean that Christ's followers are to try to put away sin by the sacrifice of themselves. That would be to push imitation to the point of identification and deny the once-for-all efficacy of Christ's own sacrifice. It does not even necessarily mean that they are to die an unnatural death; for they are called upon to present themselves "as a living sacrifice, holy and acceptable to God, which is your spiritual worship."[91] It is in life that self-sacrifice primarily occurs.

Already in the Epistles it is suggested that it is the life of love and praise which does this.

> Therefore be imitators of God, as beloved children. And walk in love, as Christ loved us and gave himself up for us, a fragrant offering and sacrifice to God.[92]

> Through him let us continually offer up a sacrifice of praise to God, that is, the fruit of lips that acknowledge his name. Do not neglect to do good and to share what you have, for such sacrifices are pleasing to God.[93]

Subsequent Christian tradition has continued to use the language of sacrifice to understand various aspects of the life of faith. Roman Catholics, for example, call their celebration of the Eucharist the Sacrifice of the Mass. The sacramental act is a sacrificial act. As such it has an interested, instrumental dimension, for it is as much an act of receiving as of giving. In the act of communion the faithful acknowledge their need of divine grace and come to receive it from the hand of God. But there is a further dimension, since sacrifice is as much a giving as a receiving. "The same Jesus is here present who dies on the Cross. The whole congregation unites itself with His holy sacrificial will, and through Jesus present before it consecrates itself to the heavenly Father as a living oblation."[94] By receiving God's gift to them the faithful offer themselves to God.

Protestantism has always been skittish about viewing the Eucharist, Communion, or Lord's Supper as a sacrifice, lest there be misunderstanding about the finality of the death of Christ. But this is Martin Luther speaking: "When I declare the Word of God I offer sacrifice; when thou hearest the Word of God with all thy heart, thou dost offer sacrifice. When we pray, and when we give in charity to our neighbor, we offer sacrifice. So, too, when I receive the Sacrament,

I offer sacrifice—that is to say, I accomplish the will and service of God, I confess Him, and I give him thanks. This is not a sacrifice for sin, but a sacrifice of thanksgiving and praise."[95]

From the mystical tradition comes the idea of "a speechless self-offering, a total oblation of personality . . . as the apex of contemplative prayer." So the author of *The Cloud of Unknowing* writes, "Thou ghostly friend in God, look that, leaving all curious seeking in thy natural wits, thou do wholly worship thy Lord God with thy substance, offering up unto Him plainly and wholly thine only self, all that thou art and such as thou art . . . and say thus: 'That I am and how that I am, as in nature and in grace, all I have it of Thee Lord, and Thou it art. And all I offer it unto Thee, principally to the praising of Thee, for the help of all mine even-Christians and of me.' "[96]

From the free-church tradition (churches supported by their members rather than by tax subsidies) comes the idea of financial contributions to the church as sacrifice. Here the levitical notion of the sacrifice that is a free-will offering is reversed and a free-will (monetary) offering is seen as sacrifice. Not that every gift counts as a sacrifice. In the background is Jesus' comparison of the rich who contributed large sums to the Temple treasury with the widow who gave but two coins: "Truly, I say to you, this poor widow has put in more than all those who are contributing to the treasury. For they all contributed out of their abundance; but she out of her poverty has put in everything she had, her whole living."[97] In this context giving becomes "sacrificial giving" only when we give "till it hurts." The point of giving "till it hurts" is not masochistic; what is at work here is an understanding that what we give to God in sacrifice is finally ourselves and that the giving of money becomes in fact the giving of ourselves only when we give enough to really feel it.[98]

Finally, from the Anabaptist tradition within Protestantism comes the idea that the self-sacrifice by which Jesus' disciples follow the way of the cross is less a matter of public worship or private devotion than of one's daily life in the everyday world. The personal and especially political non-conformity involved in imitating the non-violent, non-power seeking service through self-giving life and teachings of Jesus is the sacrifice by which we give ourselves to God and neighbor.[99]

In view of earlier discussions it should not be hard to see sacrifice in the Christian tradition as useless self-transcendence. And as in several of the other traditions we've been considering, we can see how useless self-transcendence pushes from the merely privative notion of disinterestedness to the positive concept of love. The displacement of myself from center stage becomes intrinsically valuable as my heart is drawn out in thanks, adoration, imitation, and celebration of an Other. As Augustine has put it, sacrifices are "the things which we do for the purpose of drawing near to God."[100]

Guilt and Death
in Exilic Religion

9A. Fundamental differences in dealing with guilt and death

There is perhaps nothing more obvious about religion than its relation to human need. The believing soul turns to the Sacred for help, for comfort, for hope, and for deliverance. We have noted that the human needs without which the believing soul would be unrecognizable are, roughly speaking, of two sorts. The distinction is not easy to make with precision. We have spoken of pre-spiritual needs and spiritual needs. We might, following Kierkegaard's lead, distinguish between temporal and eternal happiness, but only if we remember that "eternal happiness" signifies an absolute goal which may or may not involve everlasting life as personal survival of death.[1] Or we might, following Jaspers, distinguish between the penultimate happiness that pertains to our existence and the ultimate happiness that pertains to our *Existenz*.[2] None of these distinctions is fully satisfactory; but all of them call attention to the distinctiveness of the believing soul's concern about guilt and death. It is a central thesis of this book that the religious life is attractive to the believing soul largely because of the hope that through a proper "relation" to the Sacred guilt and death can be overcome.[3] The religious life presents itself as the promise of this ultimate happiness, which it calls salvation. That will be the term used henceforth to refer to the overcoming of guilt and death.

But while Chapters Four and Five have sought to clarify the nature of the problem to which salvation is the solution, and Chapter Six has tried to indicate its centrality to the life of faith and piety, almost nothing has been said about the way in which religion is a means to salvation or about the nature of salvation itself. There are two reasons for this.

First, the believing soul insists that the religious life is three dimensional and that the satisfaction of need concerns only two of these dimensions. Just as a line or plane would be a pale abstraction in relation to a solid figure in three-dimensional space, so the believing soul portrayed only as the pursuit of salvation, that is, engaged in commerce with the divine out of motives of self-interest, would be a caricature of the genuine article. Thus it was necessary in Chapters Two and Three, even before turning to the holy as attractive, to note that it is also repelling, that it has a dark side as well as a bright. Its sheer perfection draws us toward it in admiration, but it also humbles us and evokes our envy. The demand placed upon us to bring our own existence into proper conformity with the divine perfection excites our zeal as the one ideal worthy of our all, but it also disturbs our complacency and reveals our spiritual inertia. The threat to every complacency about our being and our behavior is the high price to be paid for any contact with the Sacred which is to be fully honest.

As a defense against a sensed inner tendency to bad faith at just this point, the believing soul keeps insisting that the *tremendum* and the *fascinans* are inextricably united. Even when the believing soul is not fully aware of what is going on, the paradoxical forms in which the experience of the numinous comes to expression give testimony to the inevitable ambivalence it evokes, all the way from the exotic images of Krishna and Kali or Dionysus to the esoteric dialectic of illusionist metaphysics.

But even when this is properly taken into account we still have only a flatland of faith, a life of two dimensions instead of three. The believing soul not only insists on the polarity of attraction and repulsion, but also on a polarity within the attractiveness of the Sacred. The religious life is not only instrumentally valuable, but also intrinsically so; it is not only a means to salvation, but the experience of salvation and thus an end in itself. To put it a bit differently, religion not only has the task of overcoming guilt and death as the most serious threats to a meaningful and happy life here and (sometimes) hereafter; it must also provide the positive content of that life. Thus in Chapters Seven and Eight we looked briefly at this dimension of the religious life with help from several other modes of experience and from the concept of useless self-transcendence. Only when this third dimension of the religious life is clearly in place is the believing soul satisfied that attempts to understand it are not abstract and thereby seriously misleading.

There is a second reason why the theme of salvation only now comes to the fore. It has been important to go as far as possible in our attempt to understand the believing soul at the generic or uni-

versal level. Though we have noted important differences among
actual religious traditions in seeking to describe the three dimensions
of the religious life, it has been possible to focus attention on structures with a serious claim to being universal (or at least very widespread) and thus to keep speaking of the believing soul in the singular.
But when we turn from the problems of guilt and death to the solutions offered to the believing soul, we find the differences among
various religious traditions pushing their way to the fore. At this
point it becomes necessary to replace the formal analysis which always
looked for some way to give expression to a common essence with
descriptions which will highlight rather than mute the disagreements
which finally require passing from the generic features of the believing soul to its specific differences.

It is in terms of a generic feature of religion already familiar to
us that we turn to focus on specific differences. In the earlier discussion of ambivalence we noted that the Sacred is apprehended as
an emphatic challenge not only to our behavior but to the very status
and being of the self we immediately find ourselves to be. Religion
tells us that we can become real only by ceasing to be that self.[4]
Frederick Franck correctly claims that each religion "speaks in its
own language of man's irrepressible concern with Ultimate Meaning,
and each one points to *the overcoming of ego* as the precondition for
the perception of this Meaning."[5]

Since we can expect each religion to speak of our true self and of
the self that must be left behind, the ego that must be overcome if
that true self is to be realized, we should not be surprised to find
these words on the lips of Jesus. "If anyone wishes to be a follower
of mine, he must leave self behind; he must take up his cross and
come with me. Whoever cares for his own safety is lost; but if a man
will let himself be lost for my sake, he will find his true self. What
will a man gain by winning the whole world, at the cost of his true
self? Or what can he give that will buy that self back?"[6] But since
each religion speaks *in its own language* of the problem of overcoming
ego and leaving the false self behind in order to find true selfhood,
we won't expect other religions to use the symbol of the cross or the
notion of following Jesus to define that overcoming and that leaving.
For the Jew, the Sioux, and the Taoist, the story will be quite different.[7]

Since this notion of finding the true self is intimately tied up with
the overcoming of guilt and death, it is another way of talking about
salvation. Just as each religion makes the distinction between the true
and false self "in its own language," so each will have its own dis-

tinctive account of salvation. The remaining chapters of this essay will describe three fundamentally different conceptions of salvation in the form of a typology of religious differences. Each type will be "larger" than any particular, historical tradition inasmuch as each is in fact exhibited in more than one such tradition. At the same time each type will be "smaller" than any of the traditions which belong to it, for the types will have a single-mindedness, a cleanness and consistency which no living, historical reality ever possesses. Virtually every living religion will have elements of more than one type within it. This fact does not refute a claim that its primary meaning and intention is to be of one particular type or another, though it is clear that there will be differences of interpretation on this matter.

That the types are both "larger" and "smaller" than the actual religions which nevertheless instantiate them can also be expressed by Ricoeur's notion that the types are both *a priori* and *a posteriori* in relation to historical reality. "The 'types' which we propose are at the same time *a priori*, permitting us to go to the encounter with experience with a key for deciphering it in our hands and to orient ourselves . . . and *a posteriori*, always subject to correction and amendment through contact with experience."[8] The use of a typology for interpreting the religious life thus highlights the hermeneutical circle in which all interpretation occurs, the dialectical interplay of pre-understanding and empirical testing.

Ricoeur's formulation highlights one of the purposes for using a typology rather than dealing with religious differences simply by moving from the generic study of religion to a survey of particular traditions such as Judaism, Islam, Buddhism, and so on. When religions are laid side by side in this way for comparison all differences tend to become equal and it becomes difficult if not impossible to know which differences are fundamental. The search for essential differences requires some sense of what the real heart of a specific religion is. (Readers who can remember that wonderful old record "What It Was Was Football" will see the point immediately. The describer of the game had no clue what a football game was all about and was therefore disappointed when, just as the game was about to begin, some idiot kicked the ball and the rest of the afternoon was spent fighting over it instead of playing football. Not knowing the essential structure of football, he watched an entire game without recognizing it as such.) One important function of the typology is to seek to locate what is essential. It thereby becomes, not simply the result of research (by virtue of its *a posteriori* character), but like Max

Weber's ideal types, an instrument of further research and interpretation (by virtue of its *a priori* character).[9]

There is a second benefit to be derived from turning to types rather than directly to historical traditions. In keeping with the existential purposes of this phenomenological interpretation,[10] it is important that the content retain as much as possible the form of possibility rather than of fact. Learning is boring and fruitless when it is reduced to the accumulation of facts. Only when facts become possibilities does learning come alive. In the natural sciences (including the social sciences when understood in quantitative and experimental terms) those possibilities are technological. In the human sciences (*Geisteswissenschaften*, the humanities and the social sciences when the latter are not assimilated to the natural sciences), to which the present discussion belongs, those possibilities concern the shape of self-formation, personal and social. They are thus essentially self-referential. If the study of religion is to involve consciousness formation and not mere ignorance liquidation,[11] its form must remain that of possibilities which lay a claim upon my (our) own existence, which invite the openness which consists of both sympathetic listening and critical scrutiny. Particular traditions can, of course, be encountered in this way. But since one is dealing with historical actuality as such, it is all too easy for understanding to give way to the accumulation of factual information. The "ideal" character of types serves as a check against this tendency.

If the types are to be our "keys for deciphering" specific religious texts and practices, we first need a key for developing the types. The key or clue adopted here for developing a schema for interpreting religious differences is the concept of world. Religious differences will be interpreted in terms of divergent attitudes toward being in the world. We will be considering types of religious life which can be called anti-worldly, semi-worldly, and worldly.

If the designation "anti-worldly" sounds pejorative to us, whether for religious or secular reasons, that only tells us something about ourselves. For those whose spirituality is of this type the term signifies wisdom and common sense at once. For they take being in the world as such to be the fundamental problem of human existence. Salvation will thus consist in liberation from the world. The false self is the worldly self and the true self is the worldless self. A qualified form of anti-worldly religion indentifies the world with the physical world and the false self with the body and the senses. Its anti-worldly impetus thus takes the shape of a radical mind-body dualism, and liberation consists in the total separation of the soul from the body. We will be looking at Orphic-Platonic-Gnostic expressions of this fundamental attitude.

A more radical form of anti-worldly religion can be found in various Indian traditions, Hindu and Buddhist, according to which the worldly self that needs to be left behind is not merely the body but also what we normally mean by the mind. These traditions understand liberation from the world not merely as freedom from the body but as freedom from that individuated selfhood which lives out any practical or theoretical comportment with that which is not itself and which thereby forms its world, whether mental or physical. Taking the correlation of self and world seriously, they recognize that the worldly self must itself be overcome if liberation is to occur, and they identify this self not merely with the body but with the whole aggregate of human capacities for knowledge of what is other, for desire, and for action. This chapter will conclude with a dramatic Hindu version of this standpoint.

Following Ricoeur, I shall speak of anti-worldly religion as exilic religion, for it views the world as a place of exile.[12] The true self is realized by awakening to the awareness that it does not belong in this place of suffering and alienation and, by virtue of that awakening, returning to its true unworldly home. In the following chapters which deal with semi-worldly and worldly religion I shall explain why I refer to them, respectively, as mimetic and covenantal religion. Both differ from exilic religion by being world-affirming. But they differ from each other in that mimetic religion affirms the world as nature (but not as history), while covenantal religion affirms the world primarily as history (and also as nature).

It is worth noting at the outset that for each of the three types we will be considering both forms which involve the notion of personal immortality in some fairly recognizable version and forms which do not. As important as the notion of personal survival of death may be, especially when the problem of death is a major focus of this study, that will not turn out to be the focus of difference. Just as in our earlier investigation of the nature of death as an existential problem we discovered that the question of personal survival was not the fundamental question, now we will discover that the deepest differences among religions are not on this point.

Cogent rationales can be given for presenting exilic, mimetic, and covenantal religion in virtually any order. One can obviously work from world-affirmation to world-negation or vice versa. But one can just as easily begin with semi-worldly or mimetic religion, for the actual religions which express exilic and covenantal attitudes emerged

historically out of contexts that were thoroughly mimetic. The problem is not so much to choose some order of presentation, but to avoid
the implication that a kind of Hegelian dialectical development from
less adequate to more adequate is involved. That would clearly be
incompatible with the non-evaluative character of the method we
have adopted. Just as it is not the task of this book to say whether
religion as such is a good or bad thing, it is not its task to say which
type of religion is superior to other types. Locating religions on a
spectrum of attitudes toward the world is one thing; determining
whether salvation is best understood to occur in history, in nature,
or outside of both in a worldless pure consciousness—that is another.
The *epoche* by which that question is bracketed, along with the question whether human existence should be understood in terms of
salvation of any kind, is not an attempt to minimize the importance
of those questions nor to escape from them. It is rather a sense of
their urgency and their ultimacy that reminds us that "our existence
is too tightly held in the world to be able to know itself as such at
the moment of its involvement, and that it requires the field of ideality in order to become acquainted with and to prevail over its facticity."[13]

9B. Exilic religion in the west: the Orphic-Pythagorean tradition

In the form associated with the Homeric literature, Greek religion
is anything but hesitant about affirming the goodness of life on earth,
the here and now. But as early as the sixth century B.C. there emerged
two traditions of sharply and self-consciously anti-worldly religious
ideas and practices. We know them as Orphic and Pythagorean. In
the fifth century Pindar and Empedocles gave wider circulation to
some of these ideas, but it was through Plato in the fourth century
that the Orphic-Pythagorean form of anti-worldly religion became
part of the mainstream of western culture.[14]

The anti-worldliness of this tradition is dramatically expressed by
Empedocles in his *Purifications*. Those born to life on earth "must
wander for thrice ten thousand seasons far from the company of the
blessed, being born throughout the period into all kinds of mortal
shapes, which exchange one hard way of life for another. For the
mighty Air chases them into the Sea, and the Sea spews them forth
on to the dry land. . . . One (*Element*) receives them from the other,
and all loathe them. Of this number am I too now, a fugitive from
heaven and a wanderer. . . . I wept and wailed when I saw the un-
familiar land (*at birth*) . . . the joyless land where are Murder and

Wrath and the tribes of other Dooms, and Wasting Diseases and Corruptions and the Works of Dissolution wander over the Meadow of Disaster in the darkness."[15] Given this view of the world as a place of painful exile, it is no surprise to hear that the ethics of the tradition is an asceticism which is "the turning away not merely from the weaknesses and errors of earthly being but from the whole of earthly life itself."[16]

Underlying this ethic is an equally anti-worldly metaphysic in the form of a radically dualistic interpretation of human nature. In its mythological form it involves the god Dionysus. "It all begins with the wicked Titans, who trapped the infant Dionysus, tore him to bits, boiled him, roasted him, ate him, and were themselves immediately burned up by a thunderbolt from Zeus; from the smoke of their remains sprang the human race, who thus inherit the horrid tendencies of the Titans, tempered by a tiny portion of divine soul-stuff, which is the substance of the god Dionysus still working in them as an occult self."[17]

Quite possibly even before this myth was developed (its date is hotly debated), the dualism it expresses was already interpreted as the dualism of body and soul. So radically new to the Greek context is this dualism that Ricoeur can say that "the Orphics *invented* the 'soul' and the 'body.' "[18] What can this mean? Surely Homeric Greeks had the concept of soul and a word to go with it, *psyche*.

But in the Greek world before the Orphic-Pythagorean "invention" of soul and body, there seems to have been no distinct concept for the body as such, and what is more important, the term "soul" had an entirely different function from the newly "invented" concept of the soul. The simplest indication of this is that the Homeric *psyche* did not in any way compromise the sharp boundary between divine and human, immortal and mortal, while the Orphic-Pythagorean-Platonic soul is divine and immortal. That divine component within the human person, which in the myth was the remnant of Dionysus among the ashes of the Titans who had just eaten him, is now given the name of soul. The results are revolutionary. In the first place the distinction between mortal and immortal no longer separates gods from humans but rather stands for a division within the human self. Second, and in consequence, I can now say that I am my soul but am not my body. This disavowal of the bodily self (and with it earthly existence) is something which would have appeared preposterous to Homeric characters, even if they had had available to them the language to express it. The startling claim of Empedocles, "I go about you as an immortal god, no longer a mortal,"[19] and the calmer but equally radical teaching of Plato about the divinity of the soul, together with the discrediting and disowning of the body that they imply, provide both the meaning and justification of the claim that we are witnessing the "invention" of the soul and the body.

This invention brings with it an inevitable element of verbal confusion, since the term *psyche* henceforth will have two very distinct, even contradictory, roles to play. But if we take account of this situation, we will find Greek philosophic thought more coherent than we otherwise could. For if we distinguish the Orphic-Pythagorean soul from the Homeric soul, "the divine psychic entity which lives on and the mortal complex in which it is embedded,"[20] there will be no reason for an Empedocles (and after him an Aristotle) not to give a thoroughly naturalistic interpretation of the soul as the totality of vital powers, including feeling, perception, and thought, tying them inextricably to the body, and a supernaturalistic interpretation of the soul as a bit of divine reality existing "unmixed and incapable of mixture, *alongside* the body and its faculties which indeed only have life . . . when united with it."[21] Empedocles himself seems to have been aware of both the conceptual situation and the potential verbal equivocation; for he refrains from referring to his true, immortal self as *psyche*. "The occult self which persisted through successive incarnations he called, not '*psyche*' but 'daemon.' This daemon has, apparently, nothing to do with perception or thought, which Empedocles held to be mechanically determined; the function of the daemon is to be the carrier of man's potential divinity and actual guilt."[22]

It is by understanding the phrase "man's potential divinity and actual guilt" that we will understand the religious significance of the metaphysical revolution we've been exploring. For therein resides the Orphic-Pythagorean doctrine of sin and salvation, the significance of the exile motif for the problems of guilt and death.

The vehemence of the Orphic-Pythagorean hostility to the body cannot be grasped in terms of the dichotomy between mortal and immortal. Earthly life is not hated simply because it comes to an end. That might well be cause for loving it all the more dearly, as Homeric experience suggests. It is rather because earthly life is conceived as punishment for some prior guilt that it is conceived as a place of exile. If Empedocles is now wandering "far from the company of the blessed," this is because "when one of the divine spirits whose portion is long life sinfully stains his own limbs with bloodshed, and following Hate has sworn a false oath—these must wander. . . . Of this number am I too now, a fugitive from heaven and a wanderer, because I trusted in raging Hate."[23] In terms of the notions of reincarnation and the transmigration of souls, earthly life is viewed as punishment for sins in previous lives. Since these lives seem also to have been earthly lives, the question arises how the whole cycle of life, death, and rebirth gets started, and no very clear answer is forthcoming. But this is not a primary question; much more important is understanding the nature of the present situation and learning how to do something about it. And the claim that earthly life as such is punishment is at the heart of this version of exilic religion. This motif comes to expression in the famous passage from Plato's *Cratylus* according to which the body is to be viewed as both a tomb and a prison for the soul.[24]

This interpretation of guilt and punishment is as radically new to Greek experience as the soul-body dualism in which it is embedded. The notion of gruesome post-mortem punishments for the wicked is already to be found in Homer. It is an important part of Orphic-Pythagorean religion. But the distinctively exilic feature is the quite different notion that earthly life, regardless of good or bad fortune, is itself to be viewed as punishment. Put simply, the point is that life in the body is hell.[25] Being-in-the-world is exile.

It is thus with good reason that Nilsson writes, "The greatness of Orphicism lies . . . in the incontestable originality which made the individual in his relationship to guilt and retribution the center of its teaching."[26] The emphasis on the individual here should not go unnoticed, for it probably provides the clue to the sociological background of the revolution before us.[27] But it is not necessary, however, to pursue the sociological question in order to grasp the central fact. "The wages of sin is in this case that life upon earth which for the soul is death. The whole multiplicity of the universe, emptied of its innocent and natural sequence of cause and effect, appears to these zealots under the uniform aspect of a correlation between crime and punishment, between pollution and purification."[28]

Reference to purification reminds us that exilic religion is not just an account of sin and punishment but also of salvation. The daemon-soul is to be "the carrier of man's potential divinity" as well as of his "actual guilt." Or, to use another phrase of Dodd's, the entire scheme was to help make sense of the feeling of being "at once a god and a criminal."[29] We must turn to the account of purification and salvation.

The first thing to notice is that punishment is not itself purifying. Socrates suggests just punishment makes the soul better by ridding it of evil. Just as the medical art cures us of illness, so punishment cures us of injustice.[30] Whether and under what conditions this is true for human punishment of humans in the family and larger society, there is no sense of its being the case for the punishments central to Orphic-Pythagorean religion. Both the punishments of the world to come and those which are constituted by earthly life as such can be viewed as the paying of a penalty.[31] In that sense they can be viewed as progress toward the release from prison which would be a permanent release from the cycle of birth, death, and rebirth. But it is not simply a matter of serving time. For the punishment of being incarnate is itself the source of new defilements.[32] It's as if serving time in prison were itself a crime for which one's sentence could be increased. Instead of accepting prison life in the hopes of getting time off for good behavior, the only way to keep from becoming more deeply mired in pollution is to make every effort to escape.

If the hope at the core of the Orphic-Pythagorean gospel does not lie in simply accepting one's punishment as just, where is it to be found? Pausanius knew. He tells us that Orpheus "reached a position of great power owing to the belief that he had discovered how to initiate into communion with the gods, how to purify from sin, to cure diseases and to avert divine vengeance."[33]

There is a threefold path of purification which marks the way of salvation. It includes ritual, moral, and philosophical purification. The distinction between the first two might well have seemed less self-evident to the original believers than to us, and we might have difficulty deciding whether the vegetarianism which was a central part of this religious life is to be understood in ritual or moral terms.

We don't know a great deal about the ritual purifications involved, but the central locus for them was the initiation rites which were so central to the cultic expressions of this religion. We do know that, at least in the eyes of Plato, they were subject to abuse and to the lapse into religious commercialism.[34]

The asceticism which defines exilic morality is more familiar. It includes abstaining from violence, and this is an important part of the rationale for vegetarianism (since in the context of reincarnation, taking the life of an animal might be taking a "human" life). It also includes that attempt to flee the pleasure of the body which is the primary connotation of asceticism and which represents the above-mentioned attempt to escape from prison so as to avoid further pollution and a renewed sentence. One catechism teaches, "Pleasure is in all circumstances bad; for we came here to be punished and we ought to be punished." And Empedocles seems to have become the first Manichee by repudiating sexual relations as such, whether within marriage or not.[35]

It is Plato who decisively gives this version of exilic religion its gnostic form by interpreting purification in terms of philosophy. The earlier forms of Orphic-Pythagorean religion prepared the way for this by the importance they placed on sacred writings and metaphysical doctrine and on the revelation of important truths as part of the initiation process.

The link between philosophy and purification (and thereby with the whole problem of guilt and worth) is revolutionary for both philosophy and religion. It means that philosophy cannot simply be science, that there must be an essential link between metaphysics and spirituality, and that the doing of philosophy cannot be an isolated skill or part-time activity, but has to be the integrating center for the whole of life. It also means that religion cannot be reduced to ritual or even to the combination of ritual with morality. In this way religion is freed from the temptation to succumb to the crass commercialism just mentioned and from the even more subtle temptation to identify the spiritual life with either civic virtue or the more strenuous heroics of asceticism. As important as ritual and morality are to the religious life, the contact with the sacred which lies at the center cannot be bought with either money or good deeds. And for Plato and a long tradition after him, the something more that is needed is philosophy. He summarizes his dual revolution in this way. "Wisdom itself is a sort of purification. Perhaps the people who direct the religious initiations are not so far from the mark, and all the time there has been allegorical meaning beneath their doctrine that he who enters the next world uninitiated and unenlightened shall lie in the mire, but he who arrives there purified and enlightened shall dwell among the gods. You know how the initiation practitioners say, 'Many bear the emblems, but the devotees are few'? Well, in my opinion these devotees are simply those who have lived the philosophical life in the right way."[36]

Here, as throughout the tradition, purification from the stain of guilt is explicitly linked to the question of death. The immediate object of purification is to be permitted in the afterlife to "dwell among the gods," to participate in that "Banquet of the Pure" which connotes a kind of celestial (if underworld) carousal.[37] This underworld version of Elysium, the Fields of the Blessed, is all the more important in view of the alternative which awaits those not admitted. Plato's description of lying in the mire is about the mildest picture available. The usual accounts of the post-mortem punishments awaiting those who die polluted by their sins are a good deal more graphic, as in Book X of the *Republic* and Book VI of the *Aeneid*.

But this immediate avoidance of punishment cannot be the ultimate goal. For these two alternatives are only temporary conditions prior to rebirth to an earthly life which itself is viewed as punishment. The ultimate goal, here as in every reincarnation scheme, is permanent release from the cycle of birth, death, and rebirth.

The question which arises about this final salvation is whether the anti-worldly theme is carried through to the end or whether Orphic-Pythagorean religion is better described as other-worldly than as anti-worldly. In such a case it would not be worldly existence as such that is rejected, but life in this world, which is to be fled for the sake of life in a better world. This would clearly be the case if the "Banquet of the Pure" were to be viewed as the ultimate goal. But it clearly is not, and whether the ultimate destiny of the pure is properly described as freedom from worldhood as such is simply not clear.

At first it may seem clearer than it is. Plato's account of the life of the gods in the *Phaedrus* with the splendid procession led by Zeus and the banquets held at the very top of the heavens would appear to be a very worldly locus for the soul's ultimate destiny. Nor does Empedocles seem to suggest any unambiguous dissolution of the structure of self and world. As Kahn puts it, "Unlike his fellow believers in transmigration, the mystics of India, Empedocles does not imply that the purified spirit will lose itself in Death as a drop of water loses itself in the sea. On this point the modern Orphic scholars tend to be slightly more "Orphic" than their ancient originals. If immortality in Empedocles' view cannot be defined as the personal survival of a particular human being, still less can it be identified with the escape from individuality as such. Empedocles is no more a Buddhist than he is a Christian. The terms he uses suggest the continued, harmonious co-existence of discrete individuals, very much like the celestial cavalcade of gods and spirits in the *Phaedrus*."[38]

And yet there are indications that it is not that simple. Plato always introduces his mythological and pictorial excursions into eschatology with the kind of disclaimers which prevent our taking them at their literal face value. Moreover, in the *Phaedrus* itself the ultimate destiny of the soul is not the heaven in which the gods live but that "heaven which is above the heavens" about which Plato asks "What earthly poet ever did or ever will sing worthily?"[39] It is anything but clear that the description which he then offers of pure being and its purely intellectual apprehension can in any meaningful sense be designated as a worldly life, though the distinction between subject and object is retained, at least grammatically.

The case of Empedocles is just as puzzling. It is true, as Kahn points out, that he does not use the metaphors of absorption familiar from the Upanishadic tradition. But when we remember that all the faculties which constitute the being-in-the-world of the finite self are attributed by him to the psyche which does not survive death and not to the daemon which does, it looks as if the immortal and divine part with which he ultimately identifies may not be the sort of thing capable of or interested in personal, worldly existence. Something more like the vision of the *Aeneid's* Book VI may be envisioned, where the final hope is "to become one with the divine mind which is at the same time the fiery *aither*, at once the encompasser and the orderer of the universe."[40] Speaking of the Orphic-Pythagorean tradition, Guthrie says "there can be little doubt that the ultimate aim was annihilation of self in reunion with the divine."[41]

9C. Exilic religion in the west: the Gnostic tradition

When Gnosticism is described as "Platonism run wild,"[42] it is to the Orphic and Pythagorean elements of Platonic spirituality that reference is made. It is in the variety of writings now referred to as Gnostic that exilic religion came to expression in the west during the simultaneous decline of Greco-Roman civilization and emergence of Christianity.

There is disagreement as to how inclusive the "Gnostic" umbrella should be. Probably the most generous scholar, on this question, is Hans Jonas. When he speaks of the "oriental wave" in the Hellenistic world, he includes not only those groups which would be considered gnostic on any account, but a good deal that would not normally be, including Marcion, Manichaeism, Neoplatonism, and Christianity.[43] In what follows I shall exclude Neoplatonism and orthodox Christianity, but shall otherwise follow Jonas in speaking of Gnosticism inclusively rather than narrowly.[44] The primary reason for this is that while there are striking differences of style, image, and doctrine there is a common spirit that runs throughout. Even Arthur Darby Nock, who tends to stress differences much more than Jonas, acknowledges that the "mood" of escape is widespread, that there is a "nearness of feeling" and a common "way of thinking" which unites superficially disparate writings.[45] Others speak of the Gnostic "stance" or the Gnostic "tendency" and its recurring "structures."[46] It is clear that any substantive account of what the (inclusively designated)

Gnostic writings share would have to be in terms of anti-worldly religious themes. The salvation of the individual is to be understood as escape from the world, conceived as a place of exile in which the true self can find no true home.

In view of the oft-mentioned continuity with the Orphic-Pythagorean tradition and the description of Gnosticism as "Platonism run wild," we will not be surprised to find the sharp soul-body dualism combined with strong hostility toward the body and toward the world of space, time, and matter as the natural home of the body, and thus at once a prison and an exile for the soul. In *The Gospel of Thomas*, for example, bodily-worldly existence is described as a dreadful nightmare. "Either there is a place to which they are fleeing, or without strength they come from having chased after others, or they are involved in striking blows, or they are receiving blows themselves, or they have fallen from high places, or they take off into the air though they do not even have wings. Again, sometimes it is as if people were murdering them, though there is no one even pursuing them, or they themselves are killing their neighbors, for they have been stained with their blood."[47] Although the imagery is different here, there are echoes of Empedocles' dour description of life in this "Meadow of Disaster," just as there are in the claim that "all the parts of nature that surround us come from the impure cadavers of the powers of evil."[48] The world is already hell.[49]

There is nothing essentially new here. But Gnosticism has also been described as "a dualism more radical that Plato's."[50] What makes it so is not simply its hostility to the body and its world but the way in which the body's world is set in radical opposition to God. To the dualism of soul and body there is added the antithesis of God and world. Since the soul is divine, this serves to intensify the alienation between it and the world. Thus Plotinus' polemic against the Gnostics can be summarized by saying that they "think very well of themselves and very ill of the universe. Each of them is a 'son of God,' superior even to heaven. . . ."[51]

But it is the intensity and thoroughness of the antithesis of God and world, not its mere existence, which makes Gnostic dualism more radical than Orphic-Pythagorean-Platonic dualism. In Gnostic thought "the very origin of the world was attributed to a terrible fault, and evil was given status as the ultimate ruler of the world. . . ."[52] The world is not so much a field of conflict between good and evil as the product and permanent domain of "the Adversary." For, "to the majority of Gnostics it was unthinkable that such a world should have been created by the Supreme God: it must be the handiwork of some

inferior demiurge—either, as Valentinus thought, an ignorant daemon unaware of any better possibility; or, as Marcion thought, the
harsh and unintelligent God of the Old Testament; or again, as in
other systems, some angel or angels in revolt against God."[53]

So the conflict is not simply between God and the soul on one hand
and the body and its world on the other. The enemy is the world
and its God, and Gnosticism is a revolt against both.[54] Plotinus is fully
aware of this; he does not merely complain that Gnostics think "very
ill of the universe." It is true that they "cavil at the Universe" and
"censure the constitution of the Kosmos." But they go beyond this
"to despise this Sphere, and the Gods within it. . . ." They "revile
the Administrator of this All. . . ." While Epicurus denies Providence,
this doctrine is even worse, for "it carps at Providence and the Lord
of Providence."[55]

The world is still a prison from which escape is to be made, but
attention is shifted from the prison as such to the guards and the
warden, whose single-minded purpose it is to prevent any escapes.
The personification of the opposition is what brings the intensity of
Gnostic dualism to a new level. For the Gnostics "the universe, the
domain of the Archons, is like a vast prison whose innermost dungeon
is the earth, the scene of man's life. Around and above it the cosmic
spheres are ranged like concentric enclosing shells. . . . The religious
significance of this cosmic architecture lies in the idea that everything
which intervenes between here and the beyond serves to separate
man from God, not merely by spatial distance but through active
demonic force. . . . The spheres are the seats of the Archons, especially of the 'Seven,' that is, of the planetary gods borrowed from
the Babylonian pantheon. It is significant that these are now often
called by Old Testament Names for God. . . . The Archons collectively rule over the world, and each individually in his sphere is
warder of the cosmic prison. Their tyrannical world-rule is called
heimarmene, universal Fate, a concept taken over from astrology but
now tinged with the gnostic anti-cosmic spirit. . . . As guardian of his
sphere, each Archon bars the passage to the souls that seek to ascend
after death, in order to prevent their escape from the world and their
return to God. The Archons are also the creators of the world, except
where this role is reserved for their leader, who then has the name
of *demiurge* (the world-artificer in Plato's *Timaeus*) and is often painted
with the distorted features of the Old Testament God."[56]

This cosmology involves the systematic persuasive redefinition of
the concepts of matter, fate, and creation. In the Gnostic setting,
matter is no longer merely a passive, inertial resistance to the good-

ness of form. It is active, personified opposition. Accordingly, while the Persian Manichees speak of Ahriman, the Zoroastrian name for the god of Darkness, and Arabic-speaking Manichees speak of the Arch-Devil, Greek- and Syriac-speaking Manichees speak of *Hyle*, Matter. "There can be no doubt that Mani himself . . . used this Greek term for his principle of evil; but it is equally certain that 'Matter' has here always the function of a mythological figure and not that of a philosophical concept. Not only is it personified, but it has an active spiritual nature of its own without which it could not be 'evil.'. . . Mani ascribes to it powers, movements, and strivings of its own which differ from those of God only by being evil. . . . So far is Matter from being the passive substratum of the philosophers that the Darkness with which it is identical is even alone the originally active of the two opposed principles, and the Light in its repose is forced into action only by an initial attack of the Darkness."[57]

In similar fashion, Fate ceases to be the impersonal necessity of philosophical speculation and becomes frighteningly personified as a variety of planetary demons who are its executive agents. One can say that Matter and Fate have not merely been mythologized, but demonized.

But the most dramatic and revolutionary demonization of all is that of the Creator, who becomes the Cosmic Bad Guy in Gnostic thinking. It is virtually self-evident in Gnostic perspective that he (or they) who guards the prison and dictates its rules is the one who built it in the first place. The decisive split between Gnosticism and orthodox Christianity would have been necessary if for no other reason than that the Yahweh of the Old Testament, whom the orthodox Christians viewed as "the Father of our Lord Jesus Christ," was so far from being either his father or ours that it was the mission of Christ (in Christian forms of Gnosticism) to rescue us from his tyrannical domain.

In the Manichaean account the creation of Adam and Eve was "a deliberate countermove, in fact the grand countermove, of the Darkness against the strategy of Light." For the King of Darkness pours into them all the Light that he wishes to keep from returning to its source. The act of procreation by which this occurs "is described with much repulsive circumstance, involving copulations between the male and female demons, devouring of the progeny by their King, et cetera."[58] One might say that for Gnosticism the thought of creation conjures up images of Walpurgis Night.

In addition to being cunning and repulsive, the Creator is presented as an arrogant pretender. In unmistakable identity with Yahweh, he says, "I am God, and there is no other God beside me."[59] But when he does so he is repudiated as blind, arrogant, an impious sinner, and as both ignorant and a liar. He is called Samael, meaning god of the blind, the chief of the Authorities of Darkness and the First Father of Chaos. He is the begetter of death, and his actions lead even his own son and mother to feel shame and repent.[60]

If creation and the rule of the Creator are the original sin, then disobedience of his law would be a virtue and the serpent, who advocates such disobedience in the Garden of Eden, would have to be the hero of that story. When the story of Eden is told from this perspective, the command not to eat of the tree of knowledge is the product of malicious envy and jealousy on the part of the creator-demiurge or his cohorts, the Rulers, the Authorities of Darkness. The curse upon Adam and Eve and the serpent also comes from the "chief Ruler," the "arrogant Ruler." The serpent's role, by contrast, is that of Instructor. He is the repository of true wisdom, and he speaks the truth when he tells Adam and Eve that they will not die but be like gods. Not surprisingly, the serpent blends quite easily into the figure of Jesus.[61]

With Jesus playing Prometheus to Yahweh's Zeus, the demonization of the Creator is complete and one can see why Gnosticism can be described as "a dualism more radical than Plato's." There remain two questions about Gnosticism in relation to the present study. How does its radical exilic dualism relate to the themes of guilt and death? And is it resolutely anti-worldly, or just otherworldly? In other words, is it just this world or worldhood as such which it negates with such vehemence?

It is often suggested that Gnosticism interprets the human predicament in terms of ignorance and error rather than sin and guilt, that "the gnostic concept of salvation has nothing to do with the remission of sin ('sin' itself having no place in gnostic doctrine, which puts 'ignorance' in its place). . . ."[62] While such statements are not entirely without foundation, they are fundamentally misleading. It is true, as the very name Gnosticism suggests, that salvation is interpreted in terms of the triumph of knowledge over ignorance. And it is important to note that this saving knowledge is never the product of methodical, human rationality. It is either magical knowledge for use in outwitting the Archons in making one's escape from the cosmos, or, more frequently, it is the metaphysical knowledge about one's own true identity and current condition of exile here on earth as taught in the esoteric writings of the tradition. Jesus' identification with the Serpent who is also the Instructor fits in with this scheme. The Heavenly Savior comes to combat error with enlightenment.

But all this is misleading by virtue of incompleteness if taken to suggest that Gnostics were untroubled by guilt and, in association with it, death. Dodds has called the age when Gnosticism flourished an Age of Anxiety, characterized by moral as well as material insecurity. With reference to Gnosticism he offers two reasons for viewing it in this light. On the one hand he points to the frequency with which Gnostic writers take up the Orphic-Pythagorean theme that life in the body is a punishment for sin, sometimes for the sin of pride in choosing to become incarnate. On the other hand he suggests that the rigid dualism of body and soul is itself "an index of intense and widespread guilt-feelings" and that in response people "were able to endure themselves by making a sharp dichotomy between the self and the body, and diverting their resentment on to the latter."[63]

There is a double claim here, first, that the problem of guilt is central to Gnostic experience and, second, that it was dealt with in two nearly opposite ways. Both these claims are well supported by the evidence.

So far as the first claim is concerned, it simply isn't the case that talk about ignorance and error, knowledge and enlightenment crowds out all thought of guilt in relation to death. For example, in *The Gospel of Thomas* Jesus tells Thomas, "Whoever finds the interpretation of these sayings will not experience death." The sayings are addressed to those who are estranged from the Father by intoxication and blindness, two standard Gnostic images of ignorance. But sobering up and learning to see is not just a matter of instruction and understanding but also of repentance.[64] In *The Apocalypse of Peter* it is naturally Peter to whom the Savior speaks. Those "without perception" participate in the false kingdom of "the worker of death." They think "that they will become pure. But they will become greatly defiled and they will fall into a name of error." Such souls are not "of the truth, nor of immortality," but each "has death assigned to it." Those who are "from what is not good" face destruction and death, while those who are "in the Eternal One" face life and immortality. Those who oppose the truth are "the messengers of error," but passing over from the one side to the other is again not merely a matter of knowledge but of receiving "my forgiveness of their transgressions into which they fell through their adversaries" and thereby of escaping the "punishment" which would otherwise fall to the enemies of the truth.[65] Here and throughout the tradition, ignorance and sin are more nearly like two sides of the same coin than two separate and independent issues. And it is especially in relation to death that the matter becomes pressing.

If the centrality of the problematic of ignorance and knowledge does not in any way eliminate that of guilt and worth in the face of death but rather blends in with the latter, it does so in such a way as to permit two quite different "solutions." The first is indicated in Dodds's reference to the Orphic-Pythagorean notion of incarnation as punishment. It involves the acceptance by the individual of personal responsibility for whatever guilt or lack of worth makes life and especially death troublesome. Salvation can occur if and when, in spite of that guilt, punishment can be either terminated or cancelled all together and a sense of worth restored. In the passages we have just looked at this occurs in the mode of divine forgiveness which is made possible by human repentance on the one hand and divine mercy on the other.

The other mode of dealing with guilt as a sense of insufficient worth is indicated in Dodds's reference to soul-body dualism as a diverting of resentment (directed toward oneself and grounded in guilt) to the body. This strategy for dealing with guilt can be called shifting the blame. We have already encountered it in Section 4C as the juvenile delinquent's Denial of Responsibility.[66] By treating the body as a disposable garment quite distinct from the true self which is divine and by accounting for evil in terms of the former, the Gnostic accomplishes the same thing that the delinquent does by calling his criminal behavior a "social disease," the product of an environment for which he is not responsible. By placing the origin of evil outside themselves those who would otherwise be troubled with guilt are able "to endure themselves."

But the Gnostic "demonization" of the world means that matter and the body are not in themselves the ultimate origin of evil. Eventually the blame gets passed on to higher levels. Plotinus was especially sensitive to this aspect of Gnosticism. In the passages where he complains that they "cavil at the Universe," "revile the Administrator of this All," and "censure the constitution of the Kosmos," he notes that in doing so they "make the Soul blameable for the association with body" and teach that "guilt inheres in the Primal Beings."[67] It is important to recognize here that the Soul is a cosmic principle, one of the Primal Beings and not my soul or yours. Thus in both phrases Plotinus is noting the Gnostics' desire to shift the blame not merely from their own true self to the body they disown, but to higher and more powerful beings. The title Ricoeur gives to this strategy in Greek experience is equally apt for Gnosticism: "The Wicked God and the 'Tragic' Vision of Existence."[68]

Of all the broadly Gnostic schools of thought, the school founded by Mani is in one respect the most important. It is the only one to have any very widespread influence as an organized religion.[69] If we turn to Manichaeism to see what Gnosticism looks like as a semi-successful religion, we find that the two methods of dealing with guilt exist side by side. In its liturgy it turns to repentance and forgiveness, while in its cosmology it practices the metaphysical shifting of blame which conjures up the categories of tragedy.

Our knowledge of Manichaean liturgy comes from a remarkable collection of Coptic psalms. The most significant group of these for the questions before us is called Psalms of the Bema, "sung in honour of and at the feast of the Bema, at which Mani's death and passion were commemorated and the coming judgment of the world fore-shadowed."[70] The psalms consist very largely of calls to confession and repentance and even more of petitions addressed to the Judge (sometimes the Father, sometimes Mani, the Savior who presides at the final judgment) for forgiveness and remission of sins. The first psalm in the group opens with this line: "We pray thee, our God, the merciful, forgive us our sins."[71] In its simplicity and in its appeal to the mercy of the Judge, it is typical of these prayers.[72]

A second group of psalms takes a somewhat different tack. The editor calls them Psalms to Jesus, in lieu of the lost title from the manuscripts. They are somewhat more explicit about the presence of death as a threat, quite possibly because they were not, like the Bema psalms, used in a liturgical setting where that was so obvious as to need little mention. But they differ primarily from the first group in that instead of simply appealing to the mercy of the Judge for forgiveness they tend to recite their good deeds and the merit of their knowledge as a basis for help "in the hour of my need." But the question of worth in the face of sin and death remains primary.[73]

The emphasis on knowledge is present, though muted, in these Psalms. But here as elsewhere it is blended in with the themes of sin and forgiveness rather than being an alternative to them. We read

Forgive the sins of them that know thy mystery, to whom
  there has been revealed the knowledge of the secret of the Most High
  through the holy wisdom wherein there is no Error,
  of thy holy Church of the Paraclete, our Father. . . .
Sin mourns because thou didst suddenly escape
  and didst not follow after his error. . . .[74]

What is especially remarkable about all this is its peaceful co-existence alongside the motifs of demonic forces and divine tragedy which shift the blame for evil away from the individual, who then needs neither to appeal for forgiveness nor to list his meritorious accomplishments, moral and cognitive, in order to face death with a sense of personal worth. These motifs are implicit in the dualistic metaphysics of Manichaeism. They occasionally work their way into the Psalms, as when we read

The God of this Aeon has shut the heart of the unbelieving and has sunk them in his Error and the deceit of drunkenness. He has
made them blaspheme. . . .[75]

But it is especially from Augustine that we are made sensitive to this aspect of Manichaeism. In his *Confessions* we find echoes of Plotinus' complaint against the Gnostics for shifting the blame for evil from human to divine beings, this time directed particularly against the religion he once espoused. He acknowledges that he was attracted to the astrologers because "they say, 'The cause of your sin is inevitably determined by the stars' and 'Venus was responsible here, or Saturn or Mars.' As though man, who is flesh and blood and proud corruption, should be guiltless and the guilt should be laid upon the creator and the ruler of heaven and of the stars.'"[76] It has been suggested that the same motivation was important to his much deeper involvement in Manichaeism. "The elaborate avoidance of any intimate sense of guilt would later strike Augustine as the most conspicuous feature of his Manichaean phase. . . . The Manichees have been presented as the purveyors of the bleakest pessimism. Yet they reserved this pessimism for only one side of themselves. They regarded the other side, their 'mind', their 'good soul', as quite untarnished: it was, quite literally, a crumb of the divine substance. . . . For Augustine, the need to save an untarnished oasis of perfection within himself formed, perhaps, the deepest strain of his adherence to the Manichees."[77]

The passages in the *Confessions* which suggest such a reading are very direct. They combine the themes of human innocence and divine tragedy, repudiated now by Augustine as forms of sinful pride, but recognized as part of the powerful attraction of Manichaean teaching. "And how could anything be more proud than to assert, as I did in my incredible folly, that I was by nature what you are? . . . I preferred to think that you also were subject to change rather than I was not what you are. . . . I accused the flesh. . . . And I preferred to maintain that your unchangeable substance went astray

under compulsion, rather than admit that my own changeable substance had deviated of its own accord and for its punishment had
fallen into error."⁷⁸ For more than a decade, while living a life in
violation of the Christian and Ciceronian ideals of his childhood and
adolescence, Augustine salved his potentially troubled conscience with
these ideas.

While the centrality of the problem of guilt and death for Gnostic
experience emerges with special clarity in the Manichaean tradition,
the plurality of its answer remains striking. To those who, in the face
of death and the prospect of judgment, experienced fear, alarm, and
dread,⁷⁹ Manichaean religion offered not one, nor even two, but three
distinct replies: (1) Lord, have mercy, (2) Lord, here are the good
deeds by which I merit your favor, and (3) I didn't do it—it wasn't
my fault. The last is evidently most closely in keeping with the Manichaean world-view, but we have already seen that the first two play
a prominent role in the actual religious life of the devotees. What is
lacking is any coherent account of the relation of these quite divergent solutions to the problem of guilt to one another and to the
concept of salvation. We will find answers to these questions from
another quarter in the next section, and with them a more coherent
and complete version of exilic religion. But before we turn eastward,
there remains a final question about Gnosticism. Is it resolutely anti-
worldly? Is it worldhood as such or just this world which it repudiates?

It would be easy to find Gnostic texts which indicate that the individual—who by virtue of forgiveness, merit, or innocence, combined with the appropriate knowledge, is freed at death from life in
the body and its world—can look forward to life in a better, body-
free world, the Kingdom of God or of Light. For example, in Psalm
223, the Manichees speak of a great building which is being built
outside this world, which in turn is to be destroyed by fire when the
former is completed. Then Darkness and the Enemy will be banished
and all the Light will be reunited. "A new Aeon will be built in the
place of the world that shall dissolve, that in it the powers of the
Light may reign."

But as in the Orphic-Pythagorean case, such imagery is not in itself
decisive. There are two indications that the brave new world which
has no bodies in it may not really be a world at all, a place in which
more or less individuated experience can occur, situated in a context
of meaningful spaces and times, things and persons.

The first such indication is grounded in the fact that hatred of the
body has as its correlate the divinity of the soul. This means not only
that self-knowledge is in fact the knowledge of God,⁸⁰ but also that

in the story of the individual's redemption and rescue from the world by the Divine Messenger, subject and object, Savior and saved are one. Once free of error's bondage in this world, the true self is free to enter into God once again and become in fact what it has always been by nature, one with him.[81]

If this oneness means only that the saved have the same nature as the Savior, there can easily remain enough plurality for life beyond this world to be in some genuine sense a worldly life. But if the oneness means that the saved are parts of the divine whole, fragments of a single substance, it is not clear that one could meaningfully speak of a new and better world at all. But it is precisely the latter kind of language one finds. The divine is an immutable substance, often represented as Light, portions of which get dispersed and eventually mixed with Matter or Darkness. Salvation requires the separation and regathering of these fragments, not just for their sake but to restore the wholeness and integrity of the divine substance.[82] When "the Light shall go to the Light,"[83] it would seem that there is a oneness beyond any notion of being-in-the-world.

This possibility is strengthened by passages which seem to contain a critique of the whole realm of name and form analogous to that found in the *Upanishads* and Vedantist texts. The theme of unity without form is about as succinct a formula for worldlessness as one can find.[84]

The other indication that Gnosticism may be more thoroughly anti-worldly than some of its images would at first suggest lies in its "Empedoclean" interpretation of the dualism of soul and body. In the previous section we noted that the usual language of mind or soul-body dualism is not sophisticated enough to say what Empedocles wants to say. The *psyche* as the totality of intellectual, volitional, and emotional aspects of being-in-the-world belongs, with the body, to the order of nature. The true self, which is divine, he calls "daemon."

A similar distinction is made within Gnosticism, which regularly treats body and soul as products of the cosmos, or, as the Valentinians put it, "even the soul is a product of the defect."[85] Thus the true self is to be distinguished just as much from the "empirical soul" or the "*psychical* envelopments or garments" of the body as from the body itself.[86] It is rather to be characterized as spirit (*pneuma*, or sometimes *nous*). Thus it is spirits without souls that are the spark of the divine and which are able to re-enter the godhead.[87]

Once again a definitive interpretation is not possible. We are not told explicitly whether spirits wish to leave this world because it is material or simply because it is a world. The one clue that it may be the latter case is that in distinguishing the true spiritual self so carefully from both body and soul, both the material and the mental dimensions of the only being-in-the-world we know are denied to spiritual life. Only knowledge remains, but what kind? It is not psychic knowledge. Does this mean merely that it is not dependent upon sensation or that it is knowledge which goes beyond judgment as such because its home is in the Undivided? We cannot be sure.

Gnosticism points us in the direction of a more consistent and single-minded exilic mentality. Whether it was itself such a world-view as taught to its adherents and the ambiguity is only apparent to those trying to decipher its meaning from outside or whether it was in itself undecided we must leave undecided. We cannot say with any confidence what coherent relationship, if any, there may be among the three "solutions" it offers to the problem of guilt; and we cannot say with any confidence whether it is thoroughly anti-worldly or only otherworldly. But there are versions of exilic spirituality which resolve these ambiguities, and it is to one of them we now turn.

9D. Exilic religion in Shankara's Advaita (non-dualist) Vedanta

Like every living religious tradition, Hinduism is a rich and complex tapestry of ideas and practices that fits as a whole into no neat categories. But in the radically non-dualist interpretation of Vedanta (one of the six systems of orthodox Hinduism) by Shankara, whose dates are usually given as 788 to 820 A.D., we have one of the most systematic and single-minded expressions of exilic religion to be found anywhere.

Shankara is a gnostic. Ignorance is the source of all evil and suffering, and salvation is to be won through knowledge. "As fire is the direct cause of cooking, so Knowledge, and not any other form of discipline, is the direct cause of Liberation; for Liberation cannot be attained without Knowledge. Action cannot destroy ignorance, for it is not in conflict with ignorance. Knowledge alone destroys ignorance, as light destroys dense darkness."[88] As we shall see, among the actions and disciplines which do not bring about liberation are those of ethics and religion. Neither the deeds of moral uprightness, nor those of religious ritual, nor those of religious devotion are of any avail unless they be means to "the complete comprehension of Brahman [which] is the highest end of man."[89]

The ignorance that knowledge must overcome is not a passive lack of information but an active misperception. It involves seeing what is not there instead of what is, or to use a favorite term of Shankara's, it is the superimposition of what is not there upon what is. This notion of superimposition is explained with a series of metaphors. In the twilight one may see a rope and take it to be a snake or see a post and take it to be a man. Again, under the right lighting conditions, mother-of-pearl or oyster shells may look like silver. The moon may be "seen" to move, when it is in fact clouds that are moving, and to someone with defective vision, the single moon may appear double. The audience at a magic show "sees" effects which the magician does not see because they are in fact not happening. Wanderers on a salty steppe "see" water that is not a reality but only a mirage, just as dreamers "see" and "experience" events which their waking selves know did not really occur. All of these metaphors by which the concept of superimposition is spelled out are simply more or less ordinary human experiences of "seeing" what is in fact not there to be seen.[90] By their use Shankara tells us the whole of ordinary experience is a systematic misperception of this sort.

Brahman is the only true reality, the one object of knowledge. But just as the rope, which is really there, is given the characteristics of the snake which is not, so in ignorance we superimpose upon the reality of Brahman characteristics which do not belong. Following the *via negativa* of the Upanishads, Shankara seeks to lead us to an understanding of what Brahman is through a systematic understanding of what Brahman is not.[91] The meaning of the formulas in which Brahman may be said to be defined and the ultimate truth expressed cannot be understood apart from this dialectical process.

Since ignorance is a form of (mis)perception, it has its proper object just as knowledge does. The totality of the objects of ignorance makes up the world of ignorance. It has two names. From the experiential point of view it is *samsara*, the veil of tears in which we suffer from one life to rebirth in another in a transmigratory cycle governed by the relentless law of *karma*, according to which all good is rewarded and all evil punished. Since our continued existence in *samsara* is by itself proof that our moral debts are still unpaid, life is like that of a prisoner regularly transferred from one prison to another, or like the life of an exile who cannot even find a permanent place of exile.

From the epistemological and ontological point of view, however, *samsara* is the world of *maya* or illusion. It is the product of ignorance or misperception and it is not really there. Like the notion of ignorance (*avidya*), this notion of illusion (*maya*) is to be understood in terms of the snake-rope family of metaphors. Thus we find Shankara saying that the world of ordinary experience, in which there is a distinction between the subject as enjoyer and the object as enjoyed, does not exist in reality.[92] He appeals to the Upanishads' claim "that for him who sees that everything has its Self in *Brahman* the whole phenomenal world with its actions, agents, and results of actions is non-existent. Nor can it be said that this non-existence of the phenomenal world is declared (by scripture) to be limited to certain states."[93] From the same scriptures he concludes that "for him who has reached the state of truth and reality the whole apparent world does not exist."[94] In aphoristic form he puts it this way: "The world, filled with attachments and aversions, and the rest, is like a dream: it appears to be real as long as one is ignorant, but becomes unreal when one is awake."[95]

In these passages the totality of what is falsely taken to be there when it is not is variously described as the world of ordinary experience, the phenomenal world, the apparent world, and simply the world. That the scope of the world-negation involved here goes beyond repudiating the body for the sake of the soul will become increasingly clear as the nature of this world is spelled out in detail. But the shape of things to come is already clear. For the self as enjoyer, as agent, as filled with attachments and aversions is every bit as much a part of the dream world of unreality as the objective correlates of those modes of selfhood are. The world of *maya* is not that of the body from which the soul must seek escape. It is rather the world within which the distinction of subject and object occurs and in which subject and object are equally illusory.

Once again following the Upanishads, Shankara spells this out by identifying the world of *maya* with the world of name and form. The determinations by which anything is distinguished from anything else make possible a world of plurality. Epistemically they are names, ontologically forms. We would speak of predicates and properties. But for Shankara all duality, all difference belongs to *maya*. It is in fact the essential mark of *maya*. Brahman, Infinite Consciousness, the True Self is totally beyond all the distinctions which name and form make possible,[96] which, in turn, are to be understood solely as the product of ignorance.[97]

It goes without saying that my body is a product of name and form and thus of illusion and ignorance. But this is equally true of the distinction between one self and another.[98] No mind-body dualism enables me here to affirm my soul while saying no to my body. Both the physical conditions of presence to other bodies and the personal conditions of presence to other selves are in the final analysis unreal. But this has dramatic consequences. Not only is Shankara compelled to teach, "I am other than the body." He must complete this by teaching, "I am other than the mind."[99] Not only the physical world of space, time, and causality, but also the mental world of I-consciousness belongs to ignorance and illusion.[100]

Shankara is remarkably thorough in specifying every aspect of I-consciousness as belonging to *maya*. The cognitive self that says, I know, the appetitive self that says, I want, the active self that says, I did it, the possessive self which says, I own it, and the dialogical self which says, I and Thou—all of these capacities and the individuated self-consciousness which belongs to each are assigned, along with the body and the senses, to the ultimately unreal domain of name and form. To win Brahman is to leave all this behind.[101]

Two of these negations are of special importance. The self as agent is a fundamental presupposition of the moral life, and the self as I over against Thou is a fundamental presupposition of the religious life, understood as a relation of human persons to God or the gods. Since the self presupposed by moral virtue and religious devotion (*bhakti*) is declared to be unreal, the goal is clearly not to replace the evil self with the good or the faithless self with the faithful. It is to transcend the whole realm where morality and religion (thus understood) make sense.

It does not follow for Shankara that we should live as we please. "For an unillumined person there is an imperative need of practicing ethical disciplines, prayer, and worship. As long as he perceives a distinction between good and evil, he must follow the good and shun the evil; only thus, in the long run, can he go beyond the illusion of good and evil."[102] Virtue and devotion will bring material happiness on earth or in heaven, but only knowledge which discriminates the True Self from the upright and pious self brings liberation. For the Brahman which we truly are is entirely beyond the realm of action and thus beyond good and evil.[103] Similarly, the gods are themselves aspects of the illusory realm of name and form,[104] and the fundamental assumption that I am a self distinct from the gods whom I worship is a product of ignorance.[105] The clear and sustained insistence on this point is all the more remarkable when we discover how attuned Shankara himself was to the way of devotion. The hymns of praise and confession that he addressed to the gods are clearly an expression of his own deep prayer life and not merely exercises he constructed for the inferior many who could not understand and practice his philosophy.[106]

The purgative dialectic by which I refuse to indentify myself with my body or my mind, with my cognitive, appetitive, or active capacities, with my sense of personhood in relation to other persons, and with my ethical and worshipping tendencies, is not intended to lead, as in Buddhism, into the Void. It is rather to culminate in the discovery of the ultimate reality, of the highest truth that Brahman (or Atman) is everything.[107] Brahman is the "non-dual, indivisible, One . . . which is indicated by Vedanta as the irreducible substratum after the negation of all tangible objects."[108]

But the negation which culminates in Brahman is not so much a denial of the "tangibility" of objects as their plurality. It is not the touchability or even the general perceptability of the world which renders it *maya*, but its fundamental structure as a plurality of subjects and a plurality of objects in comportment with one another. As "non-dual, indivisible, One," Brahman/Atman is, as the Upanishads declare, "One without a second." "There is in it no diversity."[109] "When ignorance is destroyed, the Self, which does not admit of any multiplicity whatsoever, truly reveals Itself by Itself, like the sun when the cloud is removed."[110]

More important existentially, however, than either the discovery that all is Brahman or that Brahman is beyond all distinctions, is the discovery that I am this Brahman, that this Self is the True Self I have been seeking. My "relation" to this Brahman is one of identity. Shankara regularly expresses this with the upanishadic formula, "That art Thou," meaning that Brahman, all-encompassing and beyond all difference, is who I really am.[111]

Of course, even the statement "I am Brahman" can be made only by someone still at home in the world of name and form. When this truth is fully realized, it will be in a silence which finds no occasion to speak. But this silence is not oblivion any more than Brahman is the Void. The three basic affirmations about Brahman make this clear. Brahman is Existence-Knowledge-Bliss.[112] To speak of Brahman as Existence is to indicate simply that it is real while all else is not. To speak of Brahman as Knowledge or as Consciousness is to indicate that Brahman is life and not death, subject and not object, the ultimate Self. To speak of Brahman as Bliss is to indicate that this "Experience" is the salvation for which the believing soul has been seeking.

The middle term, consciousness, is clearly the crucial one. Without it there could be no meaning to the notion of bliss, and the metaphysical scheme, even if true, would have lost all touch with the religious life and its concern for salvation. But it is not at all clear how Brahman could be consciousness. For (ordinary) consciousness is always consciousness of. . . . It presupposes the distinction of subject and object and thus necessarily finds its home in the world of name and form. Brahman is said to be the ultimate self, the true subject. But how can there be a self without a world, and how can there be a subject without an object?

At this point the notion of *Turiya*, the Fourth, taken over from the *Mandukya Upanishad* becomes indispensable. *Turiya* is the fourth because it is to be distinguished from the three states of consciousness which pertain to ordinary, worldly consciousness. These are waking, dreaming, and deep (dreamless) sleep. Though we attribute a reality to the waking world which we deny to the world of dreams, both are obviously worlds of name and form, modes of *maya*. In dreamless sleep, by contrast, the distinction of subject and object falls away and "one does not behold the universe."[113] In this respect dreamless sleep is the condition in which the self "approaches most closely Its native purity."[114] Dreamless sleep can even be described as a kind of blessedness, and it is called the sheath of bliss. But it is not the bliss appropriate to Brahman, for this bliss is merely the absence of any conscious activity and thus of any suffering and pain; and it comes about not because ignorance has been transcended in knowledge, but because the mind which knows no home but *maya* is temporarily out of gear.[115]

Still, dreamless sleep is the empirical analogue for *Turiya*. *Samadhi*, meaning trance or ecstasy, is the temporary experience of oneness with Brahman. In *savikalpaka samadhi* I-consciousness and the distinction of subject and object still remain. "But in *nirvikalpaka samadhi*, absorption bereft of I-consciousness, the mind totally merges in Brahman, becomes one with It, and loses all distinction of knower, knowledge, and object of knowledge. Just as a lump of salt, when dissolved in water, so, likewise, the mental state, in the *nirvikalpaka samadhi*, taking the form of Brahman, is no longer perceived to be distinct from Brahman and cannot be separated from Brahman; it has no existence apart from Brahman. Then Brahman, or the Self, alone exists and shines by Its own radiance. Although the existence of the mind is not felt in dreamless sleep, either, yet these two states, namely, the *nirvikalpaka samadhi* and dreamless sleep, are totally dissimilar."[116]

Totally dissimiliar? The one is clearly being modeled on the other. And yet the difference is fundamental. For in dreamless sleep I become worldless by becoming unconscious, while in *nirvikalpaka samadhi* or *Turiya* I become worldless while remaining fully aware and alert. Thus the true knower of the self is the one "who sees nothing in the waking state, even as in dreamless sleep."[117] *Turiya* is thus that mode of awareness which is just like dreamless sleep except that it is consciousness. It is not consciousness of anything, nor is it I as

distinct from anyone else who is conscious. Pure Consciousness is
awareness from which all distinctions, including above all the distinction of subject and object, self and world, have disappeared as
completely as in dreamless sleep. But because it remains consciousness it can be called bliss in a literal and positive sense, while dreamless
sleep is the sheath of bliss only metaphorically and negatively.

Since it is not the abolition of consciousness but its systematic al-
teration which is to be sought, it is clear why meditation will have
primacy over the good deeds of both ascetic morality and religious
devotion as the path to salvation. For while the latter can be practiced
in the hope that somehow at death the knowledge (altered consciousness) which is liberation will suddenly occur, meditation is the
direct attempt to exchange worldly for worldless consciousness. When
Shankara continually insists on the superiority of knowledge to both
works and worship as the way to true life, he never means merely
the study and comprehension of his metaphysical scheme, but along
with that the meditational practice by which its truth can be directly
experienced.

In view of the close link suggested between the concept of salvation
on the one hand and the problems of guilt and death on the other,
it remains to ask how the bliss of oneness with Brahman is the overcoming of guilt and death. In a sense the answer is too obvious to
require stating. The false self which gets left behind in the realization
of the True Self is precisely the self which can fear death and experience the shame of guilt. Only for the self which still says I can
either guilt or death be troublesome.

It is in relation to this problematic of guilt and death that we can
understand the centrality of a cluster of predicates which emerges
in Shankara's presentation, attributed indifferently to Brahman, Atman, or myself (appropriately, since Brahman=Atman=I). This
Brahman-Atman which I myself am is eternal, changeless, immutable,
stainless, and pure.[118] The first three characteristics indicate that in
attaining Brahman I have overcome death; the latter two express my
overcoming of guilt. Immortality and innocence have been attained.
The regular juxtaposition of one or more predicates from the first
group with one or more from the second is one indication of how
closely the questions of guilt and death are linked in Shankara's concept of liberation. If we remember the meaning and importance of
the symbolism of stain, defilement, and purification as presented in
Section 6B, we will see that when Shankara says that "knowledge
purifies the embodied soul stained by ignorance . . ." and portrays

the true comtemplative as "undefiled,"[119] he is indeed talking about the problem of guilt as a question of fundamental worth.

For Shankara the "original sin" by which human existence is spoiled and from which it desperately needs to be set free is not disobedience, as in Genesis, but rather ignorance. But this ignorance is just as much the ultimate defilement of human life as that disobedience. My bondage in *samsara* is to be explained and justified just as much in terms of the ignorance which has not yet been overcome by knowledge as by the fact that, in terms of the law of *karma*, I have not yet paid the consequences of the evil I've done in this and previous earthly lives.

Shankara's use of the more obviously moral language associated with the theory of *karma* and reincarnation in parallel with the language of defilement and purification also helps us to see the moral significance of the latter. We have already seen that the agent self belongs to the realm of name and form.

The obvious consequence of this is that liberation takes me beyond the domain in which the distinction between good and evil deeds applies. Shankara places great stress on this fact that in attaining oneness with Brahman I pass beyond the scope of merit and demerit, of injunction and prohibition, of good and evil deeds. The result is that full and final liberation will assure that at death there is no return to the world in which I can be stained with evil and either rewarded for good or punished for evil.[120]

The innocence which goes with immortality for Shankara can thus be expressed either in terms of being beyond good and evil or in terms of being stainless and pure. This is how he sums it all up, using both kinds of language. "The illumined person realizes in his heart, through *samadhi*, the Infinite Brahman, undecaying and immortal, the positive Substance which precludes all negations, which resembles a serene and waveless ocean and is without a name, in which there are neither merits nor demerits—which is eternal, serene, and One." Emerging from his own *samadhi*, he cries out, "Where is the universe gone? By whom is it removed? And where is it merged? It was just seen by me; and has it ceased to exist? . . . I do not see anything; I do not hear anything; I do not know anything. I simply exist as the Self, the Eternal Bliss. Blessed am I; I have attained the Goal of my life. I am free from the clutches of transmigration . . . I am undecaying, immaculate, and eternal. I am neither the doer nor the enjoyer. I am changeless and beyond activity; I am the essence of Pure Knowledge. I am indeed Brahman, One without a second . . . beyond the illusion of 'you' or 'I,' 'this' or 'that'. . . . Like the sky, I am beyond contamination . . . I am unaffected by waking, dreaming, and deep sleep. . . . Merits and demerits cannot affect me. . . . Let this inert body drop away . . . I am not touched by what may happen to it. . . . I, Pure Consciousness, am ever free."[121]

In addition to the language of purification and of passing beyond good and evil, Shankara speaks in a third way of salvation as the overcoming of guilt, and here again the link with the overcoming of death is a close one. It is the language of confession and forgiveness in relation to a loving, personal god. We have already seen that both the moral life and the life of religious devotion are for Shankara ultimately illusory, but he consistently stresses the importance of moral rectitude and religious piety for those still within the realm of name and form where the differences between good and evil deeds and between any god and myself obtain. And we have just seen that he uses the language of the moral domain to express the meaning of salvation as liberation; so it should be no surprise that he also uses the language of I-Thou religious devotion (*bhakti*) for the same purpose.

This occurs in the various hymns to the gods (and gurus)[122] attributed to Shankara, poems of extraordinary lyrical beauty. Here, instead of liberation being solely a matter of knowledge to be attained by the disciplines of meditation, it is a gift of grace to be asked for in prayer.[123] An essential ingredient in this salvation is the overcoming of death.[124] But it is clear that it is not death as an event which comes at the end of life, but the fear of death which comes to pervade all of life which is the enemy.[125] It also becomes clear that death is fearful largely because of guilt; and in this context there emerges the penitential motif in Shankara's psalms.

Like Ramakrishna centuries later, Shankara turns with special passion to the Divine Mother. He acknowledges that he comes to her without merit and as one "lustful and foolish and greedy . . . ever enchained by the fetters of evil."

> Addicted to sinning and worthless companions
> A slave to ill thoughts and to doers of evil,
> Degraded am I, unrighteous, abandoned.
> Attached to ill objects, adept in ill-speaking:
> In Thee is my only haven of refuge,
> In Thee, my help and my strength, O Bhavani![126]

In another hymn to the Divine Mother Shankara addresses her as the "Supreme Purifier, who washest away all sins" and then as the "Giver of utter fearlessness . . . the Bestower of instantaneous Liberation, the Giver of Eternal Good!" Here the innocence of purity and forgiveness is explicitly linked to overcoming the fear of death and attaining eternal happiness.[127]

Shankara's hymns to Shiva, the Creator God of the Hindu pantheon, are much the same. They unite the request for forgiveness of sins with the hope of freedom from the fear of death.[128] But perhaps it is in his hymn to the sacred river Ganges (Ganga), addressed as a goddess, as "Thou who art stainless" and the "Savior of sinners,"[129] that Shankara's devotional piety is most succinctly expressed.

> O Mother Ganga! take away the burden
> Of wicked deeds that weighs upon me;
> Bear me across the ocean of the world. . . .
> He, Thy worshipper, O Mother Ganga!
> Never will be seized by the King of Death.
> ....
> If, by Thy grace, one bathes in the waters,
> Never need one enter a mother's womb:
> The sins of a lifetime for all annulling,
> The claims of destiny at death dispelling.
> Jahnavi! Ganga! the worlds accord Thee
> Honour and renown for the glory that is Thine.[130]

Guilt and Death in Mimetic Religion

10A. *Mimesis* as the renewal of innocent life

Mankind, everyone that exists,—what does he know?
Whether he is committing sin or doing good, he does not even know.
O my lord, do not cast thy servant down;
He is plunged into the waters of a swamp; take him by the hand.
The sin which I have done, turn into goodness;
The transgressions which I have committed, let the wind carry away;
My many misdeeds strip off like a garment. . . .
O god whom I know or do not know, (my) transgressions are seven
  times seven; remove my transgressions;
O goddess whom I know or do not know, (my) transgressions are seven
  times seven; remove my transgressions.
Remove my transgressions (and) I will sing thy praise.
May thy Heart, like the heart of a real mother, be quieted toward me
Like a real mother (and) a real father may it be quieted toward me.[1]

This Sumero-Akkadian prayer, which one editor classifies as a "penitential psalm," has come to be known as the Prayer to Every God. In important respects it reminds us of the prayers of Shankara cited at the conclusion of the previous chapter.[2] But important as these similarities are, it would be a mistake to take this confessional lament and those of Shankara as expressive of the same spirituality. The larger contexts in which they occur give significantly different meaning to the prayers despite striking similarities in word and image.

We can recognize the same kind of difference if we imagine Martin Luther King and a Grand Dragon of the Ku Klux Klan pledging allegiance to the United States flag. In this case the two rites are verbally identical, not just similar, but the two acts have radically different meanings because the worlds in which they occur are radically different. Because we know those worlds we can quite easily

194

recognize that for the Klansman "liberty and justice for all" means for all white, Anglo-Saxon, Protestant males, while for Martin Luther King it means for all without exception, and especially for those minorities which in the past have been denied the liberty and justice that others have enjoyed. In both cases "the republic for which it stands" is a nation without "niggers." But in the one case it is because blacks have been excluded, while in the other it is because they have been fully included as equals in every aspect of social life.

The task before us in this chapter is to understand the world of semi-worldy or mimetic religion well enough to be able to recognize the distinctive meanings which such common motifs as purification, forgiveness, divine favor, and eventually life after death have in that context.

Semi-worldly religion is diametrically opposed to the world-denying attitude of exilic religion. Whereas for the latter creation is the ultimate catastrophe, the former celebrates creation and the world order that emerged from that primal moment. In fact, as we shall see, creation and salvation become virtually indistinguishable.

And, yet, there is a qualification in this affirmation. For it is only the world as a constantly renewable order, that is, only the world as nature that is acceptable. In Eliade's language, it is the world as cosmos but not as history which is to be celebrated. In Hegel's language, it is the world of life but not of spirit. The unique particularity, the linearity, the contingency, the openness and uncertainty of historical existence—these are to be eliminated as much as possible. This is to be carried out by the thorough integration of human being in the world into the cyclical life of nature, especially the cycle of the seasons, where the only movement is recurring movement and change exhibits a changeless pattern. The view of Plato and Aristotle that the most perfect image of eternity in time is circular motion is a fundamental premise of mimetic religion.[3] Culture, as humanity's second nature, is to close rather than open the gap between human experience and its natural setting.

Semi-worldly religion is nature religion, then, not simply or even primarily because nature is the primary manifestation of the divine, but because through worship human existence is to be assimilated to the natural order. It is the nature of that assimilation or integration which gives rise to the name "mimetic." Eliade, who has devoted a good deal of attention to this life-world, calls it the archaic mentality, since its most thoroughgoing instances are found among ancient or "primitive" cultures. But since the term archaic is more likely to have pejorative than instructive connotations, a more descriptive term seems desirable. The term "mimetic" suggests itself because semi-worldly religion seeks to integrate human existence into the natural cosmos by means of a ritualized imitative participation in which religious rites not only come to have central importance in life but the very difference between ritual and ordinary life is not allowed to emerge clearly if at all. Thus "every act which has a definite meaning—hunting, fishing, agriculture, games, conflicts, sexuality,—in some way' participates in the sacred. . . . Thus we may say that every responsible activity in pursuit of a definite end is, for the archaic world, a ritual." In such a society "all the important acts of life were revealed *ab origine* by gods or heroes," and "not only do rituals have their mythical model but any human act whatever acquires effectiveness to the extent to which it exactly *repeats* an act performed at the beginning of time by a god, a hero, or an ancestor."[4]

In this way the whole of life becomes *mimesis* as temporal experience is given the meaning of timeless archetypes. This transfer of meaning and value is possible because ritual reiteration of mythical archetypes is no mere story-telling. "Now the cult is already a kind of action—not only a fictive re-enactment, but a renewal of the drama by active participation."[5] This means that the sacred time represented in the myth is "reattained by means of a ritual, or by the mere repetition of some action with a mythical archetype." For "a ritual does not merely repeat the ritual that came before it (itself the repetition of an archetype), but is linked to it and continues it, whether at fixed periods or otherwise. . . . In religion as in magic, the periodic recurrence of anything signifies primarily that a mythical time is *made present* and then used indefinitely. Every ritual has the character of happening *now*, at this very moment. The time of the event that the ritual commemorates or re-enacts is made *present*, 're-presented' so to speak, however far back it may have been in ordinary reckoning."[6]

It thus becomes necessary to use the same two terms that Plato uses in his theory of forms. We would misunderstand the meaning of imitation (*mimesis*) if we were to construe it as mere representation rather than as participation (*methexis*). If Plato's mystical instructions for "the transcendence of the cave" are a philosophic transcription of exilic spirituality, his moral and political instructions for "the discipline of the cave" have their roots in mimetic spirituality.[7]

In this light, we can appreciate two features of this type of religious experience emphasized by Eliade, even if we do not retain his name for it. The first is its *anti-historical* character. We are constantly referred to "the abolition of time through the imitation of archetypes and the repetition of paradigmatic gestures."[8] Of course, this abolition of time is not a metaphysical argument which draws from some putative paradox the conclusion that morning does not come before afternoon. It is only profane time that is to be abolished, that is, time that has not been rendered meaningful through *mimesis*. The striking mark of these "traditional" societies is "their revolt against concrete, historical time . . .(their) will to refuse concrete time, their hostility toward every attempt at autonomous 'history,' that is, at history not regulated by archetypes."[9] Time has a narrative structure, to be sure, but nothing new or unique in relation to what happened *in illo tempore* is to be part of the story. For the unique is worse than useless; it is the essence of chaos and the anomic, of meaningless human existence.

But for all this mimetic religion remains *worldly* religion. Because of its revolt against history it is necessary to introduce the qualification "semi," but there remains an enormous gap between this spirituality and the exilic type. The Gnostic preference for the serpent over the Creator would be as abhorrent to the mimetic mentality as to the biblical Hebrew. "The repetition of archetypes shows the paradoxical wish to achieve an ideal form (the archetype) in the very framework of human existence, to be in time without reaping its disadvantages, without the inability to 'put back the clock'. Let me point out that this desire is no 'spiritual' attitude, which depreciates life on earth and all that goes with it in favour of a 'spirituality' of detachment from the world. On the contrary, what may be called the 'nostalgia for eternity' proves that man longs for a concrete paradise, and believes that such a paradise can be won *here*, on earth, and *now*, in the present moment."[10]

It is above all the creation myth which provides the archetypes for the ritualized validating of human life in time and on earth. But the creation story typical of mimetic experience is not the familiar story from Genesis. It differs in three ways. First, it is less concerned to differentiate the gods from the nature in which they are manifest. In theological language, they tend to be immanent within nature rather than sharply transcendent to it. More important in the present context, however, is a second difference. Whereas the biblical story has a narrative setting which makes it the first of Yahweh's unique acts in history, a kind of "Prologue in Heaven" to a story whose goal is quite different from its beginning,[11] the mimetic story represents the end just as fully as the beginning. Instead of being a story which leads to other stories and thus to an ontology of reality as event, it is a story to end all stories, implying an ontology of being as order and dependable recurrence. Finally, rather than focusing on the emergence of the world *ex nihilo*, it is the story of the emergence of

cosmos out of chaos, typically via combat between a divine hero and
a demonic villain.

Vedic India provides a vivid variation on this theme in the story
of the victory of Indra over Vrtra. Nowhere is the entire myth narrated in its completeness, but as reconstructed from the many different hymns in which it is referred to, it goes something like this.[12]
There are two groups of gods, good and evil. The latter are called
Danavas, a name which signifies binding, covering, restraining. Their
leader is Vrtra, the arch-demon, portrayed as a snake or dragon lying
upon the mountains. The good gods are called Adityas, a name signifying unbinding, liberation, freedom. Their leader is Varuna. But
under his leadership things are not going well, and as is so often the
case, the stage is set for a young god to emerge as hero. Such a god
is Indra, born, apparently, of Earth and Sky.

At first he seems to be nothing special, but somehow he gets hold
of the magical drink, soma. Upon drinking it he swells to a terrifying
size, forcing Earth and Sky permanently apart, thus putting them in
their proper place. In return for a promise that he will be their king,
he agrees to be the champion of the Adityas against Vrtra. After no
easy battle he eventually prevails with the help of his special weapon,
the vajra (lightning), with which he repeatedly rips open his opponent. This opening permits the completion of the cosmogonic process
begun with the separation of Earth and Sky. Out of the carcass of
the slain beast there flow the waters which had been held in captivity.
Like lowing cattle they flow down the hillsides to their appointed
places. From them emerges the sun, which begins its regular daily
course.

Finally Sat is separated from Asat. Though these terms mean existence and non-existence and play an important speculative role in
subsequent Indian thought, they function as images rather than concepts at this stage of the game. Sat is the upper world where the gods
and humans dwell. It contains the earth and sky and the atmosphere
between filled with light, warmth, moisture, and all that is necessary
for life. Asat, by contrast, is the netherworld, into which the carcass
of Vrtra and all remaining Danavas (still alive) are cast. It is the
place of death, characterized by darkness, cold, and chaos.

The story ends, then, with even chaos finding its place in the order
of things. At the beginning there was no cosmic order, for while
everything necessary was present, nothing was where and as it should
be. Earth and Sky were too close together, while the waters and the
sun were kept from providing the earth with the moisture and warmth
it needs. The Danavas were center stage, running the show, instead

of being banished to the netherworld where they belong. With their banishment and the emergence of the cosmic order the way is cleared for the appearance of human beings within the realm of Sat. Their function is to maintain the given order through sacrifice. The name given to the whole arrangement of everything in its place and carrying out its proper function is Rta. Like the Chinese concept of Tao and the Egyptian concept of Maat, it can be translated many ways, including truth, justice, order. It is a concept in which cosmology and ethics are as yet unseparated, for the cosmic harmony which results from the creative act is the measure of right behavior of gods and humans alike. To act in accordance with this harmony, fulfilling one's proper function in one's proper place, thereby maintaining and supporting the cosmic order, is what life is all about.[13] It is, to use the Greek concepts for the same idea, the work (*ergon*) in which virtue (*arete*) and happiness (*eudaimonia, makaria*) become one.

Within the Vedic life-world the last thing one wanted was to be creative in the modern sense of the term, to perform an act of distinctive self-expression as a unique individual. "We must do what the gods did in the beginning." "Thus the gods did; thus men do."[14] While not the only mythical archetype, the cosmogonic myth is an especially important account of what the gods did. Consequently, for example, the construction of a building re-enacts the creation. With the help of an astrologer the place is found exactly above the head of the snake whose shaking would shake the world to pieces. A peg is driven into the ground to pin the serpent down. Then the cornerstone is laid exactly above the spot, now secured against the forces of disorder. But all this is simply to imitate the victory of Indra over Vrtra, bringing the building as microcosm into harmony with the divinely established macrocosm.[15]

Taking possession of newly conquered territory similarly means extending the microcosm and calls for macrocosmic validation. This is done by erecting an altar to Agni (fire) in the new territory. "But the erection of an altar dedicated to Agni is merely the microcosmic imitation of the Creation. Furthermore, any sacrifice is, in turn, the repetition of the act of Creation, as Indian texts explicitly state."[16]

This raises the question which is rapidly becoming overdue. What is the bearing of mimetic religion on the problem of death and the problem, so intimately linked to it in the present study, of guilt? Wherein does salvation from guilt and death consist in this type of religious experience? Before taking a more detailed look at two examples of mimetic religion, one with and one without belief in per-

sonal immortality, it will be useful to bring this overview to an end
with a sketch of the link between *mimesis* and salvation.

We will not be disappointed in our expectation that the universal
language for overcoming guilt will be present. There will be rites of
purification invoking the whole imagery of defilement and cleansing.
And there will be confessions of having offended the gods and re-
quests for forgiveness and a restoration of divine favor. But if we ask
what distinctive dimensions of meaning these symbols carry in this
context, we find a single answer: return to the innocence of paradise.

Among the most prominent festivals of mimetic religion is the New
Year Festival. The "New Year" may be celebrated more than once
during a solar year, for it signifies the renewal of life, and this can
occur both in the fall after summer heat and drought, and in the
spring after the deadness of winter. A typically important beginning
to these ceremonies involves purification, penance, expulsion of sin
and everything evil, sometimes in the form of a scapegoat ritual.[17]
In these rites "we witness not only the effectual cessation of a certain
temporal interval and the beginning of another, but also the abolition
of the past year and of past time. And this is the meaning of ritual
purifications: a combustion, an annulling of the sins and faults of the
individual and of those of the community as a whole—not a mere
'purifying' . . . this annual explusion of sins, diseases, and demons is
basically an attempt to restore—if only momentarily—mythical and
primordial time, 'pure' time, the time of the 'instant' of the Creation."[18]

Here we see that it is the problem of guilt which lies at the heart
of "archaic man's refusal to accept himself as a historical being."[19]
The powerful need to be delivered from the historical world so as
to live in a kind of continual present is motivated by the desire for
innocence. But the deliverance looked for is no eschatological hope
in which one returns to one's worldless (or at least bodiless) home
after a period of exile incarnate on earth. It is rather the regular
return to the primordial innocence of the earthly paradise, *herrlich
wie am ersten Tag*.[20]

Since, as Hegel has said in contrasting nature with history, only
animals are truly innocent, the question arises whether we should
see "in this tendency toward purification, a nostalgia for the lost
paradise of animality." We shall see that the Egyptian setting provides
some support for this suggestion, but the paradise of innocence can
never be reduced to merely animal innocence. "Everything that we
know about the mythical memories of 'paradise' confronts us, on the
contrary, with the image of an ideal humanity enjoying a beatitude

and spiritual plenitude forever unrealizable in the present state of 'fallen man.' In fact, the myths of many peoples allude to a very distant epoch when men knew neither death nor toil nor suffering and had a bountiful supply of food merely for the taking." There was easy communication between gods and humans until it was interrupted by human fault. "Since then, men must work for their food and are no longer immortal."[21]

It should come as no surprise that the abolition of history and the return to the moment of creation concerns the problem of death as well as that of guilt. For the difference between ordinary, profane, historical time and the sacred time of myth and ritual is not only the difference between guilt and innocence, but also the difference between human mortality and divine immortality.[22] We just noticed the Vedic tradition in which Brahmanic sacrifice re-enacts the cosmogony and paradoxically re-establishes the primordial unity prior to creation so that life and worldly order can be established but the threat of death not introduced. It is natural, then, that rites renewing the creation of the world should accompany all important new beginnings, such as birth, initiation, marriage, and enthronement. It is just as natural to turn to such rites in times when life is threatened by illness or bad crops or a barren womb.[23] The mimetic possibility of "living at the heart of the *real*," of "living an eternal present," means that somehow death can be abolished along with sin and guilt.[24] It remains continually possible to turn over a new leaf, to obtain a new lease on life unspoiled by sin and (therefore) unthreatened by death.

10B. Mimesis in ancient Mesopotamia

The initial sketch of the mimetic *Weltanschauung* has been derived primarily from Eliade, whose presentation is something of a classic. Its substance, if not always its rhetoric, is widely shared by scholars from a striking diversity of academic disciplines and intellectual traditions. In and through the scholarly debate which goes back at least as far as Frazer's *Golden Bough*, and dependent upon no single individual or school, there emerges a fairly consistent picture of a type of religious experience exemplified in "primitive" societies, ancient China, ancient India, and the ancient Near East.[25] Because the latter area has been the object of most intense study, two examples will be drawn from it to illustrate the type in more detail. These will be Mesopotamia and Egypt, which perhaps exemplify the type all the more clearly when the important differences between them are fully acknowledged.

One of the most important of these differences is that whereas in Egypt there develops a full-fledged theology of personal immortality, first for the King and eventually for everyone, belief in life after death is not part of Mesopotamian religion. To be sure, death is not oblivion, but the shadowy underworld, more familiar to many in its Greek version, is anything but attractive. In the *Gilgamesh Epic*, the hero is twice given a picture of the netherworld by his friend Enkidu. The first time it is the report of a dream in which he is taken to the "House of Darkness."

> To the house which none leave who have entered it,
> On the road from which there is no way back,
> To the house wherein the dwellers are bereft of light,
> Where dust is their fare and clay their food.
> They are clothed like birds, with wings for garments,
> And see no light, residing in darkness.[26]

Later Enkidu refuses to tell Gilgamesh what he has seen in the underworld.

> (But) if I tell thee the order of the nether world which I have seen,
> Sit thou down (and) weep![27]

The reason is simply that in the netherworld the body he loved so dearly was devoured like an old garment by vermin and filled with dust.

It is no wonder that Gilgamesh should seek to find the secret of sharing in the immortality of the gods, but the decisive answer to this quest is bluntly negative.

> Gilgamesh, whither rovest thou?
> The life thou pursuest thou shalt not find.
> When the gods created mankind,
> Death for mankind they set aside,
> Life in their own hands retaining.
> Thou, Gilgamesh, let full be thy belly,
> Make thou merry by day and by night.[28]

This gloomy view of what eventually awaits us all seems to have been unchallenged, but it hardly needs to be added that Mesopotamian religion does not consist of the advice to eat, drink, and be merry. While it can be said that "in both Mesopotamia and Egypt religion centered round the problem of maintaining life,"[29] that cannot be taken in a merely biological sense nor even in the hedonistic sense of the secular advice given to Gilgamesh. Even where the major religious activities consist of those seasonal rites associated with what Gaster calls "reviving the topocosm,"[30] and even where these rites appear to be given a quasi-magical meaning by their participants,[31] they are properly viewed as religious because they can never simply be reduced to the securing of secular goals by magical means. For as Gilbert Murray has said, "The instinctive fundamental desire of the human group to ensure that it shall survive and not die is a great thing in itself, and passes in almost all this primeval literature into something more: a consciousness that man, though he desperately needs bread, does not live by bread alone, but longs for a new life, a new age, with young gods, not stained by the deaths and impurities of the past."[32]

In the ancient Near East "the purely secular—in so far as it would be granted to exist at all—was the purely trivial. Whatever was significant was embedded in the life of the cosmos. . . ."[33] For this reason Frankfort can subtitle the study from which this statement is drawn, A Study of Ancient Near Eastern Religion as the Integration of Society & Nature. This integration is a functional matter, to be sure, but the function is not merely to maintain life and make it pleasant, but above all to make it meaningful. In this context life becomes meaningful through a sense of belonging (i.e., participation), and belonging is achieved through *mimesis* (imitation). It is not the least bit demeaning to this religious self-understanding to suggest that just as children seek to participate in the adult life which seems superior to their own by impersonating grown-ups, playing house, dressing up in high heels, and so on, so the ancient Sumerians and Akkadians sought to participate in the life divine by acting it out.

In Mesopotamia the New Year's Festival, often referred to by its Akkadian name, *akitu*, "must be considered the most complete expression of Mesopotamian religiosity."[34] In this case the link between myth and ritual is explicit. The Akkadian epic poem, *Enuma Elish*, was recited on the fourth day of the festival and provides the content for most of the subsequent action. Also known as the Babylonian Creation Epic, it tells a story very similar to that of Indra and Vrtra, with Marduk and Tiamat in the lead roles. In gratitude for Marduk's victory the gods built him a temple at Babylon, called the Esagila, and they all celebrated with a festive banquet.[35]

But the *akitu* begins with neither the tenseness of combat nor the jubilation of victory. It begins rather in an atmosphere of mourning and with the sounds of funereal wailing. Marduk, the expected hero, is missing, held captive in the mountain. His role at this point derives,

not from the story of his combat with Tiamat, but from his identification with the fertility god Tammuz, whose dying and rising again
are intimately related to the disappearance and reappearance of vegetation during the seasonal cycle. By incorporating the popular myth
and rites of Tammuz into the New Year's Festival, Marduk, the high
god, is merged with Tammuz, the fertility god, and the cosmic myth
is blended with the agrarian myth into a single, very complex story
of the natural order into which society seeks to be integrated.[36]

The two stories interact throughout the festival. The agrarian elements derived from the Tammuz myth can be summarized as follows:

Day 5:   The people search for the missing god and re-enact
           the descent of the goddess into the netherworld to
           find him.
Day 7:   Marduk is liberated from the "mountain" of the
           netherworld.
Day 10:   After banqueting with the gods, Marduk celebrates
           the hierogamy, the ultimate rite of fertility religion.

The elements of the festival which derive directly from the story of
Marduk's combat with Tiamat are the following:

Day 8:   The First Determination of Destiny for the follow-
           ing year takes place and Marduk is established by
           the gods as their leader.
Day 9:   The victory of Marduk over Tiamat is celebrated
           with mock battles and a triumphal procession to the
           special hall erected for the celebration of this fes-
           tival.
Day 10:   Marduk celebrates his victory with a banquet for all
           the gods.

On the eleventh day the Second Determination of Destiny takes
place, at which the gods determine the fate of society for the up-
coming year. The purpose of this part of the festival is to enable
society to participate in both victories, that of life over death and
that of order over chaos, victories in all likelihood not nearly so
distinct in the mimetic life-world as in our own thinking. On the
twelfth and final day the gods return to their temples.[37]

But what takes place during the opening days of *akitu*? For our
purposes these days are especially important. Fully to appreciate their
importance we need to be clear about the role of the king throughout
the festival. He is always the representative of the people. But there

are two distinct dimensions of this. During the events just described he is identified with Marduk. The story of Marduk's new life, of his victory over his enemies, and his enthronement is also the story of the human king, whose vitality and sovereignty, and thereby the strength of the entire community, are re-established. Therefore, the king is often if not always the impersonator of Marduk in the ceremonies that make up the festival. Through his imitative identification with Marduk the whole of society participates in the life-renewing order of nature.

But the king is also the representative of the people in their sheer humanity, in their distinctness and divergence from the sacred cosmos. Thus he becomes the bearer of their sins, the one who makes atonement as scapegoat, priest, and "grand penitent." This is an important part of his regular function.[38] So it is natural that he plays a prominent role in the rites of purification and atonement which take up the first five days of *akitu*. What better use to make of the time during which the god is dead or held captive, signifying the triumph of death and chaos over life and order, than both to acknowledge the link between human sinfulness and society's participation in these evils and to seek to regain the favor of the gods.

Fully to appreciate this aspect of the New Year's Festival we need to know how the confessions of sin which sought the favor of the gods were understood. This chapter began with excerpts from a Babylonian liturgy of confession. A prominent feature of that Prayer to Every God is a defense of ignorance. The petitioner claims only to know some of the gods and goddesses but not others, and not to know fully what the will of the gods is. There is a knowledge that some "sin" or "transgression" has been committed, but no clear awareness of just what it is or who has been offended. With reference to this prayer, Frankfort has written, "The Mesopotamians, while they knew themselves to be subject to the decrees of the gods, had no reason to believe that these decrees were necessarily just. Hence their penitential psalms abound in confessions of guilt but ignore the sense of sin; they are vibrant with despair but not with contrition—with regret but not with repentance."[39]

But the evidence does not support this conclusion. We need to remember Oedipus. The link in our own minds between ignorance and innocence is by no means universal in human experience. And just as Oedipus nowhere suggests that there is any injustice in his having to suffer for an act done in ignorance, we find no hint in the Prayer to Every God that the disfavor of the gods is unjust. On the contrary, we find the gods represented as having a special concern

for justice, appointing kings in human society especially for its sake.[40]
And in another penitential psalm, this one addressed to Ishtar, the
justice of the goddess is explicitly affirmed.

> The judgment of the people in truth and righteousness thou indeed
>   dost decide.
> Thou regardest the oppressed and mistreated; daily thou causest them
>   to prosper.

The prayer then continues as follows:

> Where thou dost look, one who is dead lives; one who is sick rises up;
> The erring one who sees thy face goes aright . . .
> To thee have I prayed; forgive my debt.
> Forgive my sin, my iniquity, my shameful deeds and my offence.
> Overlook my shameful deeds; accept my prayer;
> Loosen my fetters; secure my deliverance;
> Guide my steps aright; radiantly like a hero let me enter the streets
>   with the living.[41]

We can turn our attention back to the opening days of the New
Year's Festival with the assurance that a crucial part of what the
ancient Mesopotamians sought to achieve through the integration of
society into nature was freedom from that disapproval of the gods
which they could themselves only approve.

For the first five days of *akitu*, activity takes place in Marduk's
temple, Esagila, where the solemnity of the god's absence is inten-
sified by rites of purification and penance. We have the texts of
prayers offered early in the morning on the second and fourth days.
The first of these has been called the "Kyrie Eleison" for obvious
reasons. "Bel" is another name for Marduk.

> Bel, without equal in his anger;
> Bel, merciful king, lord of the lands . . .
> Have mercy on thy city, Babel!
> Turn thy face toward thy temple, Esagila!
> Establish the liberty of the children of Babel, objects of (thy)
>   protection![42]

The similar prayer on the fourth day ends with a request that
Marduk be gracious to Babylon and have mercy on his temple, Esagila, causing the light to shine on the children of Babylon. It is
followed by a prayer to Marduk's consort Beltia (Zarpanit), which
opens with hymnic praise of her justice and compassion along with

her majesty and splendor, and asks her to intercede with Marduk on behalf of the king and all his people.[43] It is after this that the *Enuma Elish* is recited to the god, anticipating his return, his victory, and the people's participation in it all.

But penitential preparation is not yet completed. It reaches its climax on the fifth day, which Frankfort calls the Day of Atonement. The day begins with a prayer to Marduk and Zarpanit that they may be appeased. Then the temple is purified by the priests through rites of exorcism and washing. A sheep is then sacrificed in a "scapegoat" ceremony which includes its complete removal along with that of the sacrificers from the city until the entire festival is completed. After a hymn in honor of the temple's purification, offerings are made to Marduk, who is again invited to be favorable.[44]

At this time the king is brought into the temple. The priest deprives him of all the royal insignia, which are placed before Marduk. Then the priest strikes the king on the cheek, pulls his ears, and makes him kneel before the god and say:

> I have not sinned, lord of the countries; I have not despised thy
> divinity;
> I have not destroyed Babel; I have not caused it to be scattered;
> I have not shaken Esagila; I have not forgotten its rituals;
> I have not smitten suppliants on the cheek;
> I have not humiliated them;
> I care for Babel; I have not broken down its walls.[45]

The priest then recites the assurance that his prayer is heard and accepted, that Marduk will bless his kingship, the temple, and the people of the city, who are also recognized in the person of the king as suppliants. The royal insignia are restored.

Whether the recital of innocence is taken to have magical powers in itself to make the statement true as it is said, or whether it presupposes that atonement has already been made for all the sins of the king and his people, perhaps through the scapegoat, perhaps through the king's humiliation, it is clear that his mimetic participation in the renewal which follows, and that of his people, presupposes that together they stand in innocence before the gods. On the very day when all this happens the festival breaks out of the temple and the search for the captive (dead, suffering) god begins. The way for his appearing is clear. The removal of guilt prepares for the triumph over death.

It has been said that in the celebration of the New Year's Festival "the people place their whole existence under the sign of the drama of creation," and that in this context "there is no problem of salvation distinct from the problem of creation; there is no history of salvation distinct from the drama of creation."[46] We must remember that there are two dramas of creation blended into one here, as the original emergence of cosmic order out of chaos is blended with the biannual emergence of life from aridity and death. The rites by which human existence is placed under the sign of the dual drama of creation constitute salvation for they mean participation in a life of purity and innocence on which the favor of the gods shines. This is no permanent achievement. Like nature itself and even the gods whose life it manifests, this life must ever be renewed. The good news of mimetic religion in its Mesopotamian version is that it is indeed renewable.

10C. Mimesis in ancient Egypt

The religion of ancient Egypt focuses around a very similar gospel. One of the major differences between the two concerns life after death. Whereas the Mesopotamian view, like the Greek conception of Hades and Hebrew view of Sheol, portrays the grave as entrance to a dark and dismal netherworld, devoid of hope or happiness, Egyptian religion held out the hope of personal blessedness in the life to come, at first for the king, but eventually for everyone.

In view of this "otherworldly" hope, it is especially important to notice the worldly character of Egyptian religion, especially as expressed in its attitude toward creation and the body. Creation is not the exclusive mark of any single deity in the pantheon. This honor, and it clearly is an honor, the highest mark of divine greatness, is attributed to a variety of gods, including Ptah, Khnum, Atum, and Re (later Amon-Re).[47] Here, of course, "creation does not necessarily mean the bringing forth of something out of nothing; to the eastern mind it contains the idea of regulation, of cosmos. To a large extent the material is there already and the act of creation consists in forming the chaotic material into a living organism."[48] Understood in this light, Egyptian religion is a continuous celebration of creation, and every creation story does what Frankfort attributes to one of the earliest, namely, it imparts "the character of an established order, valid for all time, to the phenomenal world."[49]

Equally distant from the spirit of anti-worldly religion is the Egyptian attitude toward the body, especially in connection with death. Far from seeing death as a liberation from the body, "the Egyptians could not abstract the survival of man's immortal parts from the continued existence of his body. . . . So, while they admitted that man suffered physical death and nevertheless survived, they could not imagine such a survival without a physical substratum. Man without a body seemed incomplete and ineffectual. He required his body in perpetuity, as if it were the concrete basis of his individuality."[50]

Another aspect of the same affirmation of the body comes to light in a linguistic oddity which expresses an absolutely fundamental belief. An Egyptian word which originally meant "body" or "physical appearance" came to function, with a possessive pronoun, as the eqivalent of "His Majesty" or "Your Majesty." This is, of course, but one expression of the notion that the king is an incarnation of the god Horus. But we miss an important part of the meaning of this as we read it only to mean that the king is divine. It also means that the divine is embodied. The very "physical frame of Pharaoh" is the god incarnate, and the king can thus be addressed as "the Embodiment of the Lord of All."[51]

But if the created world order, including its physical aspects, are affirmed and celebrated in Egyptian religion, it remains "semi"-worldly religion. For the world it loves is not the world of history but that of nature. Here, at least as emphatically as in Mesopotamia, the task of religion and of the kingship, which was so vital a part thereof, is "the integration of society and nature."[52] The Egyptian story is a chapter in the larger account of how "during a very considerable period, humanity opposed history by all possible means."[53] For "no actuality, no incident of history, could ever equal the dignity of the unchangeable order of creation."[54]

From our perspective the Pharaohs are historical individuals, but this dimension is submerged in the typical for Egyptian thinking. Already at the coronation we find "a deliberate attempt to fuse the historical event, the coronation of one particular Pharaoh, with the perennial truth that Horus succeeds Osiris" in the familiar myth.[55] Because "the incidents of history . . . lacked ultimate reality" for Egyptian chroniclers, their inscriptions are long on clichés and short on specific information.[56] The king is reduced, from our perspective, to being a myth in his own lifetime, and both the artwork and the written records depicting, for example, great battles, eliminate the unique in order to portray the ideal and typical. Even when the vanquished enemy chiefs are mentioned by name, the list turns out to be historically useless, since it is used again and again. Pharaoh's victories represent an unchanging truth. He "acts out and realizes a prefigured course of events."[57] It is thus possible to speak of the Pharaoh's coronation as being "not an apotheosis but an epiphany."[58]

For the emphasis falls upon the manifestation of the deity who has always been, rather than on a unique event in this human biography.

This systematic assimilation of change to the changeless quite naturally evokes the suggestion that the ancient Egyptians viewed the *static* order of the world as divine.[59] But where the opposite of static is dynamic, this language will seriously mislead us. The Egyptians venerated the eternal, to be sure, but as eternal life; and the world of these believing souls was overflowing with a life in which they wished to share. It is necessary and appropriate that Frankfort, who often uses the term "static" and who says that for Egyptian religion "only the changeless is ultimately significant," should correct himself. It is true that "single occurences, odd events, historical circumstances were ephemeral, superficial disturbances of the regularity of being and for that reason unimportant." But that was not true of "recurrent changes, the life rhythm of a universe which had gone forth, complete and unchanging, from the hands of its creator. The alternation of night and day, of drought and innundation, of the succession of the seasons, were significant changes; their movement was part of the established order of creation."[60]

The continuous participation of human society in this established order of creation is the goal of Egyptian religion. Although there are important differences in the understanding of kingship from that in Mesopotamia, the king plays the same lead role in renewing society's share in the cosmic life, especially in the variety of festivals which occur at the "new year's" periods of the year. Egyptian ethics likewise rests entirely on the concept of imitative participation in the cosmic order which is ultimate reality, pattern, and imperative. Nature is the norm, and the name for this standard is Maat.[61]

In all these respects Egyptian religion reinforces the picture of mimetic piety we get from Mesopotamia, but it adds little, if anything new. Its distinctive contribution to the type of which it is a species is the already-mentioned concepts of the life to come. It is necessary to speak here of concepts in the plural, for just as there is no single idea of the divine, so there is no single image of life after death. What we find instead is a remarkable correspondence between representations of the gods and images of immortality. Just as the (unhistorical) life of nature has three forms, so there are three fundamental modes of representing the gods and the same three models for portraying human immortality. These are the life of the heavenly bodies, animal life, and vegetation. Since our task is interpretation rather than explanation, we need not address the questions why these beliefs arose here but not, for example, in Mesopotamia or why and how these beliefs, which in the Pyramid Texts referred only to Pharaoh, and perhaps the royal family, came in the Coffin Texts to apply to the ordinary person.

Of the heavenly bodies, of course, the Sun above all was the visible expression of the regular rhythm of cosmic life, and the sun-god (Atum, Re) was the supreme expression of divinity. In three ways it was the triumph of life. In the first place, it was viewed as the original source of all there is, the creator *par excellence*. But beyond this the regularity of its setting and rising grounds two other powerful images. One is that of death and rebirth. Just as setting is an obvious picture of death, so rising is the birth to a new life, whether the mother who gives birth is given as Nut, the Sky, or Hathor, the Heavenly Cow. At least one text makes the Sun his own mother:

> Thou art a divine youth, the heir of eternity,
> Who begot thyself and bore thyself.[62]

In any case the Sun is not so much an argument as visible proof that death is followed by rebirth.

The final image is that of combat and victory over the forces of chaos, darkness, and death. The setting sun descends into the dangerous netherworld, there to encounter the serpentine Apophis, whom he must battle all through the night before he can once again sail triumphantly across the sky.

The same verb, meaning to shine forth, is interchangeably used to refer to the rising of the sun and of the appearing of Pharaoh at his official functions. This indicates an intimate relation between the two, but though the king is divine, it is not one of identity. He is rather the son of Re. It is only natural that in death he should be reunited with his father. Thus the Pyramid Texts describe the process by which the deceased Pharaoh rises from the earth of mortals to the sky of the gods. His father, the sun-god Re or Atum, has prepared either stairs or a ladder for him to ascend, though he is also represented as flying like a falcon or goose. The double door entrance to the sky is wide open and messengers hasten to announce his coming to Re, while the other gods greet him warmly with the words, "Our heart was not glad until thy coming." Sometimes they themselves present him to his father. "O Re-Atum! This king Unis comes to thee, an imperishable glorious-one, lord of the affairs of the place of the four pillars (the sky). Thy son comes to thee." The Pharaoh then says, "I, O Re, am this one of whom thou didst say . . . 'My son!' My father art thou, O Re. . . . Behold king Pepi, O Re.

This king Pepi is thy son. . . . This king Pepi shines in the east like
Re, he goes in the west like Kheprer." Then the gods say, "O Pure
One, assume thy throne in the barque of Re and sail thou the sky.
. . . Live thou this pleasant life which the lord of the horizon lives."[63]

Just as the Pyramid Texts thus assure the king that he will rejoin
Re in his perennial journey, so the Coffin Texts express the hope of
commoners "to enter and leave by the Eastern Gate of Heaven in
the retinue of Re." In either case, whether king or commoner, the
hope is "to be absorbed in the great rhythm of the universe" by
becoming a permanent member of the party which sails with Re
across the sky each day.[64]

The stars are another visible expression of nature's eternity. The
Pyramid Texts use this image as well in lines addressed to the Pharaoh.

> Thou risest with Orion in the Eastern part of Heaven;
> Thou settest with Orion in the Western part of Heaven;
> O Unas, thou art that great star, the Companion of Orion,
> Which crosses Heaven with Orion. . . .[65]

In other cases the departed are said to have become polar stars,
which never set. The waxing and waning of the moon is still another
example of the same kind of phenomenon. It gets included as well,
as in the text in which a god says to the departed king, "I grant thee,
that thou mayest rise like the sun, rejuvenate thyself like the moon,
repeat life like the flood of the Nile." In all of these cases the theme
is the same, achieving immortality through "participation in the perennial life of the universe."[66]

But the heavenly bodies represent only one aspect of nature's vitality. Animal life represents another, and awe before animal life is
a distinctive feature of Egyptian religion. The gods are often represented as animals, including the falcon, ibis, jackal, ram, bull, and
cow. The animal world (in the absence of any evolutionary theory)
is the kind of changeless change so important to the Egyptians.
Through continuous replacement, the species lives on in and through
the coming and going of its members. The immortality of society's
life is of the same sort, but when the question comes to be that of
immortality for the individual, a different connection needs to be
found. For the Egyptians it is the notion of eternal life through
rebirth. We have already noticed that the cow-goddess, either Hathor
or Nut, is represented as giving birth to the Sun and to the stars.
She is also represented as the mother of Pharaoh, and this "mother-
image fulfills a distinct function in the Egyptian beliefs of life after

death. It does not bear witness to the king's divine origin, but it holds out a promise of immortality . . . the divine mother is concerned, not with the king's birth, but with his rebirth after death."[67] The image of animal reproduction becomes an indispensable part of the pictures of solar and stellar immortality. One of nature's recurrent movements becomes the entry way to another as the reproductive cycle and the heavenly orbits are blended into a powerful symbol of belief and hope.

Finally, there is vegetative life, whose regular appearance, disappearance, and reappearance provides yet another image for thinking about the problems of life, death, and the hereafter. It is in the worship of Osiris that fertility rites become mortuary rites and a god of vegetation becomes the hope of personal salvation for both the king and the commoner.[68] The myth of Osiris tells of his death in combat with the wicked Seth. Osiris does not return to his throne, as Marduk does, but neither does he remain dead. He is resurrected to a new life as Chief of the Westerners, the leader, protector, and prototype of the dead, the hope and savior of all mortals who seek eternal life. He is also numbered among those who accompany Re on his daily journey. His new life has its visible symbols in the regular growth of the grain crops, the regular rising of the Nile, and the regular return of the moon to the fullness it had lost.[69]

In the identification of every living Pharaoh with Horus, Son of Osiris, we can easily see the importance of this story for the divinity and legitimacy of the king. But beyond its political importance the myth has an existential meaning. This derives from the identification of the dead king (and eventually commoners as well) with Osiris, who dies to be sure, but is reborn to eternal life. The Pyramid Texts are most direct. "O King Unis, thou hast not at all departed dead, thou hast departed living! For thou sittest upon the throne of Osiris, with thy scepter in thy hand. . . ." The same theme can take the form of a presentation to the gods. "Atum, the one here is that son of thine, Osiris, whom thou hast caused to survive and to live on. He lives— (so also) this King Unis lives. He does not die—(so also) this King Unis does not die. He does not perish—(so also) this King Unis does not perish." These formulae are repeated again and again as the departed king is presented to each of the gods in turn.[70]

Through a rich variety of symbols, then, the believing soul in ancient Egypt expressed the hope of a permanent participation in the changeless change of the world we call nature, therein finding eternal happiness. Ritual *mimesis* in cult and festival is anticipatory. It looks toward the time when one will "imitate" Osiris, for example, by being reborn to heavenly life as he has been and imitate Re by joining him on his daily circuit.

But this hope of happiness was not separated from the question of the individual's worthiness. Because the blessedness of life in harmony with the cosmic order is drawn on a larger scale in Egypt than in Mesopotamia, including not only this life but also the life to come, the problems of sin and judgment play a correspondingly larger role. The chapter on ancient Egypt makes up one of the more dramatic contributions to the world's literature on the judgment of the dead.[71] The presentation formula just cited from the Pyramid Texts takes this seriously into account. For it not only repeats again and again the refrain, Osiris lives, and so does King Unis. It immediately continues, "He is not judged—(so also) this King Unis is not judged. (But) he judges—(so also)—this King Unis judges."[72]

The notion that evil is punished is built into the concept of Maat. The believing soul is taught that "Maat is good and its worth is lasting. It has not been disturbed since the day of its creator, whereas he who transgresses its ordinances is punished."[73] So far as this life is concerned, this often enough requires no direct involvement of the gods, for Maat is a kind of self-sustaining order in which virtue is its own reward and vice its own punishment. But the gods are clearly on the side of Maat, and Egyptian wisdom literature not only notes this—for example, "Speak not to a man in falsehood, the abomination of God" and "hated of God is the falsifier of words, his great abomination is the dissembler. . . ."—but also identifies the gods as those who punish transgressors in this life. So it is not quite right to say that "the theme of God's wrath is practically unknown in Egyptian literature."[74]

In fact, when attention is shifted to the life to come just the opposite is true, and "the whole funerary literature of Egypt," including the Coffin Texts and the famous "Book of the Dead," "is a literature of the fear of death. One of the imagined dangers is a judgment hereafter." In anticipation thereof a devout Egyptian might well sing a prayer to Thoth to be defense attorney.

> Would that I had Thoth behind me tomorrow (when I die)!
> Come to me when I enter before the Lords of Maat (the judges
>   in the hereafter).
> And so shall I come forth justified . . .
> Thou who bringest water to a distant place, come deliver me, the
>   silent man.[75]

A Pharaoh warns his son to "do justice so long as thou abidest on earth." For "the judges who judge the deficient, thou knowest that they are not lenient on that day of judging the miserable, in the hour of performing (their) duty. It is hard when the accuser is possessed of knowledge. Put not thy trust in length of years: they regard a lifetime as an hour. A man surviveth after death and his deeds are placed beside him in heaps. Eternal is the existence yonder. He who makes light of it is a fool. As for him who reaches it without doing wrong, he shall exist yonder like a god, striding forth like the Lords of Eternity."[76]

There is an historical development from fairly simple pictures of a post-mortem judgment in which one's deeds are weighed before "the Great God," to the very elaborate scenario in the "Book of the Dead" of judgment before the forty-two fearsome judges and of the gruesome consequences that await those who are not vindicated.[77] But throughout the whole story there persists the clear notion that death poses not so much the question of survival but of worthiness. The approval or disapproval of the gods, along with the consequences of these verdicts, is the question that death brings forcefully and inescapably to the fore. One could face death with something less than total fear and anxiety only if there was a basis for hoping to be justified.[78]

We can distinguish five different patterns of hope in this regard. They are not entirely distinct from each other, and they are by no means mutually exclusive. As in the variety of images for the nature of the divine and of eternal life, here also it seems to be assumed that the truth is a complex whole which no single account can exhaust.

Three of these are essentially rituals of sanctification. One of these consists of the rites of purification that the Pyramid Texts prescribe for the Pharaoh on his way to Re. In one of them we read

Pepi has come that he may purify himself in the Reed Field;
He descends to the Field of Kenset.
The Followers of Horus purify Pepi;
They bathe him, they dry him.

It is only after this that we read of the god's jubilation as

Pepi ascends to Heaven.
Pepi embarks on this boat of Re.[79]

No doubt this is associated with the process of embalming, and it may well be that the ritual washings were all there was to it, the king remaining passive. But it is also possible that he was conceived as taking a conscious role in the rites, and that these consisted in acts of confession and penance. It is no objection to this possibility to say that the king is already divine and has no need of confession and penance. The rite in itself bears witness to the fact that he cannot enter his eternal happiness without purification, which implies the real possibility of impurity.

The second and third ritual "strategies" for dealing with guilt at the time of death are directly related to the concept of the judgment. One of these involves "vicarious justification" through identification with Osiris. As Osiris is justified and Seth convicted in the trial which legitimates the kingship of Horus, so anyone identified with him could hope to win the approval of the gods. This identification is again achieved through the rituals of embalming. So the funeral liturgy of one of the Coffin Texts (concerning someone outside the royal family) reads, "O Thoth, justify Osiris against his enemies! Justify Osiris N against his enemies, in the great tribunal which is in Heliopolis. . . ."[80] N is the dotted line in which the name of the individual is to be filled in.

The third ritual way of dealing with the judgment consists in the Declaration of Innocence. This motif, which goes back to the Old Kingdom, is best known from the famous Chapter 125 of the "Book of the Dead." First an elaborate protestation of innocence is made before Osiris, "the great god, lord of the Two Justices!" And then a very similar declaration is made before the forty-two gods who sit with him in judgment. The deceased denies, in essence, having committed any of the sins that can be thought of, and, at the end of the first part, declares four times, "I am pure." At the end of the second declaration, the forty-two gods (as a jury) are told in no uncertain terms that they will report nothing evil of the deceased, for "I have come to you without sin, without guilt, without evil, without a witness (against me), without one against whom I have taken action. I live on truth, and I eat of truth. I have done that which men said and that with which gods are content." The defendant is then introduced to Thoth, to whom he says, "I am pure of sin." Thoth then presents the deceased to Osiris, with the notation, "He shall be ushered in with the Kings of Upper and Lower Egypt, and he shall be in the retinue of Osiris. Right and true a million times."[81]

There is no question that these rites are open to magical interpretation and that they were so understood by the ancient Egyptians. The hope was that the proper performance of the rite or incantation of the spell would automatically produce the desired result, for example, that the Declaration of Innocence would make one in fact innocent, or at least appear so to the gods. This is likely to seem rather crass to our ears, whether religious or secular, and we might well take offense in something like the manner of our response to the medieval sale of indulgences. But since our task is neither to denigrate nor to defend the Egyptians, as Frankfort and Brandon are disposed to do, respectively, but rather to understand them, we simply need to take note of the whole situation. It can be summarized in three points. (1) A magical interpretation of these rites is conspicuously present. (2) There *may* be more than that involved in these rites. We have already noted the possibility that rites of purification may involve an act of confession and/or penance, though there is no firm evidence of this beyond the acknowledgment of a need of purification. In the case of the Declaration of Innocence, the instructions prescribe that "this spell is to be recited when one is clean and pure."[82] While this may simply refer to ritual purification which in turn is given a magical interpretation, we cannot be sure that it does not presuppose some more inward form of purity. In any event, there is the notion that after the spell is recited, there still remains the weighing of the heart against Maat to see whether it is truthful.[83] (3) This reminds us that even if the ritual side of the encounter with death and judgment is wholly absorbed by magical conceptualization, there remain at least two other ways of dealing with guilt and death. One involves the concern to make sure that the Declaration of Innocence is true. The other involves a non-ritualized way of dealing with the points at which it isn't true.

The fourth model for justification at the judgment, after the three kinds of ritual of sanctification, we can call salvation by good works. The gods preside over a weighing of the good and evil deeds of one's earthly life. This is described as a weighing of the heart or conscience, suggesting that there is an important subjective dimension to innocence and guilt, as well as the objective dimension indicated by the specifications of Maat itemized in the Declaration of Innocence. The magico-ritual responses may well have developed alongside this notion that we all face a final moral judgment out of anxiety about being able to pass such a test. But the test itself is placed upon impartial, moral (non-magical) grounds.[84]

Fifth and finally, there remains a non-magical eradication of our failures to live up to the exacting standards of Maat. We can call this salvation by grace. This is not nearly as prominent in Egyptian thinking as the notion that we must pass the moral test and will simply get what we deserve. But the notion that one can hope for forgiveness because the gods are merciful is there. In a hymn to Amon-Re, whose immediate occasion is gratitude for the healing of a son, but whose deeper concern is that of justification and rescue from the underworld, we read: "Though it may be that the servant is normal in doing wrong, still the Lord is normal in being merciful. The Lord of Thebes does not spend an entire day angry. As for his anger—in the completion of a moment there is no remnant. . . ." And in a penitential hymn to a goddess, a man acknowledges that he has transgressed against her and she has severely punished him. "(But) when I called to my mistress, I found her coming to me with sweet breezes. She showed mercy unto me, after she had let me see her hand. She turned about to me in mercy; she made me forget the wickedness which had been (upon) me. Lo, the Peak of the West is merciful, when one calls to her."[85]

We might say that the Egyptians hedged their bets and left no stone unturned. But throughout their rites of sanctification and their concepts of salvation by good works and by the merciful grace of the gods there runs a common concern—in the face of death to win the approval rather than the disapproval of the gods. And it is clear that we are dealing with approval or disapproval of which the individual approved in advance. For throughout the variety of images of the judgment, and even when the forty-two gods are portrayed as most fearful, the gods are never represented as being other than the Lords of Maat.

Whether the images are those of purity, innocence, or forgiveness, the believing Egyptian was persuaded that there must be freedom from that divine disapproval of which humans can only approve if the journey is to be made safely from our temporary, earthly participation in the changeless life of nature to our permanent, heavenly participation.

11

Guilt and Death in Covenantal Religion

11A. Biblical religion as worldly but not mimetic

> The infant Savior comes again,
> Takes to Himself the hearts of men,
> Brings in a year of life and peace,
> And grants to Christian men release.
>
> Oh, sing for joy the angels call;
> Who gladly guard and keep us all.
> Resounding joy breaks forth in song,
> That God and man again are one.[1]

These sixteenth-century lyrics express something of the powerful attraction mimetic thinking has had within the Christian tradition. Indeed the whole concept of the church year brings with it the idea of yearly re-enacting the events of sacred history.

But in the Roman Catholic understanding of the Eucharist, ritual re-enactment occurs on a weekly or even daily basis, for each time the Mass is celebrated the sacrifice of Christ upon the cross is repeated.[2] As Augustine writes, "Was not Christ offered in His Person only once, yet in the sacred mysteries He is offered for mankind not only on every Easter Sunday but every day?"[3] More recently, Pope Leo XIII writes that "the Church prolongs the priestly mission of Jesus Christ" in the sacred Liturgy, "where constantly the Sacrifice of the Cross is re-presented, and, with a single difference in the manner of its offering, renewed"; and Vatican II confirms that Christ instituted this rite "in order to perpetuate the sacrifice of the Cross throughout the centuries until He should come again."[4]

In his lengthy discussion of the Eucharist, Thomas Aquinas asks "whether Christ is sacrificed in the celebration of this mystery."[5] The major objection to this is the teaching of the epistle to the

219

Hebrews (9:26–28 and 10:12–14) that Christ offered himself once and for all and by this one sacrifice accomplished human salvation. His reply is in terms of *mimesis* and *methexis*.[6] Citing Augustine to the effect that images are called by the names of what they represent, so that we say of a picture, That is Cicero, or, That is Sallust, Thomas writes, "Now, as we have said, the celebration of this sacrament is a definite image representing Christ's Passion, which is his true sacrifice." The sacrament can therefore be called the sacrifice of Christ. But this is not representation for its own sake, but with regard to its effects. "By this sacrament we are made sharers of the fruit of the Lord's Passion." As a liturgical prayer puts it, "Wherever the commemoration of this sacrifice is celebrated the work of our redemption is carried on." Or, as Pius XII later puts the same point, "The faithful participate in the oblation" because they both "offer the Divine Victim in this Sacrifice" and add to this act "the offering of themselves as a victim."[7] In short, the rite can be called a sacrifice because it is an imitative participation in the sacrifice of Christ which is its archetype, or, in Thomas's own words, the exemplar (*exemplum*) of our sacrifice.

To call the Eucharist a sacrifice is therefore not to violate the teaching of Hebrews about the once for all character of the death of Christ. For since there is but one victim, offered by Christ and by us, "What is offered everywhere is one body, not many, so there is one sacrifice."[8]

There is an important consequence of this idea which underscores the mimetic understanding of time at work here. If the sacrifice on Calvary and the one at the altar are one and the same, then the time separating them is in an important sense annulled. "After His departure, the disciples were to make liturgically present this same mystery" of his sacrificial death. "Christ can no longer die . . . but His sacrificial death is made present. . . ."[9] So Karl Adam can write, "In the Sacrifice of the Mass we are not merely reminded of the Sacrifice of the Cross in a symbolical form. On the contrary the Sacrifice of Calvary, as a great supra-temporal reality, enters into the immediate present. Space and time are abolished. The same Jesus is here present who died on the Cross. The whole congregation unites itself with His holy sacrificial will, and through Jesus present before it consecrates itself to the heavenly Father as a living oblation. So Holy Mass is a tremendously real experience, the experience of the reality of Golgotha."[10]

The teaching of the Orthodox Church agrees entirely with this understanding of the Eucharist. It is not "a bare commemoration nor an imaginary representation of Christ's sacrifice, but the true sacrifice itself; yet on the other hand it is not a new sacrifice, nor a repetition of the sacrifice on Calvary, since the Lamb was sacrificed 'once only, for all time'. The events of Christ's sacrifice—the Incarnation, the Last Supper, the Crucifixion, the Resurrection, the Ascension—are not repeated in the Eucharist, but they are *made present*. 'During the Liturgy, through its divine power, we are projected to the point where eternity cuts across time, and at this point we become true *contemporaries* with the events which we commemorate.' 'All the holy suppers of the Church are nothing else than one eternal and unique Supper, that of Christ in the Upper Room. The same divine act both takes place at a specific moment in history, and is offered always in the sacrament.' "[11]

And yet, for all this, we are not entirely in the world of mimetic spirituality. For though "all the holy suppers of the Church are nothing else than one eternal and unique Supper, that of Christ in the Upper Room," one need only mention the Upper Room to be reminded that it took place "at a specific moment in history." The archetypal narrative recounts what took place, not *in illo tempore*, but during the days of the Roman occupation of Palestine, when Pontius Pilate lived in dread of Tiberius Caesar. We are not dealing with myth but history.

Furthermore, it is also the teaching of the churches (in this case Protestant as well as Catholic and Orthodox) that at the Last Supper Jesus inaugurated a New Covenant between God and his people, and that the Eucharist is an eschatological feast anticipating a future fulfillment of the Kingdom of God.[12]

When that to which we look back is a unique historical event and that to which we look forward is a culmination of history quite different from the paradise which emerged at Creation, a significant break with the mimetic world-view has taken place. Mimetic language and imagery will continue to be found, but history is replacing nature as the locus of salvation. It will be the argument of this chapter that biblical religion, both in its ancient Hebrew and primitive Christian forms, is decisively different from mimetic spirituality and that neither Judaism nor Christianity can allow the structure of mimetic religion to be the primary framework of its self-understanding without departing radically from its biblical roots. This argument will be developed in detail from the Old Testament. Its application to the New Testament in subsequent sections is implicit and by extension. But it is important to remember that the Old Testament is not only part of the Christian Bible, but a part without which the New Testament message would be unintelligible.

Yet this is not because biblical religion is a species of exilic religion. To be sure, it shares a sense of divine transcendence with exilic religion which sets the two together off from mimetic religion. For neither of these types does the Sacred have the immanence within nature characteristic of mimetic faith. Instead there tends to be a fairly sharp distinction between God and world. But on two crucial points the interpretation of this distinction is entirely antithetical. In the first place, exilic religion seeks to find a crack in the world's defenses through which to slip into ultramundane freedom, whereas covenantal religion sees the gap bridged in the opposite direction, as God enters into the world to save his people, not by freeing them from the world, but by being with them in it.

It is obvious that this first antithesis rests on a second. In the first instance, there is hostility between the world and God, who is not its maker but its alternative. In the second case, God is the maker of a world of which he approves and for which he cares. In short, it is the worldliness of biblical faith which sets off its understanding of divine transcendence from the exilic view.

If we turn to the origins of biblical faith we find that the Old Testament is rightly described as a "worldly book."[13] It differs from exilic anti-worldliness in three fundamental ways. There is first the celebration of creation. This occurs not only in Genesis, where everything that God makes is declared to be not just "good," but "very good." It is also found in the praise of Israel, both in the Psalms which celebrate the created world itself and in those where God is praised as "Maker of Heaven and Earth" as well as "Guardian of Israel."[14] And it is found in the working assumption that the world is the proper stage for human life and fulfillment, as well as in the intimate link between the people and the land.[15]

Second, in contrast to the mind-body dualism characteristic of anti-worldly thought, Israelite thought views the human person holistically as a psycho-physical unity.[16] Correspondingly, sexuality, though no longer a part of the divine life and therefore no longer the basis of mimetic rituals, is a legitimate and important part of family life, which is itself viewed as one of God's richest blessings.[17]

Third, there is Israel's hope for the future. The absence of belief in life after death other than in the shadowy realm of Sheol and the corresponding importance placed on life here and now is a mark of Israel's affirmation of this world. But even in the canonical writings there emerge the beginnings of the belief that Yahweh and not death has the final word about our lives. And in the apocalyptic tradition this develops into a full-fledged hope for personal happiness in a life to come.[18] Is this the beginning of hostility toward the world? "In all this has Old Testament faith abandoned the world and arrived at a belief which takes a stand on the 'beyond'? An overall view of these different expressions of hope, even of those which burst the limits of a life bound by death, should have make it clear that this world is in no wise sacrificed. Even the hope which seems to burst the boundaries of death is directed to the world, to the fidelity of God to the world that he has created, and to the people that he has called there."[19]

The two most important indications of this are the continued affirmation of creation and the body in hope beyond death. For personal survival is almost without exception understood in terms of the resurrection of the body, and something of the same notion is applied to the world as well. Ancient Israel had no word equivalent to our "world." To speak of the totality of what God had created, they spoke of heaven and earth. This world, like our own bodies, is viewed as mortal, transitory. But just as our bodies are to be raised again to new life, so in the final part of Isaiah, we find the hope of a new creation.

> For behold, I create
> new heavens and a new earth.
> Former things shall no more be remembered
> nor shall they be called to mind.
> Rejoice and be filled with delight,
> you boundless realms which I create;
> for I create Jerusalem to be a delight
> and her people a joy.
> I will take delight in Jerusalem and rejoice in my people;
> weeping and cries for help
> shall never again be heard in her.[20]

For some, the story is quite different when we turn to the New Testament. The worldliness of ancient Judaism is clear enough, but precisely at this point lies its decisive difference from biblical Christianity.[21] After all, didn't Jesus say, "My kingship is not of this world"? And are not the early Christians instructed, "Do not love the world or the things in the world. If any one loves the world, love for the Father is not in him. For all that is in the world, the lust of the flesh and the lust of the eyes and the pride of life, is not of the Father but is of the world. And the world passes away, and the lust of it;

but he who does the will of God abides for ever"?[22] We can scarcely be surprised if an early Christian, in a letter to a curious pagan, quite possibly the tutor of Marcus Aurelius, describes his fellow-believers in this manner. "They dwell in their own countries, but simply as sojourners. As citizens, they share in all things with others, and yet endure all things as if foreigners. Every foreign land is to them as their native country, and every land of their birth as a land of strangers. . . . They are in the flesh, but they do not live after the flesh. They pass their days on earth, but they are citizens of heaven."[23]

Yet, though it is not difficult to find the language and imagery of exilic religion throughout the Christian tradition, the faith of the New Testament remains a worldly faith in keeping with its Hebrew origins. This can be indicated by a look at three dualities which sometimes lead to viewing Christianity as species of Gnostic (exilic) religion. These dualities are heaven and earth, spirit and flesh, and church and world.

Heaven and earth do not become paradise and hell but remain the totality of the created order for which God is praised. While this created world is of limited duration, the Old Testament hope of a new heaven and a new earth, including a new Jerusalem, continues.[24] Thus the cosmos is subsumed within history.

Consistent with this is the absence of exilic hostility to the body. Instead of defining salvation in terms of escape from the body, the Jewish hope of a resurrection of the body becomes the form of hope for the life to come, and the bodily resurrection of Jesus is taken to be the paradigm of every believer's destiny. For "Christ has been raised from the dead, the first fruits of those who have fallen asleep."[25] In her study of the sharp contrast between Gnosticism and orthodox Christianity, Elaine Pagels writes of the latter, "They even went so far as to insist that he rose *bodily* from the dead. Here again, as we have seen, orthodox tradition implicitly affirms bodily experience as the central fact of human life."[26] The resurrection throws a retrospective light on the incarnation. Why did Jesus take on bodily form in the first place? In contrast to the Gnostic view that it was to deliver us from bodily-worldly existence altogether, the early Christians "saw Christ not as one who leads souls out of this world into enlightenment, but as 'fullness of God' come down into human experience— into *bodily* experience—to sacralize it."[27]

But what about the war between the flesh and the spirit which is so central to Pauline theology? Is this not simply another version of the mind-body dualism so characteristic of exilic faith? Not in the least. One only needs to read the Pauline list of the sins of the flesh to see that the duality between flesh and spirit stands in no correlation at all with that mind or soul and body. Paul says that "the works of the flesh are plain." And they include "immorality, impurity, licentiousness . . . drunkenness, carousing, and the like." If we define "puritanism" in its popular sense as the special horror of these bodily sins, then it can be looked upon from the Pauline perspective as a heresy of selective reading. For the works of the flesh are equally plainly to be found (for Paul at least) in "enmity, strife, jealousy, anger, selfishness, dissension, party spirit, envy. . . ."[28] If party spirit is as much a work of the flesh as the bodily sins of partying, all attempts to assimilate Pauline hostility to the flesh with exilic hostility to the body founders. Paul can quite consistently affirm the created goodness of the body and the hope of its resurrection, while denouncing the works of the flesh.

The story is quite similar with the duality of church and world. Paul warns the Roman Christians, "Do not be conformed to this world," and gives regular instructions about being "in" but not "of" the world.[29] The opening chapters of I Corinthians carry a sustained contrast between the spirit of the world and its wisdom and the Spirit of Christ and his wisdom. But this polemic is not directed toward the world as the totality of the created order, but toward the world as the totality of fallen humanity.

Nor is human sinfulness equivalent with being-in-the-world. Reminding his readers of the difference between creation and the fall, Paul writes that "sin came into the world."[30] Sin is not an intrinsic character of the *kosmos* even when this term refers to sinful humanity. Instead of giving up on the world, "God so loved the world that he gave his only Son." That son comes as "the Lamb of God, who takes away the sin of the world." The Christian gospel, then, can be summarized in these words: "God was in Christ reconciling the world to himself."[31] Not to be conformed to this world means to accept this reconciliation and to become an ambassador of God in seeking to extend it. But it has nothing whatever to do with fleeing the bodily conditions of presence to other bodies or the spiritual conditions of presence to other selves.

If biblical religion does indeed stand with mimetic religion in its world affirmation, the central difference between the two concerns the kind of world affirmed. We have already seen mimetic religion affirm the world as nature, as cosmos, as cyclically recurring order. We turn now to biblical religion for the affirmation of the world as history, as unique event, as linear teleology.

11B. The faith of Israel and the world as history

It has been claimed that "the Bible relates a certain history in a confessional manner, because the recounting of this history is the central religious act of the worshipping community. Hence it is here maintained that Biblical theology is *the confessional recital of the redemptive acts of God* in a particular history, because history is the chief medium of revelation."[32] In this context confessing refers to confessing one's faith in a *credo* as distinct from confessing one's sins. And in view of reference to the "redemptive acts of God" it would be more adequate to designate history as the "chief medium of revelation and salvation." But the crucial point is simple and clear, that biblical faith involves the believing soul who meets God within history.

This faith originates in ancient Israel, which "is distinguished by the fact that it experienced the reality of its God not in the shadows of a mythical primitive history, but more and more decisively in historical change itself. . . . The presuppositions of the historical consciousness in Israel lie in its concept of God. The reality of God for Israel is not exhausted by his being the origin of the world, that is, of normal, ever self-repeating processes and events. Therefore this God can break into the course of his creation and initiate new events in it in an unpredictable way. The certainty that God again and again performs new acts, that he is a 'living God,' forms the basis for Israel's understanding of *reality as a linear history moving toward a goal . . .* history arises because God makes promises and fulfills these promises."[33]

We are dealing here with the very complex notion (1) that reality is primarily to be conceived as history rather than as nature or as cosmos, and (2) that history is not merely the continuous sequence of humanly significant events but the stage upon which or the medium within which the movement from God's promise to fulfillment occurs. It is because I believe the concept of covenant as developed in the Hebrew Bible best integrates all the varied aspects of this faith which affirms the world not only as nature but especially as history, that I have chosen the term "covenantal" to designate worldly religion.

It is just this aspect of the religion of ancient Israel which makes it possible to speak of the double exodus (of Abraham from Mesopotamia and of Moses from Egypt) at Israel's origins as being doubly significant.[34] For it concerns not only geography but also spirit, as the covenantal faith of Israel distinguishes itself from the mimetic faiths of Mesopotamia and Egypt. This is also the heart of the conflict between Yahweh, who will be Israel's only god, and the Canaanite Baalim with their mimetic fertility cults. (For Israel did not leave mimetic religion behind by moving to Palestine.)

We can see this new and different faith at work in one of the earliest "creeds" of Israel, taken from the liturgy for the presentation to God of the harvest's firstfruits. "A wandering Aramean was my father; and he went down into Egypt and sojourned there, a few in number; and there he became a nation, great, mighty, and populous. And the Egyptians treated us harshly, and afflicted us, and laid upon us hard bondage. Then we cried to the Lord the God of our fathers, and the Lord heard our voice, and saw our affliction, our toil, and our oppression; and the Lord brought us out of Egypt with a mighty hand and an outstretched arm, with great terror, with signs and wonders; and he brought us into this place and gave us this land, a land flowing with milk and honey. And behold, now I bring the first of the fruit of the ground, which thou, O Lord, has given me."[35]

In these simple lines both warfare and agriculture are removed from the realm of myth and *mimesis*. In the mimetic view of things one's chief god is a warrior hero who does combat against some demonic monster *in illo tempore*, and the human combat of "our" side against our enemies is validated as the imitative participation in that original battle. Here, by contrast, there is only one battle, and it is by Yahweh against first, the Egyptians, and eventually, the Canaanites. As in so many Old Testament contexts, "Yahweh defeats historical, human enemies."[36] God's action occurs in human history, which, correspondingly, becomes the place where salvation is experienced.

In the mimetic context, agriculture is both the earthly parallel to the mythical victory of the god over a demon of drought and the earthly parallel of the sacred marriage between that god and his consort. Ritual combat and copulation are the chief ingredients, often magically interpreted, of a fertility cult designed to be sure that earth succeeds in imitating heaven. Again, it is different in Israel. "As the farmer carried the produce of the soil in his basket, his thoughts would turn to the mysterious power of growth in the soil; he would be reminded of the showers of rain that had been sent by the heavenly powers to water the soil at the proper time. The devotee of the religion of Canaan, of Mesopotamia, or of Egypt would have seen the power of the nature divinities at work here and praised them. What a striking contrast is the prayer of the Israelite farmer. He does not waste a word on this. With the produce of the field before him, he thinks exclusively of his history: Yahweh, in an act of pure grace, has led him out of the oppression of Egypt into the abundance of this land, and has made it possible for him to bring to the sanctuary the fruit of the land 'which you, Yahweh, have given me.' "[37]

We can speak of a demythologizing of the divine here, insofar as the divine activity is transferred from the heavenly time of myth to the earthly time of concrete history.[38] But this does not mean either that Israel ever succeeded in living in isolation from the myths of mimetic religion or that all uses of her mythological heritage were at odds with her covenantal faith. For side by side with the battle against the mimetic cults closest to her, the Canaanite worship of Baal, was a process in which the images and symbols of the mimetic "creation" myth were put to use in reciting the mighty acts of Yahweh in history. "Israel drew upon available symbols and language which retained power and meaning even when the old mythic patterns which gave them birth had been attenuated or broken by Israel's austere historical consciousness."[39]

This is especially true of that one historical experience of redemption which stands at the heart of Israel's self-understanding as the people of Yahweh, the deliverance from the Egyptians at the Reed Sea. Martin Buber calls it the "holy event" which above all others gives rise to Israel's affirmation of history.[40] A well-known Midrash contrasts the experience of Israel in this event with that of Ezekiel when the prophet saw visions of God. The claim is that "what Ezekiel once saw in heaven was far less than what all of Israel once saw on earth. Ezekiel, and indeed all the other prophets, did not see God but only visions and similies of God. . . . In the sharpest possible contrast, the Israelites at the Red Sea had no need to ask which one was the King: 'As soon as they saw Him, they recognized Him, and they all opened their mouths and said, This is my God, and I'll glorify Him' (Exod. 15.2). Even the lowliest maidservant at the Red Sea saw what Isaiah, Ezekiel, and all the other prophets never saw. . . . The cited Midrash has special significance, however, because it affirms God's presence in history in full awareness of the fact that the affirmation is strange, extraordinary, or even paradoxical. The God of Israel is no mythological deity which mingles freely with men in history. He is beyond man. . . . Nevertheless, the Midrash insists that not messengers, not angels, not intermediaries, but God Himself acts in human history—and He was unmistakably present to a whole people at least once."[41]

An event of this kind can be described in the sober prose of Deuteronomy, "The Lord brought us out of Egypt with a mighty hand. . . ." But the magnitude of the event in Israel's life and the emotions it engenders require more picturesque speech. In the Song of the Sea there is a peculiar mixture of restraint and freedom in this regard. There is no attempt to take advantage of the fact that in the combat between Marduk and Tiamat and between Baal and Yamm the dragon slain by the hero god represents the waters of sea and river. Rather "the sea is not personified or hostile, but a passive instrument in Yahweh's control. There is no question here of a mythological combat between two gods. Yahweh defeats historical, human enemies."[42] Still in verses 17 and 18, after completing the story through the settlement in Canaan, there is reference to Yahweh building a sanctuary for himself on his mountain and to his enthronement as king forever. These two elements are especially prominent in the Canaanite myth of Baal.

In other Old Testament contexts there is less reticence with regard to the combat motif from the mimetic creation myth. In Nehemiah 9:11 and Psalm 78:13 Yahweh divides or "splits" the sea to let the Israelites pass through, the verb evoking images of Baal or Marduk (or Indra) in combat with the Sea-Dragon. More explicit are those passages which, without in the least diminishing the historical particularity of Yahweh's victory over the Egyptians and Israel's deliverance, portray Yahweh's control over the sea in the mythological language of combat. For example,

Awake, awake, put on strength, O arm of the Lord;
awake, as in days of old, the generations of long ago.
Was it not thou that didst cut Rahab in pieces, that didst pierce
    the dragon?
Was it not thou that didst dry up the sea, the waters of the great deep;
    that didst make the depths of the sea a way for the redeemed to
        pass over?[43]

And when Isaiah wants to warn the king against a foreign policy of dependence upon Egypt, he calls to mind Yahweh's victory over the Egyptians at the time of the exodus. Only this time the Sea-Dragon is not the sea but Egypt herself, whose help is worthless because she remains "Rahab Quelled."[44]

If Israel's historical consciousness governs her use of the creation myth of her mimetic neighbors, with whom she shares the celebration of creation, it also shapes the meaning of her own creation story. The Genesis stories are best approached from the perspective of Israel's praise of Yahweh as Creator. Occasionally, this stands as a subject matter in its own right.[45] More typically, it is part of a larger whole in which it plays a subordinate role and from which it derives a special meaning. This larger context occurs especially in certain Psalms and in the second part of Isaiah. There the praise of Yahweh as Creator passes over into celebration of his redemptive acts and thus to praise of God as Lord of History.[46]

This praise implies a remarkable ontology, one in which nature, if it does not drop out of the picture altogether, is given an entirely different meaning from the one it enjoys in mimetic nature mysticism. If we say that the theme of creation stands side by side with that of redemption, we betray a tendency to separate what the texts unite. The act of creation is simply the first of a series of acts which make up the salvation history of Israel. "God's activity in the creation and direction of his works is the same as his activity in the history of the nations. What is created and what occurs have not yet been separated from one another; the special realm 'nature' does not yet exist."[47] Moreover, because especially the Isaiah passages make creation the introduction not only to Israel's redemption but also to Yahweh's sovereignty over all of human history, we can say that it is history in its totality which replaces nature as the primary and essential character of the world.[48] This same ontology can also be expressed by saying that for Israel "the world and its fullness do not find their unity and inner coherence in a cosmological first principle . . . but in the completely personal will of Yahweh their creator . . . for Israel the 'world' was much less Being than Event . . . Israel did not see the world as an ordered organism in repose."[49]

When we turn to the creation stories of Genesis, we find literary analysis confirming what is required by the creation theology of the Psalms and Isaiah. The narratives telling how heaven and earth, plants and animals, man and woman came into being are but the opening act in the hexateuchal account of the redemption from Egypt and the eventual settlement in the promised land. The story goes back, not only to the patriarchs, but beyond them through the primeval history to creation itself. "Creation is part of the aetiology of Israel!"[50]

Like her mimetic neighbors, Israel tells the story of creation. But for them it is paradigm, while for her it is prologue. For them everything has meaning as the imitative return to that moment, while for her everything has meaning as part of the ongoing story of God's involvement in the world which began with its creation. Neither ontology is speculative in its origin or contemplative in its purpose. Both are "theories" intended to guide human praxis. And both call, in the first place, for the celebration of creation and praise of the

Creator. But here the ways part sharply. For mimetic faith the practical consequence, beyond praise, is ritual or ritualized imitation. For covenantal faith it is being prepared to meet the God of creation in ever new historical encounters.

In keeping with the ambivalence associated with the divine in general, this prospect has two sides. In Amos, for example, the message goes something like this. Prepare to meet your God, O Israel. He comes in judgment unless you return to him in repentance. And you should not take his coming lightly, for He who comes is the very power of creation. It is a fearful thing to fall into the hands of the living God.[51] By contrast, Second Isaiah speaks to an Israel which has already been punished for her sins and is forgiven. He proclaims a new act of salvation, a new exodus and a return home through the wilderness. Prepare to meet your God, O Israel. He comes to deliver you once again from captivity and exile. Do not doubt his power to do this, unlikely as it may look in terms of political realism. For He who comes is the very power of creation. It is a wonderful thing to be led forth by the living God.

There turn out to be two meanings, then, to the claim that in relation to her nearest neighbors Israel's faith is a demythologized faith. For, on the one hand, she plunders their creation myths for images and symbols with which to speak of the past and future redemptive acts of God in history; and, on the other hand, she replaces the creation myth with a creation story which no longer functions as myth but is treated as the opening act of the drama which is human history. In view of the close link between myth and ritual, the question inevitably arises what the consequences of all this for Israel's cultic life might be. The historical recital to accompany the offering of firstfruits, cited at the beginning of this section, suggests that history may transform ritual as well as myth.

A summary answer to this question may be given briefly: "The reenactment of primordial events of cosmogonic myth gave way to festivals reenacting epic events in Israel's past, thus renewing her life as a historical community. This was the character of the covenant renewal festivals of the league [Israel's tribal federation in Palestine prior to the monarchy]."[52] It is to be noticed that we can still speak of re-enactment, for the notion of making the past present so as to participate in it is not abandoned. Thus the Israelite farmer, settled in Palestine, is taught by Deuteronomy 26 to say, *We* suffered in Egypt, and Yahweh delivered *us* from bondage. Even stronger is the language of Deuteronomy 5, "The Lord our God made a covenant with us in Horeb. Not with our fathers did the Lord make this covenant, but with us, who are all of us here alive this day."[53] But the past to be relived is an historical rather than a mythological past.

Thus the ancient pilgrimage festivals, each of which had pre-Israelite origins in nomadic or agricultural contexts which were entirely unrelated to the history of Israel's deliverance from Egypt and covenantal relation with Yahweh, become celebrations of these moments of salvation history.[54]

For example, neither the shepherds who originally celebrated the Passover nor the peasants who originally celebrated the Feast of Unleavened Bread would have an easy time recognizing their cult in Exodus 12:1–13:6. Beyond combining the two into a single celebration, the Hebrews broke the link between the rites and the cycles of nature. Every detail of the ritual is made to commemorate some aspect of the Exodus. Perhaps the most remarkable thing of all is the word of Yahweh to Moses and Aaron in 12:2 (RSV), "This month shall be for you the beginning of months; it shall be the first month of the year for you." Whether this change of calendar came early or late, "the establishment of the Passover in any case means a regulating of the time of Nature by means of the time of history."[55]

If we add to this feature of Israel's festivals and the central role of historical recital in the Hebrew psalms of praise and lament, whose *Sitz im Leben* was the cult, it will begin to be clear how thoroughly the public worship of ancient Israel was permeated by an awareness of the mighty acts of God in history.[56]

11C. The purposes of redemptive history

We have not yet made our way to the heart of covenantal religion. That the narratives around which worship is built are recitals of divine activity on earth and in human history is clear enough. But the point of this activity remains unspecified. Yahweh becomes a warrior, taking on first the Egyptians and then the Canaanites, choosing for his human allies a people notable for their ability to complain. To what end? The answer is as simple as its full articulation is complex. Yahweh redeems Israel from Egypt and gives her a home in Canaan in order to establish a special relationship with her. Redemption is for the sake of a relationship, and the name of that relationship is covenant. Its simplest formulation, which permeates the Old Testament is this: I will be your God, and you will be my people.[57]

But what sort of relationship is it which can be designated by the formula, Yahweh, God of Israel, and Israel, people of Yahweh? Neither exilic nor mimetic religion provide any clues for interpreting this relationship grounded in historical adoption. But we can find a clue in the Hebrew word translated "covenant," which might best be translated as "obligation" or "promise." This makes it possible to say of the saving acts whose goal is covenantal relationship, "According to the Old Testament, the subject of a legitimate 're-presentation' can be only the saving acts of God himself, *to which saving acts belong also the promising and the demanding Word of God and the punitive judgements.*"[58] In short, it is in terms of promise and demand that the covenantal relationship is best to be understood. Reference to punitive judgements, crucial as it is to the concept of covenant, does not introduce a new category, for when God turns in judgement upon his own people this is only the keeping of the promise that neglect of covenantal demands would indeed bring punishment.[59]

There is a double significance in the fact that the promise and demand which belong to the saving acts have the form of speech. In the first place, God is a God who acts. But these acts are not brute facts whose meaning is the product of human construction. The God who acts is also the God who speaks, and his speech interprets his acts. "The biblical writer brackets the Exodus event with a preceding and a succeeding interpretation. He does not see the exodus as an 'act of God' distinct from the 'word of God' which explains it . . . The event is never uninterpreted."[60]

Second, through the speech of both promise and demand the relation between God and people becomes one of dialogue. The praise and petitions of the people become part of a conversation in which they are also addressed. The primary consequence of this is a radical personalizing of both God and people.

Because the concepts of Torah (instruction) and law have been so central to both the Jewish and Christian understanding of the Old Testament, we can begin with Yahweh's demand, and then turn to Yahweh's promise in seeking to interpret the covenantal relationship.[61] Whether we are thinking of the Ten Words (Ten Commandments) or of the entirety of the law codes which make up about half of the Pentateuch, we are dealing with prescriptions that Israel understood to belong to the covenant God made with Israel at Mount Sinai. The universality and the particularity of this Torah are equally important for understanding its covenantal character.

The universality of the law consists in the fact that it governs the whole of life. There is cultic law and there is social law, that is, regulations both for the proper worship of Yahweh and for the proper intercourse with fellow humans in daily life. And, in addition to this twofold direction of external behavior, there is instruction about the inner attitude of love to God and neighbor from which it is to stem. No split between sacred and secular or between inner and outer is to be permitted. The whole of life is to be shaped as part of the people's relation to God. But this is not viewed an an onerous burden. Instead it is a natural expression of the relation between the people and their God. As he had led their fathers across geographical deserts and through geographical wildernesses from Mesopotamia to Canaan and then to Egypt and back again, so, once their wanderings are over and they are settled in the land, he will not abandon them, but will continue to guide and accompany them through the uncharted existential wastelands of historical existence. It is because they viewed the law as guidance that Israel was able to see it as a gift.[62]

If the universality of the law means that this guidance extends to every dimension of human life, its particularity arises from the fact that it is not addressed to everyone. Martin Buber tells of the efforts of the young Goethe to prove "that the Ten Commandments were not actually the covenantal laws of the Israelites" on the grounds that a covenantal relationship could not "be based on universal obligations."[63] But even if one thinks that (some of) these maxims have a kind of Kantian validity for all rational creatures, the biblical text does not view them in this light. We do not read, it would be self-contradictory and therefore irrational to have any other gods before me. We read instead, "I am the Lord your God, who brought you out of the land of Egypt, out of the house of bondage. You shall have no other gods before me."[64] Buber comments, "What is said here to Israel . . . is not that there *are no* other gods: to say this would be to contradict the intentional sense and connection of the passage; Israel is told, that it is *forbidden* for other gods to exist. Forbidden that *they* should have other gods: but it only concerns *them*, who are addressed, and the whole reality of the subject under discussion is that of the relationship between YHVH and Israel."[65] This is why Westermann can say, of a related passage, "The words 'and beside me there is no god,' constitute a claim, not a statement of fact," and why von Rad can say, that "Israel's monotheism was to some extent a realisation which was not granted to her without the long discipline of the first commandment."[66] We are not dealing here with universal truths of reason but with a conversation between particular parties in a particular situation. In the speaking of vows a relationship is constituted, and the laws of Israel are the constitution of that bond. Given the difference between "spouses should be faithful to each other" and

"I vow to be faithful to you," it is the latter which expresses the form of covenant law.

Though the mutuality of vows and of dialogue indicate a thoroughly reciprocal relationship, the covenant is not an agreement between equals. It is between a god and his people. But such a relationship is not an everyday occurrence, whose nature is immediately obvious. Three models drawn from everyday experience are employed in the Old Testament as commentaries on the concept of covenant. Each indicates something of the basis upon which one party can rightfully make demands of the other. These models are lord and vassal, father and child, husband and wife. Since even the first of these represents a "quasi-familial" relationship,[67] it becomes clear that within the family created by covenantal vows, obligation rests upon love and loyalty rather than either fear or rationality alone.

The first model comes from international relations in an essentially feudal context. Parallels of structure between Hittite and Akkadian suzerainty treaties on the one hand and Old Testament texts on the other strongly suggest that the covenant was understood along the lines of the oath of fealty taken by a vassal to a more powerful king, his protector, ally, and lord. Such treaties typically have six parts: (1) a preamble introducing the sovereign lord, (2) a prologue giving the history of the relation between the two parties, (3) the stipulations governing the relationship, (4) arrangements for the preservation and public reading of the document recording the agreement, (5) a list of gods who are witnesses to the oath, and (6) a list of blessings for keeping the oath and curses for breaking it.[68]

Some scholars see the first three elements of this pattern in the Decalogue as the covenant law, beginning, as it does, (1) I am the Lord your God, (2) who brought you out of the land of Egypt . . . (3) You shall have no other gods before me. . . . A fuller expression is found in the covenant renewal ceremony at Shechem as recorded in Joshua 24. But by far the most complete patterning of Israel's covenant in terms of a suzerainty treaty is the book of Deuteronomy.[69]

There is a certain one-way character to such treaties. Though obligations as ally and protector are implied for the lord, they are left implicit, while the obligations of the vassal are spelled out in great detail. It is these which are surrounded by blessings and curses. The historical prologue may be intended to suggest that there is a basis other than force for the relationship, but such treaties can be imposed. To be sure, the biblical texts contain no such suggestion, but while the covenant is offered rather than imposed, it is just as clearly not negotiated. One can even speak of "a surrender to the divine power and grace."[70]

Such surrender is not passivity. It is rather the acknowledgment of an unconditional obligation to "love the Lord your God with all your heart, and with all your soul, and with all your might."[71] In this context "love" is not first and foremost a religious or ethical concept but a term borrowed from international politics. In the language of the suzerainty treaties lord and vassal are expected to "love" one another. The relationship is two-way but emphasis falls on the love owed by the vassal to his lord. This love can be commanded, for it consists not so much of feelings as of loyalty, service, and obedience.[72]

The second model is that of husband and wife. Israel is told that by virtue of her covenantal relationship with God, "your Maker is your husband."[73] This metaphor contains a threefold commentary on the idea of covenant. First, it portrays the people's sinfulness in terms of a wife's unfaithfulness to her husband. The prophets regularly speak of Israel's sins as adultery or even harlotry. As with the lord and vassal metaphor, Yahweh is portrayed as having a right to loving loyalty on the part of his people.

In the preaching of Hosea a second theme comes to the fore alongside this first one. The tenderness of heartbroken love, longing for reunion in spite of having been cuckolded, a motif quite impossible in terms of lord and vassal imagery, here becomes an integral part of covenantal thought.

The third dimension of this metaphor comes from Amos. He refers to the saving history in familiar words, "I brought you out of the land of Egypt, and led you forty years in the wilderness, to possess the land of the Amorite." But at the same time he indicates that this does not make Israel unique, for Yahweh, as Lord of History, has guided the migrations of other nations as well.[74] Still, Israel does have a unique relationship to Yahweh. "You only have I known of all the families of the earth; therefore I will punish you for all your iniquities."[75] In the Old Testament the verb to know signifies no theoretical cognition. It is used to speak of the union of husband and wife, as when we read that Adam knew his wife Eve. So when God speaks of knowing Israel alone of all the nations, the marriage metaphor is once again before us. And when the events of revelation and covenant making at Sinai are distinguished as this knowing from the events of deliverance and guidance from Egypt, through the wilderness, and into Canaan, we get an explicit teaching in answer to our question about the purpose of salvation history. For Amos, as Buber puts it, "the first series exists for the sake of the second."[76]

Yahweh has rescued Israel in order that he might be married to her, that a relation of loving intimacy might be established. Though Amos speaks of judgment and God's right to expect faithfulness from Israel, his prophecy, like that of Hosea, ends on the theme of restoration and the triumph of Yahweh's love over Israel's faithlessness.

Situated somewhere in between these two models is a third picture of the covenant relationship, that of father and son. Sometimes the emphasis is on the tenderness of loving intimacy, as in the happy side of the husband-wife metaphor.[77] At other times the emphasis is on the duty owed by a child to the father, the discipline that can be expected for disobedience, and the pain experienced by the father of rebellious and unfaithful children. The God of the prophets often sounds like King Lear.

> Ingratitude, thou marble-hearted fiend,
> More hideous when thou show'st thee in a child
> Than the sea-monster! . . .
> How sharper than a serpent's tooth it is
> To have a thankless child.[78]

Each of these three models represents a familial or quasi-familial relationship in which respect, obedience, loyalty, and faithfulness are the natural and appropriate role of the lesser partner, who is dependent upon the greater for protection and leadership.

We turn now to the concept of promise as the second clue to the meaning of covenantal relationship as the purpose of salvation history, for "with the various biblical covenants, promise and the resultant expectation were given as an integral part of them."[79] What further light can be thrown by this concept on the covenantal formula, I will be your God, and you will be my people?

The first thing to notice is that the formula is itself a promise. Since it is clearly within historical experience that the fulfillment of this promise is to be sought, its meaning is that God does not merely turn his people loose in history but accompanies them through it as their leader and guide.[80] It is not only his law which is to provide a light, map, and compass for the treacherous journey through historical experience; Yahweh accompanies his people on their journey in person. Hence the promise as Israel is sent on from Sinai to the promised land, "My presence will go with you and I will give you rest."[81]

In the dramatic dialogue between Moses and Yahweh at the burning bush, the sacred name of God is interpreted as expressing this very promise. Through a play on words which links the name YHWH

with the verb to be, an answer is given to the question Moses antic-
ipates from his fellow Hebrews in Egypt concerning the name of the
God he represents. The traditional translation, I am who I am, is
derived from the Greek translation of the Old Testament and im-
poses a Greek metaphysics of being upon a Hebrew ontology of event.
A more authentic rendering would be in the future tense and would
be something like, I will be there (for you) as I choose to be there.[82]

In the ancient near-eastern context the name of a god was important for magical purposes. With it one might conjure a god and
compel divine assistance. Quite possibly this was the motive Moses
attributed to the Hebrews in the question he anticipated about the
divine name. In this setting Yahweh's answer is twofold. I will be
there (for you). But I will be there as I choose to be, retaining my
sovereign freedom. "In short: you do not need to conjure Me, but
you cannot conjure Me either."[83] Or, in other words, "He who promises his steady presence, his steady assistance, refuses to restrict himself to definite forms of manifestation."[84]

This promise of a personal accompanying leadership adds to the
law a second, more personal dimension of divine guidance through
history. Beyond that, it plays a role in the covenantal relationship
quite distinct from the law. Torah instructs the people about what
kind of lives they are to live on their historical sojourn with God,
but it does not tell the goal of that journey. The promise opens up
into a preview of that goal.

At this point it is no longer possible to focus almost entirely on
the Sinai or Moses covenant. There are two other major covenant
traditions in the Old Testament, the Abraham covenant and the
David covenant. Just as the Moses covenant best illuminates the
meaning of covenant in terms of law or obligation, so the Abraham
and David covenants best enable us to understand covenant in terms
of promise. For they contain the promises which tell us about the
destination of the historical journey of the covenant partners.

It would not be strictly accurate to contrast the promise covenants
of Abraham and David with the obligation covenant of Moses, for
in both cases there is unconditional obligation, freely undertaken,
and in both cases there is promise or vow, through which the obligation is incurred. Still, the Abraham and David covenants have an
almost directly opposite structure from the Moses covenant, and the
distinction of the promise covenants from the obligation covenant is
one way to point to this difference. The Moses covenant focuses
almost entirely on the obligation the people undertake in their promise to love and serve Yahweh; while the Abraham and David cove-

nants focus almost entirely on the obligation Yahweh undertakes in the promises to bless.[85] It is these promises of blessing that indicate the goal of the covenantal journey.[86]

There are four distinct promises involved in the Abraham covenant. One of these is the covenant formula itself, at least its first half. For God promises Abraham "to be God to you and to your descendants after you. . . . I will be their God."[87] Then there are the promises that Abraham will have many offspring and that the land of Canaan will be given to his descendants.[88] The historical narrative from the exodus to the conquest, in which the Moses covenant is placed, begins and ends with emphasis on the fulfillment of these promises.[89] Finally, there is the promise which is of central importance in the present context.

> I will make you into a great nation and I will bless you;
> I will make your name great, and you will be a blessing.
> I will bless those who bless you, and whoever curses you I will
>   curse;
> and all peoples on earth will be blessed through you.[90]

The first three promises reiterate the discovery already made, that the purpose of revelation history is the establishment of the covenantal bond between Yahweh and his people. The fourth promise, however, takes us beyond that to the purpose of that relationship. It is, to be sure, an end in itself. But it is also more than that. The text just cited "indicates something of the final meaning and purpose of the saving relation that God has vouchsafed to Israel." The God of all the earth has focused his attention on one people for the sake of all peoples. "What is promised to Abraham reaches far beyond Israel; indeed it has universal meaning for all generations on earth." Here, "Abraham is assigned the role of mediator of blessing in God's saving plan, for 'all families of the earth.' The extent of the promise now becomes equal to that of the unhappy international world."[91] This is why it is necessary to speak in the plural about the purposes of redemptive history. For the mighty acts of God have a national goal which points beyond itself to an international goal. Abraham and his descendants are blessed to be a blessing to all peoples.

To be the covenant people of God means, from the perspective of law, to be in a familial or quasi-familial relation of dependency which grounds the obligation of faithful and obedient service to God as king, husband, and father. From the perspective of promise, it means to be the recipient of God's unmerited favor by virtue of which a people become partners of God in sharing his gracious blessing with

all other peoples. Thus we read in the book of Isaiah that to be the
servant of Yahweh is to be a light to the nations,[92] and we get this
lyrical picture of the universal meaning of Israel's election.

> It shall come to pass in the latter days
> that the mountain of the house of the Lord
> shall be established as the highest of the mountains,
> and shall be raised above the hills;
> and all nations shall flow to it,
> and many peoples shall come, and say:
> "Come, let us go up to the mountain of the Lord,
> to the house of the God of Jacob;
> that he may teach us his ways
> and that we may walk in his paths."
> For out of Zion shall go forth the law,
> and the word of the Lord from Jerusalem.
> He shall judge between the nations,
> and shall decide for many peoples;
> and they shall beat their swords into plowshares,
> and their spears into pruning hooks;
> nation shall not lift up sword against nation,
> neither shall they learn war any more.[93]

The reference to Zion in this text brings the David covenant into
the picture. The promises to David are given by the prophet Nathan.
After conveying a renewed promise of blessing for "my people Israel," Nathan reports the word of the Lord to David personally. His
son will rule after him, "and I will establish his kingdom. He shall
build a house for my name, and I will establish the throne of his
kingdom forever. I will be his father, and he shall be my son. When
he commits iniquity, I will chasten him . . . but I will not take my
steadfast love from him. . . . And your house and your kingdom shall
be made sure forever before me; and your throne shall be established
forever."[94]

At first glance this seems to move away from the universalism of
the Abraham covenant to a narrower particularism than even the
Moses covenant, since attention is shifted from the nation to their
ruling dynasty. But this covenant becomes the heart of messianic
hope in Israel, and in the picture of the anointed ruler (Messiah =
the anointed one) whose reign is everlasting we find another uni-
versalization of the divine promises. This occurs both in the Psalms
and in the prophets.

The point of departure in the Psalms is the kingship of Yahweh
himself. The "enthronement psalms" which celebrate this divine sov-

ereignty emphasize both the majesty of its power and the justness of its decisions. Its scope is threefold. It extends to the whole of nature, of which Yahweh is the creator. It is also an historical rule, for it involves "his people" Israel. But the glory and righteousness of Yahweh are not in any sense their exclusive possession. As the "great King above all gods" Yahweh is king of all peoples and the blessings of his reign are for them all. If all the nations are invited to clap and shout for joy because of God's grace to his chosen people, Israel, it is because all are to be included as "the princes of the peoples gather as the people of the God of Abraham." If divine faithfulness to his covenant with Israel is to occasion joyful singing throughout the world, it is because this same Yahweh "comes to rule the earth. He will judge the world with righteousness, and the peoples with equity."[95]

In like manner the "songs of Zion" celebrate the divine kingship in its universal as well as in its national significance. Once again the majesty of the divine power is related to the blessings it secures for all peoples. When God "utters his voice, the earth melts." This is good news, however, for "he makes wars cease to the end of the earth; he breaks the bow, and shatters the spear, he burns the chariots with fire!"[96] Yahweh is "terrible to the kings of the earth," but again this is good news because the purpose of God's judgment is "to save all the oppressed of the earth."[97] By relating these blessings to Zion, however, these psalms call attention to their human mediation, for Zion is the central symbol of the David covenant. It is because of this mediating role that Zion is "the joy of all the earth."[98]

A more direct reference to the role of the Davidic king in blessings for the nations is found in the "royal psalms," which direct attention to the human king. There are important differences between kingship in Israel and in other parts of the ancient near east. But it remains the case that the king's role is to see to it that the divine will be done on earth as it is in heaven. Thus the anointed one on the throne of David is to be Yahweh's "faithful viceregent."[99] As such the king becomes the bearer of the same divine sovereignty celebrated in the enthronement psalms and songs of Zion, with the result that descriptions of the human king become loaded with superlatives more appropriate to the ideal task than to the historical reality.[100] In the mimetic context the exaggerated description of the king points backward to the mythical archetype. But in the covenantal context it becomes promise that seeks historical fulfillment. In this way royal psalms become messianic psalms, expressing and evoking hope that some day through Yahweh's faithful viceregent the gap between the ideal king and the real king will be closed and the whole earth will be the beneficiaries.[101]

The form of messianic futurism is different in the prophets, but the substance is the same. In a cultic situation celebrating the king and the covenant, it occurs in the psalms by overloading historical referents with idealized descriptions. Speaking in a political situation where the human kingship is either tottering or defeated, the prophets sharply distinguish any present descendants of David from the coming one in whom the promises will be fulfilled.[102] They regularly evoke the promises to David as the basis for their hope and expectation that some day the blessings of the covenantal relationship will be renewed through the restoration of the throne of David.

This hope has an intensely nationalistic meaning in the context of defeat and exile, anticipated or already experienced.[103] But without repudiating this nationalistic hope, the prophets also rise above it to picture the coming blessing in universal, international terms. Preexilic, exilic, and post-exilic prophets share this vision. For example, Isaiah describes the "shoot from the stump of Jesse" on whom "the Spirit of the Lord shall rest," whose reign will bring justice for the poor and a peace symbolized by the wolf and the lamb lying down together.

> They shall not hurt or destroy in all my holy mountain;
> for the earth shall be full of the knowledge of the Lord
> as the waters cover the sea.
> In that day the root of Jesse shall stand as an ensign to the peoples;
> him shall the nations seek, and his dwellings shall be glorious.[104]

The promise aspect of the covenantal relationship thus has the same meaning in the David tradition that it has in the Abraham tradition. If the first purpose of salvation history is the establishment of a marriage-like relationship between Israel and her God, it is not simply that they may live happily ever after. A second purpose is intended, that the first relationship should become the means by which a second is established, this time between God and all peoples. The Abraham and David covenants, focusing on the theme of promise, bring this second goal to light. The David covenant differs from the Abraham covenant primarily by the specificity with which it describes the nature of the international blessing in terms of peace and justice.

11D. The overcoming of guilt and death in covenantal salvation

The bearing of all this on the covenantal understanding of guilt and death is direct. The close link between guilt and death in biblical religion is, as was argued in Chapter Six, anything but unique. The believing soul regularly finds the two to be inextricably intertwined, as the existential analysis of each would lead us to expect. But the distinguishing features of covenantal piety do lead to a distinctively covenantal interpretation of both guilt and death. Those distinguishing features are the historical understanding of the world (Section 11B), and the covenantal understanding of history (Section 11C).

From the exilic and mimetic perspectives, historical existence itself can be looked upon as the heart of the problem. For from the exilic point of view it presupposes natural, embodied selfhood and from the mimetic point of view it presupposes unique individuality rather than the reiteration of archetypal form. Covenantal religion will borrow images from these traditions to express its understanding of the human predicament, but they cannot be basic. For, in covenantal perspective, historical existence as such, far from being the problem, is the condition for the possibility of salvation. It is the medium within which or the stage upon which the human and divine rendezvous occurs.

As a medium or a stage, history has no meaning apart from the meeting which occurs within it. And for covenantal faith, as we have seen, the meaning of the meeting between God and his human creatures is the establishment of the covenantal bond which makes it possible for the parties to address each other, respectively, as "My people" and "Our God." This is the meaning of salvation. Thus the distinctively covenantal understanding of guilt and death will be in terms of that which threatens the covenantal bond by damaging or destroying it altogether.

With regard to death the faith of ancient Israel contains both moments we have examined in exploring exilic and mimetic piety, the absence and then the presence of a hope for personal salvation beyond death. In both cases the issue of covenantal fellowship is the central issue. According to the earlier view, which is not so much taught as assumed, Sheol is the abode of the dead. It is much like the underworld realms of the dead known to us from Mesopotamian and Canaanite mythology, which in turn are very similar to the possibly more familiar Greek Hades. Sheol is a kind of "negative replica of earthly existence," where the shades "eke out a bare existence."[105] It is a realm of silence and darkness and, above all, weakness. Since it is not oblivion one must speak of life, after a fashion, though it is life without vitality. But the worst thing about Sheol is its theological meaning. It is not a place of punishment and torment, for the righteous and wicked are there without distinction (though this will change in the apocalyptic writings). But it is a place where the shades are cut off from fellowship with God.

It has been said that "this realm remained outside Yahweh's sphere of influence for quite a long time and was only gradually opened to his sovereignty."[106] But this is a misleading way of making an important point. It implies a kind of dualism foreign to the faith of the Old Testament, as if Death and Sheol were powers beyond the control of Yahweh. But this is explicitly denied in a number of texts;[107] nor, on a close reading, is it what is affirmed by those texts which describe Sheol as cut off from God. The dead are indeed "forsaken" and "cut off from [God's] hand." But this is not due to divine impotence, but to a mutual forgetfulness "in the land of forgetfulness." God doesn't remember the dead, and they don't remember him. He works no wonders for them, and they offer no praise to him.[108] It is because there is no praise that Sheol is a place of silence, for apart from telling of God's saving works and covenantal faithfulness there is no foundation for human speech.[109] By contrast the living remember God's mercy in the past, they cry for his help in the present, and they hope for his faithfulness in the future, and for these reasons they praise God.[110] So strong is this link that it can be said, "There cannot be such a thing as true life without praise. Praising and no longer praising are related to each other as are living and no longer living."[111]

Clearly death is here viewed as a limit. But it is not the limit of God's sovereignty so much as it is the limit beyond which the covenantal bond is broken. In death there is no longer any meaning to the words, I will be your God and you will be my people. The point misleadingly expressed by describing death as "outside Yahweh's sphere of influence" is better put by saying, "Even though it is taken for granted that Yahweh's power of control extends to Sheol, this does not alter the fact that death is felt to be the ultimate bound, which excludes not only from earthly life but also from enjoyment of fellowship with God." It is as the opponent of "the will to fellowship revealed in the covenant relationship" that death is dreaded.[112] But it is precisely that will to fellowship on God's part, experienced within the covenantal relationship, which gives rise to the hope, not merely that the victory of Sheol may be delayed, but that it may eventually be overcome altogether.

This hope occurs in two forms in the Hebrew scriptures. In a couple of passages salvation after death is an eschatological event on a cosmic scale. It involves many, if not necessarily all the dead. Here we are introduced to key elements of the apocalyptic tradition which is such a major factor in Jewish faith from the second century B.C. onwards and is essentially taken for granted in the New Testament. These include the resurrection of the body and the final judgment of both the wicked and the righteous. But there is also hope on a much smaller scale, grounded in the individual realization "that in direct encounter with God life acquires an indestructible content."[113] In both cases hope grew out of the covenant people's "conviction that the fellowship they had enjoyed with God in this life could not be broken even by death."[114]

This latter hope we find in the book of Job, but only in the form of longing.[115] In the Psalms, however, this longing appears in the form of hope. For example, the Psalmist exults in praise to God

> For thou dost not give me up to Sheol,
>   or let thy godly one see the Pit.
> Thou dost show me the path of life;
>   in thy presence there is fullness of joy,
>   in thy right hand are pleasures for evermore.[116]

The basis of this "heaven-storming confidence" is the Psalmist's present experience of life in communion with God. "That moreover, which, in the present constitutes for him the content of life and the essence of all good, he knows to be allotted to him in the future also as his abiding portion. Step by step the praise rises right up to the level of sheer exultation, as he sees the limits which otherwise are set to all earthly well-being yield before the happiness of fellowship with God . . . Sheol and the grave can no longer terrify him. . . . How this happens . . . there is no unambiguous statement." But while there is no explanation, there is a certainty "built on the gift of fellowship with God here and now."[117]

In another Psalm this hope is even more explicit. Here death has its terror not merely as the end of life or as the passage to an undesirable place, but precisely as the loss of contact with God. The death of those who live outside the covenant bond with Yahweh is no mere termination or decline. It is the ruin of being swept away from God's memory and awareness like the elements of a dream when one awakens.[118] But the present experience of the covenant bond which, for the pious would make death far worse than a natural

disaster, gives rise to the hope it is somehow stronger than even the
threat of death. So the Psalmist proceeds

> Nevertheless I am continually with thee;
>   thou dost hold my right hand.
> Thou dost guide me with thy counsel,
>   and afterward thou wilt receive me to glory.
> Whom have I in heaven but thee?
>   And there is nothing upon earth that I desire besides thee.
> My flesh and my heart may fail,
>   but God is the strength of my heart and my portion for ever.[119]

The language used here is that of being translated or snatched
away from death as Enoch and Elijah were.[120] But here as before
there is no inclination to speculate on how death is overcome or on
where and in what condition God will be the portion of the pious
for ever. The idea of snatching away simply expresses "an expectation of a bond with Yahweh which even physical death cannot
interrupt."[121]

This same hope appears in its eschatological, cosmic form in the
book of Daniel and in chapters 24-27 of Isaiah, the so-called "apocalypse of Isaiah." In the Isaiah passage the central theme is the decisive judgment of God upon those who resist his purposes and the
historical victory of his covenantal kingdom. This positive side of the
story is portrayed through the image of a covenant banquet that God
hosts on Mount Zion. It evokes memories of the covenant meal celebrated on Mount Sinai when Moses and the elders of Israel ate and
drank with God.[122] But there are two important differences. This
banquet is for all the nations, not just for Israel. And this banquet
celebrates not simply Israel's victories over the Egyptians and the
Canaanites, but the God-given victory of all peoples over their ultimate enemy. "And he will destroy on this mountain the covering
that is cast over all peoples, the veil that is spread over all nations.
He will swallow up death for ever, and the Lord God will wipe away
tears from all faces, and the reproach of his people he will take away
from all the earth; for the Lord has spoken."[123]

But can this historical fulfillment of the covenantal promises be
fully satisfactory without the participation of the righteous who have
gone before? Apparently this question is an important part of the
belief in the resurrection which gets perhaps its first clear expression
here.

> Thy dead shall live, their bodies shall rise.
> O dwellers in the dust, awake and sing for joy!

> For thy dew is a dew of light,
> and on the land of the shades thou wilt let it fall.[124]

In the Daniel passage the scope of the resurrection is extended to include the wicked as well as the righteous. "And many of those who sleep in the dust of the earth shall awake, some to everlasting life, and some to shame and everlasting contempt. And those who are wise shall shine like the brightness of the firmament; and those who turn many to righteousness, like the stars for ever and ever."[125] Of these two passages it can be said, "At last the biblical writers had found that mould, as it were, into which they could pour their hopes and longings and which alone could give real shape to the belief that man's fellowship with God would not be broken by death."[126]

The Old Testament understanding of sin and guilt has the same distinctively covenantal form as the understanding of death. They are dreadful because sin is the cause of and guilt the experience of a breach in the covenantal bond. On the other hand, the experience of God's will to fellowship is strong enough to support the belief that the initiative to heal the breach comes from God's side and that the will to forgiveness and reconciliation is part of the meaning of the covenantal formula, I will be your God and you will be my people.

This personalizing of the understanding of sin and guilt finds eloquent expression in the fact that one of the root words for sin in ancient Israel has the meaning 'to rebel.'[127] This means that "sin was comprehended as a conscious and responsible act, by which Man rebelled against the unconditional authority of God in order to decide for himself what way he should take, and to make God's gifts serve his own ego . . . now the decisive feature was the conflicting directions of two wills, the divine and the human, and this conflict could only be resolved by dealings between two persons."[128] This is why in Psalm 51, the biblical paradigm for penitence, David, who has taken both the wife and the life of one of his generals, can say to God, "Against thee, thee only, have I sinned, and done that which is evil in thy sight." His guilt finds expression in the simple statement, "I have sinned against the Lord."[129] Here as in the story of Eden, the heart of sin is to be found in a heart of rebellion against God, and guilt is the painful awareness that the bond of fellowship with God has been broken from the human side. "Thus Israel became well acquainted with the punishment of an evil conscience, which outruns the external penalty. . . . When fallen Man hides himself in order to elude God's gaze, when David's heart smites him after committing crime, these turns of phrase express eloquently the understanding of guilt as the disturbance of a personal relationship of trust."[130]

One of the distinctive forms of corporate penitence in the Old Testament is narrative confession, the recital of the salvation history interspersed with accounts of the people's sinfulness. This occurs not only in the Pentateuch and the histories of the kings, but also in the Psalms. In Psalm 78, for example, the history associated with the Moses covenant is recited, contrasting the faithfulness of God with the unfaithfulness of his people. The latter's sinfulness is consistently portrayed as the breaking of the personal bond between God and his people. Thus they rebelled against him (vv. 8, 17, 40), were disloyal to him (vv. 8, 37, 57), forgot him (vv. 7, 11, 42), and refused to believe or trust him (vv. 22, 32). In this setting, of course, forgetting has an entirely different meaning from its exilic sense. It does not mean that I (or we) forget that our true nature is divine and that we have no business here in the world but to seek liberation and the return to our true, unworldly home. It rather means forgetting the mighty acts of God in history for my (or our) salvation and with them the covenantal bond which was their purpose. Forgetting is more a matter of ingratitude than of bad metaphysics, which makes it a natural partner of distrust, disloyalty, and even rebellion against God.[131]

This covenantal understanding of sin and guilt is related to the three prime models of the covenant relationship. The root image of rebellion, of course, has its natural home in the political realm. In the many passages where it and its relatives are used without specification, the primary connotation is revolt against the king.[132] But the biblical writers extend this cluster of concepts to the parent-child and husband-wife relationships as well. Sinful Israel is portrayed as rebellious, faithless, and foolish children who do not know or honor their father and who have forsaken and dealt corruptly with him.[133] Especially in Jeremiah and Hosea the covenant breaking which can be described as rebellion and forgetfulness is regularly described as the unfaithfulness of a wife to her husband. Israel's adultery has made a lie of the covenant formula, a fact dramatically expressed when Hosea is told how to name his son. "And the Lord said, 'Call his name Not my people, for you are not my people and I am not your God.' "[134]

In this context salvation will mean forgiveness and forgiveness will mean the restoration of the covenantal bond of fellowship. Thus adultery and the break between the people and their God is not Hosea's last word. He speaks of a renewed covenant, in which God addresses his faithless people, "And I will betroth you to me for ever; I will betroth you to me in righteousness and in justice, in steadfast love, and in mercy. I will betroth you to me in faithfulness; and you shall know the Lord. . . . And I will have pity on Not pitied, and I will say to Not my people, 'You are my people'; and he shall say, 'Thou art my God.' " As the people acknowledge their guilt and seek the face of their God, they will say, "Come, let us return to the Lord; for he has torn, that he may heal us; he has stricken, and he will bind us up. After two days he will revive us; and on the third day he will raise us up, that we may live before him."[135] There is no longer the need to flee from God's presence.

Jeremiah speaks in much the same way of a renewed covenantal relationship when God will say, "I will forgive their iniquity, and I will remember their sin no more."[136] This theme of forgetting is as central to the covenantal concept of salvation as it is to the covenantal concept of sin. Just as sin involves forgetting the covenant partner, thereby breaking the relationship, so forgiveness involves forgetting the sinful partner's unfaithfulness so as to restore the relationship. To say, I will forget the wrong you did to me, is to say, I want our relationship to resume as if it had never happened. This means that forgiveness involves more than the decision to forego or terminate punishment. Thus in Isaiah the word of forgiveness has this form:

> I am the Lord, your Holy One,
>   the Creator of Israel, your King. . . .
> I, I am He
>   who blots out your transgressions for my own sake,
>   and I will not remember your sins. . . .
> Remember these things, O Jacob,
>   and Israel, for you are my servant;
> I formed you, you are my servant;
>   O Israel, you will not be forgotten by me.
> I have swept away your transgressions like a cloud,
>   and your sins like mist;
>   return to me, for I have redeemed you.[137]

God's willingness to forgive by forgetting frees Israel to forget the past as well. In the context of the renewal of the marriage bond between Israel and her God, he says to her,

> Fear not, for you will not be ashamed . . .
> for you will forget the shame of your youth,
> and the reproach of your widowhood you will remember no more.
> For your maker is your husband. . . .
> In overflowing wrath for a moment I hid my face from you,
> but with everlasting love I will have compassion on you. . . .[138]

For ancient Israel forgiveness was not only a covenantal concept in its meaning but also in its motivation. If forgiveness is the intent to restore the covenantal partnership, this intent is grounded in God's faithfulness to his covenant promises. So we find that God's willingness to forget the sins of his people is often presented as arising from his remembering his covenant promises, through Abraham, through Moses, and through David.[139] Even where references to a specific covenant are not explicit the same linkage is found where God's willingness to forgive is grounded in his steadfast love (*hesed*). This concept designates a covenantal relationship. It refers less to a general faithfulness or good will than to a loyalty to covenantal vows.[140] On the basis of promises made in the past there arise new promises which designate the future as a time of forgiveness and reconciliation.[141]

Although God's faithfulness to his own promises and the will to fellowship that those promises express ground a merciful willingness to forgive which is a major theme of Israel's praise, this does not signify any kind of moral indifference on God's part, as if covenantal promises had diminished the meaning of covenantal law. For among the covenant promises is the promise to punish the breaking of the covenant law. This is why God's mercy is less an alternative to punishment than a modification of the way in which punishment is administered.[142] Punishment is a ratification from God's side of the rupture in the relationship brought about by human sin. But the divine acknowledgment that all is not well is designed to heal the wound rather than to deepen it. Its purpose is to bring the sinner(s) to a realization of what has happened and to a desire to return. It is not really paradoxical to say that the ultimate goal of punishment is forgiveness, for this only means that its intended result is repentance and confession, the willingness to seek and accept forgiveness. For the restoring of the broken bond requires both the offer and the acceptance of reconciliation.[143]

If on the one hand the promises of the covenant include punishment as well as forgiveness, the laws of the covenant include forgiveness as well as obligation. For among the demands of the law are the prescriptions for various rites of atonement. Although the symbolism of these rites is often that of purification or the spatial removal of that which contaminates, they have a distinctly covenantal meaning as well. These rites have been specified and provided by God as part of the covenant as a means of renewing broken fellowship. If there is a willingness on the part of the human violator(s) of the covenant to seek and accept forgiveness and reconciliation, whether this has been brought about by punishment, the fear of punishment, or what Ricoeur calls "the fear of not loving enough,"[144] covenantal law has already spelled out a way for the contrite heart to act out its confession, to give public and empirical reality to its own will to fellowship.[145] It is thus through the joint action of the covenant partnership that the bond between God and his people, individually and collectively, is renewed and revived. God's role is to demand repentance, while offering reconciliation. The human role is to acknowledge guilt, while accepting forgiveness. The two agree to put the past aside, so as to resume their journey through historical existence together.

If we ask what the results of our threefold typology (Chapters 9 through 11) are, two quite general conclusions can be stated. First, some detailed support has been given for the claim made in Chapter 6 that guilt and death are a central and essentially single concern of the religious life, not only in the biblical tradition, but in religious traditions very different from the former and often thought to differ precisely by the lack of such a concern. While this is by no means a strict proof of the universality of this concern, it would seem to lend a good deal of plausibility to such an hypothesis and provide a fruitful framework for further exploration of the issue.

Second, our typology has not only shown that the form that this concern takes, and thus what we might call the form of salvation, varies from one context to another; it has also shown that these variations stand in a meaningful correlation with the basic attitudes toward human being in the world which provide the key to the religious typology developed here. In fact, the world affirmation and negation variable is so closely linked to the guilt and death variable that a closer look might reveal them not to be independent variables at all, but different faces of a single spiritual issue.

But it would not be in keeping with the existential dimension of our phenomenology to look back on our journey only in terms of possible future research. For the idea was that the phenomena to be explored were not to be reduced to data for scientific theorizing, but to be maintained as possibilities for personal and communal experience. The first eight chapters presented the possibility of the religious life generically in terms of its three dimensions, the awesome terror of the sacred as ontological and axiological *tremendum*, the attractiveness of relation to the sacred as a means for dealing with guilt and death, and the attractiveness of relation to the sacred as an end in itself, as a form of useless self-transcendence. The typology, appropriately becoming more specific, has presented three variations on the theme of religion as a means for dealing with guilt and death.

It might be argued, however, that for us these variations cannot meaningfully be said to be possibilities, "live options" in the sense of William James. There aren't many local temples, for example, where one could take up the practice of Mesopotamian or Egyptian religion; and while some westerners are attracted to Vedanta missions, exilic spirituality remains for most an exotic curiosity for historical research at best. It needs to be remembered, however, that we were not studying these particular traditions on their own terms but as especially lucid illustrations of a type of spirituality. These types of spirituality can take up their abode in almost any tradition, and it is not difficult to find forms of Judaism and Christianity, not to mention Islam, which are more nearly exilic or mimetic than covenantal. The point is simply that if there is any form of the religious life which is a "live option" for me, I can increase my understanding of it and of myself in relation to that possibility by seeking to identify its exilic, its mimetic, and its covenantal dimensions, if any, and the interrelations of these dimensions if more than one is clearly present.

Since the task of existential self-understanding is communal and not only individual, our typology will also have a bearing on the doing of theology. The theologian includes among his or her tasks the search for self-understanding as a member of and on behalf of a specific religious community or tradition. The question to what degree "we" are exilic, mimetic, or covenantal, and how more than one of these perspectives might be integrated into a coherent or incoherent blend, has essentially the same form on the individual and communal level.

Finally, for the unbelieving soul, the person who stands outside all communities of faith and piety, our typology may help to provide self-understanding on a number of issues. Perhaps the most important of these is the discovery whether what one finds either attractive of repulsive about religion belongs to religion in some generic sense or rather to a specific way of being religious.

In all of these cases the project will have been fruitful if it has helped us relearn to see the world, enlarging our understanding of the possibilities life offers us, thereby enabling us to live our lives with greater integrity.

NOTES

Chapter 1: The Art of Understanding as an Alternative Approach in the Philosophy of Religion

1. This question is the title of the Third Essay in Nietzsche's *Genealogy of Morals*.

2. The debate over the verification criterion of meaning and the factual meaningfulness of metaphysical assertions belongs in this context as well.

3. Edmund Husserl, *The Idea of Phenomenology*, trans. Alston and Nakhnikian (The Hague, 1970), p. 43. Husserl goes on to describe phenomenology as the clarification of meanings (p. 46).

4. For a discussion of some of the difficulties with the traditional approach, see Merold Westphal, "Prolegomena to Any Future Philosophy of Religion Which Will Be Able to Come Forth as Prophecy," *International Journal for Philosophy of Religion*, Vol. 4, No. 3 (Fall, 1973), pp. 129–35.

5. Gerardus van der Leeuw, *Sacred and Profane Beauty: the Holy in Art*, trans. David Green (New York, 1963), p. 6.

6. The quoted phrase is the subtitle to Hume's *A Treatise of Human Nature*. Among his most important followers on this point are John Stuart Mill and Carl Hempel. For an introduction to their work see William Dray, *Philosophy of History* (Englewood Cliffs, 1964), and Arnold Levison, *Knowledge and Society: An Introduction to the Philosophy of the Social Sciences* (Indianapolis, 1974).

7. Karl Jaspers, *General Psychopathology*, trans. Hoenig and Hamilton (Chicago, 1963). Max Weber speaks correspondingly of "non-understandable uniformities." *The Theory of Social and Economic Organization*, trans. Henderson and Parsons (New York, 1947), p. 94.

8. For examples of this way of speaking in the philosophy of action see the essays by Bedford and Hamlyn in V.C. Chappell, ed., *The Philosophy of Mind* (Englewood Cliffs, 1962), and by Davidson and Anscombe in Alan White, ed., *The Philosophy of Action* (New York, 1968).

9. Jaspers, *General Psychopathology*, p. 303. His italics dropped.

10. See Weber, *Theory*, p. 90; Maurice Merleau-Ponty, *The Primacy of Perception* (Evanston, 1964), pp. 58 and 62; R.G. Collingwood, *The Idea of History* (New York, 1956), pp. 213ff; and Jaspers, *General Psychopathology*, p. 28.

11. See Rollo May, *Love and Will* (New York, 1969), p. 209.

12. Erwin Straus, "Born to See, Bound to Behold: Reflections on the Function of Upright Posture in the Esthetic Attitude," in Spicker, ed., *The Philosophy of the Body* (New York, 1970), pp. 341–43. Cf. the similar comments of Hans Jonas in the same volume, pp. 323–25.

13. Herbert Read, *A Concise History of Modern Painting* (New York, 1959), p. 13.

14. Paul Ricoeur, *The Symbolism of Evil*, trans. Emerson Buchanan (New York, 1967), pp. 10 and 19.

15. In his account of hermeneutical experience, Hans-Georg Gadamer calls understanding an activity which is also a passivity because it consists of "uninterrupted listening." *Truth and Method*, trans. Barden and Cumming (New York, 1975), p. 422.

16. Our three models of understanding, the painter, the actress, and the good listener stand in an interesting relation to the history of hermeneutics as a theory of understanding. The second of these stands in an obvious and close relation to the so-called "romantic" hermeneutics of Schleiermacher and Dilthey. Ricoeur's formula, "re-enactment in sympathetic imagination," stands as a succinct summary of its three central concepts. This tradition has been subjected to a penetrating critique by Hans-Georg Gadamer, among others, on the grounds that understanding is always productive and never merely reproductive. This is because the fusion of horizons that understanding achieves never is and never wants to be total. The otherness of what is to be understood is to be retained, and the goal is to mediate between two perspectives rather than to reduce them to an identity. This means that understanding is never simply self-understanding but rather the openness of myself to the claim of the other upon me. Gadamer's own model is that of translating a text from one language to another. See ibid., pp. 147–69, 264–73, and 321–50. In his essay, "The Model of the Text: Meaningful Action Considered as a Text," Paul Ricoeur develops the assimilation of human behavior and experience to a text calling for interpretation. This comparison lies at the heart of the translation model. See *Hermeneutics and the Human Sciences*, ed. and trans. John B. Thompson (Cambridge, England, 1981), pp. 187–221.

The very idea that understanding human life is like translating a text, however, helps us to see that Gadamer's critique creates no rigid either/or. For the translation model blends easily with each of the other three. The good translator and the good listener have an obvious affinity. The painter is also a kind of translator, and it is clear that painting is always productive and never merely reproductive of its object, even when it is most realistic. But just the same is true of acting, and it can be said that acting is a translation of the written text of the play into the language of sounds and gestures. Trying to put ourselves into the shoes of another, which is what "re-enactment in sympathetic imagination" is all about, is not the attempt to conjure up an experience identical to the one we seek to understand. (This would be impossible in any case, since the original experience did not occur in the imagination.) It is rather the conscious attempt to get beyond the limits of our previous experience, to open ourselves to the life of another in such a way as to make our attempt to articulate the meaning of that life a faithful translation, remembering that a faithful translation is never simply a repetition.

17. G.W.F. Hegel, *Phenomenology of Spirit*, trans. A.V. Miller (Oxford, England, 1977), p. 18. Miller's translation differs slightly from that in the text. Cf. paragraphs 3 and 19 in *The Logic of Hegel*, trans. William Wallace (London, 1892), and the *Zusatz* to paragraph 24, where Hegel writes, speaking of the fundamental categories of all thought and being, "But things thus familiar are usually the greatest strangers." It is significant that throughout his in-

terpretation of Husserl's phenomenology, Erazim Kohak recurs constantly to the discrepancy between the evident and the obvious as motivating the phenomenological project. See *Idea & Experience: Edmund Husserl's Project of Phenomenology in Ideas I* (Chicago, 1978), pp. 4, 16, 23, 40, and 198, note 14. This theme is central to both the early and later writings of Heidegger.

18. G.W.F. Hegel, *Lectures on the History of Philosophy*, trans. Haldane and Simpson (New York, 1963), III, 171.

19. Maurice Merleau-Ponty, *The Phenomenology of Perception*, trans. Colin Smith (London, 1962), pp. xiii–xx. For the same theme in a different quarter, see Ludwig Wittgenstein, *Philosophical Investigations*, trans. G.E.M. Anscombe (Oxford, England, 1958), Part I, Sections 129 and 415.

20. F.W.J. Schelling, *Philosophie der Mythologie* (Esslingen, 1857), II, 137.

21. Sigmund Freud, *The Interpretation of Dreams*, trans. James Strachey (New York, 1965), pp. 134–36.

22. Søren Kierkegaard, *Concluding Unscientific Postscript*, trans. David Swenson and Walter Lowrie (Princeton, 1941), pp. 331–32.

23. Weber, *Theory*, p. 90.

24. Ibid., p. 89.

25. The first phrase is from Ricoeur. See note 14 above. The second is from Alfred Schutz, *The Phenomenology of the Social World*, trans. George Walsh and Frederick Lehnert (Evanston, 1967), p. 86. The third is from Charles Taylor, *The Explanation of Behavior* (New York, 1964), p. 62.

26. For a more detailed discussion of these and related statements from Nietzsche see Merold Westphal, "Nietzsche and the Phenomenological Ideal," *The Monist*, April, 1977.

27. Max Scheler, *On the Eternal in Man*, trans. Bernard Noble (New York, 1960), pp. 180–81.

28. Paul Ricoeur, *Freud and Philosophy*, trans. Denis Savage (New Haven, 1970), p. 32.

29. Søren Kierkegaard, *For Self-Examination and Judge for Yourself*, trans. Walter Lowrie (Princeton, 1944), p. 68.

30. Ernst Becker writes, "Freud is like a Biblical prophet, a religious iconoclast who spoke a truth that no one wants to hear and no one may ever want to hear." *The Denial of Death*, (New York, 1973), p. 94.

31. Peter Berger, *The Sacred Canopy* (Garden City, 1967), p. 100. Cf. p. 193, n. 33.

32. Ibid., p. 100. Cf. p. v.

33. Ricoeur, *The Symbolism of Evil*, pp. 230 and 235. Under the impact of his dialogue with Habermas, Hans-Georg Gadamer has also incorporated the "hermeneutics of suspicion" into his hermeneutical project. See *Reason in the Age of Science*, trans. Frederick G. Lawrence (Cambridge, Mass., 1981), and the closing section of my essay, "Hegel and Gadamer," forthcoming.

34. Keith Campbell, *Body and Mind* (Garden City, 1970), p. 11.

35. For a more detailed discussion of these passages in Hegel see Merold Westphal, "Hegel's Theory of Religious Knowledge," in Frederick G. Weiss, ed., *Beyond Epistemology: New Studies in the Philosophy of Hegel* (The Hague, 1974), pp. 31–33.

36. *Phenomenology of Spirit*, p. 47.

37. Antonin Artaud, *The Theater and Its Double*, trans. Mary Caroline Richards (New York, 1958), p. 8. See Kierkegaard's *Concluding Unscientific Postscript*, pp. 176–77. For Nietzsche see the essay cited in note 26, above.

38. *The Phenomenology of Perception*, pp. xiv–xv.

39. Sigmund Freud, *The Ego and the Id*, trans. Riviere and Strachey (New York, 1960), p. 13. The phrase is actually quoted from Groddeck.

Chapter 2: Ambivalence and the Sacred

1. Gershom Scholem, *Major Trends in Jewish Mysticism* (New York, 1961), pp. 146–51. Cf. Augustine, *Confessions*, I, 5. "Narrow is the mansion of my soul, enlarge Thou it, that Thou mayest enter in." (Pusey translation. Other citations from the *Confessions* in this chapter are from the Pine-Coffin translation.)

2. Cited by Mircea Eliade in *From Primitives to Zen: A Thematic Sourcebook in the History of Religions* (New York, 1967), pp. 16–17.

3. *The Bhagavad-Gita*, trans. S. Radhakrishnan, in *A Source Book in Indian Philosophy*, ed. Radhakrishnan and Moore (Princeton, 1975), pp. 138–42. My italics.

4. In this connection it is of interest that E.T.A. Hoffman, the greatest of romantic storytellers, resorts to this phenomenon in his imaginative portrayal of "the marvellous—which is likely to make the everyday life of ordinary mortals seem pallid. . . ." He not only introduces his readers to "the faerie region of glorious wonders, where both rapture and honor may be evoked," but interrupts the painting of one such scene to assure the readers that if they had seen it all taking place in real life, "in horror, the hairs of your head might have stood on end." *The Best Tales of Hoffman*, ed. E.F. Bleiler (New York, 1967), pp. 17–18, 39. Hoffman's sense of the natural difference between the ordinary world of everyday experience and the world which evokes the ambivalence we're discussing is important. See Section 3A.

5. This is the language of St. Theresa of Avila, describing her ecstatic raptures in *Interior Castle*, trans. E. Allison Peers (Garden City, 1961), p. 167. Cf. p. 186.

6. Thomas Merton, *Contemplative Prayer* (Garden City, 1971), p. 27. My italics.

7. Quoted from the Marcarian Homilies by Archimandrite Kallistos Ware in *The Power of the Name: The Jesus Prayer in Orthodox Spirituality* (Oxford, England, 1974), p. 9. My italics.

8. Augustine, *Confessions*, VII, 10. My italics. In his famous essay on beauty, Plotinus describes the emotions which accompany the apprehension of that which is at once good, beautiful, and true. On the one hand there is joy, wonder, and happiness, on the other, distress and terror. *Enneads*, I, 6, 4, and 7 (MacKenna translation).

9. See Robert J. O'Connell's suggestion that the passage from the same paragraph that Pine-Coffin translates "you raised me up so that I could see that there was something to be seen, but also that I was not yet able to see it," should be more literally translated to indicate that God raised him that "I might see that what I saw *existed*, and that I, the seer, *did not yet* exist." *St. Augustine's Confessions: The Odyssey of Soul* (Cambridge, Mass., 1969), pp. 1–3 (with notes).

10. William James, *The Varieties of Religious Experience* (New York, 1958), p. 67. My italics.

11. Mohandas K. Gandhi, *An Autobiography: The Story of My Experiments With Truth*, trans. Mahadev Desai (Boston, 1957), p. xiv. My italics.

12. Maurice Friedman, *Touchstones of Reality* (New York, 1972), p. 16. My italics.

13. Isa. 40:15 and 17 (NEB). We find an example at the tribal level among the Sioux. Their prayers, for example, are more frequently "that we may live" or "that my people may live," than "that I may live." See *The Sacred Pipe: Black Elk's Account of the Seven Rites of the Oglala Sioux*, ed. Joseph Epes Brown (Baltimore, 1971).

14. It is clear that "the believing soul," to use Ricoeur's phrase, is not simply one who believes or affirms this or that proposition. He or she is one who *sees* things in a certain way. We have bracketed the question of the veridicality of this perception, but we need to keep in mind the primacy of perception operative here. This *seeing* obviously generates both beliefs and feelings.

15. E.E. Evans-Pritchard, "Some Aspects of Nuer Religion" in *Gods and Rituals*, ed. John Middleton (Garden City, 1967), pp. 141–47.

16. Job 1:21 (NEB).

17. Friedrich Schleiermacher, *The Christian Faith*, trans. Mackintosh and Steard (Edinburgh, 1948), paragraph 3.

18. Evans-Pritchard, "Nuer Religion," pp. 145–46. My italics.

19. *The Sacred Pipe*, pp. 14 and 54. My italics.

20. Gen. 18:27 (NEB). My italics.

21. C.S. Lewis, *Till We Have Faces*, pp. 111–14. The second ellipsis is in the Lewis text. Pagination is the same in the Harcourt Brace editions of 1956, 1957, and 1980 and the Eerdmans edition of 1966.

22. The *primacy* of this *perception* in relation to the rest of experience can be illuminated by the title essay of Maurice Merleau-Ponty's *The Primacy of Perception*. It is perhaps even more closely related to Jean-Paul Sartre's notion of the pre-reflective *cogito* in *Being and Nothingness*, trans. Hazel Barnes (New York, 1956), Introduction, Section III. He there describes a self-awareness which is prior to any overt reflection on oneself and which inhabits every awareness of an object.

23. Ibn 'Ata'illah, *The Book of Wisdom* (in one volume with Kwaja Abdullah Ansari, *Intimate Conversations*), trans. Victor Danner (New York, 1978), p. 69. In her Preface to this volume Annemarie Schimmel calls attention to the tension in both these Sufi classics between two aspects of God, "his *jamal*, Beauty, Kindness, and Grace, and his *jalal*, Majesty, Justice, and Wrath," p. xiv. Thus Ibn 'Ata'illah tells us that God's Decrees of Fate are the source of trials and the suffering of affliction, and immediately continues:

> Whoever supposes that His gentleness
> is separate from his Decree of Fate
> does so out of shortsightedness. (p. 73)

24. *Confessions* VII, 11.

25. *Proslogion*, Ch. 14, in *Anselm of Canterbury*, ed. and trans. Hopkins and Richardson (New York, 1975), Vol. I, p. 103. My italics. The verb here translated as "to perceive" is *sentire*, rendered by other translators in this passage as "to feel" and "to experience." Cf. John E. Smith, "In What Sense Can We Speak of Experiencing God?" *The Journal of Religion*, Vol. 50, No. 3 (July, 1970), pp. 234–36.

26. See the selections from Shankara's Commentary on the *Vedanta Sutras*, in *A Source Book in Indian Philosophy*, pp. 509–43.

27. Verses 46 and 170, pp. 296 and 305, in *A Source Book in Indian Philosophy*. For the frequency and diversity of these metaphors, see *Buddhist Texts Through the Ages*, ed. Edward Conze, et al. (New York, 1954).

28. For the same motif in the Islamic context, see Ibn 'Ata'illah, *The Book of Wisdom*, pp. 81 and 54.

29. *The Sacred Pipe*, pp. 3–4.

30. Ex. 20:18–19, 33:18–20 (NEB). To the latter text, Augustine replies, "Do not hide your face away from me, for I would gladly meet my death to see it, since not to see it would be death indeed." *Confessions*, I, 5. Cf. Gen. 32:30; Judges 6:22ff., 13:22. There are three creation hymns in Amos (4:13, 5:5–9, 9:5–6) celebrating God's sovereignty over nature, but placing them in a setting of warnings about divine judgment. The one who will come in destructive judgment unless his people change their ways is the power of creation itself. Here again the moral aspect is present and destruction has the form of judgment.

31. *The Bhagavad-Gita*, 10:8, 9:18–19, 10:34. Both Brahma and Vishnu are also represented as the destructiveness of time and death. See Frederick H. Holck, ed., *Death and Eastern Thought* (Nashville, 1974), pp. 58ff. and 83.

32. From the subtitle to Chapter One of David R. Kinsley's *The Sword and the Flute: Kali and Krishna, Dark Visions of the Terrible and the Sublime in Hindu Mythology* (Berkeley, 1975). Kinsley views the juxtaposition of these two deities as illustrating from the Hindu tradition what Rudolph Otto had developed in relation to the Judeo-Christian tradition, p. 152.

33. Quoted in Kinsley, *The Sword and the Flute*, p. 1. For the exquisitely beautiful love lyrics of Jayadeva's *Gitagovinda*, the story of Krishna and Radha, see *Love Song of the Dark Lord*, trans. Barbara Stoler Miller (New York, 1977). For devotional narratives on Krishna's life see the *Bhagavata-Purana (Srimad Bhagavatam)*, translated as *The Wisdom of God* by Swami Prabhavananda (New York, 1968).

34. Quoted from Heinrich Zimmer in Kinsley, *The Sword and the Flute*, p. 82.

35. From two different sources, these descriptions are found in Kinsley, pp. 1 and 113. Cf. pp. 81 and 91.

36. Quoted in Kinsley, *The Sword and the Flute*, p. 111.

37. *The Gospel of Sri Ramakrishna*, trans. Swami Nikhilananda (abridged edition; New York, 1974), p. 11. Cf. p. 17.

38. Ibid., p. 35.

39. So clear is the Hindu tradition that Krishna and Kali are not two competing conceptions of the sacred but two inseparable aspects of a single divine nature that the two not only unite the attractive and the repelling features in themselves, but they become interchangeable with one another. In a hymn from Kali's most famous eighteenth-century devotee, Rama Prasada, we read,

> Krishna wearing a garland of wild flowers with a
> flute in hand becomes Kali with a sword.

And in a Tantric text we read, "I see my Mother, the mad, disordered girl, dancing with gentle movements of her body, now taking up the flute instead of the sword, or again seizing the sword instead of the flute, or yet again at times making both the sword and the flute into one in Her hand; mingling Her laughter with Her dancing; now loosening and now binding up Her hair. If I sleep, she awakens me by coming herself and playing the flute. If I commit my offense, She raises Her sword and, smiling gently, threatens me with it." Quoted in Kinsley, *The Sword and the Flute*, p. 151.

40. See Euripides, *The Bacchae*, lines 860–61. Also Walter F. Otto, *Dionysus: Myth and Cult*, trans. Robert B. Palmer (Bloomington, 1965), and W.K.C. Guthrie, *The Greeks and Their Gods* (Boston, 1950), Ch. VI.

41. Gerardus van der Leeuw, *Sacred and Profane Beauty: The Holy in Art*, p. 5.

42. *Confessions*, I. 4. Cf. Anselm, who writes, "O supreme and inaccessible Light, O complete and blessed Truth, how distant You are from me who am so near for You! How far removed You are from my sight though I am so present to Yours! You are wholly present everywhere, and yet I do not behold You. In You I move and exist, and yet I cannot approach You. You are within me and round about me, and yet I do not perceive You." *Proslogion*, Ch. 16.

43. Evans-Pritchard, "Nuer Religion," pp. 143–44.

44. *The Gospel of Sri Ramakrishna*, pp. 41–42.

45. Ex. 33:22–23 (NEB).

46. From Edward Conze's commentary on *The Heart Sutra* in *Buddhist Wisdom Books*, trans. Edward Conze (London, 1975), p. 83.

47. Ibn 'Ata'illah, *The Book of Wisdom*, p. 88.

48. Quoted in Frederick Franck, *The Book of Angelus Silesius* (New York, 1976), p. 21.

49. Ps. 100:3 (KJV).

50. Rudolf Otto, *The Idea of the Holy*, trans. John W. Harvey (New York, 1958), Chs. 3–4.

51. Otto does not use the Husserlian language of *noesis* and *noema*, but he is clearly committed to the correlativity of intentional act and intentional object. This means that the move from experience to "object" is not a move away from describing experience, since to describe the intentional object as such is to talk about the content pole of a certain kind of experience. The quotation marks around "object" in this context are not merely to remind us that all questions about the independent reality of the intentional object are bracketed while it is being described, but also that no single kind of "entity" is intended in the awareness of the holy. It may be an empirical object, such as a god or spirits. And it may be a non-empirical non-object, such as the Buddhist Nirvana. It is precisely because Otto's analysis is not bound to any single sort of "object" that I will argue below that it can serve as a generic analysis rather than a special case of religious transcendence. For the technical terms *noesis* and *noema* see Husserl, *Ideas*, trans. W.R. Boyce Gibson (New York, 1962), paragraphs 84–96. For summary and interpretation see Maurice Natanson, *Edmund Husserl: Philosopher of Infinite Tasks* (Evanston, 1973), pp. 86ff., 103, and 125, and Erazim Kohak, *Idea and Experience: Edmund Husserl's Project of Phenomenology in Ideas I*, pp. 120–31.

52. See *Flatland: A Romance of Many Dimensions* (1884; some recent editions, 1952, 1963, 1983), by Edwin A. Abbott.

53. Otto, *The Idea of the Holy*, Ch. 4. The Kierkegaard reference is from *Training in Christianity*, trans. Walter Lowrie (Princeton, 1944), p. 135. Cf. Plato, *Phaedrus*, 251 (Jowett or Hackforth translation), and Plotinus, *Enneads*, I, 6.2, 4, and 7 (MacKenna translation).

54. Otto, *The Idea of the Holy*, Ch. 6.

55. Human union with the holy can take a variety of forms. There is radical identification in some forms of mysticism, harmony and attunement when the holy is apprehended as the force of cosmic order, and personal fellowship when God is seen as numinous Thou in relation to the human I. No single term such as being "with" the holy or "united" to it does justice to the special character of each particular possibility. See Chs. 9–11 of this book.

56. Otto, *The Idea of the Holy*, p. 6.

57. There have been numerous attempts to suggest that one of these terms represents the generically religious while the others indicate special cases. I have chosen to use these terms interchangeably for the generically religious and have defended this usage in the paragraphs that follow.

58. Otto, *The Idea of the Holy*, p. 19. Freud used the electricity metaphor in *Totem and Taboo*, four years earlier in 1913. He got it from the essay on taboo in the 11th edition of the *Encyclopedia Britannica* (1910–11).

59. Ex. 19:24 and II Sam. 6.

60. The notion of *mana* was introduced to European scholarship by Max Müller in his Hibbert Lectures of 1878, when he quoted a letter from the missionary R.H. Codrington, which reads in part, "The religion of the Melanesians consists, as far as belief goes, in the persuasion that there is a supernatural power about belonging to the region of the unseen; and, as far as practice goes, in the use of means of getting this power turned to their own benefit. The notion of a Supreme Being is altogether foreign to them, or indeed of any being occupying a very elevated place in their world. . . . There is a belief in a force altogether distinct from physical power, which acts in all kinds of ways for good and evil, and which it is of the greatest advantage to possess or control. This is mana. . . . It is a power or influence, not physical, and in a way supernatural; but it shows itself in physical force, or in any kind of power or excellence which a man possesses. This mana is not fixed in anything, and can be conveyed in almost anything, but spirits, whether disembodied souls or supernatural beings, have it and can impart it; and it essentially belongs to personal beings to originate it, though it may act through the medium of water, or a stone, or a bone. All Melanesian religion consists, in fact, in getting this mana for one's self, or getting it used for one's benefit—all religion, that is, as far as religious practices go, prayers and sacrifices." R.H. Codrington, *The Melanesians: Studies in Their Anthropology and Folk-Lore* (Oxford, 1891), pp. 118–19. For discussion of such very similar concepts as *orenda, wakan,* and *manitu* among the native American tribes (Iroquois, Sioux, and Algonquin, respectively) see R.R. Marett's article on *mana* in Vol. 8 of *Encyclopedia of Religion and Ethics*, ed. James Hastings (New York, 1916).

61. G. van der Leeuw, *Religion in Essence and Manifestation*, trans. J.E. Turner (New York, 1963), I, 26–28. Quite possibly this description fits some situations. But perhaps it would be helpful to acknowledge that then we are dealing with magic and not religion. See Section 4A.

62. *Confessions*, XI, 9. The footnote in Otto, *The Idea of the Holy*, p. 28, mislocates the passage.

63. For this passage, quoting Revelation 4:11, and the following discussion, see Otto, Ch. 8. His italics.

64. *The Bhagavad-Gita*, XI, 40–42.

65. Job 42:2–6 (NEB). The "dust and ashes," which appeared in Abraham's speech earlier, are here given a different significance through linkage with repentance. Otto himself illustrates this new dimension of the numinous with two biblical examples, Isaiah and Peter. See Isaiah 6:1–5 and Luke 5:1–11.

66. See Otto's discussion of God as *exlex*, outside the law as its source, *The Idea of the Holy*, p. 101.

67. The quotation is from Paul Ricoeur, *The Symbolism of Evil*, p. 58. Cf. pp. 29ff. and 63ff. for the relation of perceived human fault to the sacred as *tremendum*, and 74ff. for the connection between the sense of sin and the sense of being nothing. Kierkegaard's argument that sin makes God wholly other is found in *Philosophical Fragments*, trans. Swenson and Hong (Princeton, 1962), pp. 57ff.

68. See, for example, R.C. Zaehner, "Why Not Islam?" *Religious Studies*, Vol. 11, No. 2 (June, 1975), p. 167; and Ninian Smart, *Reasons and Faiths* (London, 1968), and *The Concept of Worship* (London, 1972), pp. 22–26.

69. There are those rare individuals for whom the temporary taste of eternity is easy and frequent, e.g., Ramakrishna and Buddha. But these tend to become objects of worship themselves rather than paradigms of the religious life we are seeking to understand.

70. *The Gospel of Sri Ramakrishna*, p. 12.

71. T.R.V. Murti, *The Central Philosophy of Buddhism* (London, 1980), p. 6. His italics.

72. Schopenhauer, *The World as Will and Representation*, trans. E.F.J. Payne (New York, 1966), Vol. I, pp. 408–11. His italics. Cf. the discussion of the fear evoked by the pursuit of Nirvana in William Johnston, *Christian Zen: A Way of Meditation* (New York, 1971), pp. 86–89.

Chapter 3: Ambivalence, Inertia, and Resentment

1. This is the assumption on which I am proceeding. While the examples given and the conceptual analyses involved in their interpretation suggest such a conclusion they do not prove it. Nor would the further piling up of examples, as if we were performing an induction by complete enumeration. Insight into essence is in the last analysis a matter of intuition. One can give examples and show how a concept applies to cases put forward as counterexamples, but the conviction that all religion involves the numinous is a matter of judgment, not deductive or inductive proof.

2. Arthur Waley, *The Way and Its Power: A Study of the Tao Te Ching and Its Place in Chinese Thought* (New York, 1958), p. 193 (Ch. XLI). The holy often appears as the cosmic order in which power and rectitude are inseparable. Our distinction between the laws of nature, which govern what happens, and the moral law. which prescribes what should happen, seems not to have arisen in the Chinese *Tao*, the Vedic *Rta*, the Egyptian *Ma'at*, the Greek *Dike*, and the Stoic *Logos*.

3. I think the critiques of Feuerbach, *The Essence of Christianity*, and of Fromm, *Escape from Freedom*, both suffer from this latter defect. Whether or not that is so, the very possibility of developing such a criticism of them indicates that our bracketed approach is not irrelevant to evaluative questions.

4. "Cheap grace" is the term used by Dietrich Bonhoeffer in *The Cost of Discipleship* (New York, 1963), for the kind of pseudo-religion which grasps at the *fascinans* and ignores the *tremendum*, or tries to.

5. See Section 2C.

6. Søren Kierkegaard, *Concluding Unscientific Postscript*, pp. 347–493. I am obviously interpreting the relation between religiousness A and religiousness B as that of genus and species.

7. Kierkegaard, *Postscript*, p. 347. My italics.

8. Matt. 13:44–46 (NEB).

9. Kierkegaard, *Postscript*, p. 350.

10. Ibid, pp. 368–69.

11. Søren Kierkegaard, *Fear and Trembling and Sickness Unto Death*, trans. Walter Lowrie (Princeton, 1968), pp. 61, 49–51.

12. Kierkegaard, *Postscript*, p. 371.

13. In *Christian Discourses*, trans. Walter Lowrie (Princeton, 1971), pp. 179–80, Kierkegaard warns against the edifying as being "so gentle" and yet "so imperious" and "so binding." Taken seriously it leads to a self-denial which can be called "dying to the world" because it is "as bitter as death."

14. In a very early journal entry Kierkegaard makes this point in the language of conversion. "Conversion goes slowly. As Fr. Baader rightly says, one has to go backwards along the same way one went forwards. One may easily become impatient. . . . Hence it is that we are bidden to work out (gradually) our salvation with fear and trembling. Salvation is not a thing ever finished or complete. We may have relapses." Quoted in *Johannes Climacus or De Omnibus Dubitandum Est and A Sermon*, trans. T.H. Croxall (Stanford, 1958), p. 26.

15. Kierkegaard, *Postscript*, p. 412. This is not religious masochism. "Suffering as a dying away from immediacy is thus not flagellation and the like; it is not self-torture. For the self-torturer does not by any means express that he can do nothing before God, for he counts his acts of self-torture as being something." Page 414.

16. Ibid., pp. 468–93. Against the background of the Platonic theory of recollection, Kierkegaard's repeated claim that this kind of guilt is recollected and not remembered (pp. 472, 475, 480, 489) is a way of making this distinction between qualitative and quantitative guilt.

17. See Section 2C, note 73.

18. Kierkegaard, *Postscript*, p. 410.

19. Ibid., pp. 436–37, 475, 488. This is a point on which Hegel and Kierkegaard are in agreement. See Hegel's *Lectures on the Philosophy of Religion*, trans. E.B. Speirs and J.B. Sanderson (New York, 1962), Vol. I, pp. 173–75.

20. Kierkegaard, *Postscript*, pp. 475 and 488.

21. Søren Kierkegaard, *Two Ages: The Age of Revolution and the Present Age, A Literary Review*, trans. Howard V. Hong and Edna H. Hong (Princeton, 1978), p. 69.

22. Ibid., pp. 69, 94, 104, and 136.

23. *Confessions*, VII, 17. This and the following citations are from the Warner translation.

24. Ibid., VIII, 5.

25. Ibid., VIII, 5. Italics indicate biblical quotation from Eph. 5:14. Cf. VIII, 7.

26. Compare ibid., VIII, 5, with the passages quoted here from VIII, 9, and the following from VIII, 10: "So too when eternity offers us a higher

pleasure and the delight in some temporal good holds us down below, *it is the same soul which feels both impulses*; only its will for the one or the other course is not total and complete, and consequently it is torn apart and heavily distressed as truth puts one way first and *habit* will not allow the other way to be abandoned." My italics.

27. Martin Heidegger, *Being and Time*, trans. John Macquarrie and Edward Robinson (New York, 1962), pp. 164–65, 222–23.

28. This is a transcendental rather than a temporal priority, just as for Kant the pure intuition of space is prior to the empirical intuition of objects in space.

29. Heidegger, *Being and Time*, p. 213.

30. Ibid., pp. 165–66.

31. Ibid., pp. 212–17.

32. Ibid., pp. 220, 211, 224. His italics.

33. Ibid., p. 220.

34. This is not intended as either a definition or a sufficient account of the "ontological difference" in Heidegger, but only as an indication of what is crucial for this passage. Both Augustine and Kierkegaard would want to disagree with Heidegger here, insisting that while we do indeed have no ontic memory of a fall from innocence or from authenticity to everydayness, we do have an ontological recollection which enables us to speak meaningfully about such a fall. But that debate need not concern us here. For the crucial point concerns not how we came to be in the situation called everydayness, but whether we can get out of it.

35. Heidegger, *Being and Time*, pp. 168, 224, and 213. His italics.

36. *Totem and Taboo*, in *The Standard Edition of the Complete Psychological Works of Sigmund Freud* (henceforth S.E.), ed. and trans. by James Strachey, et al. (London, 1953-74), XIII, 24.

37. Philip Rieff, *Freud: The Mind of the Moralist* (Garden City, 1961), p. 281.

38. See the discussion of Nietzsche in Section 1E.

39. *The Future of An Illusion*, S.E., XXI, Ch. 4.

40. Ibid., Ch. 6.

41. Ibid., Ch. 4.

42. Ibid., Ch. 3.

43. Ibid., Ch. 6.

44. Ibid., Ch. 4.

45. For details see Ernest Jones, *The Life and Work of Sigmund Freud* in either the complete or abridged edition. (3 vols.; New York, 1953–57; 1 vol. abr. and ed. Trilling and Marens, New York, 1961).

46. Max Scheler, *Ressentiment*, trans. William W. Holdheim (New York, 1972), p. 50.

47. Job 13:15 (KJV)

48. For details see Ernest Becker, *The Denial of Death* (New York, 1973), pp. 105–16.

49. S.E., Vols. XV and XVI. On the importance of ambivalence in neurosis see also the celebrated Rat Man and Schreber case histories, S.E., X, 239–40, XII, 28–29.

50. James 1:8 (KJV).

51. Becker, *The Denial*, pp. 38, 146.

52. *The Interpretation of Dreams*, S.E., IV, 256–57.

53. Quoted from Brown's *Life Against Death* in Becker, *The Denial of Death*, p. 36. In *Being and Nothingness* Jean-Paul Sartre gives a lengthy analysis of human existence as the desire to be God and of the way in which sex is not primarily a matter of physical pleasure but of master-slave struggles for the power of domination.

54. S.E., XIII, 25. On *mana* see Ch. 2, note 64.

55. S.E., X, 20–22, 34–35, 39–40, 68–72.

56. S.E., X, 33, 41–49.

57. Friedrich Nietzsche, *Thus Spoke Zarathustra*, in *The Portable Nietzsche*, trans. and ed. Walter Kaufmann (New York, 1954), p. 198 (Upon the Blessed Isles). My italics. Cf. Ludwig Feuerbach, *The Essence of Christianity* trans. George Eliot (New York, 1957), p. 115. This is the same sentiment that comes to expression in Queen Orual's complaint against the gods. "That there should be gods at all, there's our misery and bitter wrong. There's no room for you and us in the same world. You're a tree in whose shadow we can't thrive. We want to be our own." C.S. Lewis, *Till We Have Faces*, p. 291. See Ch. 2, note 21.

58. Scheler, *Ressentiment*, p. 48.

59. Ibid., pp. 39 and 74.

60. The phrase "psychic life" implies no dualistic theory of human experience. Since we are embodied consciousness, I'm assuming that resentment will not only affect our perception and behavior but also our ulcers and blood pressure. Scheler also recognizes the physical effects of resentment. See *Ressentiment*, p. 71.

61. John 3:30 (NIV).

62. *Two Ages*, pp. 81–82.

63. It is Kierkegaard who states this relationship most explicitly, both in *Two Ages*, pp. 82–83, and in *The Sickness Unto Death*, trans. Howard V. Hong and Edna H. Hong (Princeton, 1980), p. 86.

64. Gabriel Marcel, *Creative Fidelity*, trans. Robert Rosthal (New York, 1964), pp. 47–49.

65. Kierkegaard, *Two Ages*, p. 82. In view of the importance self-sacrifice will come to have for the religious life in Ch. 8, this is of added importance.

66. The essentially comparative nature of envy is presupposed by Kierkegaard who consistently sees the modern movement for social equality as a passion for leveling born of envy directed toward all forms of excellence. See *Two Ages*, pp. 81–96, and Scheler, *Ressentiment*, pp. 50–53.

67. Spinoza, *Ethics*, Box III, Def. 23, Prop. 55. Cf. Prop. 24 (Gutman translation.)

68. Ibid., Book III, Prop. 32.

69. Scheler, *Ressentiment*, pp. 52–53. His italics.

Chapter 4: The Existential Meaning of Guilt

1. See the discussion of "cheap grace" and "cheap shots" in Section 3A. For a classic instance of such a critique see Ludwig Feuerbach, *The Essence of Faith According to Luther*, trans. Melvin Cherno (New York, 1967), especially in relation to his more famous book, *The Essence of Christianity*.

2. Philip Melanchthon, *Loci Communes Theologici*, in *Melanchthon and Bucer*, ed. Wilhelm Pauck, Vol. XIX in *The Library of Christian Classics* (Philadelphia, 1969), p. 21.

3. Sir James George Frazer, *The Golden Bough: A Study in Magic and Religion* (abridged edition; New York, 1960), Ch. 4. Originally published in 1922; complete edition in 1890.

4. Bronislaw Malinowski, *Magic, Science and Religion and Other Essays* (Garden City, 1954), pp. 37–38. Title essay originally published in 1925.

5. Luke 1:68–79 (NEB).

6. This formula comes from Kierkegaard, *Concluding Unscientific Postscript*, p. 371.

7. *The Random House Dictionary of the English Language* (unabridged edition; New York, 1967).

8. The remainder of this chapter is taken, with a few changes, from Merold Westphal, "The Phenomenology of Guilt and the Theology of Forgiveness," in *Crosscurrents in Phenomenology*, eds. Bruzina and Wilshire (The Hague, 1978). Copyright © 1978. Reprinted by permission of the publisher, Martinus Nijhoff Publishers.

9. See Max Scheler, "Repentance and Rebirth," in *On the Eternal in Man*, trans. Bernard Noble (New York, 1960). The distinction between "done" and "become" will become important in the discussion of Freud below.

10. "Guilt and Guilt Feelings," reprinted in *Guilt: Man and Society*, ed. Roger W. Smith (Garden City, 1971), pp. 90 and 102.

11. If there is any important distinction between guilt and shame it is not that only the former involves internalization, so the difference may not be pertinent to the present discussion. See Margaret Mead, "Some Anthropological Considerations Concerning Guilt," in Smith, *Guilt*, p. 125.

12. Scheler, "Repentance and Rebirth," pp. 49ff.

13. See his commentary on Psalm 51, especially verse 4. *Luther's Works*, ed. Jaroslav Pelikan (St. Louis, 1955), Vol. 12, pp. 336–37. Also pp. 319, 324, and 332. Cf. Ch. 11 of *The Theologia Germanica of Martin Luther*, trans. Bengt Hoffman (New York, 1980). This classic was edited by Luther, not written by him. Its influence can easily be seen in comparing the passages cited in this note and the next.

14. These are from the 1935 *Lectures on Galatians* in *Luther's Works*, ed. Jaroslav Pelikan and Walter A. Hansen (St. Louis, 1963), Vol. 26, pp. 36, 126, and 314. My italics.

15. In addition to the last two quotations above, see Vol. 26, pp. 131 and 148.

16. "Punishment is not pain in and for itself; the same pain or suffering can happen to another merely as a vicissitude of life. Punishment is the conception that this particular suffering is punishment." *Søren Kierkegaard's Journals and Papers*, ed. Hong and Hong (Bloomington, 1970), Vol. II, p. 52. Gandhi agrees. He writes, "When I merited, or seemed to the teacher to merit, a rebuke, it was unbearable for me. I remember having once received corporal punishment. I did not so much mind the punishment, as the fact that it was considered my desert. I wept piteously." *An Autobiography: The Story of My Experiments with Truth*, p. 15.

17. Ricoeur, *The Symbolism of Evil*, pp. 25–46, especially pp. 42–43.

18. It would be begging important questions simply to label guilt masochistic on account of this. See Ch. 3, note 15.

19. *The Genealogy of Morals*, Second Essay, Section 14.

20. This is suggested in a study of rehabilitation by Lloyd W. McCorkle and Richard Korn, who argue that "much as he protests bad prison condi-

tions, the adaptive inmate *requires them*, because his system of adaptation creates in him a *need to protest.*" The reason for this is that "in many ways, the inmate social system may be viewed as providing a way of life which enables the inmate to avoid the devastating psychological effects of internalizing and converting social rejection into self-rejection." "Resocialization Within Walls," *Annals of the American Academy of Political and Social Science*, Vol. 293 (May, 1954), pp. 95 and 88.

21. This phrase is from an essay by Gresham M. Sykes and David Matza entitled "Techniques of Neutralization: A Theory of Delinquency." What follows is drawn from that essay along with "The Ache of Guilt" by J. Glenn Gray about soldiers. The two essays are found in *Guilt: Man and Society*. When the Sioux Indians return from the warpath, they paint their faces black, for, as their wise man Black Elk explains, "By going on the warpath, we know that we have done something bad, we wish to hide our faces from *Wakan-Tanka.*" *The Sacred Pipe*, recorded and edited by Joseph Epes Brown, p. 92. Cf. Freud's treatment of rites of appeasement of slain enemies in Ch. 2 of *Totem and Taboo*.

22. We are reminded not only of Eichmann but also of the para-military organization of the crime "families" known popularly as the Mafia, where those who do the dirty work are always carrying out the orders of others.

23. Sykes and Matza, "Techniques of Neutralization," p. 145.

24. This is the only parallel between the soldier and the delinquent not suggested by Gray's essay, "The Ache of Guilt."

25. See the splendid interpretation of "What! do I fear myself? there's none else by": from Shakespeare's *Richard III* in Michael Gelven, *Winter, Friendship and Guilt* (New York, 1972), pp. 181ff.

26. At the end of C.S. Lewis's *Till We Have Faces*, Orual, Queen of Glome, has the opportunity to present her complaint against the gods. As she reads her brief it turns into a confession, "and the voice I read it in was strange to my ears. There was given to me a certainty that this, at last, was my real voice." Part II, Chapter 3.

27. Quotations are from the Ralph E. Matlaw translation of Dostoyevsky, *Notes From the Underground*.

28. Is this the meaning of Kafka's *The Metamorphosis?*

29. Jean-Paul Sartre, *The Words*, trans. Bernard Frechtman (Greenwich, 1964), p. 57.

30. Cf. Shakespeare's use of ghosts in *Hamlet* and *Richard III*.

31. Whether his approval is well founded or neurotic is an important question, though not in the present context, where all guilt, healthy and neurotic, is under examination.

32. *The Genealogy of Morals*, Second Essay, Section 16.

33. Ibid., Section 18.

34. Ibid., Sections 21–24.

35. Ibid., Section 1.

36. Ibid., Section 4. Cf. Freud's discussion of atonement rituals in *Totem and Taboo*, Chapter Two, Section 2.

37. *The Genealogy of Morals*, Second Essay, Section 8.

38. *Civilization and Its Discontents*, Chapter VIII.

39. The same is implicit in *The Problem of Anxiety*, Chapters VII–VIII, where guilt is discussed in terms of "social anxiety" and "loss of love." But

since the latter phrase is interpreted in both *The Ego and the Id* and *Civilization and Its Discontents* as loss of protection rather than loss of recognition, respect, and approval, the implication tends to get diluted.

40. *New Introductory Lectures on Psychoanalysis*, Lecture XXXI.

41. See Rudolf Otto, *The Idea of the Holy*, Ch. VIII, "The Holy as a Category of Value."

Chapter 5: The Existential Meaning of Death

1. Gabriel Marcel, *Creative Fidelity*, p. 241.

2. All quotations from *The Death of Ivan Ilich* are from the translation by Leo Wiener.

3. Plato, *Phaedo*, 64a (Tredennick translation).

4. Kierkegaard, *Postscript*, pp. 147–52.

5. Ps. 90:10 and 12 (RSV).

6. Jean-Paul Sartre, *Being and Nothingness*, trans. Hazel Barnes (New York, 1956), p. 546. Sartre is mistaken, however, in thinking this is a criticism of Heidegger, for whom death is by no means the exclusive sign of human finitude.

7. Martin Heidegger, *Being and Time*, p. 495. It is problematic to bring Heidegger together with Sartre and Jaspers under the existentialist rubric. Their projects assume the Cartesian self as starting point and belong more or less clearly to the Socratic tradition of "tending the soul." His project, by contrast, like the religious life we are seeking to understand, challenges the obviousness of the self-knowing, self-positing I and gives primacy to the question of the meaning of Being over that of the meaning of human life. In spite of these and other important differences, Heidegger's analysis of *Dasein* as finite freedom is genuinely related to those of thinkers like Sartre and Jaspers who are less problematically identified as existentialists.

8. Ibid., pp. 297–302. Following Tolstoy's story, Heidegger also stresses that death is not just an event at the end of life. Rather, "death is a way to be, which Dasein [human existence] takes over as soon as it is. 'As soon as man comes to life, he is at once old enough to die' " (p. 289). This means that the question of death is a question of how one lives one's life. Correspondingly, Heidegger, again like Tolstoy, gives priority to the this-worldly aspect of the problem of death over the other-worldly question of life after death. See p. 292.

9. Walter Kaufmann, "Existentialism and Death," in Herman Feifel, ed., *The Meaning of Death* (New York, 1965), p. 47. I have changed Ilyitch to Ilich so as to retain a standard transliteration. We have just noted in the previous paragraph that Heidegger's indebtedness to Tolstoy is by no means unacknowledged.

10. Aristotle, *Poetics*, 1451b5 ff. (Bywater translation).

11. As Walter Kaufmann suggests in "Existentialism and Death."

12. Heidegger, *Being and Time*, p. 311.

13. Ibid., p. 308.

14. Paul Tillich, *The Courage to Be*, Ch. 5.

15. Ibid., Chs. 4 and 6.

16. The two major sources for Jaspers's view of death are *Psychologie der Weltanschauungen* (1919) and *Philosophy*, 3 vols. (1932). There are no substantial differences between the two. Heidegger acknowledges his indebt-

edness to the former book in a footnote to *Being and Time*, p. 495. It remains unavailable in English, though Jaspers himself has described it as the first genuinely existentialist work. *Philosophy* has been translated by E.B. Ashton (Chicago, 1970). See Vol. II, Part III, Ch. 7.

17. *Philosophy*, II, 178. His italics.

18. Ibid., II, 179–80, 183. His italics.

19. Ibid., II, 178–81.

20. Ibid., II, 195–96. First italics his, second and third mine.

21. It is Kierkegaard, I believe, who first recognized the paradox that selfhood is at once a gift and a task. See *The Concept of Irony*, trans. Capel (New York, 1965), pp. 293ff.

22. Jaspers, *Philosophy*, II, 198–99. His italics.

23. This second meaning of the boundary concept is especially suggested by Marcel's essay, "The Fundamental and Ultimate Situation in Karl Jaspers," *Creative Fidelity*, pp. 231–37.

24. Peter Berger, *The Sacred Canopy: Elements of a Sociological Theory of Religion*, p. 52.

25. Ernest Becker, *The Denial of Death*, pp. 4 and 7. My italics.

26. Ibid., pp. 7 and 3. His italics.

27. Cf. ibid., Ch. 8 and pp. 212–13.

28. Aristotle, *Nichomachean Ethics*, Book I, Ch. 4–5.

29. Hegel, *Phenomenology of Spirit*, Ch. 4.

30. Hobbes, *Leviathan*, Part I, Ch. 13.

31. Becker, *The Denial of Death*, pp. 109 and 156.

32. Ibid., p. 11.

33. Ibid., pp. 4–7.

34. Ibid., p. 168.

35. The term is from Herbert Marcuse, *One Dimensional Man*, though he understands the problem of heroics rather differently from Becker. See also Marcuse's essay, "The Ideology of Death," in Feifel, *The Meaning of Death*.

36. Becker, *The Denial of Death*, p. 109. Referring to his father's disparaging remark, "The boy will come to nothing," Freud writes, "This must have been a frightful blow to my ambition, for references to this scene are still constantly recurring in my dreams and are always linked with an enumeration of my achievements and successes, as though I wanted to say: 'You see, I *have* come to something.' " *The Interpretation of Dreams*, Ch. 5, Sec. B., James J. Strachey translation.

37. Becker, *The Denial of Death*, Ch. 4.

38. From the Matlaw translation of Dostoyevsky's *Notes From the Underground*. My italics.

39. Becker, *The Denial of Death*, p. 212.

40. Ibid., pp. 198 and 6–7.

41. Jaspers, *Philosophy*, II, 199–200.

42. Translated by Walter Kaufmann in his essay, "Existentialism and Death," p. 59. The poem is entitled *"Nur einen Sommer ..."* Kaufmann's essay is in *The Meaning of Death* edited by Herman Feifel. Copyright ©1965. The poem is reprinted by permission of the publisher, McGraw-Hill Book Co.

Chapter 6: The Believing Soul's Encounter with Guilt and Death

1. See Arthur A. Cohen, *The Myth of the Judeo-Christian Tradition: and Other Dissenting Essays* (New York, 1971), and Martin Buber, *Two Types of*

Faith: The Interpretation of Judaism and Christianity, trans. Norman P. Gold-hawk (New York, 1961).

2. *Luther's Works*, Vol. 14, p. 86.

3. Unless otherwise indicated, biblical quotations in this section are from the Revised Standard Version.

4. See Ch. 4, note 17.

5. See Section 4B.

6. Walther Eichrodt, *Theology of the Old Testament*, trans. J.A. Baker (Phil-adelphia, 1967), II, 406. His italics. Cf. II, 503–04, and Karl Barth, *The Epistle to the Romans*, trans. Edwyn C. Hoskyns (Oxford, England, 1977), p. 167, ". . . in its inevitability we are reminded of the wrath which hangs over the man of the world and the world of man."

7. *Luther's Works*, Vol. 12, pp. 310–11, and Vol. 14, pp. 142–43. From commentaries on Psalms 6 and 51, traditionally called "penitential psalms."

8. Artur Weiser, *The Psalms: A Commentary*, trans. Herbert Hartwell (Phil-adelphia, 1962), pp. 598–99.

9. Ps. 51:4.

10. Rom. 6:23 and I Cor. 15:56. Cf. James 1:15, " . . . sin when it is full-grown brings forth death."

11. In Rom. 5:12–21 and I Cor. 15:20–28, 42–50. The verses quoted are Rom. 5:12 and 8:2.

12. Matt. 1:21.

13. For example, Matt. 7:21ff.; 10:15, 28; 12:36; 13:37ff., 47ff.; 16:27; 19:28ff.; and all of chapter 25. Not all of these sayings specifically link the theme of judgment to death, but against the background of Dan. 12:1–2, which links the judgment with the resurrection of the dead, the main thrust is that of Heb. 9:27, that "it is appointed for men to die once, and after that comes judgment."

14. John 3:16–18.

15. I Cor. 15:26.

16. Rev. 1:5 and 18.

17. Rev. 22:3–4.

18. Rev. 22:1–3.

19. Rev. 21:8, 27; 22:11–15.

20. See Plato, *Republic* 614d ff., *Phaedo* 80d ff. and 107d ff., *Phaedrus* 248b ff.; Vergil, *Aeneid*, Book VI., esp. lines 730ff.; *The Egyptian Book of the Dead*, Ch. 125; *Siva Purana*, Umasamhita, 9. 2ff.; *Atharva Veda*, v. 18. 13.; *The Dhammapada*, Ch. 9–10, 18, and 22; and *The Tibetan Book of The Dead*, Book II, Part I. Hindu sources quoted or referred to are in Frederick H. Holck, ed., *Death and Eastern Thought*, pp. 87 and 125.

21. Paul Ricoeur, *The Symbolism of Evil*, p. 25.

22. For the "primitive" sense of defilement, see G. Van der Leeuw, *Religion in Essence and Manifestation*, Vol. I, Ch. 4, and Sigmund Freud, *Totem and Taboo*. In the Deuteronomic law and Holiness Code of ancient Judaism ritual purity served "as a symbol and outward expression of moral perfection." Eichrodt, *Theology of the Old Testament*, I, 137. See also Pss. 51:2, 7, 10; Isa. 1:15–18, 6:5; Heb. 9:13–14; and I John 1:7–9, 3:3. Plato, in the passages referred to in note 20, among others, and Plotinus, *Enneads*, I, 6.5–9, give philosophic expression to the Orphic-Pythagorean concern for purity; and in the east the *Upanishads*, to give but one example, depend heavily on this symbol in their metaphysics of Brahman and Atman.

23. St. Thomas Aquinas, *Summa Theologica*, First Part of the Second Part, Q. 86, Art. 1.

24. Ps. 51:2 and 7.

25. Joseph Epes Brown, ed., *The Sacred Pipe: Black Elk's Account of the Seven Rites of the Oglala Sioux*, pp. 83–84. *Wakan-Tanka* is the Sioux name for God. Significantly the word *wakan* by itself is the exact equivalent of *mana*. For the Sioux the path of purity is distinguished from the one traveled by "one who is distracted, who is ruled by his senses, and who lives for himself rather than for his people." p. 7. In other words, defilement is understood morally in terms of sensuousness and selfishness, not in terms of literal physical contact.

26. Ricoeur, *The Symbolism of Evil*, pp. 31 and 35.

27. See the Preface and Ch. 2 of Freud's *Totem and Taboo*.

28. Ricoeur, *The Symbolism of Evil*, p. 31.

29. Van der Leeuw, *Religion in Essence*, I, 46ff. Cf. Kurt Latte, "Schulde und Sünde in der griechischen Religion," *Archiv für Religionwissenschaft* 20 (1920–21), pp. 263–64.

30. See Section 3C.

31. Ricoeur, *The Symbolism of Evil*, p. 42.

32. From *Oedipus the King*, trans. David Grene in *The Complete Greek Tragedies, Sophocles I*, ed. David Grene and Richard Lattimore (Chicago, 1954), lines 95ff. and 190–215.

33. Ibid., lines 353, 821ff., 1360ff.

34. Rudolf Otto, *The Idea of the Holy*, pp. 54–55 and Freud, *Totem and Taboo*, Sec. 4 of Ch. 2.

35. Otto, *The Idea of the Holy*, pp. 54–55.

36. See note 13 above.

37. *Ibsen: The Complete Major Prose Plays*, trans. Rolf Fielde (New York, 1978), pp. 853ff.

38. *Hamlet*, Act III, Scene 1.

39. Plato, *Republic*, 330d f. (Shorey translation).

40. S.G.F. Brandon, *The Judgment of the Dead: The Idea of Life After Death in the Major Religions* (New York, 1967), pp. 193–94. For examples of the cross-cultural gruesomeness of hell, compare the following: Plato, *The Republic*, 614b ff.; Homer, *The Odyssey*, 11:576ff.; Vergil, *The Aeneid*, 6:540ff.; *The Tibetan Book of the Dead*, Evans-Wentz edition, pp. 165ff.; *The Buddhist Tradition: In India, China and Japan*, ed. William T. De Bary (New York, 1972), pp. 297, 322–23; and *The Shiva Purana*, quoted in Holck, *Death and Eastern Thought*, pp. 85–87. For examples from Egypt and China, see Brandon, *The Judgment*, pp. 43–46 and 184–85.

Chapter 7: Religion as Means and as End

1. John E. Smith, "The Structure of Religion," *Religious Studies*, I (1965), p. 68, and Kathleen Bliss, *The Future of Religion* (Baltimore, 1972), Preface.

2. Paul Ricoeur, *The Symbolism of Evil*, pp. 167–68. In speaking of the unhappy consciousness, Ricoeur refers to a famous section of Hegel's *Phenomenology of Spirit*, which carries that title.

3. Walter Otto, *Dionysus: Myth and Cult*, pp. 19–21, 37.

4. Ibid., pp. 34 and 46. Among those whose contrary opinions Otto undoubtedly has in mind is his great predecessor in the study of Greek antiquity,

Erwin Rohde, who writes "It is true of the cult of the dead, as of any other sacrificial custom, that its perpetration is due solely to the hope of avoiding hurt and obtaining assistance at the hands of the Unseen." *Psyche: The Cult of Souls and Belief in Immortality Among the Greeks*, trans. W.B. Hillis (New York, 1966), I, 16.

5. Evelyn Underhill, *Worship* (New York, 1936), pp. 5 and 8.

6. Ibid., pp. 17–18, 9, and 14. Tagore, speaking from a very different tradition praises useless activity. He wants to begin the day with this invitation: "Brothers, let us squander the morning with futile songs." And he writes, "Like Brahma himself, [man] takes joy in productions that are unnecessary to him, and therefore representing his extravagance and not his hand-to-mouth penury. The voice that is just enough can speak and cry to the extent needed for everyday use, but that which is abundant sings, and in it we find our joy." *A Tagore Reader*, ed. Amiya Chakravarty (Boston, 1966), pp. 37 and 231. It's not clear whether Tagore speaks here as a poet or believing soul. In view of the analysis which follows, both would be appropriate.

7. For a profound description of the unity of presence and absence, see Henri Nouwen, *Reaching Out: The Three Movements of the Spiritual Life* (Garden City, 1975), pp. 90–91.

8. *Dionysus*, pp. 19 and 37.

9. Job 1:9–11 (RSV).

10. Job 13:15 (KJV).

11. Job 1:21 (RSV).

12. *Luther's Works*, Vol. 12, p. 345, and Vol. 14, pp. 148–49, 172. It is of special interest that all these comments (see previous note as well) are on passages in the "penitential" Psalms, which have the forgiveness of sins as their theme. Luther is here fighting against what I've been calling *spiritual materialism*, making the God-relation a means to spiritual benefits. In the same tradition Karl Barth has written that "the yearnings of religion are of the same order as our sexual and intellectual and other desires." *The Epistle to the Romans*, trans. Edwyn C. Hoskyns (New York, 1968), p. 213. From the rather different tradition of Russian Orthodoxy we hear the same message. These are the words of a humble, nameless pilgrim, seeking to help a brother in the faith. "I set out to prove to him the uselessness and vanity of avoiding sin merely from fear of the tortures of Hell. . . . I added that according to the holy Fathers, one who performs saving works simply from the fear of Hell follows the way of bondage, and he who does the same just in order to be rewarded with the Kingdom of Heaven follows the path of a bargainer with God. The one they call slave, the other a hireling. But God wants us to come to Him as sons to their Father, He wants us to behave ourselves honourably from love for Him and zeal for His service, He wants us to find our happiness in uniting ourselves with Him in a saving union of mind and heart." *The Way of a Pilgrim and The Pilgrim Continues His Way*, trans. R.M. French (New York, 1974), p. 27. The pilgrim later speaks of "spiritual greed," p. 56. For an almost exactly identical concern from within the Buddhist tradition, see Henry Clarke Warren, *Buddhism in Translation* (New York, 1979), pp. 269–72.

13. Plato, *Euthyphro*, 14b–14e (Church-Cumming translation). Cf. Book II of the *Republic*.

14. See Plato, *Symposium* 202d ff., and the remarks of the Platonist, Cotta, in Cicero's *De Natura Deorum*, I, 116, who says, "I fail to see why the gods should be worshipped if we neither have received nor hope to receive benefit from them."

15. A.E. Taylor, *Plato: The Man and His Work* (New York, 1956), p. 148.

16. From the Lord's Prayer. Matt. 6:9–13. (RSV).

17. *Bhagavad-Gita*, XVII, 11 (Radhakrishnan translation). The Kantian flavor of this distinction between self-interest and duty should be noted.

18. Ibid., III, 9. Cf. IV, 23. Work and sacrifice are linguistically linked in the Hindu tradition. See R.C. Zaehner, *The Bhagavad-Gita: With a Commentary Based on the Original Sources* (New York, 1969), p. 165.

19. *Bhagavad-Gita*, II, 47.

20. Ibid., II, 71. Cf. II, 55–57, III, 30, 39–40, and IV, 19–22.

21. Ibid., VI, 2 and V, 1–3. Cf. the Buddhist notion of the "unsupported" giving of gifts as a spiritual perfection. Such giving is disinterested and self-less, forgetful of the self, its interests, and its rewards, and wholly devoid of any sense of achievement, attainment, or merit. See *Buddhist Wisdom Books*, trans. and ed. Edward Conze (London, 1975), pp. 26–27, 35, 38, 43, 54, and 94.

22. For a western statement of this point in the Kantian tradition, see H.A. Prichard, "Does Moral Philosophy Rest on a Mistake?" reprinted from *Mind*, XXI (1912), 487–99, in many anthologies.

23. *Bhagavad-Gita*, IX, 27.

24. Ibid., III, 20–25.

25. *Nicomachean Ethics*, 1140b6 (Ross translation). For a fuller account, see 1176b3 ff.

26. Lewis, *An Experiment in Criticism* (Cambridge, 1961), p. 19. His italics.

27. Shaftesbury, *Characteristics*, ed. John Robertson (London, 1900; reprinted by Bobbs-Merrill, 1964), II, 126–28.

28. Ibid., I, 274, 317, 78.

29. Ibid., I, 296. In response to the objection that this pleasure is the end and contemplation the means, Shaftesbury continues: "And though the reflected joy or pleasure which arises from the notice of this pleasure once perceived, may be interpreted a self-passion or interested regard, yet the original satisfaction can be no other than what results from the love of truth, proportion, and symmetry in the things without." In the same vein Wittgenstein writes of religious ritual, "It aims at some satisfaction and it achieves it. Or rather, it does not *aim* at anything; we act in this way and then feel satisfied." "Remarks on Frazer's 'Golden Bough,'" trans. A.C. Miles and Rush Rhees, *The Human World*, 3 (1971), 31. His italics.

30. See Jerome Stolnitz, "On the Origins of 'Aesthetic Disinterestedness'" *The Journal of Aesthetics and Art Criticism*, 20, No. 2 (1961), 134–35.

31. *Critique of Judgment*, trans. J.H. Bernard (New York, 1951), pp. 38–43. This formulation is followed by Croce in "Aesthetics," reprinted from the 14th edition of the *Encyclopaedia Britannica* in A. Hofstadter and R. Kuhns, eds., *Philosophies of Art and Beauty* (Chicago, 1976), p. 557, and by Collingwood in *The Principles of Art* (London, 1958), pp. 135–37.

32. Lewis, *An Experiment in Criticism*, p. 15.

33. In a formulation Kant was almost surely aware of, Moses Mendelssohn refers to a faculty of the soul between knowledge and desire (*Begehren*) which

is "nevertheless far removed from desire [*Begierde*]. We view the beauty of nature and of art, without the least stirring of desire, with pleasure and satisfaction. It appears rather to be a distinctive mark of beauty that it is viewed with calm satisfaction, that it pleases even though we don't possess it and are ever so far removed from even the desire to possess it." *Morgenstunden* (Frankfurt and Leipzig, 1790). (*Veranderte Auflage*), Sec. VII, p. 120.

34. Kant, *Critique of Judgment*, pp. 39–44.

35. Schopenhauer, *The World as Will and Representation*, trans. Haldane and Kemp in *Philosophies of Art and Beauty*, ed. Hofstadter and Kuhns, paragraph 38. Paragraph numbers refer to materials from Vol. 1.

36. Ibid., Vol. II, Ch. 34. Chapter numbers refer to materials from Vol. II.

37. Ibid., Vol. I, paragraphs 38–39. Cf. 41, 43, and 49.

38. Stolnitz, "On the Origins of 'Aesthetic Disinterestedness,' ", p. 132.

39. Kant is clear that interest is not in the mere existence of the object but in the "connection of the subject with the existence of the object." *Critique of Judgment*, p. 43. Bullough even goes so far as to suggest that in "psychical distance," his term for disinterestedness, we interpret "even our subjective affections not as modes of *our* being but rather as characteristics of the phenomenon." " 'Psychical Distance' as a Factor in Art and an Aesthetic Principle," reprinted in various anthologies from the *British Journal of Psychology*, 5 (1912), 87–98. This quotation is from Section I.

40. Lewis, *An Experiment in Criticism*, p. 19.

41. Gabriel Marcel gives a profound analysis of receiving and giving as identical. For a brief summary and references, see my essay, "Existentialism and Environmental Ethics," in *The Environmental Crisis: The Ethical Dilemma*, ed. Edwin R. Squiers (Mancelona, 1982).

42. Schopenhauer, *The World as Will and Representation*, Vol. I, paragraph 39.

43. Shaftesbury, *Characteristics*, II, 129.

44. Clive Bell, *Art* (New York, 1958), Ch. 1.

45. Bullough, " 'Psychical Distance', " Sec. I.

46. Kant, *Critique of Pure Reason*, B xiii–xvi.

47. This formulation is Rudolf Makkreel's in *Dilthey: Philosopher of the Human Studies* (Princeton, 1975), p. 23. Cf. *Critique of Judgment*, paragraphs 6–9, 16–22, in relation to Section IV of the Introduction.

48. Croce, "Aesthetics," p. 559. Alison adds the art historian and the critic to the list of those whose theoretical purposes interfere with the openness of disinterest. See Stolnitz, "Origins" pp. 137–38.

49. Shaftesbury, *Characteristics*, I, 77–78.

50. Ibid., I, 269.

51. Ibid., I, 66–69, 266–69. Cf. 55–56 and 273–74. It is with Shaftesbury's voice that Dewey speaks, "Being 'good' for the sake of avoiding penalty, whether it be going to jail or to hell, makes conduct unlovely." *Art As Experience* (New York, 1958), p. 198.

52. Aristotle, *Nicomachean Ethics*, X, 6. Cf. *Politics*, VIII, 3.

53. Hans-Georg Gadamer, *Truth and Method*, pp. 93–94, 97, 101. In his protest against viewing play as a means to an end, especially a biological one, Huizinga speaks of the fun, disinterestedness, seizure, and absorption which characterize play. *Homo Ludens* (Boston, 1955), pp. 2, 9, 16–17. Cf. pp. 13,

28, and 49. He also stresses that activities such as hunting can have a utilitarian function and the form of play at the same time, with the latter even assuming primacy. But he notes the tension between playing to win or to earn money and the pure spirit of play he is describing, pp. 46 and 50–51.

54. Gadamer, *Truth and Method*, p. 92.

55. Hans-Georg Gadamer, *Philosophical Hermeneutics*, trans. and ed. David E. Linge (Berkeley, 1976), p. 53.

56. *Truth and Method*, pp. 95–98.

57. Ibid., p. 101. *Philosophical Hermeneutics*, p. 55. His italics.

58. *Truth and Method*, pp. 111–12. For Huizinga's discussion of religious rite as play, see *Homo Ludens*, pp. 4–5 and 14–27. He also brings in the disinterested feature, quoting Guardini's description of liturgy as "zwechlos aber doch sinnvoll"—"pointless but significant." p. 19.

59. Job 1:9 (Good News Bible).

Chapter 8: Prayer and Sacrifice as Useless Self-Transcendence

1. Chuang-Tzu, quoted by Fung Yu-Lan in *A Short History of Chinese Philosophy*, ed. Derk Bodde (New York, 1948), p. 64. Cf. Ch. 7, note 6 of this book.

2. Henri Nouwen, *Reaching Out: The Three Movements of the Spiritual Life*, p. 97.

3. In addition to the discussion of Socrates in Section 7A, see the discussion of Frazer in Section 4A and the Codrington quotation in note 60 of Ch. 2.

4. Royce, *The Problem of Christianity*, (Chicago, 1968), I, 385–86.

5. Matt. 6:9–13. Biblical quotations in this chapter are from the Revised Standard Version.

6. *Koran*, Surah I (Arberry translation).

7. *Self-Knowledge*, trans. Swami Nikhilananda (New York, 1970), pp. 200–01. These are the first and last stanzas of a hymn to Shiva. Shankara also gives expression to useless self-transcendence in this prayer to Vishnu, p. 188:

> Even when I am not duality's slave, O Lord!
> The truth is that I am Thine, and not that Thou art mine:
> The waves may belong to the ocean,
> But the ocean never belongs to the waves.

8. For the hymn form in the Psalms see Artur Weiser, *The Psalms*, pp. 52ff. There are also hymns in the New Testament, e.g., Phil. 2:5–11; Rev. 4:8, 11, 5:9–10, 12, 13, 7:10, 12, 11:17–18, 19:1–8; and I Tim. 3:16. Mircea Eliade gives hymns from Sumeria, ancient Egypt, Vedic India, Homeric Greece, and the Zoroastrian and Islamic traditions in *From Primitives to Zen*, Ch. I, Sections B-D. Some are "pure" hymns. Others have self-interested petitions included as in the three prayers we first looked at. But the elements of adoration and awe are very strong in all these traditions.

9. Ps. 33:1. The NIV reads "it is fitting for the upright to praise him." Cf. Ps. 147:1, "Praise the Lord! For it is good to sing praises to one God; for he is gracious and a song of praise is seemly."

10. *Worship*, p. 5.

11. Elizabeth O'Conner, *Search for Silence* (Waco, 1972), p. 120.

12. Nouwen, *Reaching Out*, pp. 89–90.

13. Merton, *Contemplative Prayer*, pp. 20, 24, 30, 33, 41, 68. Merton quotes an extreme version of this idea from St. Anthony, who says that "the prayer of the monk is not perfect until he no longer realizes himself or the fact that he is praying" *The Wisdom of the Desert* (New York, 1970), pp. 8–9.

14. Thomas Merton, *Contemplation in a World of Action* (Garden City, 1973), pp. 345–46.

15. *The Gospel of Sri Ramakrishna*, pp. 177–78.

16. Underhill, *Worship*, pp. 9–11.

17. *The Sacred Pipe*, pp. 12–16, 65–66, 82–84.

18. Weiser, *The Psalms*, p. 404, commenting on Ps. 51:4.

19. Nouwen, *Reaching Out*, p. 105.

20. Quoted by O'Conner in *Search for Silence*, p. 170.

21. Ibid., p. 151. Cf. pp. 152–53.

22. Thomas Merton, *Contemplative Prayer*, pp. 89 and 29. My italics.

23. This is the central theme of Brother Lawrence, the seventeenth-century French contemplative.

24. Edward Conze, *Buddhist Meditation* (New York, 1969), p. 11. The very first of the "tacit assumptions" which westerners need to grasp if they are to understand Indian thought (Hindu and Jain as well as Buddhist) is that it "treats the experiences of Yoga as the chief raw material for philosophical reflection." Conze, *Buddhist Thought in India* (Ann Arbor, 1967), pp. 17–19.

25. *Dhammapada*, I, 8. Cf. XIV, 12, XXI, 7–12, and Conze, et al., ed., *Buddhist Texts Through the Ages*, pp. 51ff.

26. *Buddhist Meditation*, pp. 45–51. Further instructions are given for reflection on each element of these acts of praise. See pp. 56ff. for further worship liturgies. On Buddhist faith and devotion see also *Buddhist Texts Through the Ages*, pp. 52–54 and 185–206.

27. *Buddhist Meditation*, p. 21.

28. Ibid., pp. 23, 29, 34, 107, 167.

29. *A Source Book in Indian Philosophy*, ed. Radhakrishnan and Moore, pp. 281–84. See also the verse on p. 289.

> Misery only doth exist, none miserable,
> No doer is there; naught save the deed is found.
> *Nirvana* is, but not the man who seeks it.
> The Path exists, but not the traveler on it.

30. See previous note.

31. Radhakrishnan and Moore, *Source Book*, pp. 339 and 344.

32. *The Three Pillars of Zen*, ed. Philip Kapleau (Boston, 1967), pp. 18, 174, 179. Unlike traditional Buddhism which teaches concentration on the repulsive aspects of the world, excrement, corpses, etc., Zen teaches us to see each object as of absolute value, pp. 64, 144, 199. This not only serves to challenge the self-centeredness which relativizes everything to the self, the Cartesian posture; it also opens the way to viewing every moment as of absolute value, its own end.

33. Ibid., pp. 6, 14–16, 43, 48, 65, 177, 201, 207, 215, and 309. This theme is especially prominent in the interviews between Yasutani-Roshi and his western students, which Kapleau records on pp. 96–154.

34. Quoted by W.R. La Fleur in "Japan" in *Death and Eastern Thought*, ed., Frederick H. Holck, pp. 240–41. La Fleur stresses the continuity between this theme and the broader Mahayana equation of Nirvana with Samsara;

see pp. 237 and 255, note 31. For the Chinese background and the relation to Taoism, see Fung Yu-Lan, *Chinese Philosophy*, pp. 259–61 and note 77, below. For the same theme in contemporary Zen, see Kapleau, *Three Pillars*, pp. 46 and 57.

35. Roland de Vaux, *Ancient Israel* (New York, 1961), p. 451.

36. *Rig Veda*, X. 127. 8 (Griffith translation).

37. Ps. 141:2.

38. See "Sacrifice," *Encyclopedia Britannica*, 15th Edition (1975), pp. 16, 129.

39. Henri Hubert and Marcel Mauss, *Sacrifice: Its Nature and Function*, trans. W.D. Halls (Chicago, 1964), p. 100. Cf. de Vaux, *Ancient Israel*, p. 448, and E.O. James, *Sacrifice and Sacrament* (London, 1962), pp. 13–14.

40. E. Tylor, *Primitive Culture* (London, 1871).

41. James, *Sacrifice and Sacrament*, p. 13.

42. W. Robertson Smith, *The Religion of the Semites* (London, 1859).

43. John S. Mbiti, *African Religions and Philosophies* (Garden City, 1970), p. 75, and E.E. Evans-Pritchard, *Nuer Religion* (Oxford, 1956), p. 197.

44. Evans-Pritchard, *Nuer Religion*, pp. 276, 228, 222–23.

45. *Gods and Rituals*, ed. John Middleton (Garden City, 1967), pp. 7 and 22.

46. Evans-Pritchard, *Nuer Religion*, pp. 283–84.

47. Ibid., p. 277.

48. Ibid., pp. 277 and 282.

49. The first phrase is from a hymn by William W. How; the second is from the concluding essay of Kierkegaard's *Either/Or*.

50. Evans-Pritchard, *Nuer Religion*, pp. 278–79. My italics.

51. Underhill, *Worship*, p. 52.

52. These examples, from the hymns of the *Rig Veda*, are taken from the selection given in *A Source Book in Indian Philosophy*, pp. 7–34.

53. Charles Eliot, *Hinduism and Buddhism: An Historical Sketch* (London, 1921), I, 66–67.

54. F.H. Holck, "The Vedic Period," in *Death and Eastern Thought*, p. 38.

55. Alain Danielou, *Hindu Polytheism* (New York, 1964), p. 63.

56. Ibid., p. 67.

57. For example, see *Satapatha-Brahmana*, V, 1, 1, 1–11.

58. The Freudian metaphor is suggested by James in *Sacrifice and Sacrament*, p. 46.

59. See Paul Deussen, *The Philosophy of the Upanishads*, trans. A.S. Geden (New York, 1966), pp. 61–63.

60. See *Brihad-Aranyaka Upanishad* 1. 5. 16; and *Mundaka Upanishad*, 1. 2. 5–13.

61. *Brihad-Aranyaka Upanishad*, 1. 4. 10 and 3. 9. 21.

62. *Isa Upanishad*, 1; *Katha Upanishad*, 1. 26–27; *Brihad-Aranyaka Upanishad*, 2. 4. 5.

63. *Brihad-Aranyaka Upanishad*, 1. 5. 2. The "merely" in square brackets is part of Hume's translation.

64. *Mundaka Upanishad*, 2. 1. 1—7; *Brihad-Aranyaka Upanishad*, 1. 4. 7, and 2. 4. 6.

65. *Bhagavad-Gita*, III, 10–12 (Radhakrishnan translation).

66. Ibid., III, 17–18.

67. From the *Book of Odes* in *A Source Book in Chinese Philosophy*, trans. Wing-Tsit Chan (Princeton, 1963), p. 5. For pre-Confucian reservations about this see pp. 11–12.

68. Confucius, *Analects*, 2:5, 3:12, 17 (Wing-Tsit Chan translation).

69. Ibid., 4:16. Cf. 4:12: "If one's acts are motivated by profit, he will have many enemies."

70. Ibid., 12:22 and 2.

71. Wing-Tsit Chan, *A Source Book in Chinese Philosophy*, p. 633.

72. Taoism uses a different vocabulary, but its response to traditional sacrificial ritual is virtually identical to the Confucian response. Lao Tzu's theory of right action as non-action is a sophisticated theory of disinterested action in the context of subordination to the cosmic Tao.

73. Lev. 1:1–14, 4:1–5:13.

74. Lev. 7:12–17.

75. Walther Eichrodt, *Theology of the Old Testament*, I, 147.

76. Ibid., I, 152.

77. See Lev. 25:23; I. Chron. 29:14; Ps. 50:8–15; and Isa. 66:1–2.

78. See the liturgy for this offering in Deut. 26:1–11.

79. See de Vaux, *Ancient Israel*, p. 454.

80. I Sam. 15:22.

81. Isa. 66:1–4; Ps. 40:6–8; Prov. 15:8; Hos. 8:11–13; Jer. 7:21–23. Cf. Weiser, *The Psalms*, p. 337. "It is God and his revelation and not man who in this is at the centre of the cult; and for that very reason man can only listen and obey. There is but *one* attitude of man which renders to this God what belongs to him of right . . . it is the attitude of obedience and of submission to his will," that is, the giving of oneself.

82. Amos 5:21–24; Isa. 1:10–17; Micah 6:6–8; Prov. 21:3.

83. Ps. 69:30, 51:17; Isa. 66:2; Micah 6:8.

84. Hos. 6:6.

85. Martin Buber, *The Prophetic Faith*, trans. C. Witton-Davies (New York, 1960), p. 119.

86. Ibid., p. 92.

87. Hubert and Mauss, *Sacrifice*, p. 101.

88. John 1:29; I Cor. 5:7; Isa. 53:10; and Heb. 9:26.

89. Mark 10:45; Phil. 2:5–8.

90. Luke 14:27. That the New Testament ethic is one of imitating Jesus by following the way of the cross is the thesis of John Howard Yoder in *The Politics of Jesus* (Grand Rapids, 1972), Ch. 7.

91. Rom. 12:1.

92. Eph. 5:1–2.

93. Heb. 13:15–16.

94. Karl Adam, *The Spirit of Catholicism*, trans. Justin McCann (Garden City, 1954), p. 197.

95. Quoted in Underhill, *Worship*, p. 58.

96. Quoted in Underhill, ibid., p. 59.

97. Mark 12:43–44.

98. See II Cor. 8:1–7 for the unity of monetary giving and giving of self.

99. See the whole of *The Politics of Jesus* in relation to its Ch. 7.

100. Augustine, *The City of God*, x, 5 (Dod's translation).

Chapter 9: Guilt and Death in Exilic Religion

1. Heinrich Zimmer makes a similar distinction when he discusses the religious philosophies of India under the two headings: "the philosophies of time" and "the philosophies of eternity." See *The Philosophies of India* (Princeton, 1951). For Kierkegaard see Section 3A.

2. See Section 5B.

3. The term "relation" has to be used carefully, for as we shall see, in some traditions the proper "relation" to the sacred involves passing beyond the modes of experience in which difference and relation have their meaning.

4. Heidegger's critique of the subjectivism of modern thought can be fruitfully read as a religious protest against the secular individualism of the Cartesian modernity. Although we'll be noting crucial differences in the way this occurs from one type to another, they will be united in challenging the ultimacy, the autonomy, and the self-sufficiency of the one we normally refer to as I and me.

5. Frederick Franck, *The Book of Angelus Silesius*, pp. 25–26. My italics.

6. Matt. 16:24–26 (RSV).

7. Similarly, when we hear Eliade emphasizing the paradox involved when the believing soul "sees himself as real only to the extent that *he ceases to be himself. . . .*" we recognize the generically religious. But when he specifies this ceasing to be oneself in terms of "imitating and repeating the gestures of another," we recognize the limitation to that type that he labels archaic. Mircea Eliade, *The Myth of the Eternal Return or, Cosmos and History*, trans. Willard R. Trask (Princeton, 1965), p. 34. My italics. For the main text, pagination is the same as in the 1959 Harper edition in which title and subtitle are reversed.

8. Paul Ricoeur, *The Symbolism of Evil*, pp. 171–72.

9. For a phenomenological interpretation of Weber's notion of ideal types, see Alfred Schutz, *The Phenomenology of the Social World*, pp. 176–250.

10. See Sections 1D and 1E.

11. I owe this distinction to Paul Holmer.

12. Ricoeur, Part II, Chapter IV, "The Myth of the Exiled Soul and Salvation Through Knowledge," in *The Symbolism of Evil*.

13. See the last two paragraphs of Ch. 1.

14. Given our phenomenological method, we can abstract from the historical debate over dates and influences. Scholars tend to agree on "the impossibility of separating Orphism from the religious beliefs of the Pythagoreans." W.K.C. Guthrie, *The Greeks and Their Gods*, p. 311, note 3. Cf. similar statements by E.R. Dodds, *The Greeks and the Irrational* (Berkeley, 1951), p. 149; and Alexander P.D. Mourelatos, *The Pre-Socratics: A Collection of Critical Essays* (Garden City, 1974), p. 9.

15. From Kathleen Freeman, *Ancilla to the Pre-Socratic Philosophers* (Cambridge, Mass., 1966), p. 65. For alternative translation and commentary on these fragments (numbers 115, 118, and 121), see G.S. Kirk and J.E. Raven, *The Pre-Socratic Philosophers: A Critical History with a Selection of Texts* (Cambridge, England, 1962), pp. 351–52, and Charles H. Kahn, "Religion and Natural Philosophy in Empedocles' Doctrine of the Soul," in Mourelatos, *The Pre-Socratics*, pp. 434–35 and 441–43.

16. Erwin Rohde, *Psyche: The Cult of Souls and Belief in Immortality among the Greeks*, II, 343.

17. Dodds, *The Greeks and the Irrational*, p. 155. For the relation of Orphism and the cult of Dionysus, see Rohde, *Psyche*, II, 335–41 and 596–98; Dodds, pp. 142 and 155–56; Guthrie, *The Greeks and Their Gods*, pp. 315–20; Ricoeur, *The Symbolism of Evil*, pp. 282 and 289–300; Martin P. Nilsson, *A History of Greek Religion*, trans. F.J. Fielden (New York, 1964), p. 4; and Nilsson, *Greek Piety*, trans. Herbert Jennings Rose (New York, 1969), pp. 22–24.

18. Ricoeur, *The Symbolism of Evil*, p. 300. His italics. Cf. p. 283.

19. Freeman, *Ancilla*, p. 64. See F.M. Cornford, "Mysticism and Science in the Pythagorean Tradition," in Mourelatos, *The Pre-Socratics*, p. 140, "It was assumed, moreover, in sharp contradiction to orthodox Olympian religion, that there was no inseparable gulf between God and the soul, but a fundamental community of nature."

20. Kahn, "Religion and Natural Philosophy," p. 436. Cf. Cornford, "Mysticism and Science," p. 146, "On the natural plane the soul acts as a vital principle, distinguishing organic living things from mere casual inorganic masses of matter. In that aspect it is conceived in Pythagorean mathematics-musical terms as a harmony. . . . But on the spiritual plane . . . it is a permanent immortal thing. The question how exactly this spiritual thing is related to the vital principle which distinguishes a living from a dead body is a question that might be put to any modern believer in immortality without the expectation of any very clear and precise answer."

21. Rohde, *Psyche*, II, p. 283. His italics.

22. Dodds, *The Greeks and the Irrational*, p. 153.

23. Freeman, *Ancilla*, p. 65.

24. Plato, *Cratylus*, 400c. For discussion of this passage, see Rohde, *Psyche*, II, p. 341; Guthrie, *The Greeks and Their Gods*, p. 311; Dodds, *The Greeks and the Irrational*, p. 148; and Ricoeur, *The Symbolism of Evil*, pp. 283–84. Cf. *Phaedrus*, 250b, and note 40, below.

25. Ricoeur, *The Symbolism of Evil*, pp. 284–87. The theoretical advantage of the new view over the old is simply put: "The post-mortem punishment did not explain why the gods tolerated so much human suffering of the innocent. Reincarnation did. On that view, no human soul was innocent: all were paying, in various degrees, for crimes of varying atrocity committed in former lives." Dodds, *The Greeks and the Irrational*, p. 151.

26. Nilsson, *History*, p. 223.

27. See Cornford, "Mysticism and Science," pp. 137–38. A similar interpretation is suggested by Dodds, *The Greeks and the Irrational*, p. 150.

28. Rohde, *Psyche*, II, 343.

29. Dodds, *The Greeks and the Irrational*, p. 156. In *Philosophical Fragments*, Chapter Three, Kierkegaard makes much out of the fact that Socrates doesn't know himself well enough, in spite of the Delphic injunction, to know whether he's a monster like Typhon or some kind of divine creature. *Phaedrus*, 230a.

30. Plato, *Gorgias*, 477a ff., and 525b ff.

31. For the former, see the quotation from Pindar in Plato's *Meno*, 81b. For the latter, see *Cratylus*, 400c.

32. See Ricoeur, *The Symbolism of Evil*, pp. 284 and 287.

33. Quoted by Ricoeur in ibid., p. 301, note 13.

34. *Republic*, 346b ff.

35. Dodds, *The Greeks and the Irrational*, pp. 152–55.

36. Plato, *Phaedo*, 69b (Tredennick translation). Cf. *Phaedrus*, 249c-250c, where Plato again uses the image of initiation into the mysteries as a metaphor for philosophy.

37. Rohde, *Psyche*, II, 344; and Nilsson, *History*, p. 218.

38. Kahn, "Religion and Natural Philosophy," p. 449.

39. *Phaedrus*, 247c.

40. Guthrie, *The Greeks and Their Gods*, p. 325.

41. W.K.C. Guthrie, *The Greek Philosophers: From Thales to Aristotle* (New York, 1975), p. 36.

42. Arthur Darby Nock, "Gnosticism," in *Essays on Religion and the Ancient World*, ed. Zeph Stewart (Cambridge, Mass., 1972), I, 949.

43. Hans Jonas, *The Gnostic Religion: The Message of the Alien God and the Beginnings of Christianity* (2nd ed.; Boston, 1963), pp. 24-27. For a more restrictive treatment emphasizing the differences between various writings rather than their similarity, see Nock *Religion and the Ancient World*, I, 444-51, and II, 940-59.

44. James M. Robinson has stated the reason for such an exclusion very succinctly. "Gnostic schools began to emerge within Christianity and Neoplatonism, until both agreed in excluding them as the 'heresy' of Gnosticism." From the Introduction to *The Nag Hammadi Library in English* (San Francisco, 1977), p. 2. (Henceforth NHL.)

45. Nock, *Religion and the Ancient World*, I, 448-49; II, 958.

46. Robinson, in NHL, pp. 3 and 10, and E.R. Dodds, *Pagan and Christian in an Age of Anxiety* (New York, 1970), p. 18.

47. NHL, p. 43. Texts from Gnostic treatises translated in this volume are broken by parentheses of various sorts to indicate places where breaks in the text have been reconstructed or words have been supplied to make the reading smoother. I have only cited passages where these are relatively few and I have dropped them altogether.

48. Jonas, *The Gnostic Religion*, p. 224. Cf. *The Gospel of Thomas*, in NHL, p. 124, "Jesus said, 'Whoever has come to understand the world has found only a corpse, and whoever has found a corpse is superior to the world.' "

49. "Indeed, we shall find that in Gnostic thought the world takes the place of the traditional underworld . . ." Jonas, *The Gnostic Religion*, p. 68.

50. Dodds, *Pagan and Christian*, p. 13. Dodds supports this suggestion by noting that the Gnostics "could condemn the cosmos as a whole."

51. Nock, *Religion and the Ancient World*, II, 943.

52. NHL, p. 4.

53. Dodds, *Pagan and Christian*, p. 16. See Jonas, *The Gnostic Religion*, pp. 131-33 and 191, on the difference between Gnostic systems which view the Creator and Ruler of the World as evil and devilish and those which view him (or them) as merely inferior, ignorant, and degenerate. But when *The Gospel of Philip* says, "The world came about through a mistake," NHL, p. 145, the point is put so gently as to be misleading even for the latter views.

54. Jonas, *The Gnostic Religion*, p. 110.

55. Plotinus, *Enneads*, II, ix, 6, 13, 15 and 16. (MacKenna translation).

56. Jonas, *The Gnostic Religion*, pp. 43-44. On the cosmos itself as an enclosing prison both spatially and temporally, see pp. 51-54, 133, and 210. What gives radical intensity to the scheme is the additional idea that the whole thing is "a Satanic order." Nock, *Religion and the Ancient World*, II, 947.

57. Jonas, *The Gnostic Religion*, pp. 210–11.

58. Ibid., p. 227. In this manner sexual activity is portrayed as the work of the devil. Cf. p. 145, "Marcion here voices a genuine and typical *gnostic* argument, whose fullest elaboration we shall meet in Mani: 'That the reproductive scheme is an ingenious archontic device for the indefinite retention of souls in the world.' Marcion is perhaps the leader of the Gnostic assault on the Creator God of Judaism." See pp. 137–46.

59. See Ex. 20:3; Isa. 43:11; 44:6–8; 45:18, 21–22; 46:9. This theme is even more central to Second Isaiah than these passages indicate.

60. See *The Apocryphon of John, The Hypostasis of the Archons,* and *On the Origin of the World* in NHL, especially pp. 105–06, 153–57, and 165–70. For brief excerpts from these texts see Elaine Pagels, *The Gnostic Gospels* (New York, 1979), pp. 34–35. For quotations and commentary on a related passage quoted from Irenaeus, see Pagels, *The Gnostic Gospels*, pp. 147–48, and Jonas, *The Gnostic Religion*, pp. 133–34. The voice from heaven that repudiates the false claims of the creator to be the one, true God is reminiscent of the voice at Jesus' baptism, but it decertifies rather than validates. See Mark 1:11 in relation to Ps. 2:7 and Isa. 42:1.

61. The central texts are in NHL, pp. 153–55, 174, and 411–12. See also Jonas, *The Gnostic Religion*, pp. 93–96 and 228, and Pagels, *The Gnostic Gospels*, pp. 35–36, where it is pointed out that one Gnostic writer takes advantage of the opportunity offered by the Aramaic language to pun on similar sounding words meaning serpent and instructor.

62. Jonas, *The Gnostic Religion*, p. 127. Cf. Pagels, *The Gnostic Gospels*, pp. xx and 149, and Nock, *Religion and the Ancient World*, II, 956.

63. Dodds, *Pagan and Christian*, pp. 3, 23–24, 29, and 36.

64. NHL, pp. 118 and 121. The promise of overcoming death is repeated three times on pp. 120 and 129.

65. NHL, pp. 341–43. For similar passages from *The Gospel of Truth* and *The Gospel of Philip*, see NHL, pp. 44–45, 48, and 140–46.

66. For the importance of this strategy in Greek experience see Ricoeur, *The Symbolism of Evil*, pp. 211ff., and Dodds, *The Greeks and the Irrational*, Ch. 1, "Agamemnon's Apology."

67. *Enneads*, II, ix, 6 and 12–13.

68. See note 66 above. When Gnosticism speaks of tragedy it is divine as well as human tragedy. See Jonas, *The Gnostic Religion*, pp. 62–63, 131, 148, 163, 174–76, and 196.

69. Ibid., pp. 206–08, and Nock, *Religion and the Ancient World*, II, 957–59, who writes, "Only with Mani . . . did such ideas find expression in a church—and it indeed spread as far as China."

70. C.R.C. Allberry, ed., *A Manichaean Psalm-Book*, Part II (Stuttgart, 1938), p. 1, note to lines 1–3. Mani was crucified in 277 A.D., and his passion came to be treated much like that of Jesus in the Christian tradition. The Bema festival takes its name from a Greek word meaning the tribunal of a magistrate. Just as Paul teaches that "we must all appear before the judgment seat of Christ," II Cor. 5:10, so the Manichees identify the Judge with the Savior throughout these psalms.

71. Psalm 219.

72. See Psalm 229, for example.

73. See Psalms 252 and 267.

74. Psalms 222 and 258. Cf. Psalm 248 where knowledge of the difference between Light and Darkness, church and world, soul and body is presented directly as the basis of divine favor.

75. Psalm 248. Cf. Psalm 223, which provides a fine summary of the war waged by the Kingdom of Darkness upon the Kingdom of Light.

76. *Confessions*, IV, 3 (Warner translation).

77. Peter Brown, *Augustine of Hippo: A Biography* (Berkeley, 1967), pp. 50–51. Cf. p. 176.

78. *Confessions*, IV, 15. Cf. v, 10, VII, 3, and IX, 4. In the latter passage the theme of divine tragedy is unmentioned but human innocence via shifting the blame is still presented as crucial to Manichaeism. "For it was not the case of some other nature belonging to the race of darkness which committed the sin in me, as the Manichees believe."

79. Psalms 247, 252, and 265.

80. Pagels, *The Gnostic Gospels*, pp. 143–62.

81. Jonas, *The Gnostic Religion*, pp. 78, 127, 153, 166, 174, and 196.

82. Ibid., pp. 45, 59, and 196.

83. Allberry, *A Manichaean Psalm-Book*, p. 215. This is from a Manichaean psalm that doesn't belong to either of the two groups mentioned earlier.

84. Important passages in this connection are found in NHL, 125, 132–33, and 38–43. See the next section for the Hindu critique of name and form.

85. Quoted from Irenaeus by Jonas in *The Gnostic Religion*, p. 176. Also see p. 44, "Not only the body but also the 'soul' is a product of the cosmic powers. . . . Through his body and his soul man is a part of the world and subjected to the *heimarmeme*."

86. Ibid., pp. 123 and 158. His italics.

87. Ibid., pp. 44 and 196.

88. Shankara, *Self-Knowledge*, trans. Swami Nikhilananda, Par. 2–3. In future references Shankara's name, followed by paragraph numbers, will be to this text. References to either the long and helpful introduction by Nikhilananda or the commentary and notes he appends to each of Shankara's paragraphs will be given with Nikhilananda's name (or ibid.) and a page number. References with Shankara's name and a page number will be to the selections from his commentary on the Vedanta Sutras found in *A Source Book in Indian Philosophy*. Where only page or paragraph numbers are given it is understood that the author is the same as in the previous note. See also Shankara, pp. 510–12, for his gnosticism.

89. Page 510.

90. Pages 509, 515, 523, 526, 528, 532, 537, 542; and Par. 6, 7, and 18.

91. Shankara is intentional about this. In Par. 29 he cites the formula from *Brihad-Aranyaka Upanishad*, II, iii, 6, "*Neti, neti*," meaning "not this, not that."

92. Pages 524–25.

93. Page 527.

94. Page 531.

95. Par. 6. Cf. Par. 7 and 63.

96. Pages 518, 522; Par. 40.

97. Pages 513, 520, 530.

98. Page 520. Page 530 indicates that the distinction between God and the world is equally illusory.

99. Shankara, Par. 31–32.

100. Nikhilananda, pp. 32–33, n. 11.

101. Pages ix, xi, 60–61, 70ff., 82ff., 94, 99. See also Shankara, pp. 514–15, 524–27; and Par. 6, 17–22, 34, and 46.

102. Nikhilananda, p. 125. Cf. p. 56.

103. Pages 8, 111, and 137. Shankara, pp. 512, 521, and 527; Par. 21 and 34.

104. Nikhilananda, pp. 5, 54, 59–60, 120–21; Shankara, Par. 58.

105. Shankara, pp. 513, 515, 518, 520, 530–33, 537; Nikhilananda, pp. x, 38, 58, 128. On p. 510 Shankara does not shrink from drawing the conclusion that "scriptural texts have for their object that which is dependent on ignorance. . . ."

106. In a lengthy Appendix to *Self-Knowledge* many of these prayers are included. They are essential to any full understanding of Shankara.

107. Shankara, Par. 48 and 63. In Vedanta the terms Brahman and Atman are essentially interchangeable.

108. Par. 57.

109. Par. 38; pp. 520 and 526. In both of the latter two passages Shankara quotes freely from the Upanishads on both the all-encompassing and nondual aspects of Brahman. See also Nikhilananda, p. 146.

110. Par. 4.

111. Shankara, pp. 514–15, 518, 526–27, and 529.

112. Par. 56.

113. Nikhilananda, p. 50. Cf. pp. 118 and 151.

114. Page 130.

115. Pages 61–62, 85, 118, 133, 139; and Par. 22.

116. Pages 99–100.

117. Page 114.

118. Shankara, p. 512; Par. 20, 23, 30–31, 34–36, 39, 68.

119. Shankara, Par. 5 and 52. Cf. Par. 66.

120. Shankara, pp. 512, 514, 535, 542–43.

121. Quoted from another text of Shankara's by Nikhilananda, pp. 107–09.

122. Prayers to one's guru can be fairly compared, I believe, to prayers to Mary and the saints in Roman Catholicism.

123. The hymns referred to are found in the Appendix to *Self-Knowledge*, beginning at page 175. The remaining references are to these hymns. For the theme of asking for salvation as a gift of grace, see pp. 177, 179–80, and 187.

124. See pp. 177 and 180 in the immediately preceding context. Cf. p. 208.

125. Sometimes the petition is to be delivered simply from fear, without qualification, pp. 187–88, 200, 212; but often enough the fear is identified explicitly as the fear of death, pp. 209, 217.

126. Pages 182–83. Cf. pp. 193–96.

127. Pages 184 and 187.

128. See pp. 197–206. Stanza II on p. 202, dealing with the sins of infancy, invites comparison with Augustine's well-known reflections on this subject in *Confessions*, I, 6–7.

129. Page 190.

130. Pages 190–91.

Chapter 10: Guilt and Death in Mimetic Religion

1. *Ancient Near Eastern Texts Relating to the Old Testament*, ed. James B. Pritchard (3rd ed.; Princeton, 1969), p. 392. (Henceforth ANET.) For an alternative translation see S. Langdon, *Babylonian Penitential Psalms* (Paris, 1927), pp. 39–44.

2. See especially the prayers on pp. 193–96 and 200–01 of Shankara, *Self-Knowledge*, trans. Swami Nikhilananda.

3. See Plato, *Timaeus*, 32c–38e; *Physics*, VIII, 7–9; *On the Heavens*, I, 2–4; and *Metaphysics XII*, 7. The last three passages by Aristotle should be compared with *On the Soul*, 415a25–416b8, where Aristotle presents the reproductive cycle as the second best imitation of eternity in time.

4. Mircea Eliade, *The Myth of Eternal Return or, Cosmos and History*, pp. 27–28, 32, and 22.

5. Paul Ricoeur, *The Symbolism of Evil*, p. 192.

6. Mircea Eliade, *Patterns in Comparative Religion*, trans. Rosemary Sheed (New York, 1963), pp. 388, 391–92. Cf. Peter Berger, *The Sacred Canopy*, pp. 40 and 113–14, for an account of this "making present" in the context of a theory of culture as the conversation by which the life-world is constructed and maintained. In *Myth*, p. viii, Eliade says that "the myths serve as models for ceremonies that periodically *reactualize* the tremendous events that occurred at the beginning of time." My italics. Cf. the very helpful comments on festival and imitation in Hans-Georg Gadamer, *Truth and Method*, pp. 103, 110, 121–27, and 134–35.

7. The quoted phrases are the titles, respectively, of the two volumes of J.N. Findlay's Gifford Lectures, published in New York and London, 1967 and 1966, in the Muirhead Library of Philosophy.

8. Eliade, *Myth*, p. 35.

9. Ibid., p. xi.

10. Eliade, *Patterns*, p. 408.

11. Gerhard von Rad, *Old Testament Theology*, trans. D.M.G. Stalker (New York, 1962), I, 137–41.

12. I'm following the reconstruction of W. Norman Brown as given in "The Creation Myth of the Rig Veda," *Journal of the American Oriental Society*, Vol. 62 (1942), 85–97, and "Mythology of India" in *Mythologies of the Ancient World*, ed. Samuel Noah Kramer (Garden City, 1961), pp. 281–89. See especially *Rig Veda*, I, 32.

13. The concept of maintaining the world order is very prominent and explicit in the Vedic layer of Hinduism. See *Bhagavad-Gita*, III, 20–26; *Laws of Manu*, III, 75, and VII, 22; *Artha-Shastra* (Kautilya), I, 3. In these passages the entire doing of the duty of one's station, from religious ritual to personal moral rectitude to performing one's social role, is enjoined and praised as world-maintaining activity.

14. Quoted from Vedic texts by Eliade in *Myth*, p. 21.

15. Ibid., p. 19.

16. Ibid., pp. 10–11 and 78–79. In view of the overwhelming importance of sacrifice in Vedic life, the equation of sacrifice with creation is crucial. See Alain Danielou, *Hindu Polytheism*, Ch. 4; Charles Eliot, *Hinduism and*

Buddhism: An Historical Sketch, Vol. I, Book II, Chapter IV; and S.N. Dasgupta, *Hindu Mysticism* (New York, 1959), Lecture I.

17. In his valuable study of mimetic religion, Theodor H. Gaster places great emphasis on this dimension. His schema for a typical seasonal festival of renewal involves four moments, two of *Kenosis*, emptying, and two of *Plerosis*, filling. The first two consist of rites of mortification or penance and of purgation. These are followed by rites of invigoration and of jubilation. See *Thespis: Ritual, Myth and Drama in the Ancient Near East* (New York, 1961), pp. 17–103.

18. Eliade, *Myth*, p. 54.

19. Ibid., pp. 85–86. Cf. pp. 75 and 155–58, along with *Patterns*, p. 401.

20. Goethe's *Faust*, line 250.

21. Eliade, *Myth*, pp. 90–91.

22. Page 36.

23. Ibid., pp. 78–85. For the link between the New Year and new life see pp. 62–63 and 72. Within the year the pattern of death followed by new life is also associated with the phases of the moon. See p. 86.

24. Ibid., pp. 95 and 111. His italics.

25. Three of the scholarly debates need to be mentioned. The first and most general arises as a reaction to scholars like Frazer, Gaster, Eliade, the "myth and ritual school" gathered around S.H. Hooke, and the "Uppsala school," including such scholars as Engnell and Widengren. In the eyes of other scholars they are too quick to see patterns, too willing to emphasize similarities, and too reluctant to recognize differences. Similarities are automatically generic, differences merely specific. Among those who want to pay more attention to the differences are Henri Frankfort, Thorkild Jacobsen, R. De Langhe, and S.G.F. Brandon. See the essays by Hooke, De Langhe, and Brandon in *Myth, Ritual, and Kingship*, ed. S.H. Hooke (Oxford, England, 1958), and especially Frankfort's masterpiece, *Kingship and the Gods* (Chicago, 1948), a sustained study of the differences between the Egyptian and Mesopotamian life-worlds. A major reason for choosing these two examples is that the generic features of the type come through, if anything, more clearly as Frankfort stresses the many real and important differences.

A second issue concerns the assumption that myths were the libretti, so to speak, for religious rites and festivals. This connection is not explicit, for example, in the Canaanite poem of Baal and Anath, which becomes one of the most interesting expressions of mimetic religion if it is indeed connected with seasonal rites, as Gaster and Engnell are persuaded. See Gaster, *Thespis*, pp. 95ff. and 114–244; Ivan Engnell, *Studies in Divine Kingship in the Ancient Near East* (Oxford, England, 1967), Ch. 5; and the reservations of De Langhe in *Myth, Ritual, and Kingship*. Fortunately there are explicit links between myth and ritual in the Egyptian and Mesopotamian materials, another good reason for focusing on these instances. See Gaster, *Thespis*, pp. 80–81 and 90–91; Frankfort, *Kingship and the Gods*, pp. 123–39; Rudolf Anthes, "Mythology in Ancient Egypt," in *Mythologies of the Ancient World*, pp. 71ff.; H.W. Fairman, "The Kingship Rituals of Egypt," in *Myth, Ritual, and Kingship*, pp. 81ff.; and S.H. Hooke, *Babylonian and Assyrian Religion* (Norman, 1963), pp. 112–15.

A third debate concerns the place of ancient Israel in all of this. Those scholars who emphasize pattern and similarity tend to include the ancient

Hebrews along with the Mesopotamians, Egyptians, Canaanites, and Hittites as a species of a generic ancient near eastern mimetic religion. The presence of such elements from their cultural milieu is undeniable, but the main thrust of Israelite religion seems to me to be in a wholly different direction. This will be clear in the following chapter where it serves as a prime instance of what I will call covenantal religion. On this question see especially Martin Noth, "God, King, and Nation in the Old Testament" in *The Laws of the Pentateuch and Other Studies*, trans. D.R. Ap-Thomas (Edinburgh, 1966).

26. ANET, p. 87. The other standard translation is found in A. Heidel, *The Epic of Gilgamesh and Old Testament Parallels* (Chicago, 1949). A very similar description is found in the opening lines of the *Descent of Ishtar to the Nether World*, ANET, p. 107.

27. ANET, p. 98. On the relation of this view to Greek and Hebrew concepts, see Walther Zimmerli, *The Old Testament and the World*, trans. John J. Scullion (Atlanta, 1976), pp. 111ff.

28. ANET, p. 90.

29. Frankfort, *Kingship and the Gods*, p. 5.

30. Gaster, *Thespis*, pp. 17 and 24.

31. See S.G.F. Brandon, *The Judgment of the Dead*, pp. 288–89; Frankfort, *Kingship and the Gods*, p. 192; and Eliade, *Myth*, p. 69, n. 36.

32. In the Foreword to Gaster, *Thespis*, p. 11.

33. Frankfort, *Kingship and the Gods*, p. 3.

34. Ibid., p. 313. As indicated in the previous section, the "new" year could occur more than once during a solar year, and at some places this festival was celebrated at the end of both winter and summer when the rains brought new life to agrarian society. See pp. 313–15, and Sidney Smith, "The Practice of Kingship in Early Semitic Kingdoms," in *Myth, Ritual, and Kingship*, pp. 41–42.

35. Frankfort, *Kingship and the Gods*, p. 319, places the recital on the fourth day. Smith, "Practice of Kingship," p. 40, says it was recited twice, and Eliade, *Myth*, p. 55, says "several times," but neither gives the place of the additional readings. The standard English translations of *Enuma Elish* are in ANET, pp. 60–72 and 501–03, and A. Heidel, *The Babylonian Genesis and Old Testament Parallels* (Chicago, 1942 and 1951). A summary, in the context of other Sumero-Akkadian myths, is found in Samuel Noah Kramer, "Myths of Sumer and Akkad," in *Mythologies of the Ancient World*.

36. See Frankfort, *Kingship and the Gods*, pp. 282–93, 314–16, 321–24; Ricoeur, *The Symbolism of Evil*, pp. 192–93; and Engnell, *Divine Kingship*, pp. 18–22. As is his custom Frankfort calls attention to differences between various versions of the dying or suffering god motif, showing a closer linkage of Tammuz with Osiris than with Attis, Adonis, Persephone, or Dionysus. In arguing against Frazer that the differences are more important than the similarities, he makes the generic core of these myths all the more impressive.

37. This summary follows Frankfort, *Kingship and the Gods*, pp. 317–18, though he does not separate the Tammuz motif as I have done.

38. For details see Frankfort, ibid., pp. 259–61 and Engnell, *Divine Kingship*, pp. 30–35. It is Ricoeur, *The Symbolism of Evil*, p. 193, who describes the king as "grand penitent."

39. Frankfort, *Kingship and the Gods*, p. 278.

40. See the hymn of Assurnasirpal II to Ishtar, quoted by Frankfort, ibid., p. 239, and the Prologue to the Code of Hammurabi in ANET, p. 164. It

is worth noting that the very "objectivist" concept of sin noted here is also characteristic of ancient Israel, which presumably is the point of contrast for Frankfort. See von Rad, *Old Testament Theology*, I, 266–68.

41. ANET, pp. 384–85.

42. For the full text see Hooke, *Babylonian and Assyrian Religion*, pp. 103–04. Frankfort gives an alternative translation, *Kingship and the Gods*, pp. 318–19, and refers to the prayer as a "Kyrie Eleison."

43. Hooke, *Babylonian and Assyrian Religion*, pp. 105–06.

44. For these and the following rites of the fifth day, see Hooke, ibid., pp. 107–11, and Frankfort, *Kingship and the Gods*, pp. 319–20.

45. "What is the meaning of this painful scene? It is clear that by his penance and confession the king cleansed himself of the taint of past sins and thus became fit to officiate in the succeeding rites. . . . But, in addition, the humiliation of the king brought him into harmony with the conditions under which the great ceremony started. Though communication with Marduk was still possible in Esagila, in the outer world the god had 'disappeared.' The people were disturbed; nature appeared lifeless. Now the king, too, was robbed of his splendor . . . and reduced to a minimum of power which corresponded to the low ebb in the life of nature, to the 'captivity' of the god and also to the state of chaos preceding creation. Five days of sacrifice, atonement, and purification culminated in the king's degradation and reinstatement. The preparatory rites were completed. . . ." Frankfort, *Kingship and the Gods*, p. 320.

46. Ricoeur, *The Symbolism of Evil*, pp. 192 and 191.

47. To ask which one is *really* creator is to misunderstand the epistemology of polytheism. Each mythical picture or story represents a partial insight and is simultaneously valid with the others which together with it adumbrate the whole. Each of the creators is a manifestation of the divine, creative power. See Frankfort, *Ancient Egyptian Religion* (New York, 1948), pp. 3–5 and 19–21.

48. Quoted from A.L.J. Wensinck by Frankfort, *Kingship*, p. 150. Frankfort's discussion of Egyptian creation theology is primarily found in pp. 146–61. This includes an account of the combat motif, not as central as in the stories of Marduk and Tiamat, Indra and Vrtra, or Baal and Mot. See Gaster's *Thespis* for the text and interpretation of this last, a Canaanite myth.

49. Frankfort, *Kingship*, p. 27.

50. Frankfort, *Ancient Egyptian Religion*, pp. 92–93. For Egyptian belief, a soul "could not be abstracted from the body, or rather, man's personality required both at all times; and to gain eternal life, man's surviving part should not be entirely dissociated from the seat of his identity, the body. Hence the rich development of Egyptian sculpture; hence mummification; hence, also, the equipment of the tomb with the necessities of daily life." *Kingship*, p. 5.

51. Frankfort, *Kingship*, p. 45.

52. See Frankfort, *Ancient Egyptian Religion*, pp. 25–29.

53. Eliade, *Myth*, p. 90.

54. Frankfort, *Kingship*, p. 56.

55. Ibid., p. 124. For discussion of the "mystery play of the succession" on which Frankfort is commenting, see pp. 123–39, and Gaster, *Thespis*, pp. 79–83 and 377–99.

56. Frankfort, *Kingship*, pp. 35 and 9.

57. Frankfort, *Ancient Egyptian Religion*, pp. 32–33 and 46–49.

58. Frankfort, *Kingship*, p. 5. Cf. pp. 18 and 23.

59. A typical statement is that of H.W. Fairman in "The Kingship Rituals of Egypt," in *Myth, Ritual, and Kingship*, p. 75.

60. Frankfort, *Ancient Egyptian Religion*, p. 50. Cf. p. 88, "Change, if it was of a regularly recurring type, like the succession of the seasons, was significant because it could be considered part of an unchanging scheme."

61. But we cannot speak of a natural law ethic, for our concept of natural law presupposes a difference between physical laws and moral laws and then the attempt to bring the two concepts back into proximity with each other. For Egyptian thinking physical laws of nature cannot be metaphors for the moral law of nature because the difference which metaphor presupposes does not exist.

62. Quoted in Frankfort, *Ancient Egyptian Religion*, p. 18.

63. Quoted in Mircea Eliade, *From Primitives to Zen: A Thematic Sourcebook in the History of Religions*, pp. 353–55. Cf. similar texts in Frankfort, *Kingship*, p. 118.

64. Quoted in and from Frankfort, *Ancient Egyptian Religion*, p. 106.

65. Quoted in Frankfort, *Kingship*, pp. 118–19.

66. Frankfort, *Ancient Egyptian Religion*, pp. 101 and 107.

67. Frankfort, *Kingship*, pp. 174–75. See the variety of texts quoted in pp. 168–77.

68. In view of the strong link between the cycles of natural life and the Egyptian hope for eternal life, the view of Fairman that this is a "natural development" makes more sense than the concern of Brandon sharply to distinguish Osiris as vegetation deity from Osiris the individual's hope of immortality. See *Myth, Ritual and Kingship*, pp. 86–88 and 275–77, and Engnell, *Divine Kingship*, p. 9.

69. For more detailed discussion of the myth see Anthes, "Mythology in Ancient Egypt," especially pp. 33–43, 51–57, and 68–90.

70. ANET, p. 32. For further texts and commentary see Frankfort, *Kingship*, pp. 110–17. On the democratization of the cult of Osiris, see Frankfort, *Ancient Egyptian Religion*, pp. 103–04, and the Coffin Texts in Eliade, *From Primitives to Zen*, p. 193, "Whether I live or die I am Osiris," and pp. 230–31.

71. Brandon, *The Judgment of the Dead*, pp. 6–48.

72. ANET, p. 32. This translation, however, is not certain.

73. Frankfort, *Ancient Egyptian Religion*, p. 62.

74. Ibid., pp. 70–78. Cf. ANET, pp. 379 and 381. One of the advantages of suicide put forth in a famous poem is that

> Surely he who is yonder shall
> Be a living god
> Punishing the sin of him who commits it.

Eliade, *Myth*, p. 533. Cf. ANET, p. 407. Once again Frankfort's proper emphasis on the difference between the Egyptian understanding and the much more personal meaning of sin in biblical thought as the breach of a personal bond should not lead us to minimize the importance of this dimension of Egyptian religion.

75. Frankfort, *Ancient Egyptian Religion*, pp. 117 and 80. Cf. ANET, p. 379. For similar prayers to Thoth and the sun-god, see Brandon, *The Judgment of the Dead*, pp. 22–23.

76. Eliade, *Myth*, pp. 551–52. Cf. ANET, pp. 414–18, and Brandon, *The Judgment of the Dead*, pp. 19–20.

77. Frankfort, *Ancient Egyptian Religion*, pp. 117–19. Cf. Brandon, *The Judgment of the Dead*, pp. 28ff. and 43ff., and E.A. Wallis Budge, *The Egyptian Book of the Dead* (New York, 1967). One advantage of Brandon's chapter on Egypt is his careful sorting of materials from the Old Kingdom, Middle Kingdom, and New Kingdom periods. For our purposes it will be the content of the ideas and images, not their sequence, that matters.

78. The Egyptians had a technical term which is usually translated "justified." It is *maa kheru*, meaning true of voice, or, presumably, honest in declaring one's innocence.

79. Frankfort, *Kingship*, pp. 117–18. Cf. pp. 121–22 for the same sequence.

80. Brandon, *The Judgment of the Dead*, p. 22. On this general concept see also pages 10, 21, 27, and 30.

81. ANET, pp. 34–36. Cf. Budge, *The Egyptian Book*, pp. 344–53; Eliade, *Myth*, pp. 239–41; and Brandon, *The Judgment of the Dead*, pp. 7–8 and 28–41. Associated with the Declaration of Innocence are the texts designed to assure that no accuser would rise against one in the judgment, including one's own heart.

82. ANET, p. 36.

83. Brandon, *The Judgment of the Dead*, p. 40.

84. Ibid., pp. 9–18, 23–25, 28–30, and 41–44.

85. ANET, pp. 380–81.

Chapter 11: Guilt and Death in Covenantal Religion

1. These lyrics by Cyriacus Schneegass have been set to music by Dietrich Buxtehude and translated by Victor E. Gebauer as "The Infant Jesus."

2. C. Bernas speaks of the Eucharist both as "liturgical re-enactment" and as "repetition" in seeking to elucidate the meaning of the rite as "remembrance." See "Eucharist (Biblical Data)," in *New Catholic Encyclopedia* (New York, 1967), V, 596. This article and a companion article by E.J. Kilmartin, "Eucharist (As Sacrifice)" read as if they were—though they are not—an exercise is stating Catholic theology in the language of Eliade. The themes of repetition, re-enactment, representation, reliving, making present, and participation recur throughout. Cf. Section 10A.

3. Augustine, Letter 98, to Boniface, in the year 408.

4. These teachings occur, respectively, in the encyclicals *Mirae caritatis* (1902), *Mediator Dei* (1947), and Vatican II's *Constitution on the Divine Liturgy* (1963). The notion of prolonging the priesthood of Christ is expressed in *The Canons and Decrees of the Council of Trent*, Twenty-Second Session, Chapter I, according to which Jesus inaugurated the Eucharist because "his priesthood was not to be extinguished by his death."

5. *Summa Theologiae*, III, 83, 1.

6. See Section 10A.

7. *Mediator Dei*. This theme of participation is heavily emphasized in the encyclopedia essays of Bernas and Kilmartin cited in note 2, above.

8. This theme that there is only one sacrifice is strongly affirmed by the Council of Trent, Twenty-Second Session, Chapter II, and by Kilmartin, "Eucharist (As Sacrifice)," p. 613. Commenting on the discussion by Thomas Aquinas, Thomas Gilby notes that since there is an identity of sacrifices and

nothing is added to the original but the spreading of its effects, we should speak less of the Eucharist as repetition or re-enactment of Calvary, "but rather as its continuation by the liturgical action of the Church." *Summa Theologiae* (Blackfriars edition; New York, 1954), p. 197.

9. Bernas, "Eucharist (Biblical Data)," p. 596. Cf. Kilmartin, "Eucharist (As Sacrifice)," p. 610. The notion of Christ as sacramentally present (*sacramentaliter praesens*) is explicit in *Trent*, Thirteenth Session, Chapter I.

10. Karl Adam, *The Spirit of Catholicism*, p. 197.

11. Timothy Ware, *The Orthodox Church* (Baltimore, 1964), pp. 293–94. His italics. The quotations at the end of this paragraph are from P. Evdokinov, *L'Orthodoxie*.

12. See Mark 14:24; Matt. 26:28; I Cor. 11:25; Luke 22:20; and Heb. 8–10 against the background of Jer. 31:31–34; and Mark 14:25; Matt. 26:29; and I Cor. 11:26 against the background of Isa. 25:6, 65:13; Matt. 8:11, 22:1–14; Luke 14:15–24, 22:30; and Rev. 3:20, 19:9.

13. Walther Zimmerli, *The Old Testament and the World*, p. 2.

14. See Pss. 8, 19, 29, 104, 121, and 124 as examples.

15. See Zimmerli, *Old Testament*, Chapters 2–4, 6, and p. 143.

16. For a brief summary see David Myers, *The Human Puzzle* (New York, 1978), Chapter 4. For detailed studies see Aubrey R. Johnson, *The Vitality of the Individual in the Thought of Ancient Israel* (Cardiff, Wales, 1964), and Hans Walter Wolff, *Anthropology in the Old Testament*, trans. Margaret Kohl (Philadelphia, 1974).

17. See Gerhard von Rad, *Old Testament Theology*, I, 27–29; Zimmerli, *Old Testament*, pp. 31–39; Wolff, *Anthropology*, Chapters 19–20; and Martin Buber, *The Prophetic Faith*, trans. Carlyle Witton-Davies (New York, 1960), pp. 71–79 and 118–21.

18. See Zimmerli, *Old Testament*, pp. 130–135; Edmond Jacob, *Theology of the Old Testament*, trans. Heathcote and Allcock (London, 1958), pp. 299–316; and D.S. Russell, *The Method and Message of Jewish Apocalyptic* (Philadelphia, 1964), pp. 353–90. The latter two items have useful bibliographies on the topic.

19. Zimmerli, *Old Testament*, p. 136. Cf. pp. 12–13, "God instructs the Old Testament believer by throwing him back on the events of the world. . . . The whole thrust of the Old Testament proclamation guards against any flight into a beyond which is turned away from the world; faith is established in the midst of the events of the world."

20. Isa. 65:17–19 (NEB). Isa. 66:22 explains why the first world can be forgotten. The new heavens and the new earth will be enduring.

21. See, for example, Rudolf Bultmann, "Prophecy and Fulfillment," in *Essays on Old Testament Hermeneutics*, ed. Claus Westermann (Richmond, 1966).

22. John 18:36 and I John 2:15–17. Unless otherwise noted, biblical references in this chapter are to the Revised Standard Version.

23. *Epistle to Diognetus*, Ch. 5.

24. On creation, see John 1:3; Acts 17:24; Rom. 11:33–36; and Col. 1:15–20. On the new creation, see I Peter 3:13 and Rev. 21:1–4. In the New Testament the term *kosmos* sometimes is equivalent to the Old Testament's heaven and earth, referring to the totality of the created universe. In this context it does not have a negative meaning, but is acknowledged to be transitory. For details on this and two other meanings of *kosmos* in the New

Testament, see *Theological Dictionary of the New Testament*, trans. Geoffrey W. Bromily (Grand Rapids, 1964–76), III, 883–95. (Henceforth *TDNT*.)

25. I Cor. 15:20, in the context of this entire chapter. For the sharp difference between the Hebrew-Christian idea of resurrection of the body and the Greek idea of immortality of the soul, see Oscar Cullmann, "Immortality of the Soul or Resurrection of the Dead?" in *Immortality and Resurrection*, ed. Krister Stendahl (New York, 1965), pp. 9–53.

26. Elaine Pagels, *The Gnostic Gospels*, p. 122. Her italics. Cf. C.S. Lewis, "We may hope that the resurrection of the body means also the resurrection of what may be called our 'greater body'; the general fabric of our earthly life with its affections and friendships." *The Four Loves* (New York, 1960), p. 187.

27. Pagels, *The Gnostic Gospels*, p. 175. Her italics.

28. Gal. 5:19–21. For this reason NEB translates flesh (*sarx*) as "the lower nature."

29. Rom. 12:2; I Cor. 5:9–11; Gal. 6:14; Phil. 2:15; Col. 2:20. Cf. I John 5:19, "We know that we are of God, and the whole world is in the power of the evil one."

30. Rom. 5:12.

31. John 3:16, 1:29; and I Cor. 5:19. Cf. I John 2:2, "And he is the expiation for our sins, and not for ours only but also for the sins of the whole world." Since the apparently anti-worldly strains of the New Testament occur mostly in the Pauline and Johannine writings, I have relied almost entirely on them in this discussion. In I John the polemical meaning of *kosmos* is so strong and clear that the NEB sometimes translates it as "godless world."

32. G. Ernest Wright, *God Who Acts: Biblical Theology as Recital* (London, 1952), p. 13.

33. Wolfhart Pannenberg, "Redemptive Event and History," in *Essays on Old Testament Hermeneutics*, ed. Claus Westermann, pp. 316–17. My italics.

34. On the symbolic significance of Israel's "double exodus" see Peter Berger, *The Sacred Canopy*, p. 115.

35. Deut. 26:5–9. On the role of this creed and several passages which recite the same history of exodus and conquest or settlement as a kind of dust particle around which the entire Hexateuch (Genesis-Joshua) gathers, see Gerhard von Rad, "The Form-Critical Problem of the Hexateuch," in *The Problem of the Hexateuch and Other Essays*, trans. E.W. Trueman Dicken (Edinburgh, 1966), or, for a shorter version, *Genesis: A Commentary*, trans. John H. Marks (rev. ed.; Philadelphia, 1972), Introduction.

36. Frank Cross Moore, "The Song of the Sea and Canaanite Myth," in *Canaanite Myth and Hebrew Epic* (Cambridge, England, 1973), p. 132.

37. Zimmerli, *Old Testament*, p. 10. Cf. von Rad, *Hexateuch*, p. 132. "The worshipper does not give thanks for the fruits which the Creator has provided for him, but simply acknowledges that he is a member of the nation which God brought into the promised land by a historical saving art, thus making him heir to the blessings of this land. This theme is important among the earliest writing prophets. Amos sees the withdrawal of agricultural prosperity as a specific historical judgment of Yahweh on his people (4:6–9), and Hosea complains against Baal worship and the "baalization of YHVH Himself," in that Israel "did not know that it was I who gave her the grain, the wine, and the oil, and who lavished upon her silver and gold which they used for

Baal." (2:8) See Buber, *Prophetic Faith*, pp. 118–20. Both passages base agricultural prosperity on the assumption of a special relation between Yahweh and Israel grounded in covenant history.

38. William Foxwell Albright speaks of an "archaic demythologizing which takes place in Israel from the thirteenth down to the sixth century." But by making this mean "eliminating specifically polytheistic elements in the narratives of Genesis as well as poetic survivals or pagan borrowings in Old Testament literature," he shifts attention away from the central point. See *Yahweh and the Gods of Canaan* (Garden City, 1968), pp. 183–93. This is very different from Bultmann's demythologizing, the end result of which is to locate the divine activity in existential inwardness and to find Israel's faith an embarrassment. See the essay cited in Note 21, above.

39. Moore, *Canaanite Myth*, p. 138.

40. This is in opposition to the view of those who see ancient Judaism as a form of mimetic religion. Thus Gaster writes, "In the course of time, the real significance of the combat tends to be forgotten and it then comes to be explained as the commemoration of some historic encounter. . . . In several of the Old Testament psalms the traditional motif of the god's victory over the Dragon—itself projected from the Ritual Combat—is historicized as the triumph of Yahweh over the enemies of Israel." *Thespis: Ritual, Myth, and Drama in the Ancient Near East*, pp. 38–40. For Buber's objection to this view, see p. 46 of *The Prophetic Faith* and Ch. 7 of his *Kingship of God*, trans. Richard Scheimann (New York, 1973). Also see note 52, below.

41. Emil L. Fackenheim, *God's Presence in History: Jewish Affirmations and Philosophical Reflections* (New York, 1970), p. 4.

42. Moore, *Canaanite Myth*, 131–32. On p. 123 Moore calls this song "one of the oldest compositions preserved by biblical sources."

43. Isa. 51:9–11. Cf. Ps. 74:13–14, 77:16–20, 106:9, 114:1–5, and from "The Psalm of Habakkuk," Hab. 3:8–15. The passage from Deutero-Isaiah is hooked up in v. 11 with the theme of a new exodus toward which the prophet looks in hope. This creates a link with those passages which use the combat images of the mimetic creation myth to anticipate new acts of judgment and deliverance by Yahweh *in history*. See Ps. 74:13–23, Isa. 27:1, and Nahum 1:4–15. Buber, *The Prophetic Faith*, p. 214, writes of the passage in Isa. 51, "the prophet uses, in order to express as vividly as possible the fusion of both ideas [the creation of the world and Israel's deliverance from the Egyptians], the same word to describe the depths of the water, *tehom*, as is used both in the beginning of the creation story (Gen. 1:2), and again in the Song of the Sea (Ex. 15:5,8), and the union of the two realms is decided by a third factor, the act of redemption immediately expected." In Isa. 25:6–10 and Zeph. 1:8–9 the image of the god's victory feast is also used for this purpose.

44. Isa. 30:7 (NEB). Cf. Ezekiel 29:2–5 and 32:1–3.

45. But see von Rad's suggestion that these passages are derivative from Canaanite and Egyptian sources and "do not spring in the first place from the heart of Yahwism, but rather come into it from outside." "The Theological Problem of the Old Testament Doctrine of Creation," in *Hexateuch*, p. 140.

46. For this pattern see Pss. 33, 74, 89, 136, and 148, along with Isaiah 40:12–31, 43:1–7, 14–20, 44:24–28, and 45:1–7. In *Hexateuch*, pp. 137–38,

von Rad speaks of the "complete absorption of the doctrine of creation into the prophetic doctrine of salvation," in which the former is "altogether swallowed up."

47. Claus Westermann, *Praise and Lament in the Psalms*, trans. Crim and Soulen (Atlanta, 1981), p. 127.

48. See Claus Westermann, *Isaiah 40–66: A Commentary*, trans. David M.G. Stolher (Philadelphia, 1969), pp. 24–25.

49. G. von Rad, *Old Testament Theology*, I, 141 and 152. Cf. *Hexateuch*, p. 135, "It is as if for *Deutero-Isaiah* the creation of the world and the redemption of Israel both exemplify the same divine dispensation, as if that which happened at the beginning of things, and those 'new things'. . . which are now about to happen to Israel, both result from one and the same divine purpose of redemption. And so in fact they do." Buber, *The Prophetic Faith*, p. 214, is describing the same creation theology when he writes, "God creates in history. There is no theological boundary in the eyes of this prophet between creation and history. Just as in the book of Genesis the story of the formation of the world is only the opening of the story of the formation of the people, and obviously the whole connection is aimed at making us follow the meaning of the origin of Israel back to the meaning of the world's origin, so and still more so all that Deutero-Isaiah has to say about the creation points to history."

50. G. von Rad, *Old Testament Theology*, I, 138.

51. The creation hymns of Amos are found in 4:13, 5:8–9, and 9:5–6. They seem isolated and out of place only when it is not seen that they "are always directed towards the identification of the Lord of creation with the Lord of chastisements and destructions, the God of nature with the God of history." Buber, *The Prophetic Faith*, p. 106. Cf. the similar conclusion of W. Brueggemann, that 4:13 belongs to the whole section of vs. 4–13 with a covenant indictment and covenant curses and serves "to motivate repentance and covenant renewal." "Amos IV 4–13 and Israel's Covenant Worship," in *Vetus Testamentum*, Vol. 15 (1965), p. 11.

52. Moore, *Canaanite Myth*, p. 143. He continues, "It will not do to describe the process as a progressive historicizing of myth. . . . The Canaanite mythic pattern is not the core of Israel's epic of Exodus and Conquest." Cf. Roland de Vaux, *Ancient Israel*, p. 506, and Buber, *Kingship*, p. 127, "Where event and memory govern, cult follows their command; where they do not, it bids myth to replace them with a timeless image."

53. Verses 2–3. For a detailed discussion of this theme of the re-presentation (*Vergegenwärtigung*) of the redemptive past, see Martin Noth, "The Re-Presentation of the Old Testament in Proclamation," in Westermann, *Essays*. G. von Rad writes, "The great cultic festivals had already taught Israel to realize that they were present at the redemptive events of the past." *Deuteronomy: A Commentary*, trans. Dorothea Barton (Philadelphia, 1966), p. 28.

54. For brief summaries see Zimmerli, *Old Testament*, pp. 102–03 and Martin Noth, *The Laws in the Pentateuch and Other Studies*, pp. 24–25. For a detailed analysis, see de Vaux, *Ancient Israel*, pp. 484–506.

55. Martin Buber, *Moses: The Revelation and the Covenant* (New York, 1958), p. 73. Cf. *Prophetic Faith*, p. 50; and Brevard Childs, *The Book of Exodus: A Critical, Theological Commentary* (Philadelphia, 1974), pp. 197 and 206.

56. See Westermann, *Praise*, and Bernhard W. Anderson, *Out of the Depths: The Psalms Speak for Us Today* (Philadelphia, 1974).

57. Ex. 6:6–7 and Deut. 29:13. Cf. Ex. 19:4–6 with Buber's commentary, *Moses*, pp. 101–09; Deut. 7:6–11, 27:1–10; Josh. 24; and Judges 5, with Buber's commentary on the latter two passages, *Prophetic Faith*, pp. 8–18.

58. Noth, in Westermann, *Essays*, p. 87. My italics. The suggestion about translating "covenant" as "obligation" or "promise" is in von Rad, *Genesis*, p. 199.

59. This is why there is no gulf between the law and the prophets. The prophetic warning of judgment is a kind of covenant lawsuit which appeals to covenant law as its foundation. See Walther Zimmerli, *The Law and the Prophets: A Study of the Meaning of the Old Testament*, trans. R.E. Clements (New York, 1967); Westermann, *Isaiah*, on 42:18–25, 43:22–28, and 50:1–3; G. Ernest Wright, "The Lawsuit of God: A Form-Critical Study of Deuteronomy 32," in *Israel's Prophetic Heritage*, ed. Anderson and Harrelson (New York, 1962); D.J. McCarthy, *Old Testament Covenant: A Survey of Current Opinions* (Richmond, 1972), pp. 35–40, 78–79; and Delbert Hilliers, *Covenant: The History of a Biblical Idea* (Baltimore, 1969), pp. 120–42.

60. Childs, *Book of Exodus*, p. 204. Cf. Westermann and Zimmerli, in Westermann, *Essays*, pp. 47–49, 96, and 112. That God's promise prepares the way for his acts is a major theme in Westermann, *Isaiah*, as well. For example, see pp. 81–87 and 174–76.

61. For extended discussion of law in covenantal context, see Noth, *Laws*, and Eichrodt, *Theology of the Old Testament*, I, 36–177.

62. See Pss. 1, 19, and 119. Since the law is a gift which presupposes divine favor rather than an account of how that favor is to be earned, grace is prior to works here. See Buber, *Moses*, p. 137, and von Rad, *Old Testament Theology*, I, 193–94 and 229–31.

63. Buber, *Moses*, p. 119.

64. Ex. 20:2–3.

65. Buber, *Prophetic Faith*, p. 22.

66. *Isa.*, p. 140, and Westermann, *Isaiah*, p. 140, and von Rad, *Old Testament Theology*, I, 210. Cf. Noth, *Laws*, pp. 11, 20–28, and Buber, *Moses*, pp. 130–37.

67. See McCarthy, *Old Testament Covenant*, pp. 33, 66, and 147.

68. The major study here is George Mendenhall's *Law and Covenant in Israel and the Ancient Near East* (Pittsburgh, 1955), along with his essay "Covenant" in Vol. I of *Interpreter's Bible Dictionary*. McCarthy and Hilliers provide helpful surveys of the discussion of his theses.

69. For an interpretation of the whole of Deuteronomy in these terms see Meredith G. Kline, *Treaty of the Great King* (Grand Rapids, 1963).

70. Buber, *Prophetic Faith*, p. 51. Cf. Hilliers, *Covenant*, pp. 30, 34–35, 49, 52, and 65; and von Rad, *Old Testament Theology*, I, 129.

71. Deut. 6:5.

72. See William L. Moran, "The Ancient Near Eastern Background of the Love of God in Deuteronomy," in *The Catholic Biblical Quarterly*, Vol. 25 (1963), pp. 77–87.

73. Isa. 54:5 in the context of verses 1–10. Cf. Jer. 31:32.

74. Amos 2:10 and 9:7.

75. Amos 3:2.

76. Buber, *Prophetic Faith*, pp. 45–48.

77. Hos. 11:1–9; Deut. 1:31, 32:5–14; Isa. 64:7–12; Jer. 3:14–22, 31:7–9, 20; Mal. 3:17; Ps. 103:13–14. In Ex. 4:22–23, Moses tells Pharaoh, "Thus says the Lord, Israel is my first-born son, and I say to you, 'Let my son go that he may serve me; if you refuse to let him go, behold, I will slay your first-born son.'"

78. Deut. 8:5, 14:1, 32:5–7, 15–22; Isa. 1:2–4, 30:1–5, 8–14, 45:9–11; Jer. 3:13–14, 19, 4:18–22; Mal. 1:6, 2:10. Perhaps Dennis J. McCarthy overemphasizes this side in pointing to the link between the father-son and lord-vassal metaphors. "Notes on the Love of God in Deuteronomy and the Father-Son Relationship between Yahweh and Israel," in *The Catholic Biblical Quarterly*, Vol. 27 (1965), pp. 144–47. The quotations from *King Lear* are from Act I, Scene IV.

79. F. Ch. Fensham, "Covenant, Promise and Expectation in the Bible," *Theologische Zeitschrift*, 23 (1967), 306.

80. For the centrality of the notion of the Hebrew God as leader and guide, see Buber, *Kingship*.

81. Ex. 33:14 and 40:34–38.

82. Ex. 3:13–14. See Buber, *Prophetic Faith*, p. 28, *Moses*, pp. 51–53 and 126, and von Rad, *Old Testament Theology*, I, 180–81. Ex. 33:19 can be viewed as an expansion of this promise, "I will be gracious to whom I will be gracious, and will show mercy on whom I will show mercy." For a very important interpretation of the significance of the name Yahweh, see the title essay of Walther Zimmerli, *I Am Yahweh*, trans. Douglas W. Scott (Atlanta, 1982).

83. Buber, *Kingship*, p. 106.

84. Buber, *Moses*, p. 52. Cf. Childs, *Book of Exodus*, p. 76, "God announces that his intentions will be revealed in his future acts, which he now refuses to explain."

85. Hilliers, *Covenant*, pp. 101–13. Cf. von Rad, *Genesis*, p. 199. This is why there can be such a strong emphasis on the everlasting nature of the Abraham and David covenants. See Gen. 17:7–8, 13, and 19; II Sam. 7:13–16, 23:5; and Ps. 89:4, 28–37, 132:11–14. Cf. Anderson, *Out of the Depths*, p. 127.

86. While there are three covenants they are so thoroughly intertwined that we can speak of only a single journey. On the continuity of the Abraham and Moses traditions, see Gen. 50:24; Ex. 1:7 and 12, 2:24–25, 3:6–18, 4:5, 5:1, 6:4–8, 13:5, and 33:1; Deut. 7:6–8, 29:13; and Ps. 105. In the so-called Priestly Document the Moses covenant is so completely absorbed into the Abraham covenant that there is no reference to a covenant at Sinai at all. See Walther Zimmerli, "Sinaibund und Abrahambund" in *Gottes Offenbarung* (Munich, 1963), pp. 205–16. For parallels between the Abraham and Moses covenants which underscore the continuity, see Fensham, "Covenant," 307–12, and Zimmerli, in Westermann, *Essays*, pp. 91–93. On the link of the David and Moses traditions, see II Sam. 7; Ps. 78; and Isa. 55:1–5. Cf. McCarthy, *Old Testament Covenant*, pp. 46 and 50; Noth, "David and Israel in II Samuel VII," *Laws*, pp. 250–59; and von Rad, *Old Testament Theology*, I, 338–39.

87. Gen. 17:7–8.

88. For the promise of posterity, see Gen. 12:2, 15:5, and 17:4. The promise that Sarah would have a son belongs to this part of the story, Gen. 17:15–21. The promise of the land is found in Gen. 15:18–21 and 17:8.

89. See Ex. 1:7, 12, and 20; 5:5; Josh. 21:43–45 and 23:14–15.

90. Gen. 12:2–3 (NIV). RSV translates "and by you all the families of the earth will bless themselves," giving as an alternate reading, "in you all the families of the earth will be blessed." The verb can be translated either reflexively or in the passive. The reference in v. 2 to Abraham's being a blessing argues for the latter. See von Rad, *Genesis*, p. 160.

91. G. von Rad, *Genesis*, pp. 154 and 160. Cf. p. 200, "Abraham's call was connected with the hope of a universal extension of God's salvation beyond the limits of Israel."

92. Isa. 42:6 and 49:6.

93. Isa. 2:2–4. Cf. Micah 4:1–4 and Ex. 17:22–24.

94. I Sam. 7:12–16. Cf. I Sam. 23:1–7 and Pss. 78, 89, and 132. Throughout these texts the everlasting nature of this covenant is stressed. Sin will lead to punishment, but the promise will stand because here, as in the Abraham covenant, it is the divine partner who undertakes an unconditional obligation. Zion was the fortified hill in Jerusalem that David captured from the Canaanites, and it eventually came to stand for the whole of Jerusalem as the home of Yahweh's temple and especially as the seat of the Davidic dynasty. It is to the David covenant what Sinai is to the Moses covenant.

95. See Pss. 29, 47, 93, and 95–99. The quoted passages are from 29:11, 95:3, 47:9, and 98:9.

96. Ps. 46:6 and 9.

97. Ps. 76:12 and 9. Cf. Ps. 146:5–10.

98. Ps. 48:2. Cf. v. 10. For the participation of other nations in the blessings of Zion, see Ps. 87.

99. Buber, *Prophetic Faith*, pp. 142–43.

100. We are thus dealing with theological vision rather than the flattery of courtly rhetoric. See Zimmerli, in Westermann, *Essays*, p. 111; von Rad, *Old Testament Theology*, I, 320–21, and TDNT, IX, 505–06.

101. In Pss. 2, 45, and 110 the international scope of the rule of the anointed one focuses on the divine power and the futility of resisting it. Psalm 72 especially portrays the blessings of peace, justice, and prosperity which accompany this universal sovereignty.

102. Haggai and Zechariah hoped for a time that the coming one had come in the person of Zerubbabel, a descendant of David sent by the Persian king to govern Jerusalem. But this hope was both short lived and an exception among the prophets. See Zimmerli, *Old Testament*, pp. 124–25.

103. See Amos 9:11–15; Isa. 9:1–7; Hos. 3:4–5; Micah 4:6–5:4; Jer. 23:1–6, 33:14–26; and Ezra 34:11–34, 37:15–28.

104. Isa. 11:1–10. Cf. Isa. 55:1–5 and Zech. 9:9–10. On the Isaiah text, see Westermann, *Isaiah*, pp. 282–88, and Otto Eissfelt, "The Promises of Grace to David in Isaiah 55:1–5," in Anderson and Harrelson, *Israel's Prophetic Heritage*, pp. 196–207.

105. Jacob, *Theology*, p. 303, and Eichrodt, *Theology*, II, 214.

106. Ibid., p. 304. Cf. Wolff, *Anthropology*, p. 106.

107. Deut. 32:39; Job 26:6; Ps. 88:6–7, 139:8; and Amos 9:2.

108. Ps. 88:3–5, 10–13, 6:5; and Isa. 38:18.

109. Ps. 30:9–12., 94:17, 115:17–18. Cf. Ps. 28:1.

110. Ps. 88:13, 115:18, 118:17, 119:175; and Isa. 38:18–19.

111. Westermann, *Praise*, p. 159. Cf. pp. 155–59 and Wolff, *Anthropology*, pp. 106–07.

112. Eichrodt, *Theology*, II, 496 and 503.
113. Ibid., II, 517. Eichrodt italicizes this passage.
114. Russell, *Method*, p. 389.
115. Job 14:9–17. On death and hope in Job as a whole, see Eichrodt, *Theology*, II, 517–29.
116. Ps. 16:10–11.
117. Eichrodt, *Theology*, II, 524–25. He italicizes the last phrase. Cf. Artur Weiser, who agrees that "the 'that' is of greater importance to him than the 'how' " and that the source of the belief in the overcoming of death is "the same source which has become manifest throughout the psalm as the foundation of the psalmist's faithful optimism—a life lived in communion with God." *The Psalms: A Commentary*, p. 177.
118. Ps. 73:12–20.
119. Ps. 73:23–26.
120. See Gen. 5:24 and II Kings 2:3–9. The same language is used to express hope in the face of death in Ps. 49:15.
121. Wolff, *Anthropology*, p. 109. Cf. Weiser, *Psalms*, pp. 514–15, and Eichrodt, *Theology*, II, 522.
122. Ex. 24:9–11.
123. Isa. 25:6–8. Eichrodt's description of this banquet as "the return of humanity to full, unclouded fellowship with God, who, with the advent of his world-wide dominion, expels all the destructive powers of death in order to communicate to men his unrestricted fullness of life," not only confirms his suggestion that the overcoming of death is grounded in God's "will to fellowship revealed in the covenant relationship"; it also suggests the end of that alienation between human and divine which goes back to the fall in Genesis 3. *Theology*, II, 510, 503, 512. Cf. Zimmerli, *Old Testament*, 133.
124. Isa. 26:19.
125. Dan. 12:2–3.
126. Russell, *Method*, pp. 356–57. The broad agreement that the unbreakability of the covenant bond is the central theme in the Old Testament hope of salvation beyond death finds expression in the broad agreement that this hope arises directly out of Israel's distinctive faith and that foreign influences are minimal and peripheral. See Russell, *Method*, pp. 385–89; Eichrodt, *Theology*, II, 514–16; Jacob, *Theology*, p. 314; and Zimmerli, *Old Testament*, p. 132. Some scholars think a concern for the destiny of martyrs is especially at issue in these two passages. See Russell, *Method*, p. 367; and Jacob, *Theology*, pp. 313–14. In that context the hints of resurrection for Yahweh's Suffering Servant in Isa. 53:10–12 and Ps. 22:29 are important.
127. TDNT, I, 270–74, and Eichrodt, *Theology*, II, 381–84.
128. Eichrodt, *Theology*, II, 383. Italics omitted. Cf. p. 400, "In Israel the nature of sin was seen unambiguously as conscious rebellion against God's order; and this order was *not* something far above the individual human life, *some impersonal, rather abstract cosmic law, but the norm*, valid here and now, *of the covenant* on which the existence of the nation rested." My italics.
129. II Sam. 12:13.
130. Eichrodt, *Theology*, II, 416.
131. Psalm 106 parallels Psalm 78 in these respects almost exactly. Cf. Josh 24:16, 20; Ps. 5:2; Jer. 2:29, 32; and Hos. 7:13–14.
132. This linkage is explicit in Ezekiel 20:33–38.

133. Deut. 32:5–7, 15–22; Isa. 1:2–3, 30:1–14; Jer. 3:14, 22, 4:22, 5:7; and Mal. 1:6.

134. Hos. 1:9. In addition to the whole book of Hosea, see Jer. 3:1–13, 20, 5:7–11, 9:2, 13:26–27, and 23:10, 14.

135. Hos. 2:19–23, 6:1–2. Cf. Hos. 11:1–9, where it is the bond between parent and child which is strong enough to survive rebellion and seek restoration.

136. Jer. 31:31–34.

137. Isa. 43:15, 25, 44:21–22.

138. Isa. 54:1–10.

139. Lev. 26:40–45; Ps. 106:44–46; Hos. 11:1–9, Amos 9:11–15.

140. See, for example, Ex. 34:6–7 and Ps. 103:6–14. For a brief survey of the concept of *hesed* see Leon Morris, *Testaments of Love: A Study of Love in the Bible* (Grand Rapids, 1981), Chapter Three, "Love and Loyalty." Cf. Eichrodt, *Theology*, II, 475, 480–84.

141. On the eschatological character of forgiveness, see Eichrodt, *Theology*, II, 390, 457–58, and 468.

142. The Jerusalem Bible's rendering of Ps. 99:8 captures this widespread motif very succinctly:

> Yahweh our God, you responded to them,
> a God of forgiveness for them,
> in spite of punishing their sins.

Cf. Weiser, *Psalms*, p. 644.

143. Eichrodt's comments on the theology of punishment in the Old Testament are most helpful here. See *Theology*, II, 425–33, 455–59, 467, and 475.

144. Paul Ricoeur, *The Symbolism of Evil*, pp. 32 and 45.

145. See Eichrodt, *Theology*, II, 443–48.

INDEX